*Reweaving
the Family
Tapestry*

Reweaving the Family Tapestry

A Multigenerational Approach to Families

EDITED BY

FREDDA HERZ BROWN

W. W. Norton & Company • *NEW YORK* • *LONDON*

Printed in the United States of America.

Library of Congress Cataloging-in-Publication Data

Reweaving the family tapestry : a multigenerational approach to
   families / edited by Fredda Herz Brown.
       p.   cm.
   "A Norton professional book" — Prelim. p.
   Includes index.
    1. Family psychotherapy.   2. Life change events — Psychological
aspects.   I. Brown, Fredda Herz.
   RC488.5.R49   1991   616.89′156 — dc20   90-46353

ISBN 0-393-70108-5

W. W. Norton & Company, Inc., 500 Fifth Avenue, New York, N.Y. 10110

W. W. Norton & Company, Ltd., 10 Coptic Street, London WC1A 1PU

1 2 3 4 5 6 7 8 9 0

To the people who make up my family tapestry:
my children, my parents, and my siblings

Foreword

WHAT FOLLOWS IS an extensive elaboration of a truly integrative and flexible family systems model of therapy. Rooted firmly in Bowen systems theory, the original model was taught to us by Phil Guerin and Tom Fogarty, along with their own conceptual additions and clinical innovations, at The Center for Family Learning in the early 1970s. Shortly after the formation of the Family Institute of Westchester in 1977,* we extended this model to include our family life cycle ideas. We found its principles ideal for understanding and working with the various new family forms created by widespread divorce and remarriage. In fact, in the 13 years that the model has been evolving at the Family Institute of Westchester, it has provided us with a framework ready to accept any new or innovative concept, viewpoint, or clinical technique consistent with systemic thinking. Thus, the model stretched (but did not bend or break) when we introduced quite radical ideas on ethnicity and gender, and when we encouraged a renewed focus on social class and race.

Many of the "trendiest" systemic techniques of the past decade (reframing, circular questioning, therapist neutrality, reversals, rituals, paradox, etc.) had already been in routine use by Bowen and his followers for many years, although we may have called them by different names. (Bowen called paradoxical interventions "talking crooked.") Similarly, the use of "reflecting" teams, the open discussion of family patterns with the client family, and the use of structural moves to shift rigid triangles were part of our clinical practice from the early 1970s. "Re-storying" fits into the model easily, as does hypnosis, psychopharmacology and biofeedback.

---

*The original founders of the Family Institute of Westchester were: Norman Ackerman, David Berenson, Fredda Herz Brown, Betty Carter, Eloise Julius, Monica McGoldrick and Kenneth Terkelsen. Betty Carter is the Institute's Director, Fredda Herz Brown is Director of Training, and Monica McGoldrick is a Senior Staff Consultant. The other founders have moved on.

The ideas of the epistemology debates and those of constructivism may have enlarged our thinking and our teaching, but they have not necessitated any basic change in our family therapy model, which includes all levels of the system from the biological and intrapsychic level of the individual, through the family level, to the social-political-cultural context, and on to the ecological. It all fits — even the concept of power, which is still disavowed by most systems thinkers except feminists. And these ideas about change can be adapted to brief therapy practice as well as to long-term work. Since the model is in no way to be confused with collections of unrelated concepts and techniques usually called "eclectic," it should be stated just as clearly that psychoanalytic, gestalt, object relations, and other theories that view the individual as the primary unit of concern and thus lead to different clinical interpretation and intervention do *not* fit into this model.

Thus Bowen theory, the most fully elaborated theoretical system in the family field, and perhaps the least understood and appreciated, has obviously tapped into something more than one person's vision of the family as an emotional system. Bowen theory provides a set of principles that are sound enough, profound enough, and flexible enough to be applied to human situations, conditions, and dilemmas not yet dreamed of.

Bowen's legacy to a multigenerational theory has been maintained and clinically elaborated in the following pages by Fredda Herz Brown and the contributors. They have put together an excellent application of his original ideas in this contemporary extension of the Bowen framework with individuals, couples and families. The book moves easily from a full description of this multigenerational clinical model to full-length case studies of its application.

Murray Bowen died on October 9, 1990, just as this was going to press. We are proud that his legacy will continue in this book and others to come. In the paradoxical way that Bowen himself so much appreciated, perhaps now that he is gone there will be a rediscovery of the significance of his seminal work in family therapy and beyond.

Betty Carter
Monica McGoldrick

Mount Vernon, N.Y.
October 1990

Contents

Foreword
    Betty Carter and Monica McGoldrick   vii
Preface   xi
Acknowledgments   xiii
Contributors   xv

I. THE MULTIGENERATIONAL MODEL

1   The Model   3
    Fredda Herz Brown
2   The Therapeutic Relationship   22
    Fredda Herz Brown
3   General Practice Principles   33
    Fredda Herz Brown
4   Stage 1: Defining and Working on the Foreground   43
    Fredda Herz Brown
5   Stage 2: Reweaving the Tapestry   53
    Fredda Herz Brown
6   Stage 3: The Client as Weaver   67
    Fredda Herz Brown

II. WORKING WITH FAMILIES THROUGHOUT THE LIFE CYCLE

7   Single Young Adults   77
    Natalie Schwartzberg
8   The Transition to Couplehood   94
    Gail S. Lederer and Jane Lewis
9   Families With Young Children   114
    Kathy Berliner

10   Families With Adolescents   131
          Pamela Young
11   Families Launching Young Adults   149
          Judith Stern Peck
12   Families in Later Life   169
          Demaris A. Jacob

      III.   WORKING WITH FAMILIES WITH DISRUPTIONS IN THE LIFE CYCLE

13   Families in the Divorce and Post-Divorce Process   191
          Judith Stern Peck and Fredda Herz Brown
14   Alcohol in the Family System   219
          Gail S. Lederer
15   Families With a Medically Ill Member   242
          Jane S. Jacobs
16   Families Facing Terminal Illness   262
          Elliott J. Rosen
17   Families With Affective Disorders   286
          David A. Moltz

Index   309

Preface

THE MULTIGENERATIONAL THERAPY MODEL that forms the framework for this book has evolved over many years at the Family Institute of Westchester, where I have been director of training. In this book, I offer my rendition of the model as it is currently practiced and taught at the Family Institute of Westchester. The contributors present variations of the model, although I expect the readers will find consistency in their perspectives and approaches.

The idea of writing a book arose within the context of a peer supervisory group of which I have been a member at the institute.* For several years, we focused on issues related to practicing and teaching multigenerational therapy. Using our own cases, we sought not only strategies but also a larger view of the family system. We struggled with how one teaches these ideas to trainees at various levels of family therapy experience. Finding the group's work challenging and provocative, I decided to describe in words the model as it was being practiced at the Family Institute of Westchester.

Of course, the model did not spring full-blown from this small group. In fact, it represents the ongoing evolution of a theory originated by Murray Bowen and elaborated most recently by Betty Carter and Monica McGoldrick and earlier by Philip Guerin and Thomas Fogarty. The model stresses the complexity of themes in the fabric of family life and the process of reweaving them into tapestry that makes for a more satisfying life for the client. Using this approach, the family therapist is able to move comfortably from the family or marital level to extended family work with an individual client. The model encourages therapists to attend to the ideas of gender, culture, class, and race as they influence how families operate and how clinicians can integrate these ideas into their work with families. It focuses

---

*The others in the original group were Dee Jacob, Jane Lewis, Natalie Schwartzberg, and Judy Stern Peck.

on broadening context while holding individuals responsible for the direction of their life.

In Part I, I give the reader some ideas regarding the basic theory and practice principles and attempt to outline a three-stage model of treatment ("attempt" because as we know demarcating anything in our business is risky at best). Human beings do not always fit into or follow stages. However, these stages are a close approximation to the movement of clients through the process of treatment.

Parts II and III present full-length case studies of clients who enter treatment at various life-cycle phases or at a time they are disrupted. In Part II multigenerational work with normative life-cycle issues is presented. Each contributor discusses how she moved the case from a particular presenting problem to a broader yet more "individually focused" definition of the problem. As the therapist shares her thinking or rationale, the reader has an opportunity to learn about principles and strategies of family-of-origin work from "inside" a case.

Part III focuses on work with clients who are experiencing major disruptions in the life cycle. The case studies allow the reader to see the way multigenerational therapy is applied when the family is dealing with multiple layers of a problem—the life-cycle issues and the process that disrupts the cycle, be that divorce, some form of illness (medical or otherwise), or death of a family member. Each of these chapters provides insights into how therapists using a multigenerational model approach the complexities of these situations. They highlight how the model organizes one's thinking and clinical approach in a way that is "grounding" in extraordinarily difficult and emotional situations.

The contributors have had their last memo from their "tormentor" (me); now it is up to you to judge the value of our contributions. While different people have different personal styles, the multigenerational model provides a framework for all of us in our clinical work. I hope you find it just as useful as we do.

—F.H.B.

Acknowledgments

MANY PEOPLE ARE OWED a debt of gratitude for bringing this book to publication. Most particularly, I would like to thank Betty Carter, Director of the Family Institute of Westchester, and Monica McGoldrick. These women, members of the institute's founding group along with me, have been intellectual and creative forces behind the model of treatment presented here.

The staff and faculty at the Family Institute of Westchester have been unswerving in their support. My colleagues not only wrote chapters but also contributed to our joint description of the model. Thanks to Lillian Fine, Cathy Hill, Lilly Dispirito, and Mary Bonnato for administrative support and to Lisa Fine and Neale McGoldrick for help with artwork and genograms. Randy Gerson's computer program, *The Family Recorder*, was used to generate genograms.

Since many people contributed basic principles to the multigenerational model as it is practiced at the Family Institute of Westchester, and since they have often made their contributions verbally rather than on paper, it is difficult to give full credit to specific individuals for particular ideas. While I have attempted to acknowledge individuals in the text, I take responsibility for the particular articulation of the model.

A special thank you goes to Judy Stern Peck, whose friendship and encouragement were unfailing and who provided the original inspiration for the book title.

My network of family, friends, and colleagues supported and cajoled me to finish this book and helped make doing so feel like a special accomplishment. They often made my work life enjoyable when my contribution to such was small.

I am indebted to the many individuals who over the years have taught me about their families and at times about my own. I would also like to thank Susan Barrows, my editor at Norton, who gave encouragement when I was down and advice and assistance when I needed it.

Contributors

Kathy Berliner, M.S.W.
Assistant to the Director of
   Training
Family Institute of Westchester
Mount Vernon, New York

Fredda Herz Brown, R.N., Ph.D.
Director of Training
Family Institute of Westchester

Demaris A. Jacob, Ph.D.
Faculty, Family Institute of
   Westchester

Jane S. Jacobs, Ed.D.
Assistant Research Professor
Center for Family Research
George Washington University
   Medical School
Washington, D.C.

Jane Lewis, M.S.W.
Greenwich Hospital Psychiatric
   Clinic
Greenwich, Connecticut
Faculty, Family Institute of
   Westchester

Gail S. Lederer, M.S.W.
Faculty, Family Institute of
   Westchester

David A. Moltz, M.D.
Assistant Professor of Psychiatry
Albert Einstein College of Medicine
Bronx, New York
Visiting Faculty
Family Institute of Westchester

Judith Stern Peck, A.C.S.W.
Director of Clinical Services
Family Institute of Westchester

Elliott J. Rosen, Ed.D.
Jansen Memorial Hospice,
Tuckahoe, New York
Faculty, Family Institute of
   Westchester

Natalie Schwartzberg, A.C.S.W.
Faculty, Family Institute of
   Westchester

Pamela Young, A.C.S.W.
Faculty, Family Institute of
   Westchester

Reweaving the Family Tapestry

I

THE
MULTIGENERATIONAL MODEL

The Model

FREDDA HERZ BROWN

THE MULTIGENERATIONAL MODEL that has evolved at the Family Institute of Westchester has its origins in the work of Murray Bowen, who not only defined the family as an emotional system operating across generations but also contributed the original ideas about triangles, differentiation, anxiety, and coaching that have guided the development of the model (see Kerr & Bowen, 1988). Many of the ideas about how families operate, as presented here, derive from Bowen's work.

Of the many people in the family therapy field who have been influenced by Murray Bowen, the most important for the development of the multi-generational model as it is described in this book are Betty Carter, Monica McGoldrick, Philip Guerin, and Thomas Fogarty. In their seminal book on life cycle issues, now in its second edition, Carter and McGoldrick (1989) elaborated Bowenian thinking to include horizontal and vertical movement of families through time. Both have contributed key ideas about the influences of ethnicity (McGoldrick, Pearce, & Giordano, 1982), class, gender (McGoldrick, Anderson, & Walsh, 1989; Walters, Carter, Papp, & Silverstein, 1988), and race on family systems. Guerin (1976; Guerin, Fay, Burden, & Kautto, 1987) explored the idea of tracking from nuclear to extended family and introduced alternative clinical methods, while Fogarty (1979) contributed many basic concepts, including the dynamics of the distancer-pursuer combination.

My own career, as well as the careers of the other authors, began with a Bowenian focus on extended family work known as "coaching." The current model, developed in our work together at the Family Institute of Westchester, expands and adapts that framework to include work with the nuclear family process.

The ultimate goal of this model of family therapy is to assist an individual in changing patterns and triangles and in understanding and shifting the themes in the family of origin. This goal is accomplished by focusing on the client's responsibility for changing him/herself in these patterns. It defines the client as the initiator and designer of change and as responsible for the direction of his/her life. This goal is certainly consistent with Bowenian work. At the same time, the model seeks to remain relevant to the problems at hand. This is true whether the client is an individual, a couple, or a family. The client is assisted in first identifying the connection between these current problems and previous family themes and patterns. These connections are then expanded by the therapist and the client into the ongoing work of the treatment process. It is assumed that changing the way one relates across multiple levels of the family has a higher emotional yield and a greater likelihood of impact on the clients' current life than change on any one level alone.

The movement from nuclear to extended family work is viewed as the natural flow of therapeutic process. The length of time necessary to deal with nuclear family problems and the client's willingness to deal directly with extended family issues will affect the ease with which this shift is accomplished. Generally speaking, the longer the difficulties have existed in the family emotional system, the more intense and rigid they tend to be and the longer it takes to make the extended family workable in the therapy process. In the meantime, the process of working on the presenting nuclear family problems helps clients to take charge of the direction in their ongoing life.

What is presented here is not a set of techniques for working with either nuclear or extended family systems but rather an integrated framework that views both in relationship to one another and either as an appropriate forum for family therapy. We do not ask simply that someone who knows one model of intervention add what is elaborated here to that model. Rather, this model, as it has evolved at the Family Institute of Westchester, demands that the reader/therapist adopt a therapeutic stance and a set of practice guidelines that move fairly easily from one level of problem definition and family generation to another. This model is useful with most clients, since it can be adjusted to match clients' pacing, timing, and capabilities at a particular moment in time.

The therapeutic process involves three phases of work, moving from the here-and-now work to the more long-term and future/past work on extended family issues. While not all clients move through all three phases, their articulation is important to an understanding of the treatment model. As we shall see, some clients enter treatment ready to begin extended family work, while others end treatment after the nuclear family issues have been resolved and stage 1 work is completed. In my experience, most clients who end treatment at this point or after some initial work on the extended family issues return to do further work at some later time. This model offers a certain amount of ease and continuity of focus in working with clients who stop and start treatments over long periods of time. In fact, it views such stopping and starting as natural and important in helping clients develop self-direction.

In this first chapter, we will examine the essential principles of the model in terms of (1) how families operate, (2) how symptoms are hypothesized to develop, and (3) how change occurs. The process by which clients reweave their family tapestry will also be outlined and described. The three stages of the therapeutic process will be defined and described briefly; they are: (1) defining and working on the foreground; (2) reweaving the tapestry; and (3) the client as the weaver.

HOW FAMILIES OPERATE

There are four main principles, each with its own corollaries, describing this model's view of how families operate (Bowen, 1978; Carter & McGoldrick, 1989a, b; Kerr & Bowen, 1988):

1. Families are the primary influence in our lives.
2. History tends to repeat itself.
3. Families move through time on a horizontal as well as a vertical continuum.
4. Each individual member must maintain both separateness from and connectedness to the family.

Let's consider each of these four and the corollaries which derive from them.

Families Are the Primary Influence in Our Lives

Through the course of our lives we interact in many systems. However, it is the first system with which we interact, our family of origin, that has the most powerful and persistent influence on how we think and feel about ourselves and how we interact with others. It is this system that has the most powerful impact, both positive and negative, on our future relationships.

The family system is driven by emotional forces; in part that is why it is so important to the development of a sense of self. The relationships between people who live together and who to a greater or lesser extent are dependent upon one another have an intensity that is absent in most other systems with which we interact. The difficulty in managing such intensity accounts for the formation of triangles, the basic relationship of an emotional system (Kerr & Bowen, 1988).

Bowen has theorized about the development of triangles in families. In short, anytime the emotional intensity between two parties cannot be dealt with, the triangling in of a third relieves tension; therefore, it is intrinsically self-perpetuating. The behavior of a third can also serve as focal point, providing a way of either fighting or joining; in this way the third party, which may be a person or a thing, begins to serve a function in the interaction of the other two.

The more rigid this tension-reducing solution, the more likely it will be that the interaction of any two parties will begin to depend on the relationship with the third. It is through this process that we all tend to come out of our families of origin having particular postures or positions vis-à-vis our parents. The more we have become part of a triangle, the more likely it is that we will have a difficult time defining our own position without considering or reacting to the position of others. Since emotional reactivity energizes the triangle, the people involved in one usually learn to respond to the emotions of others without getting clarity on what they are thinking or feeling.

Multigenerational therapy focuses not only on the impact of the primary emotional system but also on the importance of working on one's position in family triangles, issues, and patterns. While it may be helpful to understand the influence of this system on our lives, it is the shifting of patterns over at least three generations that frees an individual from an outgrown and constricting emotional tapestry.

This multigenerational model of treatment does not pathologize families. It encourages individuals to view their families in positive ways, to see the positive impact. It is generally understood that most of us come from families in which our parents and relatives did "the best with what they had." With such a lens, learning to view our parents and other relatives as people with both positive and negative qualities becomes a much easier task.

History Tends to Repeat Itself

All of us come out of our family of origin with emotional "baggage" (McGoldrick & Carter, 1989). As with real baggage, this emotional baggage is sometimes light, sometimes heavy; sometimes it contains good things and sometimes not-so-good things. Sometimes the bags are packed in an unwitting way, containing things we didn't think about. Such is the emotional baggage of life; it is made up of things we have purposefully and inadvertently picked up along the way. Sometimes we are not even sure how we came to carry it with us when suddenly we realize it is there in something we have said or done.

The field of mental health has traditionally been concerned about emotional baggage that is unneeded and therefore burdensome. That is, it has been concerned with emotional baggage that tends to affect our lives in negative ways.

The multigenerational model focuses on emotional baggage that impedes an individual's movement through life in a self-directed manner and has the dysfunctional results in the here and now. In this model, an individual is carrying a heavy load of baggage when he/she unwittingly lets certain issues, themes, and patterns dominate aspects of his/her life. Collecting and continuing to carry such baggage through life becomes increasingly burdensome, since each time one deals with a situation unwittingly or reactively the experience is added to the emotional baggage. This creates an increased sense of being out of control in one's life.

It is important to understand the processes by which families tend to repeat in the present what happened in the past. This repetition is accomplished in both direct and indirect ways. All of us are taught directly by our parents; we learn what is good/bad; what is important/unimportant; what is to be valued and what is not. Most of this is taught by what our parents say and tell us to do.

Other processes occur more indirectly, through the emotional fabric or language of the family. These are related to triangles and emotional/functional positions in the family (Bowen, 1978; Kerr & Bowen, 1988). A recent film entitled *Family Business* illustrated the emotional process by which members of one generation may seek to correct the negatives of their own parenting by doing the opposite with their children. In the film, the son, played by Dustin Hoffman, has been trying to live his life differently from his father, who was a two-bit con man and thief. Growing up, the son had been enlisted by the father to participate in many of the scams, and in fact, he had served time in jail for one of them. When the son has his own son, he vows to give his son the opposite by sending him to the best schools, giving him whatever he wants materially, and setting a good example by living a straight life. However, the grandson eventually drops out of school, comes up with his own scam involving his father and grandfather, and ends up in jail. So here's the typical scenario of life, played dramatically—what goes around, comes around. What we try to resolve by creating the opposite usually creates the same or similar outcome. How this happens involves triangles and occurs over multiple generations.

Rather than understanding what happened in his own life and trying to define a position for himself that would reflect what he thought would be good for his child, the son reactively took the opposite stance of his father. He defined his father's behavior as wrong and went to the opposite extreme with his son. But it was still a triangle, with the son's position dependent upon his image of his father's position. It certainly wasn't self-directed; he certainly wasn't free to be any kind of father he chose to be.

Issues of significance, patterns of relatedness, and level of emotional maturity are passed from generation to generation in much the same manner. For instance, in this film one of the issues that continues to repeat itself is the issue of legal vs. illegal behavior or, as the grandson begins to define it, boring vs. exciting activity. In the process of reacting to his son differently from the way his father had to him, the father had lost all sense of fun and excitement. Since he had always linked thievery with excitement, dropping it from his life led to a very staid and boring life, without much room for creativity. The grandson sought excitement in the activity he associated with his grandfather—thievery. The push and pull around this issue were played out again and again in their relationship.

Themes are repetitive, multigenerational patterns of relating. Sometimes, as in this film, themes can be related to gender. For instance, consider the myth of the good woman waiting at home for and always protecting her playful but recalcitrant man. This myth and the related theme, of "it's always better on the other side," are played out in *Family Business*, with each of the men choosing a woman who represents his opposite. In fact, the men even marry interethnically for several generations, apparently seeking to balance that which they react to as negative in their own group.

One particular aspect of relatedness, the closeness/distance dimension, is interesting to track multigenerationally (Fogarty, 1976; Guerin, 1976). Whether we liked or didn't like our family's patterns for maintaining closeness or distance in relationships will affect whether we reactively do the same or the opposite in our relationships. Closeness and distance are really positions vis-à-vis others. This dimension of relating is also defined and passed along from one generation to the next by the formation of triangles. That is, the nature of a triangle implies a pattern of distance and closeness; an individual is usual close to one person in a triangle and distant from the other. These positions develop over time. Then we tend to recreate them in other relationships; however, we may keep our same position or take the opposite position. For instance, in *Family Business*, a pattern of closeness between mothers and only sons and distance between fathers and sons exists over two generations. Each of the genders acts exactly as the parent of the same gender had acted.

Triangles also account for the development of emotional maturity (Bowen, 1978; Kerr & Bowen, 1988). The more an individual is involved in triangles in his/her family of origin, the more unlikely it is he/she will be clear on who he/she is. Instead, most of his/her thoughts and feelings will result from the movement within the triangle and thus will depend on a third party. In this model, emotional maturity is defined as the degree to which one is able to think and feel, to define oneself without emotionally reacting to the position of a least one other. One who is emotionally mature is clear about boundaries between self and other and is aware when his/her actions are in reaction to other. Since emotional maturity affects the development of symptomatology in families, we'll continue our discussion of it under that heading.

The other way in which history is repeated in families has to do with the emotional/functional positions one holds vis-à-vis others in the family. Each individual holds a particular position along the dimensions that define the inner experience of the family—generation and gender (Goldner, 1989). Generally we hold positions with our peers in the family, those of the same generation, siblings, cousins, etc.; we also hold positions with regard to at least the generation above us and, if we have children ourselves, to the one below us. In addition, our position within our gender group and in relation to the opposite gender group affects how we will experience ourselves (Walters, Carter, Papp & Silverstein, 1988).

This sense of self in terms of other family members is frequently repeated generationally. For instance, an oldest with no siblings of the opposite sex experiences a different type of family than a youngest with an older sibling of the opposite sex (see Toman, 1976). The experience of the child who is mom's favorite is quite different from that of the child who is always fighting with or distant from mother. Each of these individuals then tends to create within the context of the nuclear family and other systems a position that clearly resembles his/her position in the family of origin. In their familiarity such positions provide a sense of comfort. What they may not provide is flexibility in relating to others. The lack of flexibility implies lack of choice or self direction/control in how one chooses to act vis-à-vis others.

History is both the far past, the immediate past, and the present. The next principle regarding how families operate has to do with movement of the family in its near past and present life.

Families Move Through Time Horizontally as Well as Vertically

The model that has evolved at the Family Institute of Westchester looks at three generations in examining how the nuclear family moves through the current course of its life cycle. We assume that a moment in the life of the nuclear family is like a snapshot of three generations of shifts over previous life cycle phases (Carter & McGoldrick, 1989a, b).

While the notion of life cycle itself is circular, with each young adult beginning a family life cycle of his/her own, each beginning marks the ending of other cycles. It is the negotiation of the life cycle and the context of such negotiations that forms the basis of this principle. There are six corollaries of this basic principle:

1. The life cycle of a nuclear family defines its tasks and potential difficulties for the family at a particular moment in time.
2. Family patterns of relating affect the family's ability to move through a particular phase.
3. Symptoms are illustrative of the family's difficulties in negotiating a phase.
4. Major disruptions in the life cycle, such as illness, death, divorce and remarriage, create an additional level of stress and complicate negotiation of a phase.
5. Each phase provides an opportunity for the family to deal with the closeness/distance dimension of relationships.
6. Race, ethnicity and class affect the family's life cycle.

Life-cycle definition of tasks and potential difficulties. As the nuclear family moves through time, its organization and membership change. Each shift in organization is marked by specific emotional tasks that must be accomplished for the family to successfully move through the phase (Carter & McGoldrick, 1989a). For instance, in order to become a couple, the newly marrieds must define themselves as a twosome with all that entails with regard to their unit and to the extended family. Difficulties at this stage usually reflect the couple's failure to become a unit, with boundaries separating it from extended family and other systems such as friends, or to negotiate issues related to the functioning of the twosome.

The multigenerational model would focus not only on the families of origin (histories) of the spouses but also on a three-generational view of what is currently going on with the couple. Understanding the life-cycle tasks and potential pitfalls of this stage helps the clinician and the family to identify and work on the particular situation.

Family patterns affect movement through the life cycle. Implicit in the idea of negotiating the life cycle is the idea that there are tasks to be accomplished, emotional issues to be resolved. According the multigenerational model, historical family patterns may complicate reorganization and resolution of emotional tasks. If previous generations had difficulty negotiating a particular phase, the current one may have difficulty as well. For example, if one had difficulty negotiating one's own adolescence, how can one expect not to have similar difficulties with a child's adolescence? There has been no role model on either side — parent or child — for accomplishing this successfully.

Symptoms often represent the family's unsuccessful solution to a life-cycle task (Carter & McGoldrick, 1989a; Haley, 1987). Nuclear family members may utilize triangle(s) as a way to resolve the tensions associated with task negotiation. The degree to which this occurs will also affect the successful completion of a phase. The formation of a triangle, which we have seen is historically repetitious, makes the difficulties a focal point of family interactions. Difficulties become symptoms as they begin to serve a function in the relationship between parties.

Some family members have heightened emotional significance to the family in terms of their functional position or relationship to the parents. Consequently, the family is more likely to react when one of these individuals is involved in the reorganization. For example, when the oldest daughter, who has been very close to her mother and the caretaker of her siblings, begins to move into adolescence, there may be some extraordinary difficulty for the family. The degree to which this child's presence is important to the family affects the pulls in both directions. The more the adolescent rebels, the more the parents begin to take a position vis-à-vis the behavior — and the battle begins. Once the triangle forms with the parents and adolescent polarized around a particular issue, it is unlikely that the issue will be easily resolved; rather, it is apt to become the central aspect of their relationship. Once that happens, it becomes the way in which they relate — with any one person's position dependent upon where the others are standing.

Major disruptions in the family life cycle create complications and an additional level of stress (Carter & McGoldrick, 1989a, b). When the family experiences a major situational crisis, negotiation of additional tasks is required. This increases the stress on the family. Both the increased number of tasks and the increased stress complicate the life-cycle tasks.

In view of the complications when there is serious illness, death, or divorce, it is not surprising that it takes a family additional time — sometimes three to five years — to accomplish certain life-cycle tasks. This is not always predictable; however, there is increasing evidence (see Chapters 13–17) that some tasks are not accomplished until much later than expected. It is almost as if the family goes into suspended animation. The multigenerational model views these disruptions in a three-generational frame, seeking to understand the current and long-term impact of such disruptions on the overall course of family life.

Closeness/distance is negotiated at each phase. In some way, the move-ment of all life-cycle phases is toward the separation of family members. Each family must be able to let offspring move into their own families at the appropriate time. While some theories view separation as the central theme of the life cycle, in the multigenerational model maintaining connectedness is seen as equally important.

In some ways each of the life-cycle phases can be viewed intrinsically as either centrifugal or centripetal in nature (Combrinck-Graham, 1985). Cen-trifugal life-cycle phases are those in which family is expanding and the emotional forces are pushing outward. Typically, families with adolescents are centrifugal. Centripetal phases occur when the emotional forces pull inward, as in the case of the family with young children. In negotiating each phase the family achieves some balance in terms of the closeness/distance continuum.

Race, ethnicity and class affect the family life cycle (McGoldrick, Pearce, & Giordano, 1982). These three variables define the context in which a family lives; they define the family in relation to other families and to society as a whole. All three variables affect the family's experience of itself at any moment in time. In the multigenerational model, we pay heed to the impact of these contextual variables on the family's experience. There are clear indications (Fulmer, 1989; Inclan & Ferran, 1990) that race and class are related and that both change the nature and movement of a family through the life cycle. For instance, black single-parent families have differ-ent life-cycle phases than their white middle-class counterparts. Part of the difference derives from the fact that out-of-wedlock pregnancy is the reason for most single-parent status in the lower classes, while divorce is the reason for such a family form in middle-class white America.

Thus, any discussion of the family life cycle must note the family's race and class. The family's ethnic group will point to potential life-cycle phase difficulties (McGoldrick, Pearce, & Giordano, 1982). Cultural and societal factors will also affect the degree to which a family's ethnicity plays a part in its movement through the life cycle. For instance, a newly immigrated family may have a switch in generations, with the young functioning as the family interpreters to society. In this model, asking about a family's ethnicity is as important as asking about other contextual variables.

The Separateness and Connectedness of Each Person Needs to be Maintained

According to the multigenerational model, all relationships involve a bal-ance or imbalance of being together and being separate, of being connected to others and being separate from them. This leads to the instability of dyads that Bowen referred to in his writings (1976, 1978).

Closeness and distance are two points on a continuum and too much of one usually leads to the other (Fogarty, 1976, 1979). Thus, if two people have too much closeness, that is, they feel uncomfortably fused, the natural movement is toward distance. Sometimes the distance is achieved by conflict. When there is too much distance, it is usually followed by the individuals' moving closer to one another. Triangles can be viewed as a way in two individuals maintain closeness or distance (Bowen, 1978; Kerr & Bowen, 1988).

When there is fusion in a relationship, there is usually a misalignment of responsibility for self. The more fused a twosome, the greater the tendency to have expectations about and concern for the behavior of the other. Since each individual perceives his/her behavior as contingent upon the other's, a trading of responsibility takes place. Generally one individual begins to act as the emotionally overresponsible one, while the other acts in an underresponsible manner.

However, responsibility is contextual and depends not only on the person with whom one is relating but also on the issue being discussed. For instance, although I tend to be emotionally overresponsible, there are certain times when I end up being underresponsible around an issue such as money. As should be obvious, these concepts are gender-based; that is, most women tend to more responsible for emotional relationships than men (Walters, Carter, Papp, & Silverstein, 1988). This is partly because women in our society have been defined as adaptable to men; since some women view their definition of self as deriving from men, they tend to take increased responsibility for managing that shared portion of self. If not, who will look out for them?

Critical to the idea of responsibility are the notions that underresponsibility and overresponsibility are flip sides of the same coin and that both demonstrate a lack responsibility for self (Bowen, 1978; Fogarty, 1979; Guerin, 1976). Someone who is overresponsible for others, a central issue for women, is usually not good at looking out for and taking care of self. On the other hand, men, who tend to be underresponsible in relation to others, do not necessarily take any more responsibility for self than their female counterparts.

Translated into movement towards and away from others, responsibility underlies the concepts of pursuing and distancing. These concepts, developed by Fogarty (1979), describe the reciprocal nature of movement in a dyad. In the multigenerational model, these concepts help us to explore the separateness/connectedness of couples. It is interesting to observe what happens when one individual moves towards or away from the other.

While pursuing and distancing are contextual concepts, over time individuals tend to develop an operating style in relation to others. Thus, one can talk about pursuers connecting with people as a way of handling their tensions, while distancers connect with things as a way of handling theirs. In a relationship, the one who tends to pursue uses relationship space more readily that the one who distances. While these concepts are often gender-based, that does not detract from their importance. Each gender needs to increase flexibility in dealing with the other.

Whatever we term the notion, separateness/connectedness or the degree of closeness must be managed between individuals. This is true over the course of the life cycle and is reflected in the history of the family.

HOW SYMPTOMS ARE HYPOTHESIZED TO DEVELOP

According to the multigenerational model, most families will experience difficulties or problems as they move through the life cycle. However, only some families will become symptomatic, that is, have some difficulty exceeding the limits of what they are willing or able to handle. When that symptom appears or where in the subsystems of the family it occurs is variable. Here we will discuss four interrelated principles that offer some ideas about symptom formation. Symptoms (1) can form in any of three areas of the family, (2) represent unsuccessful solution to life-cycle issues, (3) are the result of triangulation, and (4) rigidify a position on the closeness/distance continuum.

Symptoms Form in Any of Three Areas of the Family

Most theories of family treatment focus on either the type of symptom that the family develops or the subsystem in which it develops. Multigenerational family therapy views these two issues as relevant only to the development of treatment techniques. Understanding symptoms in this framework demands that they be explained in terms of a unified theory; a new theory or concept is not necessary to describe each type of symptom. Nor is it necessary to have a theory for child-focused families and another for marital couples. One model should be able to explain why and where symptomatology develops in family systems.

Symptoms can occur in any number of areas or subsystems of the family. The three most common areas are between spouses, in one of the spouses, and with one or more of the children (Bowen, 1978). It is also possible for families to have symptoms in more than one area. The more stress on the family and the more emotionally immature the adults, the more likely it will be that symptoms will develop in more than one area. Over the years most families have developed familiar areas of symptom formation. Families also tend to develop particular issues around which symptoms tend to develop.

The area and type of symptom development will affect the length of treatment, especially during the early phase. It will also influence the treatment techniques utilized by the clinician.

Symptoms Are Viewed as Unsuccessful Solutions to Life-cycle Tasks

Families often attempt a variety of solutions to the tasks that present themselves in a particular life-cycle phase. The failure to negotiate a specific phase usually signals that a family is having some difficulties (Carter & McGoldrick, 1989a, b; Haley, 1973, 1987). These may be resolved without intervention or they may develop into problems or symptoms that bring a family into treatment. Difficulties are resolvable as long as they do not become necessary for the interaction of other parts of the system. In this model, based on Bowen theory, this occurs when a triangle forms around the difficulty, maintaining it.

We assume that the family has tried its best to resolve the difficulties and that its lack of success does not represent a purposeful act. However, having one or more symptoms will prevent the family from completing the life-cycle phase and generally make it difficult for family members to move on. For instance, if a young adult's presence becomes a solution to his/her parents' marital difficulties, it will be unlikely that the family will be able to let the young adult move on with the separation process. Such potentials exist at every phase and are influenced by the family's previous history in dealing with this phase and the amount of tension currently present in the family.

Symptoms Result from Triangulation

Since triangulation occurs so frequently, it seems to be a natural aspect of emotional system functioning. When we are in conflict or some form of upset, it is tension-relieving to involve a third party; it feels better. When the process becomes a necessary ingredient for dealing with the tension, then a symptom forms. Becoming necessary implies that the symptom's initial tension relief serves a longer-term functional role in the system. This happens as the process begins to occur more frequently, with the same set of participants developing a set of postures of closeness and distance and valence towards one another (Bowen, 1978; Kerr & Bowen, 1988).

The length of time that such a process continues determines the rigidity of the triangle and thus the intransigence of the symptom. While family members may feel pulled to change it, they also experience the fears of change and the familiarity of sameness (Carter & McGoldrick, 1989a, b).

Symptoms Rigidify Closeness/Distance Between People

By their very nature, triangles define the closeness and distance between various parties. In fact, in some ways triangles can be viewed as ways to deal with the degree of closeness between people; when things get too close one can always move off towards a third person, thing, or party (Kerr & Bowen, 1988).

In addition, through their repetitive nature triangles lead to long-term postures or positions of closeness/distance between individuals. Once these postures have developed there is a tendency for the triangle to stand as a structure ready to be used when tension develops between the parties.

For instance, when a child is triangulated into parental difficulties, he/she becomes more aligned with, say, mother, and more distant from father. When the tension decreases between the parents, the child returns to the outside position and the relationships seem calm—until the next instance of tension between the parents. After some repetition, the child begins to respond to the tension in the mother or in the parental relationship and habitually to take one person's, mother's, side and distance from the father.

In this model, closeness/distance is not a measure of feelings toward another individual. It is as possible to feel distant and negative as to feel distant and positive. The same is true for overcloseness; it can take on, and often does, an increasingly negative valence as the individuals struggle to create some distance between them. Thus, in examining triangles it is important look at the closeness *and* the valence. The idea of valence (Carter & McGoldrick Orfanidis, 1976) is embodied in the ideas of villain and victim, family angel and family bastard, the bitch and the hero. All of these imply little about position but a lot about the quality of the relationship. They also imply that in a particular triangle one person is being held more accountable for the tension than the other.

HOW CHANGE OCCURS

How are we to define change? As therapists we are certainly viewed and view ourselves as agents of change. Sometimes because or in spite of this self-definition, we tend to forget that change is intrinsic to family life. In fact, without change families would not be able to adapt to the demands made on them by their context and by the changing needs of their members. According to the multigenerational model as practiced at the Family Institute of Westchester, the role of a therapist is to capitalize on the family's strengths, its impetus toward movement and change; the goal is to mobilize the family and give it direction. We believe in the family's intrinsic ability to utilize plan and direct change in a useful way.

Several interrelated principles form the framework for our model's view of change and how it occurs (Bowen, 1978; Carter & McGoldrick, 1989a, b; Carter & McGoldrick Orfanidis, 1976; Fogarty, 1976, 1979; Guerin, 1976; Kerr & Bowen, 1988):

1. Change across multiple generations has a long-term and significant impact on current life circumstances.
2. Change involves one person's taking responsibility for shifting his/ her position in generational patterns of relating.
3. Change must be planned for.
4. Change is a three-step process.

Change Across Multiple Generations

Most of us would agree that that what happens in the present is influenced by what happened in the past. The multigenerational model proposes that these patterns not only existed in the past but also continue across multiple levels of the family system. In order for change to occur one must change patterns of relating with as many generations of the family as possible. In fact, even collecting family information over many generations seems to provide clients with a better understanding of the patterns as they existed before they became a part of their family-of-origin functioning. As a therapist I often think of the potential for extended family and other system change as allowing me more freedom with the individual. I have a broader tapestry in which to weave change and can direct the client to look with a broader perspective.

Another aspect of change over multiple generations is dealing with old unfinished business or baggage from the past that continues to plague present relationships (McGoldrick & Carter, 1989). If an individual remains reactive to an issue from the past, it is important to deal with it, involving other family members as well. A variety of techniques for accomplishing this and for the work that must occur in preparation are elaborated in the chapters that follow. It is important to note that, according to our model, confrontation and implied blame solidify behavior; they do not create change. Change is created by self-examined and self-directed behavior.

Change Involves One Person's Taking Responsibility for Self

This statement might seem selfish to those who view taking responsibility for self as acting only on the basis of what one wants and needs. Taking responsibility for self does not mean being inconsiderate of others. In fact, the term *responsibility* implies self in terms of other. (This idea is more clearly understood when we think of the term *irresponsibility*, which always implies others.) So what does it mean to be responsible for self? It means that, in any interaction or relationship, one examines one's own part and seeks to change that part which is not functional (Bowen, 1978).

In order to take responsibility for self, the individual must first be able to examine his/her thoughts and feelings in a particular situation and figure out how these influence his/her behavior. It means being accountable for one's own internal reactions and one's actions; it does not view others as "making" one feel or act a particular way. In accomplishing this aim, the individual seeks to develop as many person-to-person relationships as he/she can in the family. Authentic self-to-self relationships are the goal, rather than relationships that are reactive to the feelings and behaviors of others. Being responsible for self means not letting one's emotional reactivity to others determine how one thinks, feels, and behaves. Having feelings about someone is being clear about how one feels — not just responding to what the other does. Clearly developing such responsibility for self is a lifelong process.

Change Must Be Planned

In this model the client is the major agent of change; the therapist helps him/her to produce change in the system in which he/she interacts. For change to occur one must get "meta" to an emotional system. If the individual is unable to observe and describe the system and his/her reaction to it, he/she will be unable to resist the forces that pull him/her to react as usual.

Focusing on the cognitive aspects of the change process involves planning. Without cognition, one tends to enter the system in the same emotional position. In doing nuclear family work, the therapist is able to be meta to the system and therefore to help plan change. As extended family work begins, the client must be helped to achieve this position, since he/she will be the one who will be with the family and responsible for changing self. It is an intricate process of staying connected yet separate enough to observe self and eventually to change self (see Carter & McGoldrick Orfanidis, 1976). There are four steps involved in planning for change: planning, predicting, preparing, and processing. These steps will be discussed in Chapter 5.

Change Is a Three-Step

Change is often thought of as a two-step: I change and the other(s) react. However, as Bowen explained, it is what happens after this second step that really determines whether change occurs. If after the other(s) react the individual reacts by going back to his/her original position, then no change has occurred. This is in keeping with the idea that change involves taking responsibility for self and not being reactive to others. If after the other reacts the individual is able to hold the new position, then one can say one has changed.

One supposes that keeping this new position consistently vis-à-vis the other will lead to the possibility of new interactions. In other words, change in self in relation to other(s) usually leads to change in the overall interaction. It does not necessarily mean that the other person will change in relation to others.

The process of achieving this three-step is difficult at best; it is much easier to say one has changed one's position and the other person didn't accept it and did the same old thing. This model assumes that it is in the nature of systems that they will do the same old thing; therefore, change is doing something different in the face of the same old thing. And that is difficult.

THE THERAPY PROCESS

The ultimate goal of the multigenerational model as practiced at the Family Institute of Westchester is to change one individual's relationships over three generations. The therapy process begins where the client is, at the system level in which the presenting problem is defined. From the beginning of the process, the problem is placed in a three-generational context. The client is educated regarding how systems operate, how symptoms develop, and how change occurs. This education process utilizes what the client presents and expands it to allow the client to view the tapestry of his/her family.

The progress of treatment is from the here and now to the not so here and now. All along the way the client takes increasing responsibility for the focus of his/her work and for his/her life. The therapist continues to take responsibility for the conduct of the therapy sessions and for her/his behavior in it.

In this model, therapy does not end when the presenting problem no longer exists. In fact, the interesting part of treatment has just begun. Assisting one or more individuals to figure out the threads of their family systems, which have lead to the development of the current problem, is the heart of the three-stage model. Each stage implies some differences in the focus, the degree of client and therapist responsibility for change, and the techniques which may be utilized. The stages are briefly described here; a fuller description of each stage appears in Chapters 4, 5, and 6.

In stage 1 the work is focused on the presenting problem, the here and now. The problem is tracked three-generationally and an overall theme is noted for each of the adults vis-à-vis her/his family of origin. This will serve to keep the work on track in later sessions. The therapist is generally responsible in this phase for teaching the client(s) concepts regarding the family, symptoms, and change, as well as for the orchestration of change around the presenting problem. The most important focus in this regard is defining and changing the foreground, that is, the central triangle maintaining the symptom.

During stage 2, the client begins to work on the multigenerational threads of his/her life. The therapist focuses the client on some theme in his/her life that has affected the development of the current difficulties. In other words, the therapist helps the client to identify his/her part in the current situation as it weaves its way up in extended family relationships. What heralds this phase is the client's successful effort at changing self in the family of origin.

The client takes increasing responsibility for determining the course of treatment and for areas of ongoing work. Once change has been solidified in one or more areas, so that the client experiences some differences in the manner in which he/she interacts in the family, we are usually ready to begin stage 3.

In this model treatment never ends; there are just breaks between sessions. These breaks may be longer or shorter depending on the work the client is doing at a particular moment. The hallmark of stage 3 is that the client becomes the weaver of her/his own tapestry. He/she feels in charge of his/her own life and utilizes the therapy process to aid that effort. Therapy is directed primarily by the client, with the therapist acting as a consultant. For the most part, the client is able to apply the model to his/her life. Sessions are sought when the client is reactive and unable to get meta to the system. The therapist and the client consult each as knowledgable systems people.

REFERENCES

Bowen, M. (1976). Theory in the practice of psychotherapy. In P. Guerin (Ed.), *Family therapy: Theory and practice* (pp. 42–91). New York: Gardner.

Bowen, M. (1978). *Family therapy in clinical practice*. New York: Aronson.

Carter, B. & McGoldrick, M. (1989a). *The changing family life cycle: A framework for family therapy* (2nd ed.). Boston: Allyn & Bacon.

Carter, B., & McGoldrick, M. (1989b). The changing family life cycle—A framework for family therapy. In B. Carter and M. McGoldrick (Eds.) *The changing family life cycle: A framework for family therapy* (2nd ed.) (pp. 3–28). Boston: Allyn & Bacon.

Carter, E., & McGoldrick Orfanidis, M. (1976). Family therapy with one person and the family therapist's own family. In P. Guerin (Ed.). *Family therapy: Theory and practice*. New York: Gardner.

Combrinck-Graham, L. (1985). A developmental model for family systems. *Family Process, 24*, 139–150.

Fogarty, T. (1976). On emptiness and closeness, Part II. *The Family* 3/2.

Fogarty, T. F. (1979). The distancer and the pursuer. *The Family, 7*, 11–16.

Fulmer, R. (1989). Lower income and professional families: A comparison of structure and life cycle process. In B. Carter & M. McGoldrick (Eds.), *The changing family life cycle* (2nd ed.) (pp 545–578). Boston: Allyn & Bacon.

Goldner, V. (1989). Generation and generation: Normative and covert hierarchies. In M. McGoldrick, F. Walsh, & C. M. Anderson (Eds.), *Women in families* (pp. 42–61). New York: W. W. Norton.

Guerin, P. (1976). *Family therapy, theory and practice*. New York: Gardner.

Guerin, P., Fay, L. F., Burden, S. L., & Kautto, J. G. (1987). *The evaluation and treatment of marital conflict*. New York: Basic Books.

Haley, J. (1973). *Uncommon therapy: The psychiatric techniques of Milton H. Erickson, M.D.* New York: Norton.

Haley, J. (1987). *Problem solving therapy* (2nd ed.). San Francisco: Jossey-Bass.

Inclan, J. & Ferran, E. (1990). Poverty, politics, and family therapy: A role for systems theory. In M. Mirkin (Ed.), *The social and political context of family therapy* (pp. 193–213). Boston: Allyn & Bacon.

Kerr, M. E., & Bowen, M. (1988). *Family evaluation*. New York: Norton.

McGoldrick, M., Anderson, C. M., & Walsh, F. (1989). *Women in families: A framework for family therapy*. New York: Norton.

McGoldrick, M., & Carter, B. (1989). Forming a remarried family. In B. Carter & M. McGoldrick (Eds.). *The changing family life cycle: A framework for family therapy* (2nd ed.) (pp. 399–429). Boston: Allyn & Bacon.

McGoldrick, M., Pearce, J., & Giordano, J. (1982). *Ethnicity and family therapy*. New York: Guilford.

Toman, W. (1976). *Family constellation* (3rd ed.). New York: Springer.

Walters, M., Carter, B., Papp, P., & Silverstein, O. (1988). *The invisible web*. New York: Guilford.

The Therapeutic Relationship

FREDDA HERZ BROWN

IN THIS MODEL, the therapist functions essentially as a consultant or a coach. According to Webster's dictionary, a coach is "someone who instructs or trains a performer; a private tutor." A consultant is one "who is called upon for professional or technical advice or opinions." Both definitions suit the role of the therapist in our model. The therapist privately instructs or teachers the client about emotional system functioning and expert advice on how families function. The client is the performer, who functions as a learner and the change agent.

A broad perspective on this role is given in other writings (Bowen, 1976; Carter & McGoldrick Orfanidis, 1976). Here we further elaborate the original definition of coaching, outlining four aspects of the role of therapist in this model. Any one of these can be used throughout treatment. We do not see this role as limited to work with only one client, rather it can be applied wherever the family members are when they enter treatment. We do not believe that the therapist can avoid emotional involvement with a client; in fact, all of us would agree that it is easier to work with a client whom we like than with someone whom we find disagreeable, and certainly liking someone is an emotional involvement. However, therapists need to keep their own emotional issues out of the therapy process; the therapist must maintain the same difficult balance of emotional connection and separateness that the client is asked to maintain with his/her family.

In this model, the therapist is responsible for his/her own behavior throughout therapy. The therapist is not more responsible or concerned for the client's life decisions and actions than the client is him/herself. The therapist is also responsible for avoiding engagement in the client's problems by becoming automatically and inadvertently triangled into the process. On the other hand, the therapist may plan to use a triangle either among the client, family, and him/herself or among a husband, wife, and him/herself. (This is a fairly common practice in using reversals, as we shall see in Chapter 5.)

The primary focus of the therapy is not the client-therapist relationship but rather the client-family relationship. The therapist never wants to be more important to the client than is the extended family. The therapist acts as a teacher, a model, a detective, and a consultant. While each of these characteristics stances can be used throughout the treatment process, the therapist becomes less central to the process as the client becomes more self-focused and knowledgable about emotional systems. By the last stage of the treatment process, the client and the therapist are like two individuals who consult regarding a particular situation about which each possesses a certain set of opinions, knowledge, and perspective.

THE THERAPEUTIC ROLE

The development of the therapeutic role involves a complex organization of skills, knowledge, and sense of self in four functional areas; teacher, model, detective, and consultant. As we shall see, the functions are not mutually exclusive but, rather, tend to overlap.

Teacher

The therapist teaches about emotional systems by asking questions, giving information, and normalizing process. He/she is an expert on emotional systems and how they function and change. (S)he gets the client to understand this information by posing process oriented questions, that is, questions that lead them to describe the who, what, when, and where of the system.

Clients can be taught about triangles and other principles of emotional system functioning (as discussed in Chapter 1) as the relevant subject areas come up in treatment. Some therapists choose to teach clients these system principles and structural concepts by actually using a posterboard or blackboard. Others, like myself prefer to explain information casually to clients when the situation arises. I try not to be didactic since I find that I lose clients when I do that. In addition, concepts and principles are best learned by using the client's examples and/or by telling stories about other clients or ones made up to suit the case at hand. The way a question is asked or responded to provides the client with information about the system. Before long clients begin to use the terminology and the concepts themselves in their work.

In addition to posing questions that each process, the therapist uses what I have come to call "one-liners." These are statements that teach some system concept in one sentence and demand no response from the client. They are meta statements — outside of process and yet commenting on it. These one-liners are particularly helpful when the client is very reactive and the therapist wants to introduce an idea without increasing the client's intensity.

Clients also learn through reading articles or books about the relevant emotional process. Articles on other individuals' work on their own families or on such concepts as the life cycle are helpful (see Additional Readings list at the end of this chapter for some suggestions). Two recent books, *The Dance of Anger* (1985) and *The Dance of Intimacy* (1988), both by Harriet Goldhor Lerner, have proven to be particularly useful with clients.

Model

The therapist serves as a model for the client of the emotional stance that will be useful in family work. It is a stance that is involved yet neutral, connected yet separate. Clients often describe the therapeutic stance as one where the therapist is supportive of their work yet not handholding, encouraging but not directly so, and where approval becomes irrelevant. The therapist makes clear his own personal and professional beliefs by labeling them as such. The therapist takes "I positions" regarding his/her own principles and what he/she will or will not do (Bowen, 1976).

The emotional tone of the sessions is kept low-key, so that the client can think and so that the therapist can forestall emotional expression of issues towards him/her that belong within the family system. The therapist models nonreactivity by remaining calm even though the system may be responding with emotional ups and downs. The evenness of the coach's tone of voice and emotions in the face of the family's turmoil lends a sense of quiet competency and equanimity to the situation. It allows the coach to maintain perspective when the client does not. The coach feels and expresses emotions but does not increase the tension in the system by allowing his/her own reactivity to the situation to interfere with the therapy process. The fact that the coach asks questions that are circular in nature and focus on the emotional process, including the introduction of previously taboo and highly charged emotional issues, models a nonreactive stance for the client(s).

In order to provide this atmosphere, the therapist him/herself must trust the process that evolves during therapy. As we will see, it helps if the therapist has used this theory in his/her personal life.

Detective

For investigating with the client the emotional process in the client's relationship systems, the therapist functions as an incessant questioner, a systems detective. Questions are of several types, the major ones being those that have to do with pattern defining and with getting the client to think about a situation differently.

Therapists should know how they plan to use a particular piece of information before they ask the question; that is, every question should have a purpose in the treatment process. Even directing the client to ask questions of certain family members is aimed at defining patterns and exploring themes. Some family therapists have clients go back to their extended family and collect such historical information as dates of births, deaths, and immigration. While this information may be interesting, we should not lose sight of its function, that is, helping the client to understand his/her family. Being clear about the use of this information in terms of the current family work is important.

With several family members in the room, most therapists have a fairly easy time asking questions and formulating some hypotheses about the family process that is maintaining the symptom. In fact, the process is often observable. In extended family work most of what occurs is outside of the therapy room. Thus, the therapist must be able to formulate questions so that the client will be able to describe the emotional process well enough that the therapist can help the client shift his/her position. I often think of this therapeutic function as light bulb therapy. The therapist's job is to turn the lights on in the client; in other words, the therapist must ask enough questions so that the light begins to dawn in the client. This is different from interpretation or explanation, where the light bulb shines in the therapist who then tries to convey the wisdom to the client. If the timing is right, insight is achieved. In this method of treatment, the therapist, functioning as a detective, seeks to have the client figure out the connections or get the data to do so.

Questions are always posed in a circular manner, seeking to understand all aspects of the process and avoid placing of blame or responsibility. I often think that the therapist puts in as much time thinking about how to ask a question as (s)he does in actually asking the question. From such questioning comes the ability to direct the client in his/her work.

Consultant

One aspect of the therapist's role is helping clients shift positions that are problematic or dysfunctional for them. Early on the therapist may function as a consultant regarding some nuclear family processes within the therapy, such as directing a couple on some structural move or parents on how to handle some issue with their recalcitrant teenager. When therapy work shifts to outside of the therapy room, the therapist serves as a taskgiver to the client, who must perform the task and report back on the results.

In this consultant role, the therapist sometimes functions as a director. One way involves the management of the emotional process in the room. Another has to do with formulating ways in which the client can shift his/her position in dysfunctional patterns of interaction. Although these functions are not separate in actuality, we will consider them as such.

There are models of family therapy in which the therapist functions primarily as a director of emotional process. For instance, the structural model is known for its focus on the therapist as the mover of process in the room and outside of it; he/she is the major change agent. In the multigenerational model, the client is the major change agent. The job of the therapist in the room is to direct the flow of emotional process so that the intensity stays low. In this way the client is able to think and describe, and the therapist is less likely to get caught up in the client's emotional issues. For this reason, most of the communication early on with couples or families is between the therapist and the client(s). This keeps the intensity from increasing between family members and allows the therapist to remain in charge of the flow of information.

The therapist also functions as a consultant as the client makes changes in his/her life. After working with a client to elaborate a triangle or to define some relationship issue, the therapist assists the client in shifting his/her position in the relationship. Much of the early work in this area has to do with getting a client calm enough to deal with the issues and then to observe and work on them. An out-of-session task is usually assigned to help the client either better understand his/her position or shift that position. We will discuss the details of task assignment in Chapter 5. Here it is important to remember that the client is responsible for shifting the position; the therapist must carefully construct, with the client, a doable task to accomplish this aim.

CLIENT CHARACTERISTICS

The client is an active participant in the treatment, the principal actor/actress in a drama that is his/her life. This is especially true in the second and third stages of treatment. With therapeutic direction, clients become the weavers of their family tapestry, changing patterns and dealing with issues and themes that have plagued them in daily life with others.

In order to take part as a client in the later phases, the individual, whether alone or with a mate, must be not only motivated but also capable of certain behaviors. This work requires low anxiety, the ability to observe and describe reality, a self-focus, and the ability to follow through with plans. It should be obvious to the reader that these characteristics are interrelated; however, for the sake of discussion we will consider each separately.

Low Anxiety

Clients who come into therapy are generally anxious; however, some are more anxious than others. When anxiety is too high, it is impossible to carry out the most basic tasks of interpersonal relating, such as listening and asking questions. This is why the first task of the therapist is to focus on lowering the client's anxiety. Once that is accomplished and client is able to hear the therapeutic questions and seems interested in something other than feeling less anxious, the therapist/coach can begin the process of having the client examine the emotional field in which he/she resides. However, there are some clients who never get past the first effort at decreasing anxiety and dealing with initial symptomatology; there are others who, spurred on by some family issues(s), crisis, or life-cycle stage, will return months later to do some more work.

Ability to Observe and Describe Reality

Since the client may be seen alone, it is extremely important that he/she be able to observe and describe what is being experienced in a fairly accurate way. We all realize that one person's reality is another person's fairytale; emotions and expectations color our view of events. When more than one family member is in the room, the therapist can check each one's perceptions against the others; this provides a chance to verify and elaborate on the reality described by each.

When working with one client, the therapist must be confident that the client is able to observe a situation with attention to what he/she is feeling and thinking. Frequently, this is the first task assigned to clients who are not aware of how a situation develops and how they are feeling and responding in it.

Self-Focus

Since multigenerational therapy, especially in the second and third stages, entails a focus on self in the truest sense of the word, clients who seek this form of treatment must be interested in examining and changing self. They must share with the therapist the beliefs that therapy is change-oriented and evolves from understanding one's responses to those around him/her.

The client must be interested in changing his/her behavior and reactions to others, not in changing or complaining about the others' behavior. Since the therapeutic process over time becomes more and more self-directed, the basic interest in changing self must be present. The client may need some assistance in maintaining this in the face of family system reactions, but the overall interest needs to be sustainable.

Ability to Follow Through With Plans

In order to be engaged in the later stages of the therapeutic process, the client must be able to follow through on plans worked out with the therapist for work outside of the therapy room. Of course, this ability is related to the client's level of anxiety; the higher it is, the lower the ability to follow through. There may be other reasons for a client not to follow directions, primarily lack of interest or motivation; however, these are usually evaluated by the therapist before sending the client out to do a task.

Most of therapy occurs outside the therapy room, with the client working on changing him/herself in relation to others; in instances where the client is having difficulty following through or where the therapist thinks it might be useful, family members are brought in for sessions. It is important that the therapist clearly evaluate the client's ability to carry out the plans outside the room and that the client is well prepared for sessions with family members. Although clients frequently state that family members will not come if invited, I have never had one refuse to come.

One way that I evaluate whether clients can follow through is by having them begin with a small task, for instance, going to visit their parents and observing their own emotional reactions to the process of which they are a part.

If a client has not done the task, the therapist must question why it wasn't completed. Sometimes it is clear that the client felt unsure of the assignment after he/she left the session or got to the point of doing it but felt too anxious. The first problem can easily be ameliorated by having the client tape or take notes during sessions. Everyone is anxious working on family issues; tape recorded or written note are useful in helping one to remember those things that are hard to hear, much less to do. The second problem has to do with incomplete preparation for the work to be done. As we discussed briefly under therapist role and will do more fully in Chapter 5, part of the task of the therapist is to help clients adequately prepare for their own tasks.

Contraindications

There are times when one is referred a client who seems ideal for coaching— bright, intellectually and emotionally curious, interested in and focused on changing self, able to laugh at her/himself, and generally nonanxious or at least lacking the free-floating type. However, you can count these times on one or two hands. Most clients who are referred or refer themselves for treatment are in crisis, have little ability to think clearly, and can seldom laugh at themselves. If they aren't in crisis when they come in, the system's goings-on (just the daily complications of living in a reactive system) will soon interfere with their ability to maintain the back-and-forth motion between family-of-origin and nuclear family issues.

As one would surmise from the above, there are few contraindications for the application of this model. Certain clients who are very anxious and/or are experiencing a situational and normative life-cycle stress experience a longer period of time calming the system down and redefining the problem. Certainly anxiety interferes with self-focus, direction and definition, the very heart of the model.

While the multigenerational model can be applied with one person and generally has as its focus the individual, frequently it is most creatively applied with a couple. It is only possible to understand the process of self-definition and direction when one sees it in relation to an individual with whom one is intimately related. Mates who are fairly nonreactive to one another can support each other in understanding their own reactions to family. It is also frequently enlightening to the therapist to see the emotional process of the couple unfold before him/her. It is more difficult for the therapist to detect patterns when only one person is present and to make interventions in such instances.

In order to apply this model, the therapist must have a client who to a greater or lesser extent meets the characteristics stated above; the specifics of how to make the model applicable to particular client situations is the subject of sections II and III of the book. The therapist must also understand emotional systems well enough to know what to do and say when only one person is representative of the system.

Resistance

How can one discuss a model of treatment without considering client resistance? Resistance in the multigenerational model is viewed as the client's and/or the family's pulls toward sameness, towards the status quo, although it may also reflect a problem in the therapist's functioning with this client. Forces pulling toward sameness are always present in the family system and compete with the emotional pulls toward change. The therapist must figure out how to mobilize the family's strengths to tip the equation toward change.

In this view, the client is resisting not the therapist per se but the therapist's attempts to move toward change. In keeping with the focus on the client-family relationship rather than the therapist-client relationship, the therapist generally uses the client's resistance as a chance to gather information about the family and the client's anxiety. The therapist does not interpret resistance directly but may go about changing what he/she does or how he/she approaches the client as a way dealing with the resistance. In this way resistance is viewed not only as the client's responsibility but also as an outcome of the way in which the therapist is approaching change with the client.

Changing the way one approaches the client demands that the therapist always be aware of and ask questions about the implications of a shift in the client's position vis-à-vis the family. In Chapter 5, we will consider in detail how a client is prepared by defining the system resistances and preparing to deal with them. The reader is also referred back to the Chapter 1 discussion of change as three-step process for an understanding of the family's resistance to the individual's taking a different position.

THE THERAPIST AS A PERSON

In order to practice this model of treatment the therapist must understand the process that he/she is asking clients to work on and trust the process that evolves during therapy. This therapy model stresses the similarities between the client family and the therapist and his/her family. It suggests that the difficulties that clients experience are not very different from some that we experience. The expectation is that the therapist will be as responsible for his/her life as he/she expects the client to be.

As Carter and McGoldrick Orfanidis (1976) originally pointed out, there is no way to understand the emotional pulls and tugs of family system work as an individual unless one attempts it him/herself. One may gain some sense of the struggles that a client goes through during one's long-term work with them. However, it is extremely difficult emotionally to know what clients will go through and some of the ways in which they will react unless one has attempted to work on oneself in the same way. When a client says, "You don't know my mother/father," or, "If I say that, my mother will have a stroke," it will be difficult for the therapist, if he/she has not experienced it family work and reactions, to assess the reality of the client's anxiety and pace the work. If one's own anxiety goes up when hearing such statements, it is hard to help clients evaluate the reality of their fears or anxieties regarding change.

In addition, how can one be a responsible therapist and thus model this stance if one has not worked on becoming more comfortable with oneself in the systems in which he/she is involved? To remain emotionally clear of clients' attempts to pull one into their lives in a way that is isomorphic to their difficulties, the therapist must be emotionally aware of his/her own vulnerability. I think that over half of one's time in any therapy session with a couple or individual is spent keeping out of the emotional process. If the therapist becomes a part of the process by inadvertent side-taking or by allowing him/herself to become more central to the clients' lives than the family is, then therapy becomes bogged down. One can be doing all the right things as a therapist—using all the right techniques and focusing on the right issues—but if one is part of the process between people, that process does not get worked out.

So how does the therapist work on him/herself? In just the same manner as the clients do. That is, therapists work on their family-of-origin issues in treatment. Sometimes they work on these issues in therapist-own-family groups, where a small group of therapists meet regularly to discuss their own family issues. In this way they not only become familiar with the pulls and tugs of family work, but also learn something about the client-therapist relationship. This is a method of therapy that can be learned but not taught. Working on one's own family aids in the learning aspect.

Most other models of family therapy do not suggest that the therapist do work on him/herself consistent with the principles of the model. I think the reason for this is twofold. First, in most models of therapy, the therapist is the change agent, directing the action of the therapy sessions. The focus on the personal aspects of the therapist is decreased, and there is no sense of how family work would affect work as a therapist. Secondly, most models of family therapy have grown out of the tradition of short-term treatment with the whole family. Short treatment usually takes the focus off the intensity of the relationship between client and family. In addition, working with the whole family makes it much easier for the therapist to stay out of the family emotional process. The emotional process in these instances tends to stay between family members rather than between the therapist and the family. When the number of family members in the room is fewer, as with a couple or an individual, the emotional tension is likely to pull the therapist into some lurking triangle. The more the therapist knows about how he/she is likely to be triangled in, the better he/she will be at leaving the tension to be resolved in the family.

Knowing how one is likely to get triangled with clients demands not only knowledge of therapist/self in family issues but also a very good understanding of the clients' and one's own family triangles. The ways clients relate to members of their families tend to be repeated between the client and others, including the therapist, while triangles from the therapist's own family may be played out with clients. It is the goal of the multigenerational therapist to keep process between self and clients limited and thus keep the tendency for the client to replicate process under control. Using infrequent sessions, every two to four weeks, tends to decrease the intensity of the relationship and the importance of the therapist in the client's life. However, it is never possible or desirable totally to control the emotional relationship between self and client, no matter how influential one is as a therapist. Therefore, it behooves the therapist to be in as much control and as aware of his/her own emotional process and biases as possible.

REFERENCES

Bowen, M. (1976). Theory in the practice of psychotherapy. In P. Guerin (Ed.), *Family therapy: Theory and practice* (pp. 42–91). New York: Gardner.
Carter, E. A. & McGoldrick Orfanidis, M. (1976). Family therapy with one person and the family therapist's own family. In P. Guerin (Ed.), *Family therapy: Theory and practice* (pp. 193–220). New York: Gardner.

ADDITIONAL READINGS FOR CLIENTS ON EXTENDED FAMILY WORK

Anonymous. (1974). Taking a giant step: First moves back into my family. *The Family, 2.*
Bloomfield, H. (1983). *Making peace with your parents.* New York: Random House.
Colon, F. (1973). In search of one's past: An identity trip. *Family Process, 12,* 429–438.
Framo, J. L. (1976). Family of origin as a therapeutic resource for adults in marital and family therapy: You can and should go home again. *Family Process, 15,* 193–210.
Friedman, E. H. (1971). The birthday party: An experiment in obtaining change in one's own extended family. *Family Process, 10,* 2.
Lerner, H. G. (1985). *The dance of anger.* New York: Harper & Row.
Lerner, H. G. (1988). *The dance of intimacy.* New York: Harper & Row.
Powers, T. (1989). *Family matters.* New Hampshire: Hathaway Press.

General Practice Principles

FREDDA HERZ BROWN

THE FOCUS OF THIS CHAPTER is the eight general principles that guide the practice of the multigenerational model. The first three principles pertain specifically to the client, while the others have to do with a general stance toward the process of treatment. Stage-specific practice guidelines will be discussed in the next three chapters. The general principles are:

1. Stay relevant to the client.
2. Normalize process and focus on strengths.
3. Focus on each individual's part in the emotional process.
4. Be responsible for the therapy process.
5. Trust process; change takes time.
6. Whenever possible, connect nuclear family process to extended family process.
7. Ask questions; don't give answers.
8. Therapy is a process of constantly evaluating therapy.

PRINCIPLES

Stay Relevant to the Client

To a greater or lesser extent, all forms of therapy deal with the issue of relevancy and/or timing. In the multigenerational model, we worry about remaining relevant to the client's definition of the problem while at the same time introducing a broader view of it. Balancing where the client is and where the therapist would like him/her to be is at times like walking a tightrope. If one stays only with the client's definition, the therapy will be very short-term, with little movement toward extended family work. If there is too much or too quick a shift towards a redefinition, the client/family may balk and end treatment.

Introducing ideas regarding a family tapestry into the family's definition of the current difficulties is usually the first and most continuous task of treatment. There are skills involved in doing this, such as learning to ask circular questions and doing a genogram (these will be discussed in detail in the next two chapters). However, the multigenerational therapist must also possess a certain degree of artistry in weaving the ideas into the client's current viewpoint. Generally, the ability to do this evolves with practice. There are three ways in which the therapist stays relevant in this process: (1) use of language; (2) staying emotionally connected to each of the clients; and (3) weaving themes from what is presented by the client.

Therapeutic language is very important; it is way that we define people as belonging to a particular group. For instance, there is a language of "law-yerese," "the wheretofores and the party of the first part" which is important not only to what the lawyer does but also to who he/she is. Identification as a lawyer is in part reflected in the use of language. It is certainly true that therapists are identified by the type of therapy they practice; with each type of therapy comes a set of concepts and a language for communicating with others in the group. The difficulty is that often the language that is used inside the group, where everyone has the same knowledge base, is used outside the group with clients and others.

I have a motto that, if a concept can't be described or explained in plain, ordinary English, then it shouldn't be explained at all. At the Family Institute of Westchester, we try to promote this idea by having a third-year theory course where trainees are required to prepare a presentation on the same topic for professional and lay audiences. This opportunity to develop different ways of describing emotional systems concepts to a variety of individuals is very useful to both trainees and instructors.

It is important not only to use a nonjargoned language but also to use the "language" of the family. Family members' language, their use of words, reflects their knowledge base, their knowledge or understanding about their family and what makes it work. Listening to how they use language often will tell the therapist the way in which they view the problem. Nonevolutionary approaches to change, such as the strategic therapies, use the family's language to introduce paradoxes. In this way the family's view is seemingly accepted and yet changed at the same time.

Although it is an evolutionary model of change (Taffel & Masters, 1989), the multigenerational approach also views the family's language as important for framing a redefinition of the family's problem. The therapist's language must mirror the client's, so that a shift in definition can be accomplished. For instance, referring to what the family calls mother's "nagging," the therapist might talk about her difficult job in getting the kids "in shape." To the children, the therapist might suggest that the trick would be to show her that they are in better shape, decreasing what they call her nagging. Here the therapist uses the family's word and begins to shift their definition of the problem slightly to one that is more systemic and inclusive of other family members' behavior. Generally speaking, the multigenerational model does not seek to make leaps in the family definition of a situation, except in those cases where direct redefinitions have already been tried and failed. Then paradoxical strategies might be used.

Staying relevant and connected to each of the family members involves making each of the clients feel listened to and understood. Sometimes a therapist's biases interfere with staying connected. We all come with our own particular biases. We do not have to agree with what a client says; we simply need to listen and strive to understand. It is often helpful for the therapist to identify a personal opinion that may differ from what the client is presenting. This helps to keep the therapist connected, since emotional energy does not have to be spent masking the bias or becoming engaged in trying to convince the client to adopt a particular viewpoint. The client also feels connected to the therapist, who is usually relating directly from an "I" position.

As we shall see in Chapter 4, it is especially important for the therapist to connect with everyone in the family during the first session. Failure to do so often results in the failure of the family to return to the second session. In our culture, men and women, but particularly men, view therapy as having to do with emotional work and think that is the province of women. This idea is supported by the fact that many family therapists are females and usually the adult female in the family has initiated the treatment process. Thus, men may especially need to feel listened to and understood in the early phases, since they may be reluctant participants.

Keeping a balanced view of the problem also helps to keep the therapist connected to each family member. If the therapist finds him/herself becoming unbalanced in his/her understanding of the family, spending a little more time with the one who on the lower side of the scale will help to equalize things. An unbalanced viewpoint can result from the therapist's lack of understanding of that person's view or from some emotional reactivity on the part of therapist. If it is the latter, trying to understand the client's viewpoint will highlight the need to deal with the source of the reactivity.

Another way of staying connected and relevant is to weave a theme. Early on in the therapy process, the therapist seeks to extend the family's definition of the problem to a three-generational, systemic viewpoint. In order to do this, the therapist attempts to weave a theme (or several) from the current family functioning into the extended family tapestry. This not only broadens the definition of the problem and keeps the client relating to the therapist, but also establishes a context for ongoing therapeutic work for the adults. This process is especially important when working with couples, since so much of the therapeutic work is in dealing with the tapestries of the extended families. In working with families where the problem is focused on a child, the same weaving of extended family process is necessary, but the initial work is with the nuclear family. Therefore, getting to extended family issues occurs further along in the treatment process.

Normalize Process and Focus on Strengths

One characteristic of most, if not all, forms of family therapy is a focus on family strengths and normalizing rather than on pathologizing what goes on in the family. It is the job of the multigenerational family therapist to focus on family strengths and to mobilize these to deal with weaknesses or difficulties. The therapist practicing in this model will spend a good deal of time identifying, highlighting, and labeling family's strengths, whatever they may be. It is hoped that family members do not experience the therapist as judgmental or pathologizing; rather, the therapist should be experienced as accepting them and yet challenging them to go beyond where they are to new ways of operating with one another.

The therapist uses his/her sense of humor and playfulness to assist family members in normalizing their view of what is going on with them. Being able to laugh at oneself is the ultimate form of accepting one's foibles and viewing them as normal. The difficulty is getting each person to view the other person's foibles as normal also. This is done primarily by increasing the client's understanding of the other person and his/her position in the system. What is usually taken personally or attributed negatively to the other person can be viewed as an outgrowth of the system and that individual's position in it.

Families usually come to treatment thinking the worst of themselves. Parents with problematic kids consider themselves to be failures, no matter how much they blame the child. Each partner in a couple considers him/herself to be a failure, no matter how much the other is held responsible for the difficulties. It is imperative that a therapist using this model move toward the family in a positive way. Another important way of normalizing family process and focusing on strengths is to focus on the multigenerational nature of difficulties. This places the problem in a context which makes sense, while spreading responsibility over a broader territory. This increases the family's and the therapist's degree of freedom and expands the available options in dealing with the difficulties.

Focus on Each Person's Part in the Emotional Process

While using a three-generational frame and thus broadening the client's understanding of a problem, the therapist must also work toward focusing the client on his/her specific contribution to the repetition of a family pattern. This is a delicate balance—walking a fine line between broadening process and narrowing it at the same time.

Helping a client to define and then change his/her part in the emotional process is one of the central tasks of the multigenerational model. Achieving and maintaining a self-focus when examining interactional patterns are difficult. There is a seemingly natural tendency to think of the other person's part, to be self-referent—that is, to think of how the other individual's behavior affects us and our behavior. This tendency may derive in part from reciprocity in relationships. We tend to focus on the reciprocal of our behavior; at the same time, the very nature of reciprocity permits the therapist to focus the client on self.

Multigenerational therapy is inherently educational in nature and has as one of its goals teaching clients how to figure out a problem and deal with their behavior without the assistance of the therapist. The client is taught how emotional systems operate and how to go about changing his/her part in the dysfunctional aspects of the system. Becoming responsible for self and for the direction of one's life is the outcome of being able to focus on one's own behavior.

Be Responsible for the Therapy Process

Just as it is important for clients to clarify who is responsible for what aspects of an interaction, it is useful for therapists to remember who is responsible for what aspects of the therapy process. Clarity on this aspect of responsibility helps one to avoid a common pitfall of this model of therapy—the therapist taking too much responsibility for change while the clients take too little.

The therapist takes responsibility for the conduct of the therapy sessions by focusing and constructing each session. The client is responsible for the manner in which he/she conducts his/her life and the degree to which therapy is used in leading that life in a more self-directed way.

What does it mean that the therapist takes responsibility for the conduct of therapy? In this model, it means that the therapist does not "wing it"; that is, he/she does not leave the session to what the client presents. Rather, there is a plan for the session based on the overall treatment plan and specifically on the work of the preceding session. This does not mean that the agenda can't be shifted as some issue is raised by the client, but rather that the responsibility for the shift is the therapist's.

Typically, a client's need to shift the focus of a particular session should be viewed as part of the process of change. For instance, a fight between spouses before a session will often be related to some shift the therapist and the clients are working on in treatment. Recognizing its context and dealing with it as such help the therapist and the client(s) to maintain the focus of the therapy.

While each session must be connected to the preceding one and set the stage for the following one, it must also have a form of its own. A therapy session is somewhat like a play with three acts—a beginning and a middle leading to a climax and a denouement. The beginning usually consists of some pleasantries and involves obtaining a sense of what's happened since the previous session. The actual work of the session usually occurs in the middle part, when a particular pattern is examined and each person's part dealt with in some way. This leads to the summary of the session, the climax, and finally to the denouement in which a task is usually given to the client(s). When a therapist experiences a session as going poorly, it is usually because some aspect of this play construct is not going as planned.

Having an overall treatment plan for a particular family allows the therapist to move from session to session with a sense of focus. When direction changes or when things are not moving as expected with a family, it is always possible to go back to the plan, examine it and readjust it. Therapy becomes a purposeful process whereby the client and the therapist map out goals and the therapist takes responsibility for focusing and constructing sessions so that the opportunity for goal achievement is available.

Another aspect of therapeutic responsibility involves taking responsibility for one's own life and the issues that are significant in it. Bowen (1978) once said that 50 percent of one's work with clients, especially couples, is staying out of the triangles, and the other 50 percent is working on the client's difficulties. Generally speaking, the fewer the clients in the room and the more emotionally charged the process, the more likely it is that the therapist will be drawn into the family process. Therefore, it is important for therapists to understand what processes they are likely to get caught in and to take charge of their own life so that this will not happen with a client.

In my own case, when I find myself overinvolved with a family and caring too much that family members work out their difficulties, or when I find myself taking sides with a couple or liking one of the two better than the other, I know that I am reacting to something from my own life.

Therapeutic responsibility involves not only the conduct of the actual therapy session(s) but also the conduct of the therapist in her/his role. The reader is referred to Chapter 2 for more on the latter.

Trust Process; Change Takes Time

One way in which family therapy declared itself different from psychodynamic models was to focus on the rapid nature of systemic change. The field grew up around a proliferation of videotapes and presentations that focused on one or two-session "cures." Certainly such change is possible, especially in child-focused cases. However, trainees in family therapy are often disappointed when they are not able to create as rapid shifts in the family as the experts. When their therapy lasts longer than the "average," they begin to worry. While I'm not sure what the "average" is, it is clear to me that most trainees do not think of therapy as lasting much beyond the first stage of treatment, i.e., dealing with the presenting problem.

At the Family Institute of Westchester, we teach a course oriented around the middle phase of family treatment. It deals with process-oriented issues, such as dealing with middle phase resistance, focusing and constructing sessions, and tracking a theme, as well as content issues related to couples work, marriage, divorce, single parenting, and remarriage. This is the meat of the middle phase of most treatment, when the work is often slow and painstaking and when the change process is tied primarily to extended family work.

Change takes time; it cannot be rushed. In fact, there seems to be an organic nature to some processes such as divorce and grieving. No matter how much one tries to speed up the process of dealing with them, it still takes the family at least two to five years to master all the tasks necessary (McGoldick & Carter, 1989; Hetherington, Cox, & Cox, 1977). But, while it is not possible to rush process, it is also not useful to leave process to time. That is, time in and of itself is not healing. It may calm down reactivity between people but usually, if it is not used appropriately, time is lost. It is useful for the therapist to have some personal experience with trusting process; it enables him/her to be more patient with clients and to help clients be more patient with themselves.

In this model, change is evolutionary (Taffel, 1986; Taffel & Masters, 1988). If patterns evolve over time, change also evolves over time. Change is also a multigenerational process, since in families evolution is multigenerational in nature. Thus, according to this model, change tends to be more enduring when there is a shift in the client's role with members of the family with whom he/she interacts in the same way. For instance, if John has the same difficulty with his mother as he does with Susan, his wife, he would experience a greater and more significant life change if he were to work on his relationships with both of them. Change like this is slow, since the system tends to pull the individual back into the processes it has used for generations. It involves much anticipatory work to create shifts in one's own behavior with others. (The four steps of the change process are discussed in detail in Chapter 5.)

Clients may make several attempts before they are able to carry through with a new position. Oftentimes there seems to be no direct change in the family process as a result of the new position. It is at these points that the therapist's work on his own family issues become important to the therapeutic process. Such work will often increase the therapist's understanding of the time factor and the client's dilemmas. What I have learned from my personal and professional experiences is that, if one consistently works on one's own part in the emotional process without responding to the system pulls to return to the old way, change in self and in the process will take place. As my colleagues have been known to say, "if only we live long enough."

Connect Nuclear Family Process to Extended Family Process

Most clients do not present in treatment with extended family difficulties. It is true that there are some life-cycle phases, particularly couples in formation and families in later years, where the extended family is of central importance, even if not initially defined as such. Other life-cycle phases are occupied with concerns about marriage, kids, adolescents, and divorce. Generally speaking, it is only when the extended family forms a point of the family triangle that it is raised as an issue.

One of the difficulties inherent in Bowenian theory is helping the clinician and the family make the transition to extended family work when such is not presented as the difficulty. How does one translate nuclear family issues into extended family themes? The multigenerational model accomplishes this aim by focusing on nuclear family process as one part of the work of therapy. The connection of this work to extended family themes is made early in the treatment process and forms the basis of middle and later phase work. The therapist always attempts to understand whatever clients present as difficulties in the context of three generations. Clients are always asked about how this particular issue or theme was dealt with in their family of origin. They are always directed to understand the process in the larger context so that they can obtain more clarity on how the process works in the nuclear family.

It has been my experience that a therapist is like a fisherman when dealing with extended family issues. Looking for an issue around which to get the client to move multigenerationally, he/she casts the fishing line and sees if anything is hooked. If so, then he/she reels it in; if not, then the casting process begins again. The therapist is always looking for an opening; however, if the therapist moves too quickly toward a multigenerational redefinition, the client, who may act passively accepting, will often resist, even by dropping out of treatment.

Ask Questions; Don't Give Answers

In order for successful therapy to be practiced, "light bulbs" need to be shining in the client's eyes; if not, there is no interest, no spark in the learning and change process. The issue is how to create such a spark in the client(s). When the therapist asks questions, he forces the client to examine process and to seek answers. Stumbling upon family patterns, clients will often experience the light going on.

Questions focusing on the four "w's"—who, what, when and where— help a client to elaborate and describe emotional process. Asking questions that demand that the client examine the connections between things also create client interest in emotional process. For instance, asking a client about the connection between the way she acts toward her mother or father and her interaction with her children will force her to think through and elaborate the similarities and differences in process.

Trainees frequently complain that they never seem to have enough questions to ask of clients. I suggest that they simply attempt to elaborate process in one triangle. I suggest that every time they think about making an explanatory statement to the client or launching into some didactic presentation regarding the emotional process, they make the statement into a question. In this way, it becomes easier to understand the use of questions.

Therapy is a Process of Constantly Evaluating Therapy

Therapy is not only a process of initial evaluation, treatment planning, treatment, and final evaluation. Rather it is a process of continuous examination, on a conscious or unconscious basis, of how therapy with a family is progressing towards its goals. Acknowledging such an ongoing evaluative process permits the client and the therapist to look at their progress and make ongoing adjustments. There are two potential difficulties when evaluation is not ongoing. The first is that the family and the therapist will lose track of the goals and wander in the course of treatment. The second is that the therapist and the client will make no adjustments to the original set of goals and get bogged down in old business.

Losing track of goals and how they relate to the original treatment plan is a common difficulty of middle phase work with families. A frequent symptom is a lack of focus or direction in the therapy sessions. Open discussion about the process of treatment and current progress or stalemate will help to keep sessions on track.

Therapy that is bogged down because the client and the therapist have not shifted goals is often viewed as boring and sleep-inducing to the therapist. I would guess that clients must experience it this way as well. Rigidly adhering to goals and trying the same interventions over and over again are symptoms of this difficulty. The ongoing process of evaluating what one intended to do and whether that initial goal has been, won't be, or could be met is important in preventing this problem.

Clients often come to treatment expecting to stay an indefinite period of time. They will hesitantly ask, "How long is this going to take?" At times, it is possible for the therapist, based on clinical experience with similar situations, to estimate how much treatment time will be necessary; in other instances, it is not possible to estimate time. In this case, the therapist and the family should agree on some time frame that will enable them to stop and evaluate how the initial issue or problem has been handled and determine if and what sort of treatment is still necessary. The family and the therapist work toward an end point that may or may not lead to more therapy. This gives them both an opportunity to consciously evaluate the therapy process and to recontract.

REFERENCES

Bowen, M. (1978). *Family therapy in clinical practice* (pp. 529–547). New York: Aronson.
Hetherington, E. M., Cox, M., & Cox, R. (1977). The aftermath of divorce. In J. H. Stevens, Jr., & M. Mathews (Eds.), *Mother-child, father-child relations*. Washington, DC: National Association for the Education of Young Children.
McGoldrick, M., & Carter, B. (1989). Forming a remarried family. In B. Carter & M. McGoldrick (Eds.). *The changing family life cycle: A framework for family therapy* (2nd ed.) (pp. 399–429). Boston: Allyn & Bacon.
Taffel, R., & Masters, R. (1988). An evolutionary approach to revolutionary change: The impact of gender arrangements on family therapy. In M. McGoldrick, C. M. Anderson, & F. Walsh (Eds.) *Women in families: A framework for family therapy* (pp. 117–134). New York: Norton.
Taffel, R. (1986, Nov.–Dec.). Revolution/evolution. *Family therapy networker, 10*:6, 52–60.

Stage 1: Defining and Working on the Foreground

FREDDA HERZ BROWN

THE FIRST STAGE OF the multigenerational model, consisting of the initial assessment and the initial treatment of the presenting problem, is extremely important in setting the stage for all future work. However, as we look at this first stage, it is worthwhile to remember that, while we can define and differentiate these stages on paper, seldom is there a clear demarcation in clinical reality. Rather, therapy moves back and forth between stages, depending on the client's presenting problem and initial readiness.

THE ASSESSMENT PROCESS

The multigenerational approach begins when the client/family enters the treatment room for the first time. No matter who is defined as having the presenting problem, the client is considered to be the family system of which the identified patient is a member. The family is not defined by the number of people in the treatment room; thus, every problem is considered a "family problem," while all change is individually based.

In evaluating the family system, one begins not only to map out the treatment plan for the problem at hand but to weave the tapestry of the family, connecting themes and triangles generationally. There are essentially four goals in the assessment process: (1) to join and engage with each member of the family; (2) to define the presenting problem systemically; (3) to connect the problem to three-generational process; and (4) to develop a treatment plan. While therapists using this model may have different methods for meeting these goals, they must concur that certain information is necessary for their accomplishment. Otherwise, clinicians may discover later on that they are missing information necessary to plan treatment. In addition, having a format for assessment enables the therapist to feel more in charge of the therapy process, which is important for beginning therapists. The therapist at least looks as if she/he has some idea abut what is necessary information and what is not.

In the process of questioning clients about their family system, the therapist begins to teach them another way to understand the emotional process surrounding the presenting problem. The manner in which questions are phrased and posed sets the tone for treatment and serves to engage the client(s) in the treatment process.

I use an evaluation format that takes me about two hours to complete (see Table 4.1). Trainees at the Family Institute of Westchester sometimes take longer — up to five sessions — to complete the evaluation. More complicated

TABLE 4.1*

Family Evaluation Format

The Presenting Problem
   What is each person's definition of what's wrong? Who's involved? What have they done? Why now?

Basic Family Patterns
   What are the triangles, myths, labels, themes? What is the triangle maintaining the symptom? Has the family undergone any recent situational or developmental crisis? What is the current phase of the family life cycle that they are struggling to deal with? What is the family's socioeconomic class and ethnicity?

Interface with Other Systems
   Has the family had previous treatment? What is the involvement if any with social service agencies? How does each member perform in relationships outside the family?

Extended Family Relationships
   What are the triangles, myths, labels and themes? Particularly, what are the themes around the problem that the family is currently presenting? What are the themes around spousing, childrearing, sex and gender?

Family Strengths and Weaknesses
   What are the family strengths that will help in working with its weaknesses?

Goals and Treatment Plan
   What are the family goals? How can they be reached?

Potential Difficulties for the Therapist
   In what ways does this family touch off personal issues for the therapist? What are the life-cycle similarities and differences?

---

*Original format developed by Monica McGoldrick

situations, for instance, when there are several previous marriages or an involved psychiatric history, will require a longer assessment. However, even without complications, I have never been able to complete a session in less than two hours. It takes me at least a half-hour to connect to each family member. Then we move on to develop a family map or genogram (McGoldrick & Gerson, 1985). This serves as my guide to family data and relationship information across at least three generations.

Keeping the format that I use in mind, let's consider each of the assessment goals.

Connect With Each Family Member

The process of connecting with the family begins in the initial phone call, which sets the stage for what the therapist and the family should expect and who will come to the session. A family member calls under great duress, usually after much consideration of options. It seems too obvious to mention, but the family member needs to feel understood and listened to in the phone call. The therapist strives to find out something about the person calling, why he/she is calling, and who else is involved in the problem. While involving as many relevant people as possible may seem like the proper course of action, struggling over attendance during an initial phone call is usually useless and does not encourage the family to come.

After spending some time just connecting personally with each member of the family, I then share or ask the calling party to share with the other family member(s) what he/she has told me on the phone. I try in this way to balance the process of problem definition. It is during this process of defining the problem that the therapist really does his/her connecting with the family. When the therapist asks balanced questions that call for an elaboration of emotional process, family members have the experience of being listened to and understood.

Focusing on family strengths and normalizing family process also serve to connect the family to the therapist. Being supportive of family members' previous efforts at change and understanding of how hard change can be normalize their experience. I always look for ways to check with people about their feelings about and previous experience with therapy.

Define the Presenting Problem Systemically

Much of the first session is spent in figuring out the nature of the presenting problem and the basic patterns of the nuclear family. One assumption of the multigenerational model is that all symptoms are supported by a triangle and that the nature of the triangle is such that, while it was initially a solution to a difficulty, it has now become at least part of the problem. Once a problem or issue takes on a function between any two individuals, then a triangle exists, complicating the dissolution of the problem. An initial goal in defining the presenting problem is to define the triangle that supports it.

In order to do this, the therapist will need to know, "Who's involved with what (or whom), when and where?" Asking circular questions regarding the details of the process surrounding the presenting problem will elaborate the central triangle. It may also elaborate a few of the interlocking ones, like those in the sibling subsystem with a child-focused family or those with the in-laws in a marital case. I spend at least half of the first session elaborating these patterns and everyone's view of them. Each person, including the person defined as having the problem, must be heard.

Symptoms can occur in any or all of three areas of nuclear family functioning: the couple, the individual adults, and/or a child or children (Bowen, 1978; Kerr & Bowen, 1988). The locus of the symptom will frequently determine how long it takes the therapist to move from this stage of treatment into the second stage. If a family has problems with children, rather than marital problems, more time is required to move up the levels of the system to extended family work. In general, the more severe the difficulties, the longer it will take to track them during the first session and the longer it will take the therapist to move to extended family process. There are, however, exceptions to this rule, such as when the nuclear process is so reactive that moving to extended family issues is a way to calm things down.

Not only do most families enter treatment with problems in one or more areas, but they also enter treatment with a definition of the problem that may or may not be systemic. In order to be defined systemically, the problem must not be viewed in a cause-and-effect manner or as belonging to one person who then causes the upset in others. It is the job of the therapist to broaden the family's definition to include the participation of others in the problem's evolution and maintenance. A triangular definition is systemic; it defines at least the three central players in the pattern and how they relate vis-à-vis the problem. Broadening the systemic definition to include several interlocking triangles enlarges the problem definition and increases the range of options for interventions. Thus begins generation of a hypothesis that can be expanded in the three-generational context.

Connect the Problem to Three-generational Process

While most models of family therapy have the second goal of defining the problem systemically, the multigenerational model demands that the therapist go a step further by redefining the problem in the context of the extended family. In so doing, the therapist increases the family's understanding of the problem's evolution and current impact. This serves to further normalize the process, since once family members understand things in a context broader than the here and now, they begin to feel less "at fault" and perhaps to see a broader avenue for change.

Most people do not make the connection between their functioning in extended family patterns and their current functioning. In fact, even if the connection is made for them, they may not view work there as necessary or expected of them. Yet, unless these connections are made, therapy will usually stop at the end of the first phase, when the presenting problem is dealt with in an acceptable and comfortable manner. When the therapist makes a clear connection between process on the nuclear family level and process in the extended family, the adults in the family are more likely to stay on in treatment into the second phase.

Making such connections demands that the therapist delineate the adults' part in the current process and then look for how this relates to extended family functioning. The therapist must remain relevant to the problem at hand and yet shift into a larger definition of its context. One way to remain relevant is to ask what the extended family members' reactions to the current problem are and how they are being affected by it. Another is to ask how a similar difficulty was handled in the family of origin. For instance, if the problem is around parenting, the therapist might ask the father what his father's reaction is to his child's problem; what does his father think he should do with his child? Another question might be, what did your father do with you when you had similar difficulties?

These questions begin to map the triangles, issues, and relationships as they exist now and existed historically in the family. Developing a theme for each of the adults in the nuclear family vis-à-vis his/her family of origin functioning allows the therapist to have a personal link with that individual. Usually the client will provide the words for the theme. For instance, one client defined herself as a "crisis maven." What she meant was that she usually overfunctioned, especially in crises. "Being a crisis maven" became the personalized way of describing her position on a central issue around women and responsibility in her family. This theme related not only to her nuclear family functioning, but also to her own and her mother's functioning in the extended family.

Sometimes it helps initially to redefine the individual's difficulties in terms of other systems. Asking questions regarding the family's interaction with other systems reveals not only the degree to which the problems exist in other areas but also how the central triangle is reenacted in other areas. This is especially important in situations where the client(s) present with work/career issues, as often happens in young adulthood, as well as with couples who define work and friends as important. It is useful to track the themes and triangles in clients' interactions with other systems.

Gathering relationship information provides an avenue for collecting family biographical data while remaining relevant to the family in the here and now. I also ask clients to list significant nodal events, from the present day to as far back as they can remember. Often, looking at this list and the genogram together fills in the pieces of biographical information that have been missing. At times it highlights something of importance, such as a series of family deaths or illnesses within a short time. All of these events have a significant effect on the family relationship system; knowing about them will assist the therapist in making connections to family-of-origin issues and patterns.

Develop a Treatment Plan

The therapist needs an overall sense of where he/she is going with this family in the short and long term. Developing a treatment plan does not mean that one sets out a plan for the sake of doing one, as many of us learned to do to handle the immense amount of paperwork in agencies. Rather, this is a plan that is to be used with the family, whether or not it is shared with family members. It lends a focus to the ongoing work and keeps one on track during later stages, when the hard work of change tends to encourage getting off track.

While the treatment plan is a necessary component of the evaluation process, it is not written in stone and can be reevaluated and readjusted as the treatment progresses. A plan is no more than the therapist's idea after the evaluation period of what he/she is going to do with the client(s) and some idea of how that is to be accomplished. The therapist asks: In general, what needs to be accomplished in cases such as this one? How can we accomplish the goals with specific reference to this family and how it presents itself in therapy?

A family's reaction to the therapist and his/her questions is often suggestive of how the clients will respond to outside intervention. Sometimes making a specific suggestion or giving a task and observing how the family handles it will tell the therapist about the resistance to change and how the family functions in regard to it.

As the therapist defines the family's strengths and weakness, he/she must also examine his/her own. These do not have to be shared with the family but they do need to be known to the therapist and considered in treatment planning. For instance, I tend to have difficulty dealing with women who do not take care of their own emotional and economic needs. Women who have given up their careers, who have no preparation to return, and who stand to be economically and emotionally abandoned by their husbands often view me as "too strong." If I don't raise the issue, I am remiss therapeutically; on the other hand, coming out too strongly in favor of economic independence may crush a budding therapeutic alliance. Personal awareness prepares me to deal with these matters.

A treatment plan itself should consist of overall goals for the therapy with this family. The goals are statements of what the therapist — not the client — should be doing. Likewise, the moves by which these goals are to be accomplished are therapeutic interventions. Incorporating interventions into every treatment goal will help the therapist to consider various options with the particular family.

AFTER THE ASSESSMENT: EARLY TREATMENT PRACTICE PRINCIPLES

Four principles guide practice in the later part of this stage: (1) help the client to decrease anxiety and increase self-focus; (2) teach the client about emotional systems; (3) keep the presenting problem in focus and within the family's control; and (4) develop clients' interest in and focus on the extended family patterns and issues.

Decrease Anxiety and Increase Self-focus

Most clients enter treatment feeling fairly anxious. With anxiety high, their resilience and ability to deal with their problems are decreased (Kerr & Bowen, 1988). Anxiety can be decreased by helping clients to focus and by giving them specific tasks. Not only does such structure decrease anxiety but success in dealing with something differently also leads to an increased sense of self.

When clients are dealing with multiple stressors (see Chapters 7–12), the therapist needs to devote more time to helping them calm down and be less reactive. The therapist may need to move slowly, dealing with the most recent stressor first. The first phase of treatment may last longer than with clients who have life-cycle difficulties.

Clients, particularly couples engaged in long-standing conflicts, often come into treatment in extremely polarized positions. They are so reactive to each other that dealing with them together sets off land mines. When both are in the room, anxiety remains high and self-focus is almost impossible. The therapist begins to feel that anything he/she says will be viewed by one as siding with the other. The therapist's hands are tied. One way to deal with the situation is to separate the pair until each seems more self-focused. When that is accomplished in individual sessions, the therapist can then see them together again.

The therapist also decreases anxiety by dealing with the presenting problem adequately and by remaining fairly calm him/herself. One simple way to take control of the therapy process in a calm yet warm manner is to have clients talk mainly to the therapist rather than to each other. The assumption is that talking between the two increases the reactivity and thus the potential for the therapist to become the third leg of the triangle. For instance, I recently saw a couple where the husband looked furious and immediately stated that he was very angry with his wife. As soon as I asked him questions regarding his anger, he turned to his wife and directed his responses to her. Not only did he become even angrier, but she also felt compelled to respond to him. I suggested that doing so would only decrease their ability to get any work done and that he might find it helpful to answer me directly.

Clients who are anxious tend to focus on others. It is part of the reactive process that, as anxiety increases, the tendency to focus on the other's behavior and what it does to self is increased. Therefore, helping clients to become less anxious will increase the likelihood of self-focus; concurrently, assisting clients in achieving a self-focus will decrease anxiety. Asking clients questions about self and about the part they play in interactions is central to setting the stage for second stage work and in moving the client toward action in the first stage. Developing person-to-person relationships by very definition focuses on self; therefore to the degree that a family member is able to take an I-position in the nuclear family process he/she will increase his/her sense of success (Bowen, 1978).

Teach about Emotional Systems

Two aspects of the therapist role stand out at this phase of the treatment: teacher and detective (see Chapter 2 for detailed descriptions of these roles). Both focus on teaching emotional systems process but in different ways. As a teacher, the therapist may directly teach about emotional systems concepts from the data the family presents or use films, books and other material to accomplish the same goal. As a detective the therapist helps clients to learn about their own emotional systems process. In the first instance, the therapist uses the family information to teach about triangles and the emotional transmission process in families. The therapist can simply use throwaway lines to teach about some triangle, such as "I wonder if your mother would be less angry with you if your relationship with your father would shift," or, "We would know that you had really detriangled when you saw your parents as equaling deserving of one another." Or the therapist may use the more structured methods described in Chapter 2. In the second instance, the therapist-detective seeks to have clients become "detectives" in their own right. Through the therapist's questioning clients are encouraged to find answers, which, of course, lie in how their emotional system operates.

It may also be helpful to send clients to community workshops or groups on specific topics of relevance to them or perhaps to conduct such programs yourself. For instance, sending women to a group on "women and money" often raises their consciousness about a subject that is important to the balance of power in the marital relationship and to the ongoing financial situation of the household. Sending men to a workshop on "men's issues" often permits them to hear things that they are unable to hear from a therapist, especially a female therapist. The use of films in some community programs offers a great opportunity for families to learn something about families by watching others.

Keep the Presenting Problem in Focus and Under Control

Dealing with the nuclear family triangle(s) and diffusing the presenting problem can be accomplished through direct, compliance-based interventions or through indirect, defiance-based interventions (Papp, 1983, 1984). Direct interventions usually involve the assignment of tasks, generally as homework. Indirect interventions involve the use of therapeutic paradoxes and strategic techniques. The multigenerational therapist generally chooses the former type of intervention first.

Once a triangle has been identified and the flow of movement in the triangle is tracked, the therapist may see how each person could shift his/her part so that the process would be reversed. It is an interesting aspect of this model that, although it focuses on the family emotional system and seeks to broaden the problem context, at the same time it has individual change as a main objective. Thus, while the therapist seeks to look at the process in the triangle(s), he/she seeks to have the individuals, the adults, change their positions.

Indirect interventions are usually necessary when one has already attempted direct interventions and they haven't worked. They are also useful when families have been in treatment before and they view it as unsuccessful. When triangles are rigid there is an ongoing symmetrical escalation, strategic interventions are in order. Several books offer excellent descriptions of strategic interventions (Boscolo, Cecchin, Hoffman, & Penn, 1987; Papp, 1983).

After the presenting problem and triangle are dealt with, the therapist can move on to deal with other areas of family life. For instance, one might look at marital issues after the difficulties with a child or adolescent are under control. However, it is important to check on the status of the presenting problem from time to time and to keep it fairly well under the therapist's and family's control. As the family begins to improve, the presenting problem may pop up again. If the therapist knows this and predicts it to the family members, they may prepare to deal with it.

Develop the Client's Interest in and Focus on the Extended Family

By the end of the first phase of treatment, one or more of the adults should be interested in the ongoing work of multigenerational therapy—changing self in a three-generational context. Thus, one of the practice principles involves the therapist's beginning to weave the tapestry of family of origin.

Mapping of the presenting problem over three generations on the genogram often serves as the beginning step in reweaving the tapestry. Continued mapping of the adult's personal themes in the nuclear family process and the origin of these themes in the extended family is part of the ongoing work of this phase and it sets the stage for the homework of the second stage.

Asking the client questions that elaborate the family-of-origin triangles and patterns helps to set the stage. Each time an area of nuclear family process is discussed, the same area should be examined in each of adults' families. Making connections between nuclear family, here-and-now type issues and the extended family process prepares clients for work on their own in the extended family.

We are not talking just about past events in the family. Although there are always past events that must be placed in perspective, the major interest of this work is the "past-in-the-present." We assume that the ways of relating with family have continued into the present. Gaining understanding of the process on the extended family level increases options for reweaving those themes that have created the current tapestry in the second phase of the treatment process.

REFERENCES

Boscolo, L., Cecchin, G., Hoffman, L., & Penn, P. (1987). *Milan systemic family therapy*. New York: Basic Books.

Bowen, M. (1978). *Family therapy in clinical practice*. New York: Aronson.

Kerr, M. E., & Bowen, M. (1988). *Family evaluation*. New York: Norton.

McGoldrick, M., & Gerson, R. (1985). *Genograms in family assessment*. New York: W. W. Norton.

Papp, P. (1983). *The process of change*. New York: Guilford.

Papp, P. (1984). The creative leap. *Family Therapy Networker, 8*(5), 20–29.

5

Stage 2: Reweaving the Tapestry

FREDDA HERZ BROWN

THE SECOND PHASE of treatment is characterized by movement from a focus on the here and now to extended family process. It involves defining and working on the background of the family, the multigenerational threads of the tapestry. For the therapist using this model, this is the heart of the therapy process. However, the movement into extended family work is neither consistent nor unidirectional. In fact, it is backward and forward, with the therapist often on a fishing expedition attempting to hook the client into some extended family work (Guerin, 1976). This middle phase begins when the presenting problem is basically under control and one or more of the adults in the family has made a commitment to work on the self.

Throughout most of this phase, clients struggle with buying the idea that three-generational or extended family work is important for self-change. The aim of this phase is to have clients make at least one shift/change in a family pattern or triangle. The process is often filled with the joy of success and the tedium of just getting there. It is during this phase that the client becomes more active both as an investigator and an actor.

PRACTICE PRINCIPLES

There are five central practice principles to this stage of treatment: (1) develop clients' ability to understand the extended family functioning; (2) keep clients' expectations of change low; (3) look for opportunities for change; (4) use planned change to shift a client's position in the family of origin; (5) create tasks and strategies that clients can use outside the treatment room; and (6) create contexts for multigenerational work.

Develop Clients' Ability to Understand Extended Family

In order for clients to go about changing their position in various triangles in the family of origin, they must understand the way in which that system operates. To do this, they must observe and describe not only the system reactions but also their own responses to the way in which the family acts. While the therapist is knowledgeable about how systems function in general, clients need to become knowledgeable about the way in which their own systems respond. Lacking this information, they will be unable to initiate change.

Even though we grow up in families, most of us know little about them or about how they evolved to where they are. One reason for our ignorance is that, once we are involved in triangles, our ability to define a self and be independent is decreased. Thus, we only know someone in our family in relation to someone else. The more triangling has occurred and the more rigid the triangles, the more likely it is that we know little about the individuals in our family. I remember discussing with colleagues the fact that most of us know the least about our siblings. In fact, we relate to them as they were when we left the family. One reason for this is that we are oriented towards our parents in the family of origin. We also relate to siblings in relation to their roles vis-à-vis the parents and ourselves.

Another reason that we know so little about the members of our family is that parents tend to avoid discussing those aspects of their own lives that were painful or uncomfortable. Thus we end up with little historical sense of our family. When we are children, we do not see the need for such information. However, in general, the older we get, the more interest we have in the past. As we build our own futures, a sense of historical continuity becomes important.

Obtaining information about one's family and oneself is an investigative process in which the client acts as the detective and the therapist as the director of the process. The therapist must be aware of how and what to send the client to investigate, but the client must be the one who does the actual investigating. There are several ways to direct a client in this endeavor: (1) establishing person-to-person relationships; (2) collecting historical information; and (3) spending relationship time with family members (Bowen, 1978). While these ideas are certainly not mutually exclusive, for the sake of clarity they will be discussed separately.

In establishing person-to-person relationships, the therapist is seeking to help the client define a self and interact with others in the family from that position. The more relationships between any two people do not depend upon a third, the less the degree of triangling in the family. Thus, establishing person-to-person relationships decreases the propensity to relate to one person as part of a triangle. For instance, if my sister and I are in a distant relationship, with her closer to my father and me more distant from him, developing a person-to-person relationship with her will change not only the nature of our relationship but also the triangle. As she and I come to understand one another better, I will have the opportunity to observe my reactions to getting to know her and the connections in the triangle will shift. My connection to her will no longer be in relation to where she and I stand vis-à-vis my father.

The more person-to-person relationships one has in the family of origin, the less reactive one's relationships are. One might think of a pressure cooker: The greater the number of outlets or connections, the less the buildup of intensity in the nuclear process; the fewer the outlets for emotions, the more likely it is that difficulties in the nuclear system will be intense. This is one reason that emotional and/or physical cutoffs have such an impact on the family.

In addition, establishing person-to-person relationships means that one has to get to know oneself and to learn how to communicate that self to others. This is certainly a skill worth learning. However, often clients need a great deal of assistance in approaching family members with whom they have had long-standing distant relationships. A frequent cry is, "I don't know what to talk about," or "I don't like him/her." The therapist's response to the first statement is to direct the client to talk about him/herself. Asking family-oriented questions might also be helpful, as long as one avoids areas of high reactivity. The response to the second protest is to suggest that it is hard to know whether one likes or dislikes someone as long as the relationship to that person depends upon a relationship to a third party. That is, it is hard to know whether you like someone you don't really know. If a client says that he/she really does know the person, then the therapist might suggest that he/she experiment to see if there is *one* thing he/she can get to like about the individual.

One way in which clients can get to know people in their family is by collecting information about the family's history. Using the genogram as a map, clients can be instructed to visit various family members to complete certain information. In addition, family pictures and stories can be used to elaborate the family history. Since I began my family work years ago, I have become the keeper of old family pictures. I used to visit members of the oldest generation and they would show me pictures of family members whom I never knew and tell stories about these family members. I felt much more knowledgeable about my family after these information-gathering expeditions. In addition, I grew to know and love a number of family members I would not have otherwise known.

It is helpful to collect family information, but only when one has a framework within which to understand it. It is important to assist clients in defining what information they want and for what purpose. I have seen therapists collect information from clients and have clients collect it from the family without purpose; it becomes ancestral material rather than a resource for further examination.

Collecting information from as many people as possible always enlarges the client's view of specific situations or events. This is especially helpful to clients who have had a particularly traumatic event in their background or who for some reason have little recall of their family experiences. It is always interesting to me that siblings often have a totally different view of the family and are therefore helpful in enlarging clients' perspective.

Collecting information is one way in which clients can begin to spend some time with family members, which is especially valuable to those clients who are fairly cutoff from family, either emotionally or physically. Another way in which clients can spend time with family is by putting in "relationship time," that is, time in which the goal is just "spending time" with the other person. Guerin, Fay, Burden, and Kautto (1987) describe this time in terms of marital relationships; they suggest it is time spent on working on the relationship by being there for each other on a personal level. In common parlance this time has become known as "quality time." It is time where the focus is nothing more or less than just being with the person and observing how things go for self in being with that individual. I frequently suggest to clients that they spend time observing their own internal reactions when they are with a particular individual. This is done when they are unable to observe or describe what goes on in the relationship that makes them particularly anxious or reactive.

While we often try to devote such time to our nuclear family, not infrequently we forget that such time is necessary for relationships within the extended family. We are "too busy." One clearly has to make a commitment to spend time with extended family. And this is time that can't be done with company. That is, clients need to spend time by themselves with family members. Relationship time implies a dyad; having another person along creates the potential for a triangle. So it is better to go it alone. Clients may resist this idea at first, wondering what they can say or do with the other person.

Men, who often prefer activity over conversation, seem to have greater difficulty with this idea than women. Guerin et al. (1987) view activity oriented time as separate from relationship time; however, I think that such a distinction makes a gender difference in how time is spent into separate and unnecessary categories. In our culture men tend to feel most comfortable spending relationship time engaging in activities with the other person. They feel uncomfortable just "making time" with someone. While allowing for differences in gender, we might also note that each gender needs experience with the opposite and less comfortable form of relationship time. Having men learn the skills that women have and women those that men have increases their flexibility in relationships and their understanding of the needs of the opposite sex.

Keep Clients' Expectations of Change Low

Clients who are able to keep focused on self are better able to maintain low expectations of others. Since one cannot change another individual, trying to do so will prove fruitless, frustrating, and useless. As we have seen, the change process is individually oriented, with the client focusing on aspects of self that need to be examined and changed.

One of the main aims of the first phase of treatment is to get the client focused on self. During the second stage there is a continuing need to focus on this area. My experience suggests that clients may express their lack of self-focus differently in this phase from the way they express it in the earlier phase. Clients tend to look at self until the therapist suggests a change; then, they focus on whether the other person is likely to change. In fact, clients sometimes hesitate to do something different, suggesting that it won't work because the other person won't change. It is important to help clients make the change for self rather than to change the other. As Tom Fogarty has said, focusing on keeping the expectations of the other as close to zero as possible will help with this.

What do we mean by "zero expectations"? It means going into a situation and expecting that what one does or says will not change what the other person does/says. Now, it is difficult to get one's expectations this low. The more the other person matters to the individual, the harder it is to have few expectations of what one wants or needs from him/her. Verbalizing the expectations and working at decreasing them are the work of the change process, which we will discuss below.

Look for Opportunities for Change

Creating change in the multigenerational model often consists of waiting for the right moment to present itself. That is, while one may direct clients and have them act as detectives in their own family, circumstance often creates the moments for change.

For instance, although I had been working with a young man for several months regarding setting some limits on his mother's phone calls and visits to his new apartment, there had been few opportunities actually to try out his new "position" vis-à-vis his mother. Finally one day she called and left a message on his machine that she would be arriving that night to take him out to dinner. A hard offer to refuse. The client decided with my assistance to use this opportunity to shift his relationship with his mother. Since she was unreachable, he waited until she arrived at the apartment and then told her that he was sorry that she had traveled so far but that if she had waited for him to return his call she would have discovered that he was already busy that evening. While his mother was upset and tried to convince him to change his plans, he lovingly and warmly said that he could and would not do so; he wished she had given him enough notice so that he could spend the kind of time he really wanted to spend with her.

This is a perfect example of being prepared to jump on an opportunity. There are other times when clients are less prepared but mention some major happening in the family that provides the chance for some previously mentioned shift to occur. In these instances the client and the therapist have to move rapidly to prepare for the event.

At other times, a natural life cycle event such as a death creates an opportunity for change that the client has been unable to see or attempt before. I recently had the experience of having a male client return to treatment after a seven-month break. Part of the reason for the break was the client's inability to understand how he was playing an active part in a triangle between his wife and his family. I had suggested several options that would have shifted his position; he said none of these was useful. Now, after the death of his father, he was suddenly able to see the triangle in operation and had decided that it was time for him to work on it.

Use Planned Change to Change a Client's Position

As stated in Chapters 1 and 2, unplanned change is usually no change; without planning clients are easily drawn into the system's reaction to the shift and shift back to the old position. Change involves planning, preparing, predicting, and processing.*

PLAN. A client should not only plan the how, what, when, and where of the change but also plan how to deal with those who will be affected by the shift. For instance, if a client has been distant from her father and overclose to her mother, then any move toward father must include some plan for how

---

*The author wants to thank Gail Lederer for her ideas about the "four P's."

to deal with the effect of the move on her relationship with her mother. It may also be helpful to have the client consider the reactions in the inter-locking triangles. If the client's sister is very connected to the father, then a move toward the father will upset the balance in the triangle between the client, her sister, and her father. The client will not see these emotional interactions; it is the job of the therapist, with his/her understanding of triangles and emotional process, to assist the client in planning for all possi-ble reactions.

Clients should be assisted in planning and practicing exactly what they want to say or write to the family members involved. They should not be encouraged to enter a situation without knowing pretty much what and how they want to communicate to the other individual(s). For instance, if a client is writing a letter to a cutoff family member, I will have him/her check it out with me before mailing it so that we can jointly make sure that it communi-cates the content and feelings that the client wants communicated.

If by chance a reaction occurs that the client is not prepared for—and it sometimes happens—it is received as a useful piece of information about process. Examining how they might have planned differently is part of the debriefing. Such work prevents clients from feeling that they have failed at some task.

PREDICT. For every change clients make or plan to make, the therapist must assist them in predicting the possible range of emotional reactions. It is frequently useful to have the client predict the worst case scenario. However, we should not overlook the best possible response so that clients are not taken by surprise when good things happen.

Frequently clients say that they cannot predict what the other person will do or say. In my experience, however, if clients are walked through a scene, they usually are able to predict what will happen. If they can't, they are asked to imagine the worst possible response and to plan for that.

One of the reasons clients choose not to change is that the old way is familiar and the new way seems threatening. Predicting responses to the new way of operating permits clients to feel that they are knowledgeable about the new way as well. It also helps them to bear with the three steps of the change process, the most important of which is dealing with the system's reactions to the initial change in the client's behavior.

PREPARE. By now the reader can understand what preparation is like in general. In the specific sense, *prepare* means knowing what one is going to say or do, so that nothing unplanned tends to occur. Clients who go into situations unprepared frequently end up repeating past patterns, which in-clude attacking, confronting, defending or explaining. If one doesn't know what one wants to say, it is easy to fall into such patterns, especially when feelings run high.

Sometimes it is important to have a client prepare even the nitty-gritty details of an important event. For instance, during the course of my work with a young woman, Joan, her maternal grandmother died. Joan had not seen her grandmother for eight years, since there had been a cutoff between her mother and grandmother. Joan chose to keep her decision to go to the funeral a secret from her parents, so that they would not start reacting immediately. Such immediate reactivity would have made it very difficult for her to go. She prepared exactly what to wear, where to stay, and how to get from place to place. When Joan returned from her visit and came to the next therapy appointment, the therapist helped her to complete the fourth step—processing the change.

PROCESS. Some people consider the second stage of the multigenerational model to be behavioral in nature, that is, to be focused exclusively on the changing of behaviors. It is not. In fact, throughout the process the therapist is continuously focusing on the changing feelings and reactions of the client and the family system to the changes that are occurring.

It is true that the expression of feelings does not generally occur directly to the therapist, nor is it viewed as the major focus of the model. Rather the expression of feelings is encouraged as a description of what is or is not happening in the system and in response to some planned change.

Every move, like Joan's funeral visit, is followed by a debriefing session in which the client's reactions and feelings are dealt with directly and utilized to plan the next move(s). It is my experience in doing this work that most clients experience a far wider range of emotions than they ever have before their family work. These feelings and reactions tell the therapist something about the pacing and timing of the moves and how the family will respond.

Create Tasks and Strategies for the Client to Use

Creating tasks that clients will be able to carry out on their own is one of the most difficult functions of the family therapist. One reason is that the therapist is not the actor. Rather, he/she is a consultant, the process, acting only in the background. No matter how clear the therapist is, the client will modify the words and the task in his or her own way.

How does one develop tasks? It is easier to learn this aspect of the process from doing and watching than from reading. In order to give good and useful tasks to a client, the therapist must understand basic systems ideas such as triangles, overinvolved relationships, distance, and conflict, as well as strategies such as reversals, detriangling, reframing, and relabeling. The other ingredients of good task development are clarity about what one wants to accomplish and creativity in method.

I begin thinking of a task whenever the client is talking about the main theme and his/her difficulties surrounding it. It usually takes me until the end of the session to formulate my idea or to tell it to the client. Recently a female client was discussing the fact that she always feels left out in her nuclear family, with her husband and her kids. She explained that she also felt left out as child; she was an only child with several male cousins who "ganged up" on her and teased her. When we tracked the theme in her family of origin, it turned out that both her parents had been considered "black sheep" in their families of origin. I began to formulate a task that included talking to her parents about how they dealt with being left out. I also suggested that she think of each of her children and her husband individually. By relating to them as a unit she was likely to solidify her feelings of being left out, since, if they are a unit, then she wasn't part of it.

The tasks in this example were oriented toward shifting the flow of the multigenerational process and the nuclear family triangle. The process illustrates the necessity to continuously move back and forth between nuclear and extended families. It also illustrates the use of some detriangling, one of the four typical strategies used in work with extended family.

DETRIANGLING. In order to understand detriangling as a strategy, the therapist and the client must understand the nature and functioning of triangles (see Chapter 1; Bowen, 1978; Carter & McGoldrick Orfanidis, 1976; Fogarty, 1976). Since triangles tend to get rigid in position and valence over time, the therapist will frequently get a hint of one through the client's description of a position or feeling about a person. For instance, a client may describe one person as the villain and another as a victim, an angel or a bastard. This description indicates that the client has taken a position about the relationship of the other two and that such a position is based not on knowledge of either person but rather on their positions vis-à-vis one another.

Establishing person-to-person relationships as described above tends to detriangle a situation, since it is difficult to maintain a polarized position with more intimate knowledge of the people involved. Initially, however, getting to know each of the people may activate the triangle. For instance, if the client is overly involved to his/her mother and views her as an innocent victim of his/her cruel dominant father, then changing the view of father will change his/her relationship to mother. Getting to know each member of the triangle results in a changing view of villain and victim.

Another more succinct detriangling method involves the client's stepping out of the relationship between two others and moving them toward a resolution with each other. For instance, a young client of mine complains that her mother calls her every time she becomes upset with the client's father. The client's father is ill and does not take care of himself physically. When the client's mother gets anxious enough about it, she first pursues her husband, who distances, and then she calls her daughter. While this lowers the mother's tension about father, it does not solve their difficulty; it simply moves the tension to the daughter and the father. This client would then do her mother's bidding and call her father and appeal to his good senses to take care of himself.

At my suggestion, she told her mother that she felt very upset when she told her things like this and she wished that she would deal with dad about it and resolve the situation. Now, if the client were to stop here, the movement would be shifted between the client and her mother but she would still be anxious about her father. Therefore the function of the triangle would still be complete—she, rather than her mother, would be anxious about her father. The only way to complete the detriangling move and to take herself totally out of her parents' relationship was to let her father know that she had heard from mother about how upset she was regarding his health and that she hoped that he and mom would get this resolved between them. That completes the movement away from the client and puts the tension back between the original twosome. After several detriangling moves such as this one, the client is no longer involved in her parents' issues around health and illness.

REFRAMING. To reframe something means to take a situation that is usually viewed in one way and to put forth another view, that is, to frame the situation differently (Boscolo, Cecchin, Hoffman, & Penn, 1987). Therapists can reframe a situation for clients and help them to see it differently in a therapy session. Clients can also be taught to use reframing when dealing with situations in their families. For instance, it is more useful to view a client's mother's frequent phone calls as signs of concern and love than of intrusiveness. In the session the therapist might suggest that mothers are supposed to show their concern for their children and in fact the client might be more appreciative of such an effort, especially since not doing so only increases her mother's efforts. The therapist might suggest that the client thank her mother for her concern rather than fighting with her over the frequency of the calls. The vehemence of the client's objections to such a reframe is usually an indication of the degree to which the client feels stuck in the situation. The therapist needs to create some positive relationship time between mother and daughter before any reframe will be accepted.

RELABELING. This strategy is basically the same as reframing but involves the assignment of some label to typify the new frame or lens that is being applied, for instance, relabeling a mother's intrusiveness as her concern or protectiveness. In this manner a positive label is assigned to a behavior that is generally viewed as negative.

Recently I had a client whose father borrowed money from virtually every member of his extended family. The client vaguely knew that this situation existed. When it was confirmed in numerous visits with extended family, she began to view the behavior as very negative and to attach a villainous label to her father. With my assistance, she then examined her father's behavior as a way to stay connected to family members in a family where there were major cutoffs. This relabeling of his behavior from "villain/bastard" to "a rather connected bad boy" was very helpful to her. She was able to view the situation differently and thus to relate to her father differently around this issue.

REVERSALS. A reversal is an attempt to change a habitual pattern of relating by saying or doing the opposite of what one usually says or does in the sequence (Bowen, 1978; Carter & McGoldrick Orfanidis, 1976). A reversal tends to express the implicit, unacknowledged side of the issue and to break up repetitive and predictable sequences of communication. Reversals should not be used lightly. They should only be undertaken when the individual is in control of the feelings of hurt, anger, or resentment and only when they can be done in the style of the doer, not of the therapist. If used before the client is in control of his/her feelings, the statements often sound sarcastic or at best express annoyance. They are not to be used as a substitute for person-to-person interaction; they are simply a technique for decreasing the distance or conflict that stands in the way of intimate relationships.

For instance, I have been working with a young woman for a year. This woman has been locked in a long-term, intensely negative struggle with her mother. The struggle takes the form of mother's always putting down what the client says, does, thinks, wears, or eats. The client, of course, continuously tells her mother everything, hoping that just once she will get her mother's approval. When she fails to do so, this just reconfirms her view of her mother and sets the tone for the next skirmish. The client responds to the criticisms by either defending her choices rationally or criticizing her mother's attitude. I had been trying fruitlessly to get the client to shift this repetitive pattern. Then she called her mother to share the details of her apartment hunting. Mother immediately went into her critical mode, telling her daughter that she was spending too much, that she wasn't looking in safe areas, etc. As the daughter told me later, "Something just clicked and I knew what to say to her. I told her that I had no intention of choosing an apartment without her approval since I thought she was a much better judge than I and that she had much more experience in these matters than I had." The client said her mother stopped in mid sentence, hesitated, and then said she would love to go with her. During debriefing the client told me that she just felt it was the right thing to say and that she had a feeling of total exhilaration afterwards.

Create Contexts for Multigenerational Work

An individual can use various contexts to accomplish the overall task of being oneself in the systems in which one is involved. Common contexts for creating change are letter writing, family visits, family picture reviews and history-taking, reritualizing family holidays and life-cycle transitions. Let's review some of the more frequently encountered ones here.

Most people write letters to family members to share news. Rarely are these letters of a personal nature. However, letters are useful ways of communicating important personal items without making the other person feel that he/she has to respond or react immediately to what is being written (Bowen, 1978). Separating doing from responding creates thinking time. Such letters are usually read in a very thoughtful manner. For the writer, letters make it easier to deal successfully with issues, especially highly charged ones. In addition, since most of us live a substantial distance from some if not all of our family members, letters often become the primary method of communication.

Letters can also be used to help a client clarify issues or feelings regarding a particular person or event; however, such letters are not to be mailed under any circumstances (Carter, 1988). When letters are to be mailed, the thoughts and feeling should be under the individual letter writer's charge rather than out of his or her awareness. A good motto is, never mail a letter to which a response would not be welcome.

A client is frequently assigned a letter writing task in preparation for writing a letter that will be mailed or visiting a family member. For example, when a divorced client seems unfinished with her marriage, she may be asked to write a letter to her ex-husband focusing on her experience of the relationship, what worked and what did not. The client needs to make clear what her own responsibility was for the demise of the marriage. Usually such a letter is long and angry at first but several modifications allow her to become much clearer about her own part in the process and not to blame her former spouse for every fault of the marriage. When this is accomplished, the client certainly has the ability to meet with her former spouse to share this, if she and the therapist think it would be a good idea.

Letters are also frequently used to help a client deal with a significant family member who has died but whose relationship, as Anderson suggests in the film "I Never Sang for My Father," "struggles on within the minds of the survivor(s)" (Paul & Grosser, 1965; Rosen, 1990). After writing a letter like this, the client usually is asked to go to the cemetery and read it. Recently I had a client whose mother died when he was very young and for whom the client did not grieve. This client used his letter to his mother as the underpinning of a memorial service that he organized to provide a structure for his grieving. Many of the client's family and friends attended the service, despite the client's worst fears that he would be there all alone.

Letters that are written for mailing are person-to-person in nature and frequently ask questions and share information about self or some new understanding that the client has gained about the family and how it functions (Bowen, 1972). Sometimes letters can be used to reinitiate contact with a distant and/or cutoff relative. Clients who are given any letter writing task are asked to first share their letter with the therapist. This is especially true if the therapist has any hint that the client will have a difficult time writing it without anger or resentment creeping in. Planning, writing, and reviewing such letters form the content of many sessions.

Using a family visit for some purpose other than obligation becomes a hallmark of this phase of treatment. Any visit presents major opportunities to get to know family members and to work on one's relationship with them. However, such visits must be planned in advance and the client must be prepared to handle what might come up during the visit (Bowen, 1972; Carter & McGoldrick Orfanidis, 1976; Friedman, 1986). An unplanned visit means trouble in terms of opportunities to fall back into old patterns and triangles.

There are several basic guidelines to making visits into opportunities. The first is to stay in a hotel if at all possible so that one can keep a balance in dealing with the family. Having a place to go to, out of the family emotional field, makes it easier to gain perspective and to keep going according to the plan of the visit. The second guideline is to stay no longer than you will be able to be generous; that is, don't stay beyond the time when you are feeling able to be gracious, giving, or liberal in character. Staying too long creates a tense situation, where any small disturbance can lead to a major blowup.

Along with family visits, family holidays and life-cycle transitions can to reritualized as a way of connecting to family in a different way. Most family members observe family rituals in some predictable manner, often not even viewing these events as emotionally significant. Changing one's participation in the ritual or even adding a new ritual often shifts the family's way of viewing the client and shifts the client's view of him/herself in the system.

Imber-Black and her colleagues (1988) have written an excellent book on the creation of rituals to mark both normative and special life events that need marking. Actively participating allows the client to react emotionally and deal with the event. Using information about the family triangles, it is possible to use family rituals to shift the client's position. For example, a client who is typically overresponsible for family celebrations could try waiting and letting the family celebration take a different form. For a youngest child who does not usually take charge of family celebrations it could mean doing so or offering to do something differently for this particular celebration. A young female client of mine illustrates this point. She was always complaining that her family did not recognize her because she was single. She decided to use Mother's Day to invite her family over to her small apartment for a well planned (and well received) dinner.

Contexts for change are almost as varied as the client and the therapist are creative. All sort of situations can be utilized or created to work on some aspect of self in the extended family. The second stage of treatment permits a broad range of possibilities in these areas.

REFERENCES

Boscolo, L., Cecchin, G., Hoffman, L., & Penn, P. (1987). *Milan systemic family therapy*. New York: Basic Books.
Bowen, M. (1972). On the differentiation of self. In J. Framo (Ed.). *Family interaction: A dialogue between family researchers and family therapists*. New York: Springer.
Bowen, M. (1978). *Family therapy in clinical practice*. New York: Aronson.
Carter, B. (1988). Divorce: His and hers. In M. Walters, B. Carter, P. Papp, & O. Silverstein. *The invisible web*. (pp. 253–271). New York: Guilford.
Carter, E., & McGoldrick Orfanidis, M. (1976). Family therapy with one person and the family therapist's own family. In P. Guerin (Ed.). *Family therapy: Theory and practice*. New York: Gardner.
Fogarty, T. (1976). On emptiness and closeness, Part II. *The Family* 3/2.
Friedman, E. (1986). *Generation to generation*. New York: Guilford.
Guerin, P. (1976). *Family therapy, theory and practice*. New York: Gardner.
Guerin, P., Fay, L., Burden, S., & Kautto, G. (1987). *The evaluation and treatment of marital conflict*. New York: Basic Books.
Imber-Black, E., Roberts, J., & Whiting, R. (Eds.) (1988). *Rituals in families and family therapy*. New York: W. W. Norton.
Paul, N. L., & Grosser, G. H. (1965). Operational mourning and its role in conjoint family therapy. *Community Mental Health Journal* I (4).
Rosen, E. (1990). *Families facing death: Family dynamics of terminal illness*. Lexington, MA: Lexington.

6

Stage 3: The Client as Weaver

FREDDA HERZ BROWN

IN THE THIRD STAGE the client adopts multigenerational work as his/her own and views it as a lifelong, self-directed process (Bowen, 1978). The focus is the client's onging work on changing self in the family system. However, the therapist no longer has to sell the model or the idea of extended family work to the client; the client "buys it" and readily uses it to examine his/her own behavior. In fact, the nature of the therapist-client relationship shifts into one of consultant-consultee, with the client being the one who sets the pace and direction of the work. The principles of practice in this stage illustrate this shift: (1) keep the client on track; (2) use life-cycle transitions and family "occasions" as opportunities for change (Friedman, 1986); and (3) focus on the client as the change agent, the weaver.

PRACTICE PRINCIPLES

Keep the Client on Track

During the second stage of treatment it is often difficult to keep the client focused on him/herself and for the therapist to keep the sessions focused and on track. One of the major reasons is the client's ambivalence regarding the importance of multigenerational work. By the end of the second stage the client has accomplished at least one successful change in his/her functioning in the extended family system and is more confident.

The third stage presents some new difficulties in this area. While the client has bought the idea of extended family work, the work itself begins to take on a long-term nature. Therapy is not viewed as a cure but rather a lifetime commitment to working on self in the context of important relationships. Learning to be one's own person in the context of the family is difficult and ongoing work. Thus, the nature of the work, whether in therapy sessions or out, takes on its own pacing and timing. With this pacing comes a sense of quiet so that at times the client is lulled into thinking that he/she does not have to plan any moves but can just "take things as they come." That is a real mistake, since the family system will just pull the client into the old patterns when the tension is high.

When tension is high, it is easy to lose the focus on self and begin to focus on the other family members and how they should change. It is important for the therapist to keep the client focused on changes in self that are necessary to shift further patterns in the family. The client needs to understand that, when things are quiet, he/she has an opportunity to think more clearly about other themes or patterns that may need exploration.

It is certainly easier in times of quiet to go about developing person-to-person relationships and to begin to explore such subtle issues as gender and ethnicity in the family of origin. These times can also be used to solidify gains in relationships that were started during more troublesome periods. For instance, a client recently came for a session six weeks after her last one. During this time she had decided to spend some time with her three brothers individually. She had never been able to do this before because of the numerous crises in her nuclear and extended families. She found it not only very enjoyable but also extremely useful, since each of her siblings had a different view of the family and the relationships between the parents and the children.

I also find stage 3 work to be very integrative; that is, clients begin, with therapeutic direction and sometimes without, to bring together their own view of the family in a way that makes sense to them. In a way they develop a psychology of the family. They develop an understanding of how the family came to function as it did and what each person's part was in the overall operation.

By working on getting out of major triangles, one becomes clearer about who one is and how one feels and thinks about things. Life choices and positions are no longer dictated by the reactions to the anxiety in the triangular relationships. As one gets clearer on one's own boundaries, one also gets clearer on one's own feelings and thoughts, rather than reacting to the thoughts and feelings of others. A new definition of "I" evolves, with a much broader range of thoughts and feelings than earlier ones.

For instance, a young married professional woman came to a session after a month's hiatus, saying, "I can't believe how different I feel. I find that if I just wait a bit before jumping in to be responsible at work and home, I get much clearer on what I think and it frequently doesn't even resemble what I thought it would." She went on to describe how good she felt emotionally and physically and how for the first time she didn't feel caught in doing what others thought she should do. She thought that she was finally out of the triangle in which she felt trapped since her parents had divorced when she was 10.

This client had been in treatment with her spouse for over a year. The brief hiatus had allowed her to begin to integrate and even notice the differences in her functioning and therefore in her experience of herself. The richness, depth and breadth of her thoughts and feelings were somewhat surprising to her, though clearly enjoyable.

As with this client, sessions are spaced according to client need as determined by the therapist and the client. I usually find that clients begin stage 3 work by coming approximately once a month. Later, as the work is more sporadic and/or more self-directed in nature, therapy sessions are less frequent. Finally, clients only come to treatment sessions when they are in the midst of working on some issue or theme or are about ready to deal with a major family event or transition. The focus of their work becomes much more self-determined and sessions are scheduled more on the basis of client need. Therapist and client need to discuss the cues that the client will use to judge the necessity of sessions.

Scheduling hiatuses and shifting the frequency of sessions tend to decrease the likelihood that clients will find it necessary to drop out of treatment rather than discuss the issue with the therapist. Once clients experience some change in their overall lives, they are likely to leave treatment. By reframing these sojourns as part of the therapeutic process, one shifts their meaning into something that is expected and benign.

Use Life-cycle Transitions and Family "Occasions" as Opportunities for Change

Usually, when a client leaves the more active second stage of treatment, I review the gains that have been made and the potential times in the life cycle that future work will be necessary. New areas of work are often highlighted by shifts in the family organization or the entrance/exit of members. Thus, at life-cycle transitions, clients frequently experience some new theme requiring attention (Bowen, 1978; Carter & McGoldrick, 1989a, b; Friedman, 1986; Imber-Black, Roberts, & Whiting, 1988).

For instance, a client recently returned for a session after a two-year hiatus. She had accomplished a great deal of work on her relationship with her family and had felt comfortable enough to live and work near her parents' home. She was returning for some help with her relationship to her younger sister. It only took two sessions for her to figure out what the issues were and to do some important family work. Sessions like these serve as stations along the way where one can check in and see how one is doing. While change is long-term and continuous, it involves repeated stops and starts.

Major disruptions in the family life cycle, such as deaths, divorces, and chronic medical or psychiatric illnesses, usually throw the family into a state of disarray and thus provide a window of opportunity for change (Carter & McGoldrick, 1989a, b; Colon, 1973; Herz Brown, 1989a, b; Rosen, 1990). During one of these crises the client will often return for some additional sessions. It is a time when some family dynamics or patterns are highlighted by the shifts in structure and organization in the system.

It is important for clients to view all family transitions, disruptions, or occasions as opportunities for change. Otherwise they are likely to approach them naively expecting things to go well when the anxiety is high and the family is reactive. When clients can utilize the four steps in dealing with change — plan, predict, prepare, and process — they are able to approach the situation in the best way possible.

Using natural family gatherings or creating gatherings or occasions for a specific purpose becomes a hallmark of this stage of work (Carter & McGoldrick Orfanidis, 1976; Friedman, 1986; Imber-Black et al., 1988). The same is true with regard to rituals and ceremonies. Using or creating rituals around family events permits clients additional structure for accomplishing the family work. It always amazes me that, with minimal direction, clients are able to be extraordinarily creative in establishing ways of marking events of importance to them. They can also use rituals to mark the completion of some particular piece of family work, such as planning a memorial service to mark the past death of a loved one in the family.

None of these situations should be approached without a plan. Thus, a good deal of therapy time is spent in preparing for the change and processing the results of the shift in position and/or relationships. The client is the active one in conducting the overall plan and looks to the therapist for help in thinking through the process. Approaching a family transition or event without a plan and without preparation is setting up a no-change situation. Once clients make that mistake once they never make it again. They are usually shocked at the results and are thrown back in memory and sometimes in reality to the early stages of their family work.

Focus on the Client as the Change Agent, the Weaver

From the beginning of treatment the therapeutic focus has been on the increasing clients' knowledge of and responsibility for self. While the first stage is oriented toward nuclear family functioning, clients learn the ins and outs of emotional system functioning. In that early phase, clients are mainly learners, with the therapist functioning in a somewhat more traditional role of the change agent.

In this model the therapist is an active consultant, teacher, and detective during the early stage. In the second phase, clients become much more self-directed as they grapple with the task of dealing with the threads of the multigenerational family system. They are definitely more participants in the process of change, functioning as detectives in their own family.

In this last phase clients become weavers, responsible for self and knowing what they need from the therapeutic process in order to deal with and develop the tapestry that is their life. While not always able to determine the threads that need to be examined and rewoven, clients are able to define that a change is necessary. Furthermore they are able to view the change as emanating from self rather than from another. The therapist is not expected to identify what changes are necessary; in fact, doing so hinders clients in developing the skills of self-examination necessary for ongoing work.

While the therapist may have to direct clients to make connections between patterns in the nuclear family and work environment, on the one hand, and the extended family on the other, clients recognize the connections readily. In fact, frequently only when clients are anxious does the therapist need to direct the process of identifying the connections; at other, calmer times clients are able to do so without assistance.

While during stage 2 clients often experienced times when keeping the focus on self as change agent was difficult at best, now the therapist has much less work to do in this regard. Clients are consistently better able to hold the view that they are responsible for any change in a pattern or problem that is bothering them. The therapist's goal is to keep them focused on the self as the source of change.

There are generally two situations, both related to clients' sense of responsibility, that lead them to seek some therapeutic assistance during this phase. When clients are troubled by a sense of overresponsibility for a particular pattern, they are usually feeling overanxious and stuck regarding what to do to make a situation better. The therapist needs to direct clients to examine how they are taking responsibility for others and to assist them in decreasing the overresponsibility by redefining their position in the process. Detriangling moves or reversals (as described in Chapter 5) are helpful in this regard.

On the other hand, when clients are underresponsible, they may describe a great deal of anger and hurt regarding how another has treated them. Clearly they see the other person or persons as more responsible for what happened than they are themselves. The therapist must direct them to observe the process and to examine their part in the process. Techniques for defusing the anger are probably useful in these situations. Only after that has occurred will clients be able to go about making a shift in their relationships.

THE CHANGING NATURE OF THE THERAPIST-CLIENT RELATIONSHIP

While the focus of multigenerational therapy is the ongoing work on self in the context of the system of which one is a part, the therapeutic goal is that the client will learn enough about emotional systems and his/her own family that the therapist will become unnecessary. At the same time, anyone who has done any work on themselves in the family of origin knows that the process is ongoing and will always require the occasional intervention of the therapist.

In this regard the therapist functions much like a family doctor who sees the client throughout his/her life and gets to know him/her and the family well. Visits are based on need; as the client gets "better," the need decreases. Thus, sessions are more frequent in the beginning and become sporadic as time goes on. The third stage lasts indefinitely. The therapist is able to offer the client a clear, nonreactive lens through which to examine self in the family when the client feels most reactive. The client's need for such assistance will shift over the course of a lifetime of transitions and other changes.

At this stage of the therapy process, the therapist basically acts as a consultant with regard to the client's family. As the client's expertise increases, the therapist and client become joint consultants on the family emotional system. The therapist provides a structure for examining the tapestry and for taking charge of the weaving of the fabric. The client provides the data on how the fabric is organized and operating and becomes increasingly adept at applying systems knowledge to the weaving/change process.

The client has obtained a perspective on situations that allows him/her to not only observe self but also to do so with a sense of humor. Therapy is much more playful, as therapist and client are able to view situations in a lighthearted way. The client is much more flexible than earlier and sees situations as opportunities. There is a greater sense of understanding, acceptance, and humor when other family members are discussed and interventions planned.

In this model, the therapist attempts to equip the client with the tools necessary to deal with the transitions and shifts in life. Because of the continuously changing nature of family life, the client needs to feel in charge of the direction of his/her life as much as possible.

REFERENCES

Bowen, M. (1978). *Family therapy in clinical practice*. New York: Aronson.

Carter, B., & McGoldrick, M. (1989a). *The changing family life cycle: A framework for family therapy* (2nd ed.). Boston: Allyn & Bacon.

Carter, B., & McGoldrick, M. (1989b). The changing family life cycle—A framework for family therapy. In B. Carter and M. McGoldrick (Eds.) *The changing family life cycle: A framework for family therapy* (2nd ed.) (pp. 3–28). Boston: Allyn & Bacon.

Carter, E., & McGoldrick Orfanidis, M. (1976). Family therapy with one person and the family therapist's own family. In P. Guerin (Ed.). *Family therapy: Theory and practice*. New York: Gardner.

Colon, F. (1973). In search of one's past: An identity trip. *Family Process 12*(4) 429–438).

Friedman, E. (1986). *Generation to generation*. New York: Guilford.

Herz Brown, F. (1989a). The postdivorce family. In B. Carter & M. McGoldrick (Eds.), *The changing family life cycle: A framework for family therapy* (2nd ed.) (pp. 371–394). Boston: Allyn & Bacon.

Herz Brown, F. (1989b). The impact of death and serious illness on the family life cycle. In B. Carter & M. McGoldrick (Eds.), *The changing family life cycle: A framework for family therapy* (2nd ed.) (pp. 457–482). Boston: Allyn & Bacon.

Imber-Black, E., Roberts, J., & Whiting, R. (1988). *Rituals in families and family therapy*. New York: Norton.

Rosen, E. (1990). *Families facing death: Family dynamics of terminal illness*. Lexington, MA: Lexington.

II

WORKING WITH FAMILIES
THROUGHOUT THE
LIFE CYCLE

7

Single Young Adults

NATALIE SCHWARTZBERG

THIS CHAPTER PRESENTS a multigenerational approach to the treatment of unmarried young adults (from approximately mid twenties to early thirties) who are establishing themselves separate from the family of origin. First we will consider the normal developmental process, then situational factors that affect the family's stress level, and finally the ethnic, gender, and class factors that influence the movement through this phase.

For the average middle-class American family, young adulthood can be defined as usually beginning in the early twenties (see Chapter 11), when the young person is launched from the family of origin, and ending sometime in the early thirties, when the young adult is firmly ensconced in a job and capable of intimacy. Of course, the ability to live on one's own is more and more affected by the cost of living in certain geographical areas of the United States. This factor, combined with a rather long period of initial singlehood for most middle-class Americans, has created some vagueness about the boundaries of this life cycle phase. In addition, there are ethnic and social class differences in responsibilities and expectations for work or education placed on the young adult.

The successful negotiation of this phase entails expectations and consequences for both the emerging adult and his/her family. There is, in fact, a complex and circular relationship between the tasks required for both, since the movement of the young adult outwardly provokes intense issues for the family while the parents' capacity to move on in life has repercussions for the young adult. People, whether young adults or their families, tend to come into treatment when there is a sense that these developmental tasks are not being resolved.

THE YOUNG ADULT IN TREATMENT

Young adults tend to come to treatment because of their own ongoing personal awareness that they are not functioning as well as they would like in terms of career or relationships. There is typically an increased sense of urgency in these young adults, as if the options were closing down. For women, there is the additional awareness of the limits of biology in terms of their desire to have children.

Young people who enter treatment with severe symptomatology, such as depression, acute anxiety, and substance abuse, have similar concerns as their less symptomatic counterparts, although these concerns are often subsumed under the overwhelming distress of these symptoms. Much more therapeutic time must be devoted to handling the symptoms, as well as the underlying concerns, than with their relatively healthy agemates. Part of the reason for the differences in severity of young adult symptomatology is the fact that, while leaving home is difficult for all of us, there is some variation in the "degree" of difficulty based on the degree of family stress and level of differentiation. These two factors, level of stress and level of differentiation, significantly affect the family's flexibility and openness to change (Bowen, 1978). When families are under greater than normal stress, such as those experiencing divorce, death, or a serious illness, their capacity to remain open and functional is seriously strained (Carter & McGoldrick, 1989). Families whose general level of differentiation is lower, such that emotional independence of members is problematic, seem to experience these difficulties to a more serious degree (Kerr & Bowen, 1988). Therefore, young adults attempting to separate from less differentiated families encounter more roadblocks and usually have a more difficult experience in this phase that those separating from families with a higher level of differentiation.

Dealing With Normative Issues

The young adult expects and is expected to move away from home. For the process to occur, the young person needs to be able to establish trust and autonomy, feel competent, have a reasonably good self-concept, and expect success in life. With these qualities, the emerging adult must begin to create a life structure, including a realistic plan for the future with both attachment and a life's work. Thus the young person must separate from the family as well as pass from an individual orientation to an interdependent or committed orientation of self (Aylmer, 1989).

The dual direction that is expected adds significantly to the stress already occurring during this phase. At the same time all this turmoil is going on, the young adult must also be able to tolerate ambiguity enough so that experimentation with and exploration of life's possibilities can occur (Aylmer, 1989).

It is no surprise, then, that young people tend to have an ongoing sense of uneasiness during this period. This uneasiness typically translates into an intense overreaction to feeling dependent. Thus, there is a deeply felt reactive "pseudo independence" at this point, with a great reluctance to examine family issues. As a result of this reactivity to family issues, young adults in treatment, particularly at the earlier end of the spectrum, want to stay with the problems of here and now. When they are finally helped to expand personal issues into family processes, family-of-origin work can be very slow and difficult. The very tentativeness of their autonomy causes any move back into the family to be experienced as threatening.

For single young adults, the provisional quality of the early launching years is ending and life is experienced as a more serious venture. Young people need to become more acutely aware at this age of the fact that, if the direction of life is to change, it should start changing now.

For many people the end of this era marks the completion of developmental tasks and a diminution of anxiety. They are settling down to the task of becoming full-fledged adults within their world. With the development of an adult identity comes a more secure sense of self. Thus, people at the later end of the young adult phase can begin to spend more time with their families without reactive distance. However, for those people who continue to have great difficulties resolving the developmental tasks of the period, severe stress may develop. A moderate or severe crisis is common at the age 30 transition (Levinson et al., 1978). This is said to be related to the continued failure to carve out a life direction combined with the heightened awareness that life is moving by.

The anxieties of families also tend to increase if their adult offspring have not moved on in life. The interaction between the adult and the family at this point can become fraught with tension. Often parents, expressing their concern about developmental issues, serve to increase the anxiety of their already sensitive children. At its most extreme this process can result in emotional distancing between the young adult and his/her family.

The clinician begins by attempting to calm the anxiety. This can be accomplished by stressing the normalcy of individual differences within the range of young adulthood, as well as by helping the person observe the themes within his or her particular family affecting the movement to another phase. Treatment after the initial crisis is quieted can proceed with a better pace than earlier in this period because of the more developed sense of self at the latter end of the phase, as well as increased motivation. It typically involves paying heed to the connection between the problems of the young person and ongoing difficulties in the nuclear and extended family. When the person can identify and take responsibility for the role he or she plays within the family emotional system, therapy becomes a process of shifting that role (Aylmer, 1989). The young person's capacity to shift that role is related to the ability to be objective and to take an autonomous position. This can only be accomplished when (s)he has been able to develop a beginning sense of self and to be financially independent enough to take a position that may not be popular with the family.

Another important issue emerging for people at the latter end of the young adult phase is that they begin to encounter the notion of remaining single. This may be due to societal reactions as well as the beginning awareness by the individual that marriage and children, which had previously been thought of as automatic and natural, are now seen as less predictable. This development brings to the young adult phase numerous complications: dealing with the conflict between a heretofore experienced transient stage and a possible permanent position, financial planning, buying a home, making plans for further education, considering career choices that are not compatible with marriage, and planning for generative possibilities if children may not be in the future—to name a few. That this life course of remaining single has no role models and is ambivalently perceived by society at large makes the task of moving on much more complicated. (Stein, 1981).

The young person must continue to establish an adult life course with its commitments and responsibilities despite the lack of recognition as adults single people experience in contemporary American life. To be helpful, the clinician should be able to confront his/her own stereotypes about what constitutes healthy adulthood.

While the young adult is trying to deal with the normative issues of his/her life, the family also struggles through the normative crises. For the parents, their child's transition into adulthood brings up a number of important issues. These include the awareness of their own aging, as well as what this means to them as individuals and/or as a couple. Typically couples reassess their marriage and siblings jockey for new position in the household. Decisions about how to refocus life's energies become paramount.

The emotional separation of the adult child may create a vacuum with significant ramifications in the nuclear and extended family. These ramifications may engender anxiety in the grandparents' generation, the sibling system, or the marital system, thereby leading to dysfunction. On the other hand, the shift in relationships may also create an opportunity for people within a family to rework their relationships. Parents may have another chance to resolve their own separation issues with grandparents, siblings may have the opportunity to shift their relationships with other siblings as well as with the parents, and the parents can confront their relationship with each other.

As the young adult approaches 30, the family has to come to some sort of acceptance that he/she as to find his or her own way. This is particularly difficult when the young adult is floundering. The "automatic" parental rescuing responses will emerge, along with guilt for what might be perceived as an inadequate "job" of parenting. In order for parents to remain some-what detached from these difficulties, they must be secure in themselves and in their own life stage commitments. The clinician should monitor the rela-tionships between all three generations, since each remains so intricately connected with the others. If it is not possible for the parents to resolve these difficulties, or if there are severe crises developing in other parts of the system, it is appropriate to see the young adult within the context of the family to rework launching issues.

Dealing With Contextual and Situational Issues

When the normative crises of young adulthood are complicated by a situa-tional stressor such as divorce, serious/chronic illness, or death of a family member, the clinician must deal with the layers of stress as one would an onion, peeling away the skin to the center. For all the family members, often including the young adult, focus of attention shifts from dealing with the normative stresses to a reinvestment in intrafamily concerns. Emotion-ality in the family usually increases at these times. The result of the disrup-tion of the normative transition can manifest itself in a regression in the young adult or symptoms in other family members (Carter & McGoldrick, 1989).

While all situational crises are stressful, those in which there is immediate community support for the family, such as illness and death, often seem less complicated to resolve than those, such as divorce and job loss, which are accompanied by little support and much censure. The capacity of the young person to deal with this period depends on his or her own internal develop-ment, as well as the belief that the family can resolve this crisis.

The theme running through all these potentially disruptive situations is that in crisis anxiety rises and the capacity for families to move on develop-mentally is affected. Thus, the young adult's natural movement toward au-tonomy can be affected as well. If the therapist can lower the anxiety enough in each situation, the young person can help appropriately in the family without feeling permanently locked into a regressive position. The goal of working with the young adult in family developmental crisis is to support flexibility in moving back into the family without staying there.

Ethnic and socioeconomic status tends to affect the way in which a family presents for treatment, the types of problems defined, and the solutions sought. Cultures vary widely in terms of how much functional and emotional relatedness is expected of the young adult and may present with different kinds of intergenerational struggles (McGoldrick, 1982). Socioeconomic status tends to affect the focus of the young adult's tasks; those of lower- to middle-income groups may be more concerned with finding and maintaining a job than with developing a life career or life structure, which is viewed as important by their cohorts from higher SES groups.

Gender affects the way in which clients report problems and the areas in which they are motivated to work. For instance, young women are frequently concerned with frustrations in relationships, while young men report more anxiety around occupational choices that are not working out. These differences seem to be related to the fundamental differences in the development of males and females, as well as the different societal expectations of both sexes (Gilligan, 1982).

CASE EXAMPLE

Defining and Working on the Foreground

Al was 30 years old when he came for help, primarily around intimacy issues. In his initial call he expressed his great anxiety about feeling stuck at this point in his life. He stated that he seemed to be going nowhere with women and had, in fact, recently ended an unrewarding relationship. He felt time was passing and he wanted to confront the issue preventing him from moving on in life. He added as an afterthought that he had other issues around work that he also wished to explore.

Al said that he had been in therapy previously for these problems and felt the experience had been helpful. He did not want to return to his previous therapist, a psychoanalyst. This needed to be understood more fully as part of the assessment of Al's problem. It would be important to know whether the transfer represented a wish to stop temporarily in order to consolidate changes, a wish to change the modality of treatment, or a resistance to confronting his problems. Depending upon our joint assessment of what meaning the transfer had for Al, we would decide on a course of action that would be geared to enhancing his potential for change within this treatment experience.

When Al came in for his first session, he appeared to be an attractive, somewhat nervous young man, well-dressed in a business suit. He expanded on the problems initially described on the telephone, talking particularly about relationships with women that seemed to go nowhere. Specifically, he had trouble initiating contact; if relationships did begin, they soon died from both parties' lack of enthusiasm.

In addition, he felt his work life was stagnant. A computer engineer for a large company, he felt restless and unfulfilled. Al desperately wanted to start his own business but didn't think he had the discipline to work hard enough for his own company to succeed. He also lacked the self-confidence to be a manager of people. He was frightened of confrontations and knew that in running a business he would have to deal frequently with this kind of interaction.

As the consultation continued, it became clear that Al's difficulties occurred in any relationship where confrontation and resolution of conflict were required. This included his previous therapeutic relationship, which he felt had been useful to him. After two years of twice-a-week psychotherapy, he felt that the relationship was becoming too intense. Al brought up the possibility of going less frequently and was dismayed when the therapist did not agree. He encouraged Al, instead, to explore the discomfort engendered by the relationship. Rather than deal with this, Al terminated treatment. The therapeutic contact then moved from a meaningful experience to another unhappy and unresolved relationship. Clearly, Al needed to resolve this relationship in a more productive way.

The themes that ran through Al's life difficulties were also consistent with this abrupt flight from treatment. These themes included the inability to experience himself as a separate person with power, the inability to confront and resolve issues in intimate relationships, and the growing frustration in not being able to carve out for himself a meaningful career. These difficulties are typical of the issues that bring people into treatment in the later phase of the young adult life stage.

DEALING WITH THE PREVIOUS TREATMENT. Once Al was able to identify the areas he wanted to explore, we developed a working partnership that entailed a joint understanding of the family system in which these problems were embedded. Al was familiar with a psychodynamic method of examining problems but was uncomfortable with how pathological he felt when looking at his problems in this manner. He felt particularly sensitive about his awareness that he was too uncomfortable to continue his previous treatment. He responded eagerly, therefore, to the notion of broadening the problem and observing family patterns. Seeing his problems as part of a larger family context dissolved his feeling of being a failure and gave him a more understandable and benign context in which to understand his difficulties. Most significant, however, was the notion that he could be active in his treatment rather than passive. Given the feelings of helplessness and powerlessness his problems engendered, the very fact that he could make interpersonal changes was in itself constructive for him.

This reaction was somewhat short-lived, disappearing when I mentioned that before tackling his family system he would need to address his abrupt

separation from his previous therapist. I suggested that his capacity to understand the implications of the abrupt rupture of this relationship and deal
with it more appropriately was critical to his work with his family. In order
to help him understand the relationship and his family issues, I introduced
the notion of triangles in family systems, explaining that dysfunctional
triangles develop when two people are unable to deal with the anxiety of a
dyadic relationship and use another person to stabilize it (Kerr & Bowen,
1988). Therefore, developing a relationship with me without resolving his
previous therapeutic relationship would just be isomorphic to his relationship problems.

Because working with the anxiety in this relationship would not be too
dissimilar from working with the anxiety in family relationships (except that
it was less intense), we prepared for his return to his therapist as if we were
preparing for a reconnection with a family member. We talked about the
possible outcomes and prepared him for each of them. Then, when he
decided he was ready to talk to the therapist, he made an appointment to see
him. We agreed that he would call me for another appointment when their
relationship was resolved.

Two weeks later I received a call from an elated Al. He was thrilled that he
had actually resolved this "cutoff" with the therapist. The fact that he followed through in a difficult interpersonal situation for the first time in his
life was so meaningful to him that he felt he had been successful even though
the session with the therapist seemed generally uneventful. He was now
ready to resume therapy with me.

In the first session that we had after Al had seen his therapist, he shared
with me a dream that he had the previous night. I decided to use it in our
work because Al was offering it as a bridge between the two therapies and a
statement of his interest in working with me. In this dream, Al was in a small
Volkswagen and thieves were beating on the car to get to him. He was
terrified that they would be able to penetrate the shell of his automobile. He
told me that this had been a recurrent dream in his life. He understood this
dream to be a metaphor as to where he felt he was in his life. He felt
vulnerable with people and unable to confirm a clear boundary between
himself and the rest of the world. He believed that this was a statement
about the issues we needed to explore.

TRACKING THE PROBLEMS WITHIN THE FAMILY RELATIONSHIP SYSTEM. Keeping
Al's perceived problems in mind, we began to examine his relationships in
detail. We were looking for themes involving anxiety in interpersonal relationships and confronting difficult issues.

Al comes from a middle-class Jewish family. His father, Bill, developed
and ran a small but successful hardware store, and his mother, Harriet, was

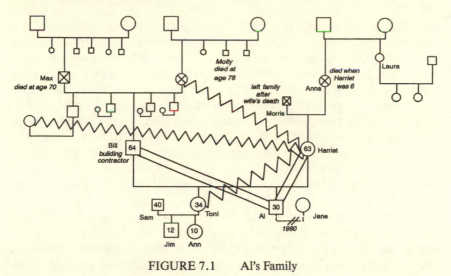

FIGURE 7.1   Al's Family

a housewife. The father was described as a hardworking and sincere man who had some difficulty asserting himself to his employees. Bill was also unassertive with his own family. Harriet was described as an intense, fearful person who was anxious about such activities of daily living as driving, cooking, and entertaining. Al described his parents as exhibiting little visible affection for each other although their marriage appeared stable.

Al is the youngest and only male of two children. His older sister, Toni, was always considered the bad one in the home while he was the child who could do no wrong. Al remembers his mother showering affection on him while Toni was always being reprimanded for her wildness.

The problem with Al's position in the home was that, while affection was showered on him, no expectations were made of him at all. Any extra effort that would be required to get an excellent grade rather than an average grade or to make money for himself was discouraged. He remembered his childhood feeling of being safe at home but frightened with schoolmates. He was particularly sensitive to competition. He ultimately moved out of his home in his late twenties but remained extremely attached to his parents and continued to be uncomfortable about competition. Meanwhile Toni married and had two children. The emotional relationship between Al and Toni was intense and negative. Although she was the older sister, Al felt he acted older than she. He always experienced himself as disapproving of her actions and reprimanded her as if she were a child. At the point that Al came for treatment Toni was going through a divorce.

Al's paternal grandfather, Max, was seen as a charismatic, forceful, and impatient businessman, whereas the grandmother, Molly, was described as bitter and complaining. Al's father's siblings received respect from the family only if they stood up to the powerful patriarch. Al's father saw himself as a bit of a "milquetoast," since he was never able to take a position for himself in the family against his father. He, therefore, became somewhat of an outcast. This position was solidified when he married Al's mother, who, although pretty and gentle, was seen as being financially unsuitable. Because of Bill's "outsider" position and his ongoing difficulty in taking a position in his family, he could not stand up for his wife so that Harriet ultimately felt unwelcome in her in-laws' home. Thus, the theme of lack of assertiveness that Al struggles with can be traced back to the patterns in the father's family.

Al's mother was an only child. She was 6 when her own mother died. Since Harriet's father felt unable to care for her alone, he left her in the care of her Aunt Laura. He disappeared from the family soon afterwards, leaving Harriet in her aunt's home. Although she was ultimately adopted by her aunt and uncle and grew up experiencing her cousins as sisters, she, like Cinderella, was always insecure about her position in her family. Harriet's original feelings of rejection by her own family added to her insecurity with her adopted family. Her subsequent rejection by her in-laws made her long for a close relationship with her own children. Toni, the firstborn child, was colicky and difficult to soothe, while Al's early passive nature made it easy for her to expect unconditional love from him. Father was also attached to Al, but this relationship didn't have the same intensity as the bond between mother and Al.

From what Al reported, mother and father were much more attached to their children than to each other. This, then, became a primarily child-focused family with positive intensity between Al and the parents and negative intensity between Toni and the parents. The level of intensity that had developed between parents and children was related to the problems in the parents' own families as well as their bonding to each other.

Our initial working hypothesis was that the emotional process between parents and children was too intense, which affected the children's ability to separate from the family in a productive way and prevented Al from moving on with his life. One possible reason for his parents' overconnection to their children seemed to be their anxiety about attachment and loss. This was related to mother's feelings of abandonment from her own family and father's ostracism from his.

This family was also a closed system: Information entering the system from the outside could not be accepted easily, and conversations between the family members were controlled by tight rules governing what was permissible and what was not. The effect was to intensify the difficulties in leaving and in forming trusting attachments outside the family. We hypothesized that this would affect the capacity of Toni and Al to develop a meaningful heterosexual relationship.

The purpose of helping Al think about his family in an objective way was to assist in moving from experiencing events in an automatic way to understanding better cognitively how his family system operated and what part he played in the family emotional process. From this cognitive, nonreactive position Al could change his part in the family system and make choices about his actions with family members rather than be flooded by the emotions of the family process. The capacity to be nonreactive to the family emotional system may also have consequences in his emotional relationships with peers (Carter & McGoldrick Orfanidis, 1976).

The next step in the process of becoming more objective about his family would be for Al to spend time with his parents and sister and observe how these relationships operated "in vivo." His tasks were to observe the interaction among mother, father, sister, and himself, to be aware of his own emotional reactions and how he became involved in the family emotional process, as well as to gather specific information on his parents' backgrounds in order to help develop an understanding of why the relationships operated in the way they did.

On a trip to Virginia where his parents and his sister lived, Al observed his parents' tremendous preoccupation with their children. Three-quarters of their conversation was about himself and Toni. Of course, they talked about Al in positive terms and Toni in negative terms. The Virginia trip was immensely productive. He saw in action his parents' clear preference for him over Toni. He was shocked to hear himself parroting their words, being parental and critical towards his older sister. Thus, he understood that the abrasive relationship between him and Toni was greatly influenced by the interaction of the relationship between his parents, their treatment of each child and the children's responses to these patterns.

Al was surprised to observe that his father's actions towards his mother contributed to his feeling that she was fragile. Father would protect mother and present a barrier against any family member's attempt to talk to her by saying "she's too tired, too upset," etc. He was shocked to learn that his mother, in fact, had been quite competent as a young women. She lived alone and worked before marrying Al's father. He discovered that it was his father who was actually seen in his youth as incompetent.

Not only was this visit Al's first move into his family but it also provided him with information to further assess his family. Essentially, the fact that Al's family was child-centered meant that his parents were more involved with their children than they were with one another. Reciprocally, he and his sister were also more involved with their parents than each other (see dia-

gram below). This type of system produces some typical triangular relationships: (1) the overly close relationship between mother and Al with his father
on the outside; (2) the overly close relationship between the parents and Al
with Toni on the outside; and (3) the triangle with mother, natural maternal
grandmother, and Al. This triangle includes mother's feeling of loss and
distance from her mother and her subsequent close relationship with Al (see
Figure 7.2). The problems that emerged out of these relationship systems
needed immediate attention, although other triangles, particularly those
including Al, his father, and paternal grandfather, were also significant. The
choice of where to begin was based on the immediacy of these problems as
well as Al's own assessment of which relationships he could work on at this
time.

    The early phase of treatment took about three months. Increasingly, Al
was able to objectify his role in his family, thus, significantly relieving his
general anxiety. He began to see his difficulties as a function of his role in
the family and was able to link this role to a broader pattern of relating with
others. Thus, a process of normalization began with his understanding that
what he saw as his pathology was an understandable aspect of that pattern.

The Middle Phase: Reweaving the Tapestry

Although one phase typically blends into another, the work of the second
phase begins when the client intentionally sets about shifting his or her own

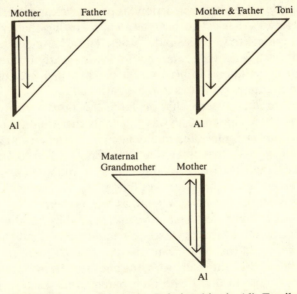

FIGURE 7.2   Triangular Relationships in Al's Family

position in those patterns he/she has identified in the first phase (Carter & McGoldrick Orfanidis, 1976).

For Al shedding his role meant breaking some of the family rules. To do this was terrifying to him because it meant he might not be considered the "good son" anymore and might, therefore, be in danger of losing the affection of his parents. In order to deal with this anxiety, he would need to know in a small but effective way that he could exist with somewhat less contact with his parents.

This young man was accustomed to calling his parents at least once a day and letting them know what was happening in his life. When he understood that being able to break the rules meant being less dependent on his family, he chose to begin this process by calling less frequently. I suggested that he think about what frequency felt most comfortable to him. His understanding was that change would come with discomfort but that he had to gauge what level of discomfort he could tolerate. He chose to call them twice a week.

To prepare him for dealing with this choice, it was necessary to help him anticipate the loneliness he would feel. When he decreased the calls, he did experience loss and loneliness. For a while his position was intensified because he wasn't used to sharing his feeling with peers and so had to deal with his sadness alone. I normalized the feelings by suggesting that there might be something positive about letting himself feel this sadness. He might be preparing himself to be able ultimately to deal with the difficult feelings that he had been avoiding in his life.

He reported having a strange dream at this point in process: He was alone on a frozen lake, ice fishing. Through the hole he had made in the ice, he brought up beautiful grapes. Although he had great enjoyment eating these grapes, he suddenly became very frightened. He thought, "I'm all alone. What happens if the ice breaks? There will be no one to help me."

He believed this dream represented his awareness of the thaw in his attachment to his parents and its potential fruitfulness. Although he felt hopeful, he was also fearful that he couldn't handle life if he lost them. He, of course, like many people going through this process, felt that changing his relationship with his parents might mean losing them altogether.

As he called less frequently, he actually began the process of loosening the intense ties between himself and his mother. The next step was to begin shifting the triangle with his parents and Toni. Since Al experienced such stress when he decided to call the parents less, he thought he might need more support before making more challenging changes. I therefore moved to shore up the sibling system. The effect would be to provide real support for Al within the family and also to upset the interlocking parental triangle.

Al was readily able to look at the patterns that were reinforced by his talking to his parents about Toni. This kept Toni in an outside position and he and his parents in a tight bond. It also prevented him from moving towards his sister. Before long he was able to refrain from negative conversation about his sister. The surprising thing to him about the change was the awareness that he more often than not was the initiator of these conversations. This had a profound effect on him, since he had never realized that he had so much influence on or was so active in the family system.

We then planned how he could directly change his relationship with Toni. It was necessary for me to work closely with him as he initiated changes, since he had previously acted as a parental surrogate in his conversations with his sister. Al planned to make a series of telephone contacts with Toni in which he would attempt to change his interactions.

I predicted that there would be resistance on Toni's part, and we planned how he would counter that resistance. The most useful first step would be for him to act more vulnerable with his sister rather than being a "preachy know-it-all." Therefore, he began by sharing his problems with Toni. Toni countered by telling him how angry she was when he sided with his parents all the time. This is typically a difficult time in a relationship change; the person who is trying to change needs to be prepared for an old reaction from the other person. In Al's case, the ability to reach out to Toni despite her anger was helped by compassion for the years of hurt Toni felt she had endured from Al. Al was able to say that Toni was right and he was sorry for the past. He was astounded by the immediate shift in Toni's attitude towards him. Shortly after that critical conversation, Toni began calling him more regularly as a friend.

Al began noticing that he was more relaxed around women. In shifting his relationship with Toni, two issues seemed to change for Al. He not only broke the tight family rules, allowing for more openness towards the outside, but, in developing an alliance with a woman on the same generational level, moved away from the intense relationship with his parents and toward a bond with a female peer. It should be reemphasized here that, as a result of three generations of relationship strains and early deaths, emotional contacts on the same generational level were weakened.

Next we began to work on the triangle with mother, father, and Al. Al needed to disentangle somewhat from his mother and get somewhat closer to his father. The parents-child triangle is potentially the most painful to shift, because the child experiences the real possibility of the loss of the parent they feel most supported by if he or she moves closer toward the other parent. The fact that this can in fact, temporarily happen, makes good preparation essential.

I believed Al was ready to work with this triangle since he had made some difficult changes with his sister and experienced himself as successful. He had been able to cope with the loneliness that shifts with his parents represented, and he now had Toni as a support.

The initial work with this triangle required that we plan for Al to be in his mother's presence and begin the process of defining himself differently with her. His capacity to do this would help him understand her pull when he wanted to move closer to his father. Al had always pictured himself as destroying his mother should he do something or say something of which she might disapprove, so this was difficult for him. The new knowledge that mother wasn't so fragile was very useful to him now.

We spent a great deal of time defining just how Al would express himself as a real person with his mother. Al had to sort out the difference between an intentionally malicious act and an act meant merely to define himself. After working through that he was not purposely "hurting his mother but merely being himself with her," he was ready to go to Virginia. Al decided to begin by sharing his dreams about his future and the fact that he didn't have the self-confidence he would like. He planned to tell her that he was opening a business despite anxieties that he would fail. His expectation was that mother would beg him not to take such chances and try to convince him to stay where he presently worked. His capacity to define himself in a real way despite her anxiety moved him further away from the "tight twosome" he and his mother had become.

Typically, when people attempt to move out of a close twosome, there is an opening for a closer relationship with the third, more distant person in that triangle. In this case. Al's changing relationship with his mother left an opening for some movement toward his father. However, one still expected resistance to this from the other member of the twosome. Therefore, Al needed to ready himself for this resistance by predicting and preparing for the specific ways in which this might happen. The next time Al visited Virginia he was able to carry out his task. Mother, as predicted, did express anxiety about his ability to succeed. Despite her escalating blows to Al's self-confidence in the form of suggestions that he would never be able to carry off a business, Al maintained his position of talking to his dad about the venture. In fact, at one point his father overheard a conversation between Al and his mother and supported Al. Such disagreements caused a problem between mother and father, with mother expressing anxiety about Al to father. Al was able to reassure mother about his capacities without being reactive to what he experienced as mother's blows to his self-esteem. His capacity to do this emerged from months of preparation, during which he became cognitively aware of how his family functioned.

Al returned from this visit jubilant. He felt much more manly and able to forge a closer relationship with his father without being fearful of hurting his mother. Shortly thereafter, he reported another dream to me. In this dream he was being attacked by people. Instead of huddling in the car and being fearful, he was standing up and throwing things back at them. He felt sure that this dream meant he felt capable of fighting back and standing up to the world.

Al continued to grow more courageous in speaking his mind to both of his parents, being careful to be assertive but not angry or rebellious. Over the next few months, he slowly developed a closer bond with his father by spending a great deal of time talking to him over the telephone about the development of a business. Since father did have his own business, he was immediately able to be helpful to Al. The next time Al visited his family he succeeded in spending some private time with his father, which was significant for both of them. He was capable of dealing with mother's occasional anxiety about this by being loving but firm with her. At the same time, he spent special, meaningful, and much more personal time with her.

The last significant triangle Al worked on was with his mother and her natural mother. The grandmother-mother-son triangle was potentially in place even before the development of the current nuclear family, since the loss of her mother left Harriet longing for her own child to mother and be mothered by. During this phase of the therapy, Al developed an apparently significant relationship with a woman. Then, alternating with the work with his mother, we spent time dealing with issues that arose in that relationship. Fortunately, his relationship with Toni had been stabilized, so he used her for advice regarding new relationships. This interaction finally placed Toni in an appropriate role in relationship to Al, that of "the wise big sister."

Much of the work with mother, Al, and maternal grandmother revolved around coaching Al to find out about his grandmother and the effect of her early death on his mother. As became clearer about the origin of mother's dependence on him, he found this to be liberating in terms of his guilt about separation. He also had some conversations with his mother about that period of her life, specifically her feelings about entering a new and possibly rejecting stepfamily.

Shortly after he began his work in this triangle, Al terminated treatment. He had started a new business and was marshaling all his forces to make it work. Al had been experiencing his relationships with women differently since the shift in his relationship with his sister. Although he had initially come into treatment with this as a problem, it had become less troublesome as he gradually became more comfortable with women. His focus had shifted to work and he believed that the attempt to open a business was a real sign of his growth. He wanted to return to family work in a year if he found it necessary. He was feeling good now but felt he would like to continue to work on issues relating to his parents. A month after terminating, Al called to report his progress. The autonomous, self-directed nature of the work he had completed allowed him to leave therapy with little discomfort. It is likely that he will be able to pick it up easily at a later point.

Summary

Al was in the second phase of therapy when he suspended treatment. Many people temporarily leave multigenerational therapy at this point. Often they experience themselves as having made enormous changes and need time on their own to consolidate the consequences of these changes. In Al's situation, becoming closer to his sister was a major change in his life. It meant he had a solid support system on a peer level, something he had never before experienced.

The capacity to put "his all" into a business venture represents his autonomy from a family system that to a large extent supported his lovableness, but not his tenacity and courage. Without the shifts with his parents it is doubtful that he would have had the requisite self-confidence. The final phase in his treatment would be for him to integrate his understanding of the changes he made in his family into his ongoing life. At this point, however, Al was finally engaging in the work of adulthood.

REFERENCES

Aylmer, R. (1989). The launching of the single young adult. In B. Carter & M. McGoldrick (Eds.), *The changing family life cycle* (2nd ed.) (pp. 191–208). Boston: Allyn and Bacon.

Bowen, M. (1978). *Family therapy in clinical practice*. New York: Aronson.

Carter, E. A., & McGoldrick Orfanidis, M. (1976). Family therapy with one person and the family therapist's own family. In P. Guerin (Ed.), *Family therapy: Theory and practice*. New York: Gardner.

Carter, B., & McGoldrick, M. (1989). Overview: The changing family life cycle—A framework for family therapy. In B. Carter & M. McGoldrick (Eds.), *The changing family life cycle* (2nd ed.) (pp. 3–30). Boston: Allyn and Bacon.

Gilligan, C. (1982). *In a different voice*. Cambridge, MA: Harvard University Press.

Kerr, M., & Bowen, M. (1988). *Family Evaluation*. New York: W. W. Norton.

Levinson, D. et al. (1978). *The seasons of a man's life*. New York: Ballantine Books.

McGoldrick, M. (1982). Ethnicity and family therapy: An overview. In M. McGoldrick, J. K. Pearce, & J. Giordano (Eds.), *Ethnicity and family therapy* (pp. 3–30). New York: Guilford.

Stein, P. (1981). Understanding single adulthood. In P. Stein (Ed.), *Single life* (pp. 9–21). New York: St. Martin's Press.

8

The Transition to Couplehood

GAIL S. LEDERER

JANE LEWIS

IN ALMOST ALL CULTURES, marriage is viewed as a joyful occasion to be celebrated and shared with family and friends. It is a time infused with great hope and expectations for the future. Because of the joy associated with this time, couples and their families frequently fail to see or anticipate the complexities and potential difficulties that need to be negotiated. "Marriage tends to be misunderstood as a joining of two individuals. What it really represents is the changing of two entire systems and an overlapping to develop a third subsystem" (Carter & McGoldrick, 1989, p. 15).

Expectations regarding couplehood vary tremendously in our society and influence this third system that the new couple embodies. Nevertheless, we are all more alike than different, and whether we are hippies, flower children or yuppies, we must find a way to work out the logistics of living. All new couples must attend to the issues of money, sex, time, power, friends, in-laws (McGoldrick, 1989), not to mention the everyday tasks such as laundry, marketing, meal preparation, and housework. To the extent that they come from similar backgrounds and life experiences, spouses may have similar expectations regarding these tasks. Yet even then, there is the potential for friction. It is the working-through of such conflicts that forms the texture of becoming a couple.

The major goal of the newly formed couple is to form a marital system and realign relationships with extended family and friends to include one's spouse (McGoldrick, 1989). In theory, for these tasks to be accomplished both partners must have developed a direction in work, be capable of intimate peer relationships, and have reached a separate sense of self in relation to family of origin—all tasks of the previous phase of the life cycle (Alymer, 1989). Thus, implicit in the initial contact with a therapist are some difficulties in negotiating the new tasks of the current phase and/or some unresolved conflictual areas remaining from an earlier phase of the life cycle.

FUSION VS. INTIMACY

One of the difficulties couples have that impedes negotiating tasks is a confusion between the "we-ness" of fusion and the "I" of intimacy. "There is a vast difference between forming an intimate relationship with another separate person and using a couple relationship to complete one's self and improve one's self-esteem" (McGoldrick, 1989, p. 213). Intimacy is the ability to be fully engaged emotionally with another person, while each maintains a separate sense of self. Fusion represents a merging of selves, with each person attempting to become more whole through the other. The more one has worked out family-of-origin issues and feels more complete as a self, the less likely he/she is to fuse with a potential mate. Individuals who enter marriage still reactive, to a great extent, to issues in their family of origin (Bowen, 1978) are more likely to seek completion of self through their spouse. It is this reactivity that influences the choice of mate. As one young woman put it: "Choosing my husband was not an intellectual decision—it was a totally emotional one." In fact, it is as if spouses are a matched set of luggage, with each mate's baggage complementing the other's.

GENDER ISSUES

No discussion of marriage is complete without mention of gender issues. In addition to the baggage of their original families, both spouses bring the baggage of societal and cultural views of marriage. Traditional views that give the promise of " . . . and so they lived happily ever after" rarely match the reality experienced in marriage. As Jessie Bernard (1973) describes it, there is "the wife's marriage" and "the husband's marriage," and the inherent differences and inequities in such an arrangement must be addressed in the therapy process. If we are to be responsible therapists, we can no longer continue the myth that men and women are equal in marriage. The world is still a patriarchal system that gives higher status to men over women and marriage is part of that system. Traditional gender roles have trained men to distance to the world of work and trained women to take care of the home and to handle the family's emotional needs. This has created a disparity of relating styles. Men tend to argue logically and women tend to argue emotionally. Men tend to blame others for what goes wrong and women tend to blame themselves. Addressing such issues validates the couple's unspoken experiences and helps the therapist to avoid becoming isomorphic to couple's issues.

The cultural view of marriage infuses itself through the romantic images of literature, movies, theater, and television. In the beginning, couples frequently make allowances for behavior that isn't quite acceptable. He may flatten and roll the tube of toothpaste from the end but keep from expressing his annoyance when she squeezes the tube in the middle. She may pick up his socks without comment when he drops them on the floor by the bed. In the beginning, each may view the other's idiosyncratic habits as acceptable or even attractive. These differences may get better or may change over time. At this early stage, couples focus on what they are getting, and differences seem enhancing. It is only later that differences become annoying and call out for resolution.

TYPES OF DIFFERENCES

Two types of differences cause problems and interfere with negotiating normative tasks: getting what you thought you wanted and getting what you thought you didn't. With the first type of difference, people get what they are looking for and then criticize the other for the very thing they wanted. The bargain might be that she will marry him if he promises to work hard and be rich; then, when he works 16 hours a day to give her the riches she expected, she turns around and berates him for working too much. This type of a bargain usually remains implicit and unstated. With the second type, people get what they didn't want; usually that is a repeat of some characteristic of a parent. For instance, he finds he married a screamer like his mother, and she finds he is distant and sarcastic like her father. Each expects the other to somehow know or understand why he/she is upset. When this fails, each is keenly disappointed.

The longer these explicit expectations and disappointments remain unstated, the more entrenched each spouse becomes in his/her disenchantment with the other. Thus, it is only a matter of time before differences become problematic. When they do, couples find themselves unable to settle their differences. The problem with most couples is *not* that they cannot agree; it is that they haven't learned how to *disagree*. Early on they were unable to acknowledge differences; now that they do, they don't know how to deal with them. Arguments boil down to a win or lose situation. Each spouse tries to win the other one over to his/her side, to convince the other one to change what he/she feels or believes in and *agree*. Or, spouses try to compromise, which means neither person gets what he/she wants. Both feel a sense of loss but console themselves with the knowledge that at least their spouse didn't get his/her way.

Spouses need to learn how to negotiate. Ideally, negotiation guarantees that each person will be happy part of the time. Negotiating a trade when a disagreement occurs ensures that one person will have it totally as he/she wishes on at least one issue. "I'll give you this if you give me that"—a quid pro quo. This does not mean that one doesn't give a little to get a little; however, when that happens it should not be done with a sense of loss or resentment. This seems very difficult for women to do because they usually are in a one-down position, with few bargaining chips and thus a greater probability for experiencing loss and resentment. It is hard for a woman to work for more equity in the marital relationship when she is struggling with issues of entitlement and/or is unable to support herself financially.

A MULTIGENERATIONAL PERSPECTIVE

Marital conflict around spousal differences is always connected to multigenerational issues. Therefore, multigenerational concepts are introduced in the very first session, as the therapist shifts back and forth from the presenting problem to genogram data and family history. As information is gathered, the therapist points out connections between the presenting problem and family-of-origin issues, explaining how these connections enable changes to be made.

A majority of the work in multigenerational couples therapy involves helping each spouse to be more insightful regarding him/herself in the family of origin. Individuals often react blindly to invisible strings being pulled from the generations above. Becoming less pulled by the family strings allows each spouse to make choices about how he/she wants to be as a person and then as part of a couple. When couples are so newly out of their families of origin, it is a good time for them and the therapist to see the parallels from their families in their own lives. They are also more frequently open, at this time, to making shifts in both relationships. Having resolved extended family issues and built a strong marital foundation, the couple will be prepared to handle subsequent life cycle phases, even if unusually stressful events occur. Also, breaking repetitive patterns in this early marriage phase, before children arrive, can prevent transmission of dysfunctional styles to the next generation. Therefore, the use of the multigenerational model at this time can benefit future generations as well.

OTHER COUPLE ARRANGEMENTS

While we are focusing on the early marriage phase of married, middle-class, heterosexual couples, we are fully aware that there are many other couple arrangements, as well as issues specific to lower- and upper-class couples. For couples who live together without marrying, the struggle we describe may be easier, since they are not making a legal or social transition, with the attendant shift in expectations. Unlike living together, marriage is a legal, as well as full-time emotional, commitment that one cannot just walk away from if things go badly. Though couples living together must still negotiate daily tasks, they do not usually have to work out the realignment with extended family. Also, their expectations of what married life is, of what "husband" or "wife" do, do not dictate behavior as strongly as when the legal knots are tied. The concept of marriage somehow encompasses the idea of added responsibility for spouse. People living together do not seem to take the same responsibility for the other's sense of well-being. When unmarried, each individual is able to remain more or less responsible for his/her own happiness. Once married, each feels responsible for keeping the other happy. Legally, couples living together have the knowledge that they can dissolve the union relatively easily. This allows for more freedom of self and less adaptive behavior.

Homosexual and lesbian couples must attend to a different set of social and legal issues than heterosexual couples do in their relationship. Relationally, they have many of the same tasks to negotiate as heterosexual couples. However, the normative tasks of making the transition to a couple are exacerbated by the addition of same-sex issues, which differ for men and women. For detailed studies, I refer the reader to the literature (Carl, 1990; Hidalgo, Peterson, & Woodman, 1985; Krestan & Bepko, 1980; Roth, 1989).

Lower-class couples must deal with economic hardships and governmental systems on top of negotiating daily tasks. The role of extended family and issues of realignment may differ in light of environmental pressures and housing arrangements (Fulmer, 1989). The transition time between forming a new couple and having children may be less or none, or children might come even before the young adult stage is reached (Hines, 1989). Thus, developmental tasks will be ill-defined and hard to accomplish.

Upper-class couples have much the same tasks as middle-class couples in realignment of extended family, but negotiating daily tasks and issues of money and power may differ. A major problem can occur when, no matter how much money the woman makes, it pales in light of the amount the man makes. Almost all women who divorce experience a downward change in economic status. However, issues of equity and power become even harder to resolve for upper-class women due to the greater imbalance of earning power and the knowledge that if the woman were to leave she would experience a drastic drop in economic and social status.

THE MULTIGENERATIONAL MODEL WITH A NEWLY MARRIED COUPLE: CARLOS AND LIZ*

Stage I. Defining the Foreground

THE ASSESSMENT. An effective couples therapist is always working on two levels—the here and now and the family of origin. The main goal of a first session is to understand the presenting problem within the larger context of the family of origin. The therapist starts by asking process questions about how the couple relationship works. Concurrently, the therapist gathers genogram data by asking focused questions about how each spouse's family behaved around the same issues that the couple presents as problematic in the marriage. As extended family issues emerge, the therapist develops a picture of how each spouse's function in his or her family of origin relates to the marriage. Thus, the framework for pointing out replication of patterns is set, and the concept of multigenerational connections is introduced within the first session.

Liz and Carlos came into therapy one week prior to their first wedding anniversary complaining of intense verbal fighting. They had both changed jobs in the past six months and were having difficulty juggling time, money, and new work responsibilities. The fighting seemed to take place over no specific issue, but it always followed the same pattern. Carlos would get angry about something Liz would do, and Liz would then get upset and yell or cry. Carlos would get even angrier at her response and this would upset Liz more. Finally, Carlos would distance because he was uncomfortable with the intensity of the conflict, and Liz would pursue him in search of a resolution until he would cut off all communication as his way of cooling things down. She would feel angry, hurt, and abandoned. Time would elapse and the couple would go back to "business as usual," until the process started all over again. Nothing was ever resolved.

Although they had argued during courtship and living together, Liz felt that fights had escalated in the past six months. Carlos felt that Liz was exaggerating and that things were not so different. He attributed most of their difficulties to the stresses of a new job, not to the relationship, and said he was coming to therapy only to accommodate Liz's needs.

---

*The following is a case study of a couple who had been in therapy with Jane Lewis.

Most couples entering therapy bring superheated emotional issues to the first session, so first moves are aimed at addressing the presenting problem and calming down the couple system. Normalizing and reframing the presenting problem as a life cycle issue and explaining the transitional steps all couples must take usually help to lower the emotional reactivity. Wherever possible, pointing out the caring that exists and the good intentions of each spouse to please the other, even if they aren't working, also helps.

Often, asking spouses to remember the "pros" at a time when they are only feeling "cons" helps balance perspective. Therefore, after Liz and Carlos explained what brought them to therapy, they were asked to describe their relationship prior to the marriage. The couple met when Carlos was Liz's supervisor at work. After dating for six months, they decided to live together. Carlos described himself as a loner who focused most of his energy on getting ahead at work and acquiring capital. He looked to Liz to provide the fun and energy he lacked in his adult life. Carlos characterized his parents as immigrants with broken English and little education. Liz, who came from an educated English family, represented a social move up for him.

Liz looked to Carlos as someone she could count on — not like her father, who had never been around. During courtship and living together she deferred to Carlos because he was older and wiser, although the stirring of conflict was evident. Liz also looked to Carlos for affirmation of her adulthood and her professionalism. Though Carlos gained class status through Liz, the societal gender roles that shape marital imbalance were clearly at work in Liz's expectations of Carlos.

In this particular case, the genogram was shared with the couple and used as a way to help them move into extended family issues (see Figure 8.1). The therapist then asked each to describe his/her extended family. Carlos told his story first. His father, in an attempt to find work, left Portugal for Brazil when Carlos was under two. Carlos and his mother joined his father the next year in Rio de Janeiro, where his brother was born. Shortly thereafter, his father again left home in search of financial security. A few years later, Carlos, his mother and brother rejoined his father in his parents' current home in Connecticut. So, much like his father, Carlos spent his early years fatherless.

Carlos' memories of childhood are dominated by arguing and physical violence. As a child he felt as if he were caught between his parents, having to protect his mother from his father. He experienced a "devastating blow" when, in spite of warnings that he would be held back in sixth grade if he missed too much school, the family left the U.S. for three months to visit his mother's family in Portugal. When Carlos returned to the States, he was indeed left back. Soon after, he began acting out and getting into trouble.

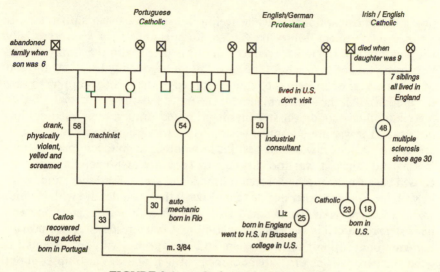

FIGURE 8.1   Carlos and Liz's Families

This behavior escalated until, by his sophomore year of high school, after having taken drugs since 7th grade, Carlos was discovered to be addicted to heroin. He was then sent to a drug rehabilitation program for the latter part of high school. By the time he graduated, he was drug-free. For Carlos, approval and achievement came primarily through excelling in school. He worked to put himself through college and earned two master's degrees. He was very proud of these accomplishments, seeing them as proof of his difference from his uneducated, immigrant parents. He never moved back home.

Carlos has little contact with his brother, whom he describes as a "hippie who works in an auto body shop, drives motorcycles and never went to college." He feels his brother has a better relationship with both his parents than he has: "I guess they accept each other." Carlos speaks to his parents monthly but remarks that he really does not have much to say to them. Though growing up Carlos felt closer to his mother, at this time he feels distant from both parents.

Liz then told her story. Her father, now a successful industrialist, emigrated to the U.S. when Liz was four months old. The family moved every few years in response to her father's business needs. Liz described her childhood as happy, despite the frequent moves. She stated, "We were expected to be close. There was no room for individuals, only family members."

When Liz was 12, she learned that her mother had multiple sclerosis. Interestingly, her mother had experienced the death of her father at a similar age. Liz reflected that her teen years were spent supporting her mother physically and emotionally, while feeling anger toward her father for his business involvement. Much like Carlos, Liz spent her early years essentially without a father. Liz was forced to move to Brussels with the family for the last three years of high school, because "mom needed my help." At the end of her first year of college, the family returned to the U.S.; according to Liz, the burden of all the arrangements for the move fell on her.

Her mother's condition steadily deteriorated until she required continuous care. Liz was not consulted when, two years earlier, her mother, father, and sisters decided it would be best for her mother to go to a nursing facility in England, since it was too difficult to keep her at home. England was chosen because the mother's seven brothers and sisters lived there and could be with her. It was further decided that Liz's father would move with her and work in Europe again, so he could visit with his wife on weekends. Liz and her sisters remained in Georgia for schooling. Liz felt responsible for providing emotional support for her sisters and was furious with her parents for what she perceived as their abandonment of her. She was also upset about her mother's condition and worried that she would die without any of her daughters being there.

Liz felt that, if she had offered to return home after she completed college to care for her mother, her mother would have stayed in the U.S. "I might have gone crazy but I wouldn't feel guilty." Her mother is currently in the terminal stage of her illness. Liz continues to speak to her sisters every week. She speaks to her father when he calls, which is usually to tell her to take care of some problem one of "the girls" is having.

Liz and Carlos had a lot of reasons for fighting. Carlos had been Liz's boss at work, creating an imbalance in the relationship, with Carlos in a one-up position to Liz. This unbalanced view was reinforced by their joint belief that men have more power than women. However, this belief may have balanced their unbalanced socioeconomic class origins. Liz's lower job and gender status may have provided a way for Carlos to remain boss even though he was from a lower socioeconomic status than Liz.

Despite being from different ethnic backgrounds, Liz and Carlos had similar cultural views of men's and women's roles. Each grew up with same-sex siblings, and both were oldests. According to Toman (1976), these constellations constitute the potential for sex and rank conflict. Both were stuck in their primary triangle, having grown up feeling responsible for their mothers, with fathers who distanced to work. Both had witnessed parents in a conflictual marriage. Both left home to escape what they perceived as untenable positions, rather than as part of a normal developmental process. The couple seemed to be extremely isolated socially and emotionally from family and friends; therefore, they were overly dependent on one another for all emotional support. This replicated Liz's family, in which members, because of moving so frequently, looked to the family to be all. The pattern of overconnectedness in Liz's family complemented the emotional distance in Carlos' family. Both scenarios contributed to the intensity that the couple invested in the relationship.

THE TREATMENT PLAN. On the nuclear level, Liz and Carlos needed to expand their social network and develop friends and separate activities as a way of diffusing the pressure on the marriage for each to be all to the other. It was unclear to me how much, if any, of Liz's reactivity to Carlos related to the stress of her mother's illness. Many people fail to connect problems in their work or marriage to the impact of death or serious illness (Brown, 1989), and Liz was no different. Liz and Carlos married what they "knew" but wanted what they didn't get. Each needed to identify what was missing and take more responsibility for satisfying his/her own needs rather than blaming or trying to change the other. Structurally, Liz needed to gain a greater sense of entitlement, so she could take more of a stand with Carlos on issues that affected her. This required a shift from seeing Carlos as "the boss" to harvesting some of her own power. Carlos needed to stop being parental with Liz and to see her as a partner. The eventual goal was for Liz and Carlos to have a nonreactive, but open and responsive, relationship with one another and with their families. If they were to form a solid couple foundation, they would need to attain a higher degree of self-differentiation from their families.

On the extended family level, Carlos needed to understand why work was a priority to him in relation to multigenerational themes and cultural problems of first-generation Americans. His family-of-origin work required becoming aware of and changing the current pattern of ritualized cutoff. Instead of reproaching his parents for their immigrant status, he needed to understand their struggles and get to know his mother and father on a personal level. A more balanced view of his parents would decrease his emotional reactivity to and embarrassment about them and free him to make different choices for himself. Carlos also needed to resolve his feelings of anger and resentment towards his parents, for taking him out of school in sixth grade. Carlos had to reconnect with his younger brother as a peer, not as a parent figure. As long as Carlos was so reactive towards his family, he would not be free to have an intimate relationship in his marriage. His emotional distance from his family would continue to affect his ability to connect emotionally with Liz.

Liz needed to open communication with her sisters and relate as a sister, not as a parent. With her father, she had to resolve her feelings of hurt and abandonment and learn to express desires as an adult daughter. She also needed to change her role as caretaker of her mother and mother to her sisters. Because of the seriousness of her mother's illness, it would be important for Liz to resolve issues with her mother as soon as possible.

THE INITIAL TREATMENT MOVES. Regardless of life cycle phase or therapist's theoretical orientation, it is generally true that after the issues and themes are defined, treatment begins by dealing with the presenting problem. In this case, the presenting problem was the couple's relationship. As we noted before, most problems stem from disappointed expectations. Since Carlos and Liz were about to celebrate their first wedding anniversary, the therapist used this event as a time for reflection and asked them to separately write down the ways their first year of marriage met or fell short of their expectations. This was a beginning step in making explicit the implicit expectations. The therapist asked Carlos and Liz to each repeat the task as he/she understood it. Liz wrote it down. Carlos said he would remember. Both agreed to do the task; when questioned, neither felt it would be a problem to do.

When Carlos and Liz arrived for the next session, they were visibly upset. Liz had completed the assigned task; Carlos had not. He attributed his failure to the fact that his boss had announced he was closing the business and all employees would get three weeks' severance pay, effective immediately. Carlos was angry and frustrated. He had never lost a job, nor had he been unemployed in his adult life. The therapist was very sympathetic and acknowledged how anyone in his position would be upset. She also added her confusion about how this event prevented him from doing the task he had agreed to do two weeks before. She was taking the assigning of a task seriously, as a model of what she expected Carlos to do. Carlos explained that he had been very busy the last week and had planned to do the task this week, but when the business closing was announced he was too distracted to remember. However, he said things had been much calmer between Liz and him since their first visit.

It was no wonder that the marital issues had calmed down as the couple focused on how to deal with this new crisis. Clearly, there was much work to be done in the here and now before any family-of-origin moves could be made. Not only did the therapist have to calm the system down, address the presenting issues, and deal with Liz's mother's imminent death, but now she had to add Carlos' job loss to the beginning work agenda.

Carlos and Liz cooled down fairly quickly and were able to work together in a crisis. However, for many couples, additional stress such as a job loss would heat up conflict even more. When conflict between spouses becomes too hot — that is, too intense — the therapist spends most of the session putting out fires. Doing therapy is impossible. In these instances it is best to see each spouse individually for a while, until each is sufficiently nonreactive that they can discuss issues together without the emotional climate overheating.

Liz was very supportive and concerned about Carlos' job problem. They were both worried about money but felt they could manage on Liz's salary and Carlos' unemployment insurance for a while. The therapist spent some time discussing Carlos' plans to look for a new job. It was too soon to know how long the job search process would take or how much of a distraction it would prove to be for the couple. The therapist reiterated to the couple the many stresses of early marriage and added that job loss, which was a major worry, made the situation that much harder. The rest of the time was used as an opportunity to refocus on them as a couple and to ask Liz about her task and what was on her list.

The next session began with the therapist's asking how Carlos' job search was going. He said he had good contacts and had begun to use his network of colleagues and friends as a way to broaden his search. He felt confident that he would eventually find a new job at his current pay and status, but realized it would take time. The therapist then shifted the session back to Liz's list of disappointments that she had read at the end of the last session. Liz felt disappointed that Carlos treated her like a child by not discussing financial matters with her but rather presenting them to her as fait accompli. He ran the show, telling her what to do, and she tagged along.

The therapist pointed out to Liz how not being consulted must remind her of how her family never consulted her about how to care for her mother. The therapist also drew a parallel between how her mother tagged along after her father, always doing as she was told, and how Liz tagged along after Carlos. Liz agreed that the situation was similar. Making comparisons between nuclear and family-of-origin issues and patterns, a major technique in this method of multigenerational therapy, helps set the stage for doing extended family work later on.

Another disappointment for Liz was that she and Carlos were not having much fun as a couple, nor were they socializing with other people. Many of Liz's friends had married and moved away. She admitted she had probably begun to lose contact with them when she and Carlos began living together; however, somehow her expectations changed once they married. Thus we see the common occurrence of changing expectations as soon as the relationship is cemented legally. Again, the therapist commented on the similarity between Liz's marriage and her family of origin. Because of moving and leaving friends so often when growing up, Liz learned that family was everything. It was natural for her to see the building of her new family as all she needed.

The last item on Liz's list was her comment that "I expected to be equal." (Yet she married her boss!) Liz's expectation that she would find equality in marriage could only lead to disappointment. Society has reinforced this myth of equality while simultaneously perpetuating inequality between men and women. As long as Liz looked to Carlos to take care of her, she could not gain more power for herself.

Carlos listened to Liz's list and then said he disagreed. He felt that he really did include her and that she just didn't pay attention when he discussed things in which she wasn't interested, such as investments. Carlos was unable to question his part or take any responsibility for what he might do that contributed to Liz's feelings. The only problems Carlos recognized were finding a job and ending the marital fights. He still distanced emotionally from Liz when things became too intense between them. One reason he was unable to see his part or change was that he was working only on the nuclear level, one step removed from where the problem started. We tell people they are welcome to try and change things on the nuclear level, but that it is a hard way to go about it because reactivity to family-of-origin issues gets transferred onto the marital relationship and muddies the water.

Carlos was ashamed of his parents' lack of Americanization and understanding of the culture, as shown in their pulling him out of school for so long or in his father's only being a machinist and his brother an auto mechanic. He did not understand that his focus on success at work was his way of gaining status as an American and differentiating himself from his immigrant parents. He also did not connect his emotional distance from his family to his fights with his wife. His main focus was on the present.

In couples work, it often happens that spouses are not ready to work on their family issues at the same time. It is not unusual for one spouse to move and the other to hold still. Women usually go first because they have been trained to deal with problems on the emotional level. Men are slower to show willingness to do family-of-origin work because they have been trained to deal with problems on a logical and functional level. Despite Carlos' unwillingness to do family-of-origin work, he continued to attend most sessions with his wife. He experienced the sessions as helpful. He felt he understood Liz better and was more aware of how his behavior might be experienced differently from what he intended. Usually, we support a husband or wife in continuing to come to joint sessions, even when one spouse is doing family-of-origin work, but often he/she drops out, perceiving it as the other spouse's problem.

Carlos acknowledged that he needed to connect with his family differently but he did not want to do anything specific right now. However, he was willing to work with Liz on the marriage to end the fighting, since this was more relevant to him than family-of-origin work. Therefore, to decrease the distance in the couple relationship, each was given the task of reaching out to the other daily: Liz to Carlos about work; Carlos to Liz about her mother.

Liz arrived alone at the next session. She was apologetic for not calling and asking if she should reschedule because her husband had a temporary job that required his working at the time of the appointment. The job began the day prior to the scheduled session and he did not feel he could change his hours so soon. The therapist told Liz she was sorry Carlos could not keep the appointment. She taped the session so Carlos could review it sometime in the future, hopefully before the next meeting. Taping the marital session when one spouse is scheduled to attend but cannot prevents the therapist from being perceived as allied with one spouse against the other.

Since Carlos was not there, the therapist elected to concentrate on Liz's family-of-origin issues rather than on the marital issues. Liz was very worried about her mother's impending death and wanted to work on getting things resolved with her mother before she died. The therapist gave Liz the task of writing a letter to her mother, not to be mailed, about the things she wanted to say to her mother before her death.

Stage 2. Reweaving the Tapestry

Beginning to resolve issues in one's family of origin is stage II work and generally does not occur so early in the therapy. However, Liz's mother's imminent death was a situational crisis that forced the therapist to deal sooner with Liz and her family of origin. Liz brought the assigned letter to her mother to the next session. The letter was a clear, poignant statement of love, sadness, disappointment, and a genuine willingness to make peace and say goodbye. During the reading, she reflected on the good times of her childhood and early teens and how much she now misses the mother she remembered having. It was during the writing of the letter that she became aware of how much more of her functional mother she had experienced than had her two younger sisters. She realized that growing up must have been a lot harder for them.

The therapist used this as an opportunity to suggest to Liz that she share her concerns about her mother's deteriorating condition with her sisters. Liz had never been in an equal position with her sisters. In keeping with her idea that her sisters never had a mother, she had always felt as if she was "the other mother." Sharing her concerns with her sisters, rather than keeping them to herself, would begin to reverse this process.

Carlos and Liz came in together for the next session. The couple had been able to carry out the assigned task of asking each other about areas of concern. Liz had discussed her letter to her mother and found Carlos helpful.

At this session, Carlos appeared quite depressed. He was still only able to focus on his need to find a job. Although being out of work is a struggle for anyone, the severity of his depression indicated that Carlos had a high degree of reactivity to being out of work. The therapist commiserated with Carlos while simultaneously connecting his depressed response to his family-of-origin issues. Without a job, Carlos had lost his status and his image as a bona fide American.

We didn't give up on family-of-origin work just because Carlos was able to focus only on finding a job. Carlos and Liz planned to visit his parents the following weekend. Carlos had not mentioned his job loss to his mother when she called the previous week to invite them for Easter dinner. He felt it would have only worried her and he did not feel comfortable telling her over the phone. This showed how stuck Carlos was in his original triangle with his parents, still protecting his mother. The therapist asked Carlos if he was planning to tell his mother and father about his job loss in person, when he visited. He said he was.

After their visit with Carlos' family, Liz was called to England. She spent four days with her mother before her death. Carlos arrived the day before his mother-in-law died and was helpful and supportive of Liz. Telling of this later, Liz was tearful, saying, "I am glad it's over; I will miss her." During her stay in England, she spent time with her sisters, her mother's family, and some of her father's family. She reported that she was able to use the time after her mother's death to look at how different her mother's and father's families were. She described her father's family as: "WASP intellectual, but the alive group and the one I like better. I'm not sure how I fit in. I also learned how important it is for me to feel needed." Liz emphasized that, during the time surrounding the funeral, Carlos was able to fit in well with her father's family and that she felt jealous and simultaneously pleased. She saw Carlos as a way of gaining status or entrée with her father. Liz would need to learn how to be close with her dad independent of either Carlos' or her mother's relationship with him. It was strikingly apparent as she retold the events that the couple had once again pulled together during this period of stress.

Liz was ready to continue looking at her family relationships. She was particularly interested in shifting her position with her sisters. She was tired of being their "mother" and thought that being a sister sounded nice. She was not ready to work on her relationship with her father but acknowledged the need to do so at some time in the future. Carlos, on the other hand, had, by bringing friends along, avoided the earlier suggestion to speak about his job loss with his parents during his visit home at Easter. He was still unable to "rock the family boat."

To keep the couple work balanced with Liz's family-of-origin work, the first part of all joint sessions focused on issues in the marriage, helping define the process between Liz and Carlos and holding each responsible for his/her part in the transactions. The marital issues paralleled family-of-origin issues. The content of Liz and Carlos' fights changed continually, but the process between them usually boiled down to either Carlos' "telling" Liz what was best for her and Liz's feeling hurt and unloved but going along or Liz's digging her heels in and insisting that things be done her way. Either way there would be an escalation of conflict and fighting. In the former example, Liz's acquiescence to Carlos evolved out of her family's message to be a "family member, not an individual," and to the societal message that women should be adaptive. For Carlos, taking over related back to his family-of-origin role as protector of his mother and to the societal message that men should "rule the roost." The latter example shows what happens when two oldests, who are used to running the show in their original families, butt heads. Neither stance represents a differentiated position.

Carlos' allergy to open conflict with his subsequent emotional distancing from Liz was a method of handling conflict learned in childhood from witnessing the violent fights between his parents. Neither Liz nor Carlos knew how to get emotional support from each other. Carlos had never learned how to get it from his parents, finding support only from outside systems. Liz, who had been the caretaker of her entire family, also had never learned. Both Carlos' distancing to school and work and Liz's reversed hierarchy left them isolated from their families. These isolated positions intensified their expectations for emotional support from each other and magnified their disappointment when support was not forthcoming.

The therapist listened to the content of their fights, always looking at the process, pointing it out to each, and connecting the process between them to their family-of-origin issues. On the nuclear level, the therapist challenged each to come up with new solutions. She coached Carlos on how, when conflict occurred, he might state his position clearly, neither retreating nor moving in by taking over. She validated Liz's right to differ from Carlos, helping her speak for herself, neither deferring to Carlos nor digging in her heels.

On the extended family level, the therapist helped Liz come up with tasks designed to define herself as an individual within her family. If she could stay connected with family members and still state differing views, she would find it easier to do the same with Carlos. During the first year of therapy, the therapist reminded Carlos from time to time of the difficulty of changing his part in the marital process without working on his extended family where it all got started. Once Carlos decided to begin family-of-origin work, he would need first to reconnect with his parents and then to connect as a son who did not have all the answers. If he could gain approval without being "the golden boy," he would find it easier to tolerate differences between himself and Liz.

Liz was able to use the insights that she had gained in England and begin to pull back from the triangulated caretaking role she had played in her family. She could see how her desire to be needed by the family fostered a position she no longer wanted—that of mother to her sisters and mediator for her dad. Liz began to redefine her expectations of her dad and sisters and thereby minimize her disappointments. Over the next eight months she refused to take responsibility for her father's relationship with her sisters or theirs with one another. In sessions, she practiced various ways to approach her father and sisters and anticipated potential problems. She was able to tell her father to stop calling her about "the girls," and she did not approach her father for her sisters when there were problems. At different times she was able to ask for emotional support from each of her sisters. She visited each sister individually, and all three of them spent time together, without husbands or boyfriends. On one of her father's visits, she planned time alone with him to talk about her career. During another visit, Liz shared her concerns with him about her marriage and Carlos' unemployment. Over time, her father became somewhat more available to her, taking on the role of a consultant.

Liz's family-of-origin moves affected the couple's relationship. As Liz began to shift from reactive stance of a disappointed child to the more entitled stance of an adult daughter, the emotional distance from her father decreased. Moving closer to her dad lowered her reactivity to Carlos' distancing. This enabled her to take more of an "I" position with Carlos regarding her needs. As Liz became more of a peer to her sisters, she was able to share her concerns and ask for advice. By realigning her position with her father and sisters, she no longer looked to Carlos to be a parent figure, wanting instead to relate as a peer. By bridging the emotional distance with her father and sisters, she no longer looked to Carlos for all her emotional needs, thus lessening the pressure on the couple relationship and the disappointment too much pressure brings. Liz was taking more responsibility for what she wanted. During this time Liz felt more confident at work and began to explore future career options as well as the possibility of returning to graduate school and getting an advanced degree.

As Liz became more focused on her own family-of-origin issues, she stopped being so responsible for Carlos, leaving the stage set for him to take more responsibility for himself. Carlos did not find permanent employment for seven months. During that time, the search for work occupied most of his time and energy and he remained unavailable to explore issues with his family. He did make several unsuccessful attempts to get together with his younger brother for lunch and dinner. His brother failed to keep the appointments and Carlos did not care to pursue him further at that time.

However, several months after he had been working at his new job, Carlos began to do some real work with his family of origin. Carlos' parents had retired to Florida and his contact with them remained polite and superficial. Carlos agreed to do a task. He was to spend time alone with each of his parents during a planned visit. The purpose was to get to know his parents as people who had their own struggles. He was to talk to his father about his father's childhood and what his life was like growing up fatherless. He was also to discuss how hard it must have been for his father to be away from his family during the early years of his marriage. He was to speak with his mother about how she managed alone with two small children in a strange country while her husband was trying to get established in the U.S.

The therapist referred to Carlos' parents as pioneers, not immigrants, pilgrims of their time. The intent of this reframe was to decrease Carlos' reactivity to his parents' lack of Americanization by presenting a new perspective. If Carlos could see his parents in a more human and less critical light, he would be able to shift his position in the triangle between himself and his parents. He would not need to distance from them as a way to show his own Americanization. He would be able to stay more connected and still feel separate. This would relieve him of looking to Liz to fill all his emotional needs.

The therapist strategized with Carlos on ways to be open and nonconfrontive with his parents by asking him to anticipate potential difficulties he might encounter. They discussed alternative approaches to each of his anticipated problems and spend part of several sessions preparing for his next visit. Carlos and Liz left for Florida with clear tasks. Liz was to practice being an observer and spend time relaxing and reading. If needed, Liz was to spend time with the parent Carlos was not working with. Liz had always felt comfortable with Carlos' family so she felt her task would be easy. As it worked out, Carlos was able to spend some time alone with each parent without needing help.

Carlos was eager to report back to the therapist and share the experience he had with his family. "It was nice to talk to them like real people." He had even brought up his anger and upset about sixth grade. He felt that he better understood his parents' behavior at that time, even if he did not agree with them. Carlos had been slow to start, but once he committed to the work, he moved forward quickly. This is often true of men who have been conditioned in the workplace to move in a straight line to achieve goals directly. Women, on the other hand, often agonize over every move they make and only move after they have looked at the issues upside down, inside out, backward, forward, and sideways.

Since his visit, Carlos has maintained bimonthly contact with his parents. He initiates at least half of the communication and makes sure that he speaks with each parent. He has been able to ask his father's advice about remodeling his home and is looking forward to his next visit with them. Carlos is still working on a strategy to engage his younger brother in some sort of relationship. It is hard for Carlos to approach him as an equal, "I think of him as a wild kid."

As Carlos became more accepting of his family, he became more critical of Liz's family, since he no longer needed her family for his own status. However, Liz developed a way of not becoming caught in their old verbal "tug of war." Carlos' need to be correct and in charge was now acknowledged by both and treated with humor, respect, and some verbal battles. The necessity to expand their social network of friends and acquaintances continues to be an area for work. Liz hopes the move to a new house will finally settle them into a community. The couple is beginning to talk about having children, the next phase of the life cycle.

Summary and Conclusions

A couple married almost a year came to therapy under appreciable stress in almost all systems: work, family of origin, social and marital. There was intense reactivity and fighting between them. Complicating this was Carlos' job loss and Liz's mother's imminent death. On the extended family level, Liz's father abdicated parenting and emotional support, leaving parenting of his younger daughters to Liz. In Carlos' family, there was a ritualized cutoff from his parents and brother since adolescence. Neither Carlos nor Liz had social contacts outside the marriage. In this collapsed system, the couple needed to be everything to one another, neither a possible nor desirable state.

By working with Carlos and Liz, individually and together, and dealing with several crisis along the way, we reframed and shifted perspectives and decreased the degree of triangulation of both spouses with their families of origin. Liz's mother died after a long illness and Carlos was out of work for a half year. Yet, in the face of these stresses, added to the normal adjustments of early marriage, they both showed substantial progress in resolving unfinished work with their families of origin. Carlos was able to increase his emotional connectedness with his parents. Liz shifted to a more equal relationship with her sisters and achieved a more personal and satisfying relationship with her dad. Since each was now less reactive to his/her family of origin, they were more emotionally available to each other. They were able to be more responsible for their own part in fights and to differ with each other without feeling as if they both must agree. In differentiating a separate self from family of origin, both were able to have a more solid sense of self within the marital dyad, joining together as a "we" without loss of self to the other.

Generally, the difficulties of early marriage hark back to family-of-origin issues that have not been satisfactorily resolved; these are complicated by the reality that early marriage is at variance with the romantic perception of blissfulness. Many couples have work to do that pays large dividends if accomplished before the addition of children.

REFERENCES

Aylmer, R. (1989). The launching of the single young adult. In B. Carter & M. McGoldrick (Eds.), *The changing family life cycle* (2nd ed.) (pp. 191–208). Boston: Allyn and Bacon.

Bernard, J. (1973). *The future of marriage*. New Haven, CT: Yale University Press.

Bowen, M. (1978). *Family therapy in clinical practice*. New York: Aronson.

Brown, F. H. (1989). The impact of death and serious illness on the family life cycle. In B. Carter & M. McGoldrick (Eds.), *The changing family life cycle* (2nd ed.) (pp. 457–482). Boston: Allyn and Bacon.

Carl, D. (1990). *Counseling same-sex couples*. New York: W. W. Norton.

Carter, B., & McGoldrick, M. (1989). Overview: The changing family life cycle—A framework for family therapy. In B. Carter & M. McGoldrick (Eds.), *The changing family life cycle* (2nd ed.) (pp. 3–30). Boston: Allyn and Bacon.

Fulmer, R. (1989). Lower-income and professional families: A comparison of structure and life cycle process. In B. Carter & M. McGoldrick (Eds.), *The changing family life cycle* (2nd ed.) (pp. 545–578). Boston: Allyn and Bacon.

Hidalgo, H., Peterson, T. L., & Woodman, N. J. (Eds.). (1985). *Lesbian and gay issues: A resource manual for social workers*. Silver Spring, MD: National Association of Social Workers.

Hines, P. (1989). The family life cycle of poor black families. In B. Carter & M. McGoldrick (Eds.), *The changing family life cycle* (2nd. ed.) (pp. 513–544). Boston: Allyn & Bacon.

Krestan, J., & Bepko, C. (1980). The problem of fusion in the lesbian relationship. *Family Process, 19(3)*, 277–90.

McGoldrick, M. (1989b). The joining of families through marriage: The new couple. In B. Carter & M. McGoldrick (Eds.), *The changing family life cycle* (2nd ed.) (pp. 209–234). Boston: Allyn and Bacon.

Roth, S. (1989). Psychotherapy with lesbian couples: Individual issues, female socialization, and the social context. In M. McGoldrick, C. M. Anderson, & F. Walsh (Eds.), *Women in families* (pp. 286–307). New York: W. W. Norton.

Toman, W. (1969). *Family constellation* (2nd ed.). New York: Springer.

9

Families With Young Children

KATHY BERLINER

HAVING CHILDREN IS TRULY a family affair; when a new generation is born, every relationship in the extended family network is affected by the automatic assumption of new roles. Parents become grandparents, brothers and sisters become uncles and aunts, sons and daughter become dads and moms (Bradt, 1988). Childbirth joins the couple to the extended family system in a permanent way. Parent, grandparent, aunt, uncle—these roles define relationships extending beyond the bonds of marriage (McGoldrick, 1989b).

Parenthood, which places so much emphasis on our children's tomorrow, also forces us to confront our history and the way family legacies, themes, and myths will or will not be carried forth. Decisions regarding the observance of religious traditions or family rituals take on new significance when the decision maker is now a parent and not just a daughter or son. While couples may cling to the illusion of being totally separate or different from their families of origin, family patterns emerge nonetheless to influence both being a parent and relating to a spouse who is now a parent. When we become parents, therefore, there is perhaps more motivation to examine and change family relationships than at other stages of the life cycle. The specter of repeating a bad relationship with your parent in relation to your child can be a powerful incentive to reappraise and repair family rifts.

While having children makes a couple a permanent part of a larger family system, it also makes a couple a discrete family unit. It is often now easier for a husband and wife to carve out their own identity in the larger family, whether around creation of their own rituals or in making their home the center of family life. Children help bestow adult status and can legitimatize boundaries with which single or newly married adults may struggle. Finding a comfortable connection with the larger family and defining the integrity of the nuclear family are the two seemingly opposite tasks a couple faces together and as individuals in making the life cycle transition.

A number of societal factors have contributed to a growing sense of disconnection between generations as well as an uncertainty about how best to function in the nuclear family. Women's greater presence in the workforce, ready access to birth control, and legal abortion have all increased women's options beyond those of their mothers and grandmothers. It is also no longer acceptable for men just to be breadwinners for the family. They are expected to have relationships with their children and participate in childcare tasks in ways their fathers never did. While it can be disputed as to whether there has been any significant altering of gender-specific roles in modern marriages, particularly once children are born (McGoldrick 1989a), expectations that marriage can and should be different contribute to very different pressures on this generation. Women, for example, feel pushed to "do to all" without changes in social climate to make that possible. Men may feel robbed of prerogatives they witnessed their fathers enjoying, with no real preparation for their families' increased demands for intimacy. The difference in experience between the generations also can result in a decrease in support from the extended family.

For a successful passage through this phase, couples need to feel connected to and enriched by family relationships and heritages, as well as free to challenge and experiment with role definitions and models of parenting. Because therapy with couples can easily be absorbed by the uproar and intense stress of forming a nuclear family, the therapist should take advantage of the generational pulls activated by having children to broaden the therapeutic lens. That lens must also take in the societal pulls that influence and shape the marital and parental contract. The disequilibrium occurring during this time of transition can provide the best opportunity for change. Old definitions of relationships are called into question. Struggles over alliances and influence become much more overt and therefore easier to address.

PROBLEM DEFINED IN THE COUPLE RELATIONSHIP

Although new parents may approach therapy with a variety of conflicts, at the root is the pressure of having a new role. For many couples, the addition of children precipitates or solidifies a traditional gender-specific role division of tasks (Bradt, 1989). This is perhaps most jarring to couples who enter the marriage as two wage earners and with an egalitarian view or expectation of the partnership. Their conflicts will frequently be about managing the increased responsibility and negotiating a comfortable division of labor. Traditional couples will also feel an impact on the marriage, as the differences between his realm and hers increase. Here the fight may be more typically about affairs, alcohol, or symptoms that balance the power between the spouses.

The role of the parent has historically been a limiting one for women who must either choose between career and home or somehow juggle both jobs. For men, parenthood has never meant giving up career or other interests (Braverman, 1989; Holder & Anderson, 1989). The consequences for marriage are significant, as women become oriented toward children and men become increasingly oriented toward the world of work. Because these spheres are not equally valued or respected, the balance in the marriage becomes skewed. Several studies done on the impact of children on marriage have documented a drop in women's self-esteem, as they feel less valued by the world in their roles as mothers (Entwistle & Doering, 1981). If the balance remains tipped and is reinforced by an economic disparity, with the woman not able to keep pace with the man's earning, the power differential begins to structure the relationship. This structure, with its overloading of responsibility for each partner in areas of different status, impedes a real reciprocity and satisfaction between adults.

There also is a natural loss of closeness in the couple when children, with their inherent dependence, are inserted into parents' lives. Moving from a dyad to a threesome automatically leaves one person on the outside at times. If women do the caretaking, then men most often will find themselves in that outside position. Because this is the most typical pattern in families, the struggle for fathers and children to have genuine relationships is all the harder. Men have few models and little support for being central with their young children, and they may experience the birth of a child as a loss rather than a gain. Mothers often feel caught in the middle, trying to be all things to all people, i.e., primary to their children and primary to their spouse.

In therapy it is important to address how parent and spouse roles were handled in the family of origin and how each spouse related to the parental-marital dyad. Balancing role definitions is easier for the spouses when they an emulate or differ from parental models based on thought rather than emotional reactivity. Getting a more objective and realistic picture of who their parents are and the choices they made in balancing their role goes a long way toward taking patterns of parenting less personally and rigidly. Furthermore, placing these patterns in a cultural, ethnic, and gender context can decrease the potency of the generational legacies.

For those individuals who used marriage as a way to escape their families of origin, coping with the role shifts of new parenthood can be more problematic. In an effort to define themselves, "escapees" often erect very tight borders around the marriage, with little available space for family, friends, or children. Without a definition of self apart from and in relation to the family or origin, it is much harder to tolerate fluctuations of intensity in current relationships (Bowen, 1978; McGoldrick, 1989b).

For some couples, the birth of a child represents an attempt to resolve early marriage and couple difficulties. Children may become the vehicle for mediating intimacy and defining the relationship. Failure to negotiate any previous life cycle phase intensified the current life cycle issues (Carter & McGoldrick, 1989). Thus, it is important to investigate these transitions when doing an initial assessment.

PROBLEM DEFINED WITH THE FAMILY OF ORIGIN

The most common presentation of the problem with family of origin is the in-law triangle. The spouse takes on the conflict with the other's family and allows the son or daughter to react from a safe outside position. "Everything would be fine if my mother and wife could only get along." "My husband hates to see me upset with my family so we don't visit." "Who comes first — the children and me or your family?" These positions take on more intensity and a sense of validity once children have defined the couple as a legitimate family.

A mother-in-law and daughter-in-law are most apt to find themselves at odds because this is a socially sanctioned competition. Women fight over the emotional caretaking of men and family, while men take a back seat in assuming personal responsibility for emotional relationships. Helping a wife disengage from the conflict is often, therefore, difficult to do, as there may be little assurance that the husband will fill the void. By the same token, a man may need to be actively invited in and pushed to take charge of his family relationships. A wife may also feel blamed by the therapist if her "overfunctioning," as it is usually termed, is not framed as a woman's dilemma. This frame may also help the couple be less reactive to a mother-in-law's difficulty in redefining her role (Walters, Carter, Papp, & Silverstein, 1989).

Couples who are fighting about or with in-laws have in all likelihood been struggling with boundary issues since courtship (if not adolescence). Again, the addition of children organizes the issues differently, with heightened concern over how to manage the influence of the family of origin. The locus of conflict may shift to the children as early as the announcement of pregnancy, with an uproar and intense lobbying over name choice as a prime opportunity for the couple to work on defining connections to the extended family.

For many spouses, conflict with the in-laws is often a sign of flight or disappointment with their own family of origin. It is therefore essential to gather family information on both sides as to the individuals' role and importance in the parental triangle. A cutoff or distance on one side of the genogram will increase intensity on all other relationships and can function like a time bomb in the marriage.

In fact, while marriage is often an attempt to create distance from the family of origin (McGoldrick, 1989b), having children shifts the emphasis from the safe harbor of the marriage back to the family each had hoped to escape. The inevitable question is: Will I be a parent like my parent? The first time you find yourself sounding exactly like your parents can be a humbling experience, challenging the illusion that your marriage and your partner can save you from all that.

Babies usually mean increased contact with the family of origin. While a husband or wife as an in-law may always be an outsider, a child is a blood relation (Herz & Rosen 1982). Boundaries drawn after marriage are frequently redrawn once grandchildren enter the picture. Whether the grandparents are seen as supportive or intrusive depends largely on how those relationships have been handled before the children.

It is not uncommon for the children to become the new means for handling relationships with the family of origin. Children provide a safer, less conflictual arena in which to relate, particularly when they are young and less self-conscious actors in the system. They also may be the focus of unresolved conflicts between the parents and the grandparents. The battleground shifts to how the parents parent and how the grandparents are behaving as grandparents. For grandparents and grandchildren to develop a real one-to-one connection, the relationship between the other two must be sorted out.

The following case provides an example of a presenting problem defined in both areas: the impact of the child on the relationship and the intensification of unresolved family-of-origin issues.*

THE CASE

Defining and Working on the Foreground

THE ASSESSMENT PROCESS. Roberta and Mark, both 31, came into therapy about 15 months after the birth of their daughter, Sara. They had been married for three years before having children, felt that they had a good

---

*Most of the "three-generational" interventions used in this case were first taught to me by Fredda Herz Brown and Betty Carter.

marriage, and as a result were in a state of panic about their current level of conflict. The argument that precipitated the call was about Mark's serious consideration of a job that would involve extensive overnight traveling.

In the first session Roberta and Mark appeared friendly and relaxed with one another, but a bit perplexed by the struggles they were having. They described fights and misunderstandings clearly related to the stresses of becoming parents and said they needed a new quid pro quo to manage the increase in responsibility. They took advantage of time in the session to acknowledge how their lives had so profoundly changed since the birth of their daughter. With all the change, they had not been able to rely on familiar pathways of solving problems and had less time to talk out issues. Although the job offer had fallen through before the first session, discussion of that possibility provided a perfect framework to clarify their values as parents.

The job represented a good career move and some increase in pay; therefore, it was hard to turn down. Roberta understood this and felt guilty for objecting to the job change. She was ambitious herself and respected that quality in Mark. They had been supportive of each other's career struggles before their child's birth and were outwardly now as well. Mark, for example, never questioned Roberta's return to part-time work after the baby was born. His even considering the job, however, signaled to them how their individual experiences of having a child and of the responsibilities involved were quite different. Roberta constantly struggled in her mind about the balance of time with the child and time for herself and career. Mark, to his surprise, focused on financial security as a way to organize his anxiety about the change in their lives. Given our society's messages about how mothers and fathers should behave, it is not at all surprising that men and women experience the addition of children differently.

The emerging differences between them were also fueled by a growing conflict between Roberta and Mark's mother, Hannah, who lived in a nearby town. This in-law triangle had taken on new intensity with Sara's birth. Roberta had always felt that Hannah did not like her but had hoped that producing a grandchild would bring them closer. When it did not, she pushed on the other side of the triangle, voicing her concern that Hannah demanded too much of Mark and did not respect their nuclear family unit. Adding a child to the unit gave new legitimacy to the complaint. We looked at how they made decisions as a couple and how this was done in their families of origin, giving them an opportunity to start placing their issues in a multigenerational context. Each could begin to see the "emotional baggage" brought to the marriage. The intensity over what each felt they needed from the marriage increased with having a child, while options for fulfilling each other's needs had diminished. I saw their difficulty in negotiating a new quid pro quo as related both to the problems couples in our society all face at this phase of the life cycle and to the awakening and intrusion of generational themes.

MARK'S FAMILY BACKGROUND. Mark grew up as an only child in a middle-class Jewish family of German descent. His father was an outgoing, charismatic man who made all the decisions in the family, acting as its buffer with the world. Mark's temperament more closely matched his mother's reserved, less confident style. The similarity between Mark and his mom had always been seen as a negative, particularly by his mother, who pushed him to be like his father. While he greatly admired his father, Mark felt that he could never measure up and that he had little in common with him. His father was a sports fan; Mark was not an athlete. His father barely graduated high school before going to work; Mark excelled academically.

In his early twenties, Mark had let himself become quite remote from both parents in an effort to detach himself from the powerful shadow of his father and establish himself in a career. His marriage at age 27 began a reconnection with his family. The contact increased partly because Roberta liked the idea of a closer family and partly because Mark was more relaxed with his family with his wife around. Finding common ground with his father as two adults was finally beginning when his father became sick and died of a heart attack at age 58, when Mark was 28. The father's death created a tremendous vacuum in the family; Mark feared being sucked in as his mother's caretaker. Not only did he not want to take care of her, but this

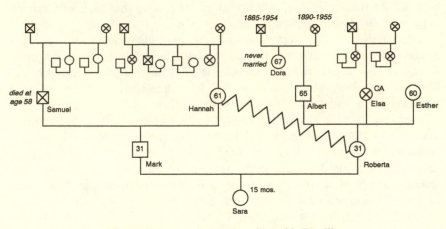

FIGURE 9.1   Roberta and Mark's Families

also reactivated all his issues regarding not being able to fill his father's shoes. It was, of course, easier to push Roberta to take over for him.

ROBERTA'S FAMILY BACKGROUND. Roberta's conflict with her mother-in-law was certainly fueled by Mark's distance from Hannah and Hannah's dependence on Mark, but it also reflected a disappointment in her own family. Roberta was an only child from a Russian Jewish heritage. When she was only three her mother died. She had been raised by her father, with the help of his older sister, Dora. Her aunt and her father never had a close relationship, and their distance often left Roberta feeling lonely. Little connection was maintained with her mother's side of the family. Robert's father remarried when she was in high school and set up a new household for the new wife and his daughter that did not include Dora. Quite predictably Dora and the new wife did not get along, and Roberta's father did little to ease the territorial dispute between them. Contact fell off with Dora. While Roberta was pleased that her father had a new partner, she was never really sure of her own place with him and often felt like an outsider.

After college, physically on her own for the first time, she because depressed and entered therapy. She spent some time mourning the loss of her mother, a loss never discussed in the family, but focused little on improving her relationship with her father. Concentrating on her own development of autonomy (a young adult development task), she was content to reconcile herself to her father's marriage and maintain ritualized visits with her father and stepmother in Florida.

Gathering genogram and nodal event information in the first interview helped put not only Mark and Roberta's conflict but also the conflict between Roberta and Hannah in a more manageable perspective. Roberta's entry into the family, for example, came at a time when the family was closing boundaries in response to Mark's father's illness and then death. The birth of their child only exaggerated the stakes in the conflict about insiders and outsiders. Their experience is a good illustration of how the timing of life cycle events, e.g., births, deaths, greatly influences a family's ability to accommodate change.

As we examined their struggles with each other and their family histories, several themes emerged. Like many couples, Mark and Roberta were uncomfortable with the traditional division of labor based on gender that was emerging between them. Yet at the same time they found it difficult to alter either their thinking or their behavior. Discussion of this, revisited and expanded in ensuing sessions, included a look at the historical, societal context of this and the specific family legacies that locked them in. For example, pulling Mark back into the marriage as an equal partner meant he couldn't pass his mother off onto his wife. He had hoped, and Roberta had feared, that a job with time on the road would leave the two women to work out some kind of coexistence. It is a very typical expectation in marriage that a woman will handle all family relationship responsibility because she presumably has the skill and time for doing so.

Mark's mythologizing of his father was another theme that kept him distant in his own parenting. Never sure he could measure up to his father as a son, he wasn't sure he could as a parent either. Letting Roberta take over eased the anxiety. Repeating, over generations, father-son distance is one of the legacies of the traditional divisions of family roles — women connected to children and men connected to the world outside.

At the same time, if they wanted as a couple to be more equally involved with the baby, Roberta also had to allow room. Her style of looking for and creating intense relationships left less space for Mark and the baby. Many women struggle with relinquishing control of children, particularly if it is one of the few areas in which they have power and control.

Treatment: From Nuclear to Extended Family Work

At the end of the first session, a two-hour consultation, we identified two areas of work. The first was on the level of the marriage and the specific adjustments needed to weather this phase of the life cycle. The second involved addressing tensions between Roberta and Hannah and between Hannah and Mark and more generally looking at how and why family relationships were affecting their marriage at this point. The first was easier to examine, as they had fairly good, nonreactive communication and the level of conflict was not high. They spent several sessions working out new ways to divide up tasks and to allow time for themselves, alone and as a couple. As a result they felt much closer and calmer with each other. During these sessions family-of-origin patterns, prescriptions, attitudes were more clearly articulated. Because nuclear family demands are high and family-of-origin themes are intensely experienced at this phase of the life cycle, it is helpful to address both from the beginning. This keeps the context broader than the couple and may increase the motivation to work on family-of-origin triangles. The most pressing triangle was with Roberta, Hannah and Mark, with Roberta as the outsider trying to get in. Sustaining a shift in this triangle would of course mean addressing two other major triangles: Mark and his mother, with the distance regulated by his idealized father; and Roberta on the outside from her father and another woman (stepmother or memory of her mother).

About four sessions into therapy, a shift to working on the first triangle came easily after the couple began to identify what they saw as a typical but unpleasant pattern. Roberta would reach out in a variety of ways to Mark's mother and be rebuffed or simply not acknowledged. Hannah would increase phone calls to Mark with stories of sadness about his father or worries about how to handle household problems. Mark would initially respond to Hannah but then would become overwhelmed by his mother's needs. Roberta would feel protective of Mark and furious at Hannah. When Mark would back off, Roberta would feel vindicated for a time. Then, partly out of concern for Mark and her sense of his depression about the loss of family, partly for her own need to give her child a grandmother, Roberta would slowly begin to try to connect with Hannah again.

Moving Roberta out of the middle of Mark's relationship with his mother seemed a fairly straightforward move and certainly a classic one in marital therapy. However, while both experienced great relief at the suggestion that Roberta back off and Mark take the space to define his relationship with his mother, a number of issues had to be kept in mind to make the shift workable. Because women are expected to take charge of emotional relationships, encouraging a wife to relinquish that role must be done supportively. In Roberta's case, she also had to be prepared for an increase in discomfort and blame from Hannah, who also expected her to take a traditional role in the house. Invitations, for example, should come from Roberta, whether Hannah wanted to accept them or not. Roberta and Hannah had already experienced the generational mismatch discussed earlier, thus interfering with a joining as women who are mothers. In addition, Mark needed to be prodded to fill in the distance with his mother, a distance he had cultivated for years, and take responsibility for his part in the conflict between his mother and his wife.

The sessions took two tacks: helping Roberta redirect her emotional energy and helping Mark move in to deal with his mother more directly. Since each had an equally difficult task, it was important to keep the pressure balanced, although they moved at different paces. For Roberta, her first major obstacle was her anger at Hannah. Not surprisingly, someone who has been relentlessly pursuing usually builds up a good store of anger and hurt about the lack of success. To deal with the anger, Roberta had to place what she saw as Hannah's rejection of her in the context of the mother-Mark-father triangle. There she could see it not as a personal rejection but as a situation where *any* daughter-in-law would have failed. Hannah, still mourning the loss of her husband, wanted Mark to take his father's place. There was no room for an outsider yet.

Roberta and Hannah also had the very different style of German and Eastern European Jews. Hannah was reserved, seen as cold by Roberta. Roberta was warm, alive, seen as intrusive and noisy by Hannah. Roberta also needed Mark to back off from his investment in having his wife and mother "get along." If Mark could accept the distance, then Roberta would not have to push and then take everything Hannah said to heart. Not feeling so criticized, Roberta could be less critical of Hannah, giving Mark a chance to decrease his own anger at his mother.

To help Roberta get clear about her contribution to the anger, she was instructed to write down her needs and expectations of the relationship with Hannah and to think about where else these might be satisfied. The idea was both to increase her resources for fulfilling those needs and also to begin to address her family-of-origin role in satisfying those needs. It was in fact easy for her to place these needs on friends and her husband, and initially she felt relief at not having to try so hard with Hannah. She acknowledged her father as there but distant and was dismissive of my attempts to see her remoteness with her father as connected to her present problem with Hannah. She could see her position as an outsider in both systems but was more interested in getting immediate help in handling Hannah. We did discuss new stances to take with her mother-in-law so that she would not get hooked into her anger and frustration, such as keeping expectations low and not trying to solve Hannah's problems. After particularly difficult phone calls, she devised phrases to say to herself to keep from feeling like a failure with Hannah: "Mark still loves me." "Hannah can't be who she is not." At the same time, I kept trying to make the connection to her family by tracking a feeling or thought into the prior generation or posing "what if" questions. "What if you were closer to your father?" "What if your mother were still alive?" "In your family, how do the wives handle . . . ?" This at least kept her family present in the therapy.

Moving Mark toward his mother was initially easy. As Roberta's anger decreased, Mark was no longer barraged with complaints. He allowed himself, for the first time in a while, to have some positive feelings about his mother. The first task of building a relationship seemed innocuous enough because the distance was so great between mother and son that the emotions were also remote. Both of them were still mourning the loss of his father. While Hannah's grief had been ongoing since her husband's death, Mark's had been reactivated by the birth of his daughter. The birth marked another opportunity lost of knowing his father differently and his father knowing him. He didn't want to feel that void when his mother died as well, and it pushed him to increase his contact. With Roberta out of the organizing role, Mark made attempts to talk about his father and his own experiences of being a father. However, the interaction made it more apparent to Mark that a vacuum existed between Hannah and himself and that filling it with talk of his father would not significantly alter his relationship. We talked in sessions about how to take his father out of the middle of his relationship with his mother and what they could talk about that would be between them. Mark decided to try to let Hannah know more about him and tried to include more personal information in his phone calls. He also made a point of discussing his work and challenging the long-held assumption that she wouldn't understand it.

Mark's initial enthusiasm in trying to define a new relationship with his mother surprised Roberta. While she felt good about not being so angry at Hannah, Roberta did have some concern that Hannah would overwhelm Mark with his demands and she would lose Mark (as she had her father). Roberta would quietly fall back into being critical of Hannah lest Mark become too involved. We had predicted ways both of them might experience discomfort with these moves toward their families, Mark had been coached to develop ways to reassure Roberta of his connection to her, but politely tell her to back off. Watching Mark struggle to define what kind of relationship he wanted with his mother helped Roberta, probably more than anything I did, to acknowledge her sense of loneliness regarding her own family.

No longer trying to get Hannah to have an intimate relationship, and feeling the loss of Mark as a "fox hole" buddy, Roberta could talk about how giving birth had activated many thoughts and feelings about her mother. She had shared little of this with Mark because her mother was not a real person to her, much less to Mark. She also felt that she had supposedly resolved her loss of her mother in therapy before. Her experience with the reawakening of feelings is a very good example of how relationships are never really resolved; rather, different aspects of them become important at different points in the life cycle.

Once Roberta became refocused on her own family, several issues emerged. First, she wanted more information about her mother now that she was a parent, but nobody in her family talked about her. She and her father had an unspoken agreement not to discuss the loss. Also, as a parent she was curious about the relationship she had had with her Aunt Dora, her "adoptive" mother. The cutoffs from both her mother's memory and Aunt Dora were contributing to the intensity of her relationships with Mark, Hannah, and her daughter.

Roberta's most powerful stalemate, however, was with her father. Their relationship was distant but cordial and she was afraid to disrupt the calm. At the same time, she was quite angry about his remoteness but had difficulty seeing how she participated in keeping the relationship cool. This anger was a significant catalyst to her reactivity with Mark in the way he parented. It therefore had to be addressed to sustain changes they had made as a couple. This is a good example of how cutoffs and stalemates in relationships function like time bombs in a family. Unresolved issues with parents easily get activated when we become parents and then get played out in the new parent-child or marital relationship.

Since Roberta had been sitting on her anger at her father for so long, she needed to be convinced that working on the relationship would loosen up her nuclear family process. She was more interested and motivated to talk about her mother or Dora but felt an active move in their direction might alienate her father. I gave her a number of tasks during this phase of the therapy to sharpen her understanding of the family emotional context. We talked at length about her father's family and how men parented on that side of the family. In phone calls with her father, she tried in a neutral way to fill out his side of the genogram. In those same cells she was also to track how she contributed to the distance in the relationship. She noticed almost immediately her attempts to push her stepmother and father apart. For example, she made only perfunctory contact with her stepmother and had little patience for her father's chat about their life together. Roberta's sense of exclusion frequently contributed to her shutting down in the conversation and not sharing much about her own life.

Seeing her father in the context of his extended family helped to neutralize some of her anger. She could take his behavior less personally when viewed as part of his family's baggage. Recognizing her part in the distance also gave her some hope of being able to change the relationship. To further reduce her storehouse of anger, she was asked to write a letter to her father, not to be sent, about all her hurts and disappointments with him. She was to keep writing it until she felt all the hurt was expressed. This task had several purposes. One was to contain and focus the anger by putting it on paper. Another was to push her toward the anger, something she had always tried to suppress. In this way, she could fully experience it, to the point of saturation, and then be in a better position to let part, if not all, of it go. It must be clear when using this task that the letter is never meant to be sent. Trying to connect to people while full of anger, under the guise of finally telling them off, inevitably pushes them away. Only when the anger is under control can someone take an "I" position regarding his/her feelings and thoughts and have any hope of being heard by the other person.

The next phase of the task, once she felt the letter was complete, was to have Roberta pick out how she participated in the hurts being perpetuated. This is not meant to be an exercise in assigning blame; rather, the goal is to look at the parts someone has within his/her control to change. Many of hurts were about losses (of her mother in body, her father in spirit) that she had no control or choice about as a child. She could see, however, how not discussing the losses continued the gulf between she and her father.

During this phase of the work, Aunt Dora came to town and wanted to see the baby. After all our discussions, Roberta felt ready to break the family rules regarding discussing the past. She welcomed the visit. We spent some time preparing for the visit with respect to goals, expectations, and worst case scenarios. Her most pressing goal was to get information about her mother. Dora and her father were the only possible sources, as all her mother's relatives were deceased. She realized that Dora might be offended by her interest in her natural mother, as Dora had put in more time in actual parenting. So she prepared herself to make a speech recognizing and appreciating what Dora had done for her. Her second agenda was to get a perspective on her father as a parent and more information about what kept him so distant. As necessary with any move toward a family member, Roberta also prepared herself to keep her expectations low — at a minimum get a glimpse of the person, Dora, who contributed to her growth.

The visit actually turned out to be very successful and Dora was a wealth of information about both sides of the family. To her surprise, Roberta also experienced her acknowledgment of Dora's role in her upbringing as heartfelt. She allowed herself to appreciate the difficulty of Dora's role in her unofficial status of surrogate parent. She came away from the meeting wanting more contact with her.

After Roberta had the successful visit with Dora and was thinking about making a move with her father, Mark, nor surprisingly, found himself more and more mired in difficulty with his mother. Roberta had less interest and need to regulate the distance in that relationship, so Mark was left to fend for himself. As is usually the case with someone not particularly in touch with his/her feelings about a significant family member, just the attempt to build a relationship will activate the dormant but still conflictual issues. Mark did well with the steps of moving towards his mother by sharing more of himself. With more contact the struggle quickly became how not fall into his father's shoes and take care of his mother. Hannah was very good at trying to turn over easy decisions to him regarding household worries. He needed experience setting boundaries; however, to do this Mark had to respond less reactively to Hannah's dependence.

Through our discussions, Mark began placing the "incompetence" in the context of Hannah's history and her family's expectations of her. His mother, the youngest of five children and very much the baby in her family, became depressed shortly after his birth and was in and out of hospitals during his childhood. Her older siblings filled in on Mark's care and she had difficulty reasserting her position as mother when back in the home. Deferring to her husband's "competence" became one way to set boundaries with her family. Mark's use of Roberta to set boundaries with his family was repetition of this triangle.

To shift his position, Mark had to experience other options beside caretaking or fleeing his mother. He was coached to take an "I don't know" position or to ask "How are your friends in similar straits dealing with this?" Mark also made attempts to acknowledge his mother's role as a parent by asking for help or advice. In conjunction with this, he was asked to make a list of positive qualities about himself that he could attribute to his mother's influence. The list was short and contained "feminine" characteristics like sensitivity and empathy. Hearing this list was particularly interesting to Roberta, who prized these qualities in Mark. The couple playfully thought of ways they could thank Hannah for her contribution to their marital happiness, although they did not follow through on any of those.

Mark also decided to "complete" his mourning of his father independent of his mother. He made contact with members of his father's family to reminisce and complete his picture of the man. He then made a graveside visit to tell his father something about himself, particularly as a father, and the ways they were similar and different. This helped him to own his competence and take a further step out of the triangle with his mother and father. Satisfied at this time with the work he had done on his family of origin and his marriage, Mark took a break from therapy.

I continued to meet with Roberta to plan a visit with her father and stepmother. Roberta had many goals for the visit, including getting to know her father differently and learning more about her mother. To come anywhere near accomplishing these Roberta had to shift her position in the triangles with her father and Dora and with her father and stepmother. She first wrote a letter to her father discussing her visit with Dora. She told him she had been worried about seeing Dora because of what seemed like an old fight between them that she didn't understand. In thinking about it she realized that, if there were still a fight, he could take care of it himself and certainly didn't need his daughter to protect him. Besides, Dora had only positive things to say about him. She also talked in the letter about how much she was looking forward to the visit with the two of them. She followed it up with phone calls in which she made deliberate positive comments about the second marriage. She mentioned how much she liked her stepmother, how well her father and stepmother seemed to get along, and other comments that would reinforce the boundary around the couple. Once in their home, she did not want her interest in her mother and in family history to be seen as divisive or as an attempt to pull her father away from his wife.

During the visit, she found that the more she pushed her father and stepmother together the more time her stepmother gave her alone with her father. One of the times they were alone, Roberta told her father of her need to know more about her mother now that she was a parent. She wasn't sure if it was too painful for her father or whether he was being thoughtful of her in not talking about her mother. If it was the latter, Roberta reassured him that talking about her mother would in fact be helpful. She also shared her curiosity about how he managed as a single parent and her new appreciation of what the loss must have been for him. Her father responded to this with his own grief, saying how hard it was for him to share it with her. Watching her father cry really challenged Roberta's resolve not to back away and shut down herself. Her not doing so allowed the conversation to progress further than it had ever gone before. In the presence of the stepmother, her father also shared some family photographs Roberta had not seen. She ended the visit feeling as though a taboo had been lifted and experienced a great sense of relief in her relationship with her father.

CONCLUSION

The treatment took place over the span of two years, with contact toward the end structured around planning for specific visits and tasks. Both Roberta and Mark experienced a loosening of tension in their marriage and an increase in options in how to negotiate with each other as spouses and parents, particularly as Roberta felt better connected to her family of origin.

It is both arduous and interesting for the therapist to keep motivation going and watch how far a client will go toward exploring issues in the family of origin. It is the therapist's job to make the work relevant. While tasks and specific moves with the family are very significant, the whole preparation process is essential in shifting perceptions and expanding boundaries of what is possible in a relationship. As in all life cycle phases, couples with young children experience both the expanding (the pull to connect to the wider system) and constricting (drawing boundaries) elements of the phase. In doing the therapy, it is important to capitalize on the expanding side and to define the connections as emotional resources to benefit the new nuclear subsystem.

REFERENCES

Bowen, M., (1978). *Family therapy in clinical practice*. New York: Aronson.
Bradt, J. (1989). Becoming parents: Families with young children. In B. Carter & M. McGoldrick (Eds), *The changing family life cycle* (2nd ed.) (pp. 235–254). Boston: Allyn and Bacon.
Braverman, L. (1989). Beyond the myth of motherhood. In M. McGoldrick, C. Anderson, & F. Walsh (Eds.), *Women in families* (pp. 227–243). New York: W. W. Norton.
Carter, B., & McGoldrick, M. (1989). *The changing family life cycle: A framework for family therapy* (2nd ed.). Boston: Allyn & Bacon.
Entwistle, S. G., & Doering, D. P. (1981). *The first birth: A family turning point*. Baltimore: Johns Hopkins University Press.
Herz, F., & Rosen, E. J. (1982). Jewish families. In M. McGoldrick, J. K. Pearce, & J. Giordano (Eds.), *Ethnicity and family therapy* (pp. 364–392). New York: Guilford.
Holder, D., & Anderson, C. (1989). Women, work, and the family. In M. McGoldrick, C. Anderson, & F. Walsh (Eds.), *Women in Families* (pp. 357–380). New York: W. W. Norton.
McGoldrick, M. (1989a). Women through the family life cycle. In M. McGoldrick, C. Anderson, F. Walsh (Eds.), *Women in families* (pp. 200–226). New York: W. W. Norton.

McGoldrick, M. (1989b). The joining of families through marriage: The new couple. In B. Carter & M. McGoldrick (Eds.), *The changing family life cycle* (2nd ed.) (pp. 209–234). Boston: Allyn and Bacon.

McGoldrick, M., Anderson, C., & Walsh, F. (Eds.). (1989). *Women in families*. New York: W. W. Norton.

Walters, M., Carter, B., Papp, P., & Silverstein, O. (1988). *The invisible web*. New York: Guilford.

⌗ 10

Families With Adolescents

PAMELA YOUNG

ADOLESCENCE IS A TIME in the family life cycle stage when there is a great deal of turmoil and change for both the adolescent and his or her family. For the adolescent, it is a time of immense intellectual, physical, and emotional development. The adolescents' central developmental tasks are to begin self-definition and to develop a stable and healthy identity and adequate social relations despite continued dependency on the family for emotional and financial support. The family's task is to reorganize itself and change its structure to permit the adolescent some independence, while at the same time recognizing and dealing with his/her dependence.

During this stage there are also other changes in family relationships. It is at minimum a three-generational process: Children become adolescents; parents face midlife issues; and grandparents face issues of retirement, moves, illness, or death. The changes within generations force changes across generations. Also, as adolescents become more emotionally independent, they begin to develop their own relationships with members of their extended family. This change requires a realignment in the relationship between the parents and the grandparents. It is therefore not unusual for adolescence to reactivate old emotional issues between the first and second generations and to set the triangles in motion within the entire family system.

Since at this life cycle stage there are so many shifts in intergenerational familial relationships, it is hard to predict where any one shift begins or will end. For example, the demands and neediness of the grandparents may affect the parents' relationship with their adolescent child. At the same time, it is equally possible that the adolescent's conflict with his/her parents will affect the couple's marital relationship and the parents' availability to the older generation. This in turn may add additional stress to the relationship between the parents and grandparents.

The adolescent's paradoxical desire to be a child *and* an adult creates external turmoil, because the adolescent's behavior tends to be contradictory, inconsistent, and unpredictable and to be marked by ambivalence, confusion, and generational conflict. This behavior, an inherent part of the adolescent's struggle for independence, produces a shift in all familial relationships. The family boundary between parents and children, which previously had been clearly defined, must now become more permeable, so as to allow adolescents to be dependent and also to experiment with independence.

The adolescent's exposure to the external world represents another aspect of his/her struggle for independence. Through increased contact with and reliance on the adolescent subculture, peers, and school, there begins a genuine questioning of family values and norms. Through their involvement with their peer group adolescents become more self-reliant and subsequently desire more control in making decisions about their own life. While this may compel the parents to recognize the fact that they can no longer maintain complete authority over their adolescent child, usually they have no clear-cut guidelines for making judgments about age-appropriate behavior and decision-making responsibility. Establishing revised boundaries requires a new process of negotiation between parent and child (McGoldrick & Carter, 1982). Familial struggles over rules and relationships are therefore a hallmark of this stage. In fact, parental authority and control are almost always issues during this life cycle stage.

In reality this life cycle stage is probably the greatest test of the family's adaptability and flexibility. This experience exposes the family to different ideas, attitudes, and values, which often serve as a catalyst for change within the family system. However, parents often err — either on the side of trying to keep the boundaries too permeable, providing minimal structure, or on the side of rigid adherence to rules, providing too much structure. Since either of these solutions creates problems, families that choose them frequently seek treatment.

TREATMENT OF FAMILIES WITH ADOLESCENTS

Because of the adolescent's increased involvement in the world at large, referrals for treatment may come from a variety of sources, i.e., the school, courts, other outside agencies, physicians, clergy, parents, siblings, friends, and/or the adolescents themselves. Since any part of the family may be experiencing difficulty, families usually initiate treatment for one of the following reasons: (1) marital difficulties, (2) symptomatic behavior of a younger sibling, (3) symptomatic behavior of one of the parents, or (4) symptomatic behavior of the adolescent (Ackerman, 1980). How a problem manifests itself depends upon a number of factors, including the vulnerability of a particular relationship, role, or person. However, problems in one area are related to problems in the others and are frequently related to the shifting boundaries characteristic of this stage. In fact, due to the interconnectedness of relationships, it is rare that problems occur in just one area.

In this chapter all four presenting problems will be viewed from a multigenerational perspective. In working with any of these problems, the therapist makes a family assessment, paying specific attention to both the nuclear and extended families, the multigenerational patterns and themes, and the triangulation processes. The first three problems will be addressed briefly. Then we will focus on the treatment of the symptomatic behavior of the adolescent.

MARITAL DIFFICULTIES

Adolescence is a time of stress for couples. Marital conflicts frequently surface around the issue of parenting and are often precipitated by the couple's difficulty in adjusting to parenting an adolescent and dealing with their child's unpredictable behavior and numerous challenges of authority. This difficulty may reactivate unresolved emotional conflicts between a couple. The more overt the marital conflict and the greater the tendency for the spouses to deal directly with each other, the less need there will be for the couple to triangulate around the adolescent. If the marital conflict is not openly acknowledged, this triangulation process may take the form of disagreements between the parents about the adolescent's behavior or involvement of the adolescent in the marital issues. When this occurs, some adolescents remain in an emotional stuck position by actively taking sides with one parent against the other.

In working with the couple, the therapist must always explore the spouses' relationships and unresolved issues with their own parents. The therapist must also explore the role of the adolescent in the couple's marriage. It is important to note that adolescence is difficult for intact families and is inherently more complex and difficult for divorced and remarried families.

SYMPTOMATIC BEHAVIOR OF A YOUNGER SIBLING

As the adolescent begins to become more independent and to separate emotionally from his/her family, the problem may begin to center on a younger sibling. This sibling may be triangled into the parents' marriage as a result of the adolescent's natural distancing or because the adolescent attempts to align with the younger sibling, thereby triangulating him/her into the parent-child relationship conflicts.

The therapist must meet with the entire family to assess the family dynamics and the degree of the withdrawal of the adolescent. If it is too great, i.e., a cutoff, the adolescent must be helped to reconnect to his/her family. This change may reduce the intensity of the mother-father-younger sibling triangle and thereby solve the problem. However, if the adolescent is appropriately distant from the family, the therapist must help to detriangulate the youngest sibling and help the family to connect the recent change in his/her behavior to the older sibling's adolescence and withdrawal (Ackerman, 1980). If the younger sibling is allied with one parent or with the older adolescent, the therapist must help to shift that relationship so that the child is free to relate individually to both parents and to the adolescent as an older sibling.

Although in some ways stepparenting may cut down the intensity of the parent-child relationship, the stepparent relationship may also be a ready focus for adolescent parental struggles. The stepmother-daughter relationship is especially difficult; in other cases the adolescent male may compete with his stepfather for his mother (McGoldrick & Carter, 1989).

SYMPTOMATIC BEHAVIOR OF ONE OF THE PARENTS

Adolescence is a time when parents truly begin to become aware of the fact that their child will eventually leave home. Therefore, during this life cycle stage, adults begin to refocus on midlife and career issues and to reevaluate their own life apart from their children. The normal stress of adolescence is exacerbated when the parents experience acute dissatisfaction with their own lives and subsequently feel compelled to make changes in themselves. Frequently in upper- and middle-class families many women initiate careers while their husbands are in the process of maximizing their business success, thinking of early retirement, or dealing with their inability to further career advancement.

There is also a shift in the parents' concern toward the older generation as grandparents begin to deal with issues of retirement, moves, illness, or death. The parents must renegotiate their own relationships with their adolescent child and with their parents simultaneously. Frequently they must also adjust to the new role of being their parents' caretakers. Caught between the generations, one parent may develop symptoms. In fact, a major number of problems, e.g., depression and anxiety, occurring in this stage are related to the unresolved but intensified issues with the extended family (Ackerman, 1980). If a child is the stabilizer of the couple's marriage, the child's adolescence and withdrawal will create a shift in the triangle and a new balance must be reestablished. In response to the threat of fusion, one parent may become symptomatic. Although either parent may seek treatment, their relationship with their adolescent child must be addressed during the course of therapy. When this does not occur, the therapist may often find that the adolescent will act out as he/she gets caught up in his/her parents' difficulty.

SYMPTOMATIC BEHAVIOR OF THE ADOLESCENT

Adolescents can present symptomatic behavior in a variety of ways, ranging from minor behavioral difficulties to serious psychiatric problems. In fact, the range of presenting problems has grown as our society has become more complex and the available options for adolescent rebellion have expanded. It is therefore not surprising that during this life cycle stage the symptomatic behavior of the adolescent tends to be the most frequent precipitant for seeking treatment (Preto, 1989).

Defining and Working on the Foreground

INITIAL ASSESSMENT. Regardless of the presenting problem, the therapist's first task is to assess the extent to which other parts of the system are involved. The therapist must do a thorough evaluation because the presenting problem may not be the major or most significant familial problem. In fact, it may be just the tip of the iceberg. To understand the choice of symptoms, the therapist must look at the presenting problem from a multigenerational perspective, examining the triangles, multigenerational transmission process, patterns and themes spanning generations.

In making an initial assessment, the therapist must remember that changes in the family are related not only to the adolescent's changes but also to the changing relationships, expectations, and tasks faced by the family members during this period. In addition to the usual assessment of social, economic, occupational, and ethnic issues affecting the family, the therapist must assess whether the problem is primary, i.e., the family is simply having difficulty adjusting to adolescence, or secondary, i.e., adolescence has precipitated the emergence of an underlying unresolved problem.

An example of the latter would be adolescent rebellion embedded in marital issues.

This clinical assessment will determine the focus and length of treatment. If the problem is of the first type, primarily one of life cycle transition, the focus of treatment will be on helping the family deal with the adolescent phase by normalizing age-appropriate behavior, as well as family turmoil and conflict, and educating all family members about the inherent difficulties of adolescence. Parents will be encouraged to support age-appropriate behavior and to set limits on that behavior. Treatment will be relatively short.

If the adolescent problem is secondary to other unresolved problems, the first step is to calm down the presenting problem, i.e., the adolescent's behavior, by utilizing the previously mentioned techniques. Concurrently, the family must be helped to view the problem within a larger context, with the therapist connecting the adolescent's problem to the system's problem.

The more difficulty the family has negotiating new boundaries, the more likely it will be that rigid triangle(s) have formed. The more rigid the particular triangle, the fewer the options for solving difficulties and the more dysfunctional the family will become under stress. Therefore, the therapist needs to clarify the individual and generational boundaries to decrease the amount of triangulation occurring within the family. The therapist helps family members shift their individual position in the major triangle maintaining the problem.

In this life cycle stage there are several major triangles that tend to stabilize the problem: (1) the adolescent, the father, and the mother; (2) the adolescent, the parent of the same sex, and the grandparent of the same sex; (3) the adolescent, a sibling, and their parents; and (4) the parents, the adolescent, and his/her peers (Guerin & Guerin, 1976). Any of these triangles can become the major triangle that not only stabilizes the adolescent's behavior but also "hides" other areas of conflict or relationship difficulties.

In general, one can identify triangles and concomitant boundary problems by first meeting with the entire family to assess family dynamics and interactional processes. At some point the therapist should also meet separately with the adolescent and the parents. This clinical move supports and begins to clarify individual and generational boundaries uniting the couple in their executive functioning and in their working together (Minuchin, 1974). It also supports the adolescent's separation from the parents and helps prevent him/her from viewing the therapist as allied with the parents or from engaging in a power struggle, as sometimes happens in joint sessions when the adolescent gets belligerent or refuses to speak (Nicholson, 1986). Separate sessions with the adolescent and his siblings may also be held to allay fears and to encourage support in that subsystem (Preto, 1989).

Working Individually With the Adolescent

In meeting individually with the adolescent, the therapist has the opportunity to assess the extent of the adolescent's problems and his/her functioning outside of the family system and to identify the areas of conflict and generational differences. In individual sessions, the adolescent usually feels less judged or criticized by the parents and thus freer to express his/her self. He/she subsequently tends to be more comfortable in revealing his/her own secrets or concerns about him/herself or the family. The therapist can utilize the individual sessions in conjunction with family sessions or joint sessions with the parents to begin to coach the adolescent on how to deal more effectively with his/her parents.

Adolescents cannot be coached in the traditional Bowenian way to do extended family-of-origin work because the developmental struggle inherent in this stage is their own difficulty in assuming an "I" position. Although the issue of attaining appropriate autonomy from one's parents and establishing independence remains central throughout adolescence and young adulthood, its intensity is greatest in adolescence (Bowen, 1978). It is a time when one has the least distance from one's parents and the greatest intensity in dealing with them.

Part of the difficulty centers on the adolescent's mood lability and reactivity. Adolescents tend to become emotionally reactive and repeatedly to get caught up in an "I won't change if they won't change" position. They also tend to be in a position with their parents that is overconforming or overrebellious. Either way, the adolescent's behavior is reactive and determined by the parents' behavior. Neither position offers any flexibility, since one is the opposite of the other. However, in adolescence they often become rigified.

In addition, adolescence is also a time of marked changes in the adolescent's ability to understand one's relationships with important other people. While adolescents tend to be self-centered, they are continuously readjusting their behavior in terms of their "importance" to others. Although they experience cognitive growth, their sense of themselves is often fluctuating and reactive and their intellect cannot rule their emotions (Friedenberg, 1959). They are inherently unable to keep any position for any length of time. They have difficulty taking responsibility for their own feelings and being objective about their own parents. They also have no real power. They are both financially and emotionally dependent upon their parents and are unable to take the risk of possibly losing their approval or becoming too vulnerable with them. Their parents are in control and their parental advice still governs them.

Adolescents can be helped to do some multigenerational work, by developing an understanding of the family's emotional system and how it functions. They may also be helped to identify and change their own role in the system. They can be taught the concept of triangles and how they may get triangled into their parents' marriage or extended family relationships. Teaching them to recognize boundaries will help them to see how they intrude upon them and how this intrusion may become dysfunctional for themselves and for all family members. As adolescents begin to gain an awareness of multigenerational patterns and themes, the differences in their parents' background and how they may influence their different operating styles and ability to foster the adolescent's independence become evident. This therapeutic work with the adolescent may help to ameliorate the problem, to calm down the system, and to begin improving familial relationships. There will be additional benefits if the parents are simultaneously beginning to deal with their own conflicts and the adolescent is able to avoid being triangled into their marital issues.

Working With the Parents

In joint meetings with the parents, the therapist addresses their specific concerns and works toward increasing the emotional support between them. If the parents deny conflict and present a united front, the therapist should assess what is being said and whether or not conflict is being detoured. If the parents display conflict, the therapist should assess the level of caring and guide the parents toward recognition of how their conflict in parenting may triangulate the adolescent into their relationship. Unless the couple has already defined marital issues as a presenting problem, the therapist should focus on the parental differences. Sometimes, even when marital issues are labeled, it is best to avoid them until after the presenting problem is under control.

The therapist should encourage the parents to be clear about their expectations of each other and help them to negotiate their differences in parenting. Teaching the parents to adopt a listening stance, to ask questions, to listen to explanations, and to encourage the adolescent to verbalize his/her feelings will enable them and the adolescent to begin to negotiate differences and conflict (Offer, Ostrove, & Howard, 1981).

If the parents' rules seem too rigid, they should be helped to recognize the need to change, to negotiate, and to promote their child's autonomy and individual growth. On the other hand, frequently the therapist must correct the myth that a family should operate as a democracy and support the parents' executive functioning and right to set limits without justifying their behavior. However, it is often essential to elicit the adolescent's viewpoint if rules are to be followed.

Exploring parents' differences in limit-setting may lead to discussion of their own experiences in their families of origin and how these have influenced their relationships with their children. The therapist may point out how patterns in one generation resemble those in the next. Parents with a strong sense of self are less reactive to their adolescent child's challenges and personalize them less frequently. Conversely, parental tolerance is low if parents have a less developed sense of self due to their not having become emotionally independent of their own parents (Bowen, 1978).

The therapist often needs to coach the parents to deal with the school system and their child's peer group, especially if difficulties exist in those systems. Another vital task is to educate the parents regarding appropriate adolescent behavior, i.e., challenging parents' authority; experimenting with new behavior, dress, and music; wanting to spend more time with friends rather than family; and exploring different gendered roles.

Helping parents to reflect on their own adolescence often results in more parental empathy for the adolescent. The therapist should ask about each parent's adolescence, focusing on how they relate to their parents. This will offer new connections and insights for understanding the present situation. It will also enable the parents to become more objective about each other as they make the connections between the present and the past.

As the therapist tracks relationships across generations, he/she connects present conflict to past unresolved conflicts. This permits the parents to become more objective about their pattern of interaction with their adolescent child. Seeing the discrepancy between their adolescent experience and their child's enables the parents to gain a cognitive understanding of why it has been so difficult for them as parents. It also deflates the competitive issue of who is the better parent.

The therapist should teach parents about reciprocity in relationships, the multigenerational transmission process, the concept of triangles, the impact of sibling positions, and the cultural differences regarding normative behavior for adolescents. The therapist needs to remember that parents can only be helped to hold back or pull back from their adolescent child. Parents cannot give their child a sense of being an adult. Only the child can emotionally define him/herself as an adult. This identity struggle is the developmental task of adolescence (McGoldrick & Carter, 1982).

CASE ILLUSTRATION

Mrs. Cohen initiated treatment when she phoned and stated that she was concerned about Aron, her 16-year-old son. She described him as verbally abusive and unwilling to abide by any family rules. During this phone conversation the therapist did not request that the four-year-old son attend the first session because his behavior would make it difficult for the family and the therapist to focus on the presenting problem.

At the initial session, Alfred Cohen, 42, Joan Cohen, 40, and Aron appeared. Mrs. Cohen looked unkempt and presented herself as extremely anxious and somewhat depressed. By contrast, her husband was impeccably dressed and displayed overt contempt for his wife. Aron was also neatly attired and appeared to be an extremely bright 16-year-old. He was a junior in high school and considered himself to be a superior student. His parents agreed with his academic assessment but were concerned about a recent drop in grades. They also agreed that he was disrespectful to his mother and rarely listened to her commands. Aron assumed a superior attitude toward his mother. In the course of our discussion he acknowledged that he viewed her as stupid and illogical.

The parents said that they have been married for 20 years and that they have only the one other child, Jerry, age 4. Mrs. Cohen had two miscarriages prior to her youngest son's birth. Mr. Cohen is a computer consultant; his wife is a psychologist who has recently resumed a part-time job. The Cohens describe themselves as having few friends and rarely socializing with others.

Mrs. Cohen is the youngest of two children. She had a close but conflictual relationship with her mother, who died in 1981. She has a distant relationship with her father, who is 80 years old and resides in Massachusetts. Her brother Harry, age 43, has a history of psychiatric hospitalizations and has been diagnosed as having schizophrenia. He is currently in a group residence in Massachusetts. Mrs. Cohen maintains minimal contact with him.

Mrs. Cohen describes her parents' marriage as very unhappy and very conflictual. Her mother was the inconsistent but critical boss, while her father assumed a passive stance. During Mrs. Cohen's adolescence, her parents' marital conflicts increased and her father openly disagreed with his wife's rules. Mrs. Cohen states that at age 17 she became very depressed and dropped out of school for a year. She does not recall specific details about that year or any specifics about her brother's illness. She also denies any present or past concern about her own or her son's mental health.

Mr. Cohen is also the youngest of two children. His brother Dick, age 44, is married and resides in West Virginia. He is described as being the family rebel. He is very outspoken but minimally involved with the family. Mr. Cohen's parents reside in North Carolina. His father, age 70, a recovering alcoholic, is described as having had a violent temper. The alcoholism is an open family secret and has never been addressed. Mr. Cohen states that he has a distant relationship with his father and a close but conflictual relationship with his mother, who is ill with tuberculosis.

Mr. Cohen describes his parents as having a distant and unhappy marriage. He describes himself as having been an excellent student and always respectful of his parents. He reluctantly admits that in his early twenties he had a drinking problem and a violent temper. In fact, he physically assaulted his wife during the early years of their marriage. He is fearful of his temper but over the years has learned to distance himself when he feels that he might lose control.

In the initial session, Aron allied himself with his father and appeared in conflict with his mother. His father often supported Aron's complaints and rarely supported his wife's position. Mr. Cohen also complained of his wife's jealousy of his relationship with Aron and stated that she frequently complained of being left out of the father-son relationship. Mrs. Cohen agreed with this view and stated that being the only female in the family has been difficult for her. In fact, she frequently feels attacked by all.

Although Mrs. Cohen initially labeled Aron as the problem she also quickly identified long-standing marital and parenting difficulties. Mr. Cohen agreed and stated that they had previously been in marital therapy. He attributed its failure to his wife's refusal to change. She, on the other hand, blamed her husband for disqualifying her feelings and treating her as if she were incompetent. The couple also acknowledged problems coping with their four-year-old son, who was having difficulties adjusting to nursery school. Both parents described themselves as overly permissive and not wanting to deal with Jerry's temper tantrums. Interrupting, Aron stated that the problem was his mother. He described her as intellectually inferior and "crazy" and then went on to say that she was too inconsistent and illogical and that he could not wait to go away to college. Mr. Cohen agreed that his wife was the problem but added that he was also concerned about the behavior of both of his children. He stated that Aron was verbally abusive towards his mother and that Jerry was out of control and having difficulties adjusting to nursery school and relating to children his own age. Mrs. Cohen stated that her husband repeatedly undermined her parenting and limit-setting with the children.

When the family was asked what happened when the parents assumed a united stance, all admitted that this never occurred. Aron again stated that he had the right to make decisions, to choose his friends, to stay out late, and to decide what type of afterschool job he needed. After commenting about the myth that a family is a democracy, I said that the parents have the responsibility to set limits even though neither Aron nor Jerry would approve. Both parents admitted that they have no idea what is appropriate, that they don't trust the other's judgment, and that they doubt that they could follow through with a united stance for any length of time. The need for sessions alone with the parents and individual sessions with Aron appeared evident to all.

Throughout this interview my questions focused not only on obtaining factual data about the family but also on mapping the relationships, alliances, and triangles within the familial system. As the data on the genogram were filled in, we gained a multigenerational perspective of the presenting problem, i.e., the adolescent's lower grade performance and disrespect towards his mother (see Figure 10.1).

In the interview it quickly became evident that the children were triangled into the parents' marriage and that there were boundary problems at both ends of the age spectrum. The parents were unable to support each other's executive functioning and therefore set few consistent limits for their children. Mr. and Mrs. Cohen were overly permissive with Jerry and were unable to support Aron's need to make a few independent decisions for himself. In fact, Aron's adolescence and independent strivings appeared to precipitate a family crisis and to reintensify the unresolved marital issues. Adolescence was considered a secondary problem because the father-mother-son triangle intensified around this issue.

During the first interview the couple's unresolved marital problems were quite evident. However, I was aware of the fact that, initially, dealing with parental rather than marital issues would be less threatening to them. I also

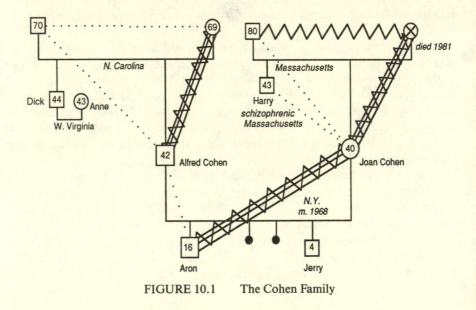

FIGURE 10.1   The Cohen Family

hypothesized that the couple's social isolation and distant relationships with their extended families intensified the nuclear familial relationships. In addition to adolescence, Mr. Cohen's mother's illness, Mrs. Cohen's recent employment, and Jerry's involvement in nursery school were viewed as current stressors on the family. In the initial and then in subsequent interviews, I used the genogram data to highlight for the family the repetitive themes and patterns spanning the generations.

The initial goal of treatment was to calm down the presenting problem, to support the generational boundaries, to help the parents work together and unite in their parental stance toward their children, and to detriangulate Aron and Jerry from the marital relationship.

Defining and Working on the Foreground: Individual Sessions With Aron

In the first individual session, Aron described his lack of respect for his mother and his embarrassment about bringing any friends to the home because of his mother's intrusive behavior and poor housekeeping. He admitted feeling allied with his father but fearful of his father's temper and the possibility that Mr. Cohen might physically assault him. He also acknowledged his own fear of assaulting his mother and his resentment towards his father, who tended to avoid any individual contact with him. He described his father as working long hours and only talking to him whenever he and his mother had some type of conflict. He also spoke of his brother's behavior and his refusal to assume a parental role with him.

In the five biweekly individual sessions that followed, I began to teach Aron about the family emotional system. First I explained the concept of triangles and stated that Aron appeared to be triangled into his parents' marriage and that he might be expressing a lot of anger towards his mother for his dad. I also pointed out how Aron's active involvement in his parents' marriage prevented his parents from having to work out their own relationship. It was suggested that he might be creating a conflict in order to have more contact with his father. It was also pointed out that, if his parents' relationship improved, they would assume a united stance and set limits and make expectations for him that he, as any normal teenager, might object to.

Aron denied that he would prefer them to argue. I then helped Aron to recognize the need to detriangulate himself from the marital relationship. In the individual sessions that followed, Aron was helped to detriangulate himself from his parents' relationship and to deal directly with each parent separately. He was also encouraged to bring friends to his home and to consult his parents prior to committing himself to an afterschool job.

Defining and Working on the Foreground:
Joint Sessions With Mr. and Mrs. Cohen

In addition to the individual sessions with Aron, his parents were seen together initially weekly and later biweekly and then bimonthly for a total of 19 sessions. These sessions focused on helping the couple begin to unite as parents and to recognize how their marital problems were interfering with their parenting. A great deal of time was spent on trying to calm down the situation with Jerry and to detriangulate Aron from the marital relationship by encouraging each parent to deal directly with the boys and supporting each other in doing so. The parents worked on defining role expectations and negotiating who was in charge of the children. They also began to set specific tasks and role expectations for each other. Mrs. Cohen began to work on her housekeeping skills, while Mr. Cohen began to help out more with Jerry. The couple also assigned Aron specific tasks and household chores, e.g., unloading the dishwasher, taking out the garbage, and keeping his room neat. The parents-Aron-Jerry triangle was calmed down by encouraging each parent to spend more time with each child and to no longer expect Aron to automatically assume a parental or babysitting role with his brother.

Utilizing the data from the genogram, the parents were helped to reflect upon their own parents' marital relationship and parenting skills. They then became aware of the similarities between the central triangles spanning the generations (mother-father-child) and the intergenerational patterns, e.g., conflictual marital relationships, distant relationships with fathers, close but conflictual relationships with mothers, difficulty dealing with feelings and separation issues. They were also sensitized to the idea that their sibling position, i.e., both being the youngest child, as well as their gender differences, contributed to their own struggles over power and control. They were helped to recognize their own difficulty in dealing with their sons' growing up and the need to realign their relationship so as to cope effectively with the parental demands of adolescence. Through the identification of parental issues, they were helped to reflect upon their own adolescence and their relationships with their family of origin.

Adolescence was a difficult time for both sets of families. Mrs. Cohen recalled that her parents' conflictual relationship intensified during her adolescence. She also recalled her own difficulties in sharing feelings and separating, which eventually led to her teenage depression and her need to leave high school during her senior year. She was subsequently able to identify difficulty dealing with feelings as a familial theme, i.e., depression, schizophrenia, and separation issues.

She also became aware of the fact that Aron's adolescence reactivated her unresolved past emotional issues. Her son's request for autonomy precipitated her fear of loss. Aron's adolescent conflict with his parents reactivated an earlier pattern of relating in her family of origin. Mrs. Cohen was eventually able to acknowledge her fear of letting Aron go and its connection to her past relationship with her parents. Through continued discussion about her family she also became aware of the intensity of her nuclear relationships because of the lack of other familial and social relationships. She was not, however, willing to discuss any feelings, issues, or past events with her father or brother.

Mr. Cohen realized that his family was similar to his wife's since both had difficulties dealing with feelings, i.e., temper, violence, secrets and alcoholism. However, in contrast to his wife, Mr. Cohen dealt with his adolescence by being "the good son." In recalling his fear of his father, he began to express concern that Aron might have similar feelings towards him. He spoke of his wish for his son to feel differently towards him and his desire to have Aron view him as a "buddy." He also became more aware of the marked discrepancy between his being the perfect, respectful teenager and his son's disrespect towards his mother. However, he had difficulty looking at his own contribution to this process.

Reflecting upon their own adolescence enabled the Cohens to assume a more objective stance towards Aron. Both heightened their awareness of their own desire to have had a better relationship with each of their parents. Mrs. Cohen began to feel less threatened by her son's desire to have a relationship with his father. Mr. Cohen also began to recognize the impact of his wife's being the only female in the family and her need to have a separate relationship with Aron. The couple then began to work more effectively as parents in supporting each other's decisions and in developing separate relationships with their son. This work enabled each parent to recognize his/her own role and to shift position in the triangle so that each could have a separate relationship with his/her spouse and son.

During the course of treatment, the parents were encouraged to support Aron's involvement with his peers. This was especially necessary in light of the family's own tendency toward social isolation. The spouses were also encouraged to spend some time together apart from their children and to plan one night a week just for themselves. They were eventually helped to reconnect to old friends and to begin a social life outside of their nuclear family. They were not, however, willing to pursue family-of-origin work.

As the parents united, as might be expected, Aron began to act out. He had his first sexual relationship and was discovered by his parents with a girl in his bedroom. His acting out was seen as a response to the recent shift in the couple's relationship. It was Aron's attempt to remain triangled into his parents' relationship and to protect them from having to deal directly with each other. Mrs. Cohen was quite upset by this incident, while Mr. Cohen appeared proud of his son's sexual prowess but annoyed that the event occurred in their home. The parents were helped to deal with this event and to negotiate their differences in gender expectations. Aron was also seen with his parents in order to evaluate the situation and to calm down the system.

At the present time Aron and his parents have been symptom free for one-and-a-half years.

SUMMARY OF CLINICAL WORK

In this case example, as with most families, I initially dealt with the parental rather than the marital system because that was less threatening for the couple. However, through the identification of differences in parenting, marital issues were highlighted. I focused on the presenting problem and repeatedly connected it to extended family issues. However, the couple chose to work only on those issues that would immediately calm down the familial system. Although I repeatedly conveyed the need to do some family-of-origin work, this idea was too anxiety-provoking for the couple. Their resistance seemed to be related to the fact that the presenting problem was ameliorated and the emotional power and intensity of each spouse's familial system were extremely strong. Although this resistance often occurs, especially when the adolescent's behavior is no longer perceived as a problem, many couples or individual spouses choose to do some family-of-origin work at a later date. This is especially true when the problems with the adolescent reemerge.

Future Work: Reweaving the Tapestry

If, at a later date, this couple or even one spouse chooses to do family-of-origin work, the initial preparation phase has already been completed. The individuals are already aware of familial patterns, themes, and triangles that are repeating themselves in the next generation. They have taken an "I position" and have displayed some motivation to take responsibility for their own behavior and a desire to work on changing their own role in their relationships with both their nuclear and extended families. They are therefore ready to do extensive family-of-origin work (Carter & McGoldrick Orfanidis, 1976). If they sought treatment as a couple, Mr. and Mrs. Cohen would be coached in each other's presence to find out more about their own families, e.g., membership, who's in the family, historical facts, relationships, alliances, details about their grandparents, especially Mr. Cohen's father's relationship with his father and Mrs. Cohen's mother's relationship with her mother. This very act of seeking additional familial information would begin to open up the familial system and help each spouse to feel more connected to his/her extended family. This in turn would diffuse some of the intensity of the nuclear system.

Both Mr. and Mrs. Cohen would be coached to learn more about their parents from living relatives in their grandparents' generation, parents' generation and their own. The intent of this contact would be to help them gain more objectivity about their parents as people and to understand why their parents act or acted as they did. Potentially they would start with relatives in the grandparents' generation because this contact would be less emotionally charged. However, due to the ages of Mrs. Cohen's parents, this would be impossible. Since this is a frequent occurrence in families with adolescents, the parents would then be coached to seek contact, through phone calls, letters, or in person, with other relatives in their parents' generation.

In doing multigenerational work with Mr. Cohen, the therapist would help him to understand his father as a person and why he became an alcoholic with a violent temper. This understanding would diffuse some of Mr. Cohen's rage toward his father and would help him to view his parents differently. It would also help him to relate to his father in a different way and in turn would make him more emotionally available to his own son. He would then be taught to apply multigenerational principles in dealing with his mother and her family. Mr. Cohen would also be helped to reconnect with his brother, initially by phone and later in person.

Mrs. Cohen would be assisted in learning more about her mother's family. She would be coached to contact any relatives to find out more about her mother's relationship with her parents, her own experiences with adolescence and separation, her parents' marriage, and how her parents dealt with her adolescent depression. She would be assisted in working in a similar fashion on her father's family. Due to his age, she would probably choose to work with his family first. Special attention would be given to coaching her to reconnect with her elderly father and eventually to visit her mother's grave. In addition, she would be encouraged to visit her brother and to explore with her father his concerns and plans for his son's future. Throughout the entire process, Mr. and Mrs. Cohen would be told to expect the worst possible response and coached how to deal with it if it did occur.

CONCLUSION

Adolescents can be helped to understand their behavior and its relationship to the nuclear and extended familial system. They can be taught about the family emotional system and can be sensitized to the concepts of triangles, reciprocity of relationships, sibling positions, generational patterns, and multigenerational transmission processes. This new awareness may enable the adolescents to make some behavioral changes, which, in turn, may begin to calm down the familial system.

Although the inherent turmoil of adolescence creates disruptions, it continues to provide an opportunity for the transformation of the family structure and the promotion of growth for all family members. This is especially true for the parents since they have the most power in the family system. If they change the way they deal with their adolescent child, this relationship may improve. In addition, adolescence can provide them with the impetus to do family-of-origin work. This work not only enables the parents to make lasting changes for themselves as individuals but also affords them the opportunity to improve their relationships with their children and in turn to alter generational patterns.

REFERENCES

Ackerman N. J. (1980). The family with adolescents. In E. A. Carter & M. McGoldrick (Eds.), *The family life cycle: A framework for family therapy*. New York: Gardner.

Bowen, M. (1978). *Family therapy in clinical practice*. New York: Aronson.

Carter, E. A., & McGoldrick Orfanidis, M. (1976). Family therapy with one person and the family therapist's own family. In P. Guerin (Ed.), *Family therapy, theory and practice*. New York: Gardner.

Friedenberg, E. Z. (1959). *The vanishing adolescent*. Boston: Beacon Press.

Guerin, P., & Guerin, K. (1976). Theoretical aspects and clinical relevance of the multigenerational model of family therapy. In P. Guerin (Ed.), *Family therapy, theory and practice*. New York: Gardner.

McGoldrick, M., & Carter, E. A. (1982). The family life cycle. In F. Walsh (Ed.), *Normal family processes*. New York: Guilford.

McGoldrick, M., & Carter, B. (1989). Forming a remarried family. In B. Carter & M. McGoldrick (Eds.), *The changing family life cycle*. (2nd ed.) (pp. 399–429). Boston: Allyn and Bacon.

Minuchin, S. (1974). *Families and family therapy*. Cambridge, MA: Harvard University Press.

Nicholson, S. (1986). Family therapy with adolescents: Giving up the struggle. *Australian and New Zealand Journal of Family Therapy*, 7:1–6.

Offer D., Ostrove, E., & Howard, K. L. (1981). *The adolescent: A psychological self portrait*. New York: Basic Books.

Preto, N. G. (1989). Transformation of the family system in adolescence. In B. Carter & M. McGoldrick (Eds.), *The changing family life cycle*. (2nd ed.) (pp. 255–284). Boston: Allyn and Bacon.

11

Families Launching Young Adults

JUDITH STERN PECK

LOU CALLED BECAUSE of his concern about his 23-year-old daughter, Julia, who was just beginning her last year at college and was very depressed. Julia had reached out to her father to ask for help. She was the third of four children ranging in age from 22 to 28. Her father wanted to know if I would see her.

Lou had called me six months earlier for marital therapy, but he and his wife, Lila, had never made it into the office. I suggested to Lou that he have Julia call me to set up an appointment. It is important, in any case but especially when beginning treatment with young adults, to have them make contact with the therapist, so that they will view the process as their responsibility/commitment. It is equally important to see the young adult alone initially because being separate from the family is a central issue during this developmental phase. It is for these reasons that I asked that Julia call me. When the young adult presents as the problem, he/she should be seen alone for the initial interview.

Family therapists receive calls like this one often, and even before the first session begin to hypothesize in the most general way about what may be the central issue in the family. My own initial consideration of a case involves an appraisal of the social context, the clinical context, and the family therapeutic context. I try to ascertain the degree to which each of these factors has an effect upon the others, as well as the potential use of a multigenerational model as a treatment modality.

For instance, the thoughts that came to mind as I heard Lou talk about his family related to the family's life cycle stage. I made the assumption in this case that the children were in the process of leaving home and that the family was in its initial launching stage of the family life cycle. How was this being handled by parents and children? I knew from my previous conversation with Lou that the marriage was troubled. Why was Julia the one seeking help? How was her problem related to the marital problem? What was happening with the other three children? Before I explore the clinical and family contexts, let me set the stage by considering the social context of this family, the messages and expectations generated by living in our society.

THE SOCIAL FAMILY CONTEXT

Within the paradigm of family development called the family life cycle (Carter & McGoldrick, 1980, 1989), the launching stage has as its central focus the process of separation — both children from parents and parents from children (Aylmer, 1989). The launching stage is experienced most intensely as the younger generation leaves the family home to begin adulthood. The family makes the transition from being a family with adolescents to being a family with young adults. This stage in a family's life can last anywhere from 10 to 20 years, depending on how many children there are and how long it takes for the children to make their place in the world (McCullogh, 1980). It is a process that includes three and sometimes four generations. It is due to these variables of time and intensity of the shifting relationships that the launching stage is considered one of the most complex stages of the family's life cycle.

For our understanding and application, it seems appropriate to divide the launching stage into subunits of phases with respect to the younger generation and to assign particular tasks to each generation. Young adulthood, defined as encompassing the 21- to 33-year-old age range, may be divided into two phases. During the first phase, the "launching phase," which usually lasts from about age 21 to age 26, the young adult focuses on leaving home, experimenting, and finally overcoming the fears of being on his/her own and becoming functionally independent; this phase is the focus of this chapter. In the second part of this stage, the 26- to 33-year-old builds his/her own independent foundation for the future; this was the focus of Chapter 7. Needless to say, these processes can overlap, but they encompass the tasks for the young adult.

While all this may be going on for the children, the middle adults, the parents of the young adults, are often acting as a bridge between two generations, experiencing pulls and tugs from both. They are separating from their children who are leaving home and leaving a void in the family's life, often the mother's life in particular. At the same time, these middle adults may be called upon to care for elderly parents who are aging and may be chronically or terminally ill (Neugarten, 1968). In addition, they are frequently faced with their own career/role changes. If one adds a full array of economic and cultural particulars to this already complex situation, it is clear that the interrelationship among these issues presents the therapist with a complex puzzle.

The primary objective of young adulthood is for the family to move the young adult into the adult world and for the young adult to make a place for him/herself within that world. This transition involves many tasks, all of which relate to the process of separation and differentiation from one's family of origin. As one grows older, certain aspects of one's relationship to parents and siblings must also be changed, while others must be nurtured or preserved. The aim of these familial changes is the creation of an adult-adult relationship based on mutual respect, a change in status that requires an emotional shift on everybody's part. The challenge for the young adult is to strike a balance between autonomy and attachment. The challenge for the parents is the same — to maintain attachment yet acknowledge autonomy. In order to facilitate this balance, each young adult must create an adult life structure for him/herself. This entails developing an intimate life structure of friends and, if one follows the typical middle-class path, eventually a mate, as well as a work life structure.

Many children who have reached the chronological status of early young adulthood (21–26) have failed to achieve the emotional status of young adulthood. They do no move toward independence but get stuck somehow in their developmental process. Staying home or marrying prematurely may short-circuit progress into young adulthood and independence. Either might occur as a result of the young adult's fears around his/her pursuit of autonomy. Young adults sometimes view the world as an overwhelming place, especially when they consider the "functional" responsibilities of taking care of themselves and creating emotionally supportive life structures.

On the other hand, Erik Erikson reminds us that "the fashionable insistence upon the dependence of children upon adults often blinds us to the dependence of the older (middle) generation on the young one" (1963, p. 266). All too often we see the young adult wanting to move on, and one or both parents unwittingly getting in the way of that process because of their own individual or marital difficulties. A future without children can seem quite empty for some middle-aged adults. More often than men, women define their age status in relation to the status of their family life cycle (Neugarten, 1968). Married women with children, relating the commencement of middle adulthood and the launching of their children to the end of their childbearing and rearing phase, often experience a sense of being nowhere and of having no purpose. Women at this stage in life may also feel an increased freedom (not without trepidation, perhaps): the sense of beginning a new period of their lives, in which they can test talents and capacities that had earlier lain dormant.

While many women turn outward at this phase, many men turn inward. Men associate middle age with increased pressure and obligation. Professionally, they are often at their peak, with increased responsibility and seniority. They view middle age as "a time to take stock" of their personal lives. Their concerns for their own physical health may intensify as they struggle with issues of self-awareness, mastery, introspection, and the inevitable downward trend of the future. They review their relationships with their children as well.

Looking at the process of launching as a reciprocal or circular one between generations, rather than a linear, cause-effect one, provides a complex and satisfactory model for clinical interventions. Understanding this process and using it in clinical work will be the focus of the rest of this chapter.

THE CLINICAL CONTEXT

As stated earlier in this book, "coaching" is a term coined by Murray Bowen to describe how a systems therapist does family therapy with an individual client (Bowen, 1978). Like the Bowenian model, our multigenerational model emphasizes staying connected in important relationships while maintaining one's own values and beliefs and developing new person-to-person relationships with each member of one's family. I introduce this therapeutic process early in my work with most families by focusing on one person's role in the patterns of his/her family. It is generally the treatment of choice for young adults, even though they are usually financially dependent, because as a modality it encourages the very tasks of young adulthood. Often the young adult, after completing his/her education, is in the process of making the transition to becoming financially independent. The consideration of socioeconomic context is quite an important variable in how the therapist attempts to intervene. One of the frequent goals of treatment is to move the young adult toward financial independence by encouraging the natural instinct toward independence or challenging continued dependence.

Paradoxically, this method emphasizes reengaging the family during this life-cycle stage of emancipation. This paradox becomes the challenge of the clinical context, for, although the young adult may have left home in a physical sense, he/she has not yet established him/herself in either the work world or a relationship. One could suggest that the young adult is "in process" and that direct regeneration of preexisting emotional ties is essential to establishing a lifelong balance of autonomy and attachment. At the same time, the therapist must consider whether the parents may have some unfinished business that does not allow them to let go.

Young adults often present with symptoms of depression, difficulty with relationships, or general malaise. During the first phase of treatment, which involves evaluation, engagement, and education, the therapist should attempt to see the entire family after engaging with the young adult. This can be done only after the therapist has established an alliance with the young adult — and even then only cautiously. A multigenerational evaluation allows for a more complete assessment of a family's consistent patterns and unresolved problems and a sense of each member's role in the inability to move through the transitional phase of launching. Even while looking at generational patterns, it is imperative that the therapist start with the presenting problem, tracking it within the family system.

The therapist should use the genogram, which maps the entire family system and suggests the family's interrelatedness, past, present, and future. "Genogram questioning goes to the heart of family experiences: births, illnesses, deaths, and other nodal events that have affected the family's natural movement through transitional phases" (McGoldrick & Gerson, 1985, p. 126). It allows the therapist to expand his/her own view of the presenting problem by broadening the context being considered. It also helps a therapist to evaluate behavior and relationships, both for his/her own understanding and for that of the family. Lastly, genogram questioning engages the parents and young adults in the therapeutic process. This leads the family to a clearer understanding of where it is "stuck" as a unit within the developmental process.

In an initial evaluation consultation with a young adult and his/her family, the issues of entanglement become clear to both therapist and family. All too often, the intensified triangle surfaces, and the therapist has the opportunity to see the alliances in progress.

Differentiation entails the establishment of personal authority, taking responsibility for one's own actions, and defining one's own thoughts, feelings, and opinions. It is not something that happens overnight. The challenge at the family life cycle stage when children leave home is for the clinician to loosen the system in order to allow young adults to remove themselves so that they have some perspective on the entanglements that make up the family. Once young adults have a concept of these entanglements, they can begin to disentangle themselves and move toward separation.

The other dimension of the clinical context that requires consideration is the therapist's own relationship to the life-cycle stage and the family (Simon, 1989). Bowen states that 50 percent of a therapy session is devoted to working on the client's family, while the other 50 percent is devoted to keeping oneself out of the family process (Bowen, 1978, pp. 529–47). In helping families to "move on," the therapist must consider how his/her own stage in the family life cycle might affect working with these families.

A potential pitfall for the therapist is alignment with one or the other generation, the young adult or the parents. The therapeutic context could become contaminated by its own triangle and thus impinge on the disentanglement of the primary triangle. Needless to say, it is easier to treat families at a point in the life cycle that the therapist has already experienced; the therapist's own life experiences broaden his/her perspective. The challenge for the therapist is to recognize the subtle ways in which contamination of the therapeutic process can occur, to maintain as neutral a position as possible, to view each family member's position with tolerance and respect, and to hear and evaluate all points of view.

In addition, the therapist would do well to have a flexible view of how to treat families. While the young adult usually presents as the problem, once the initial problem has been redefined as "letting go," either the parents or the young adult child might continue in treatment, depending on who is more motivated to do the work. It may be necessary to see varying dyads during the clinical process, and it is best that the therapist be comfortable with the notion of treating different family members at different times.

A therapist who has been chosen to treat a young adult may be faced with breaks in the process, which may relate to the young adult's going off to do his/her "own thing" or merely taking time to integrate what has been discussed in therapy. If the therapist does not feel comfortable with such potential breaks in the treatment, the young adult will certainly feel constrained. It is important that the treatment process, painful as it is, be experienced as a positive, growth-inducing one, so that the young adult will be encouraged to reenter therapy at a later time. There exists "an instinctual rooted life force that propels the developing child to grow to be an emotionally separate person . . . " (Kerr & Bowen, 1988, p. 95). The therapeutic context must be respectful of this force within the young adult and his/her fear of becoming as emotionally connected to the therapist as he/she feels to the family.

The rest of this chapter is devoted to a detailed consideration of how I used a multigenerational approach to help Julia and her family move toward differentiation. This case addresses the issues of whom to see and how to work with a young adult who is enmeshed in her family and having trouble "leaving home."

The Family Therapeutic Context: Defining the Foreground

As noted earlier, the initial phone call came from Julia's father. I asked him to have her call me, which she did. I saw her alone for the initial interview to assess the depth of her depression. Initially young adults need privacy to feel free to talk about their feelings. Also, for them to be comfortable in bringing in their family, they first need to know why they are doing so, that is, to understand their difficulties from a family perspective. Lastly, before treatment with the family can commence, the young adult needs to experience the therapist as potentially helpful to him/her.

Julia presented herself as a young adult without purpose in her life. She told me that she was sleeping a good deal of the time and feeling scared and insecure. She had been involved with a spiritual cult but had dissociated herself from that group and was feeling alienated, with no sense of belonging anywhere. She had been involved in therapy earlier during the summer, but her therapist had moved out of town. That was when she had decided to give up her commitment to the spiritual organization. While she had been able to return to college for her last year, she had trouble concentrating on her work, attending classes, and connecting socially. During this first interview, I questioned Julia about her depression, expressing my concern about any suicide ideation. She confessed that from time to time she had suicidal thoughts but she refuted any possibility of acting on them and claimed she had no specific plans.

We talked about whom she would contact if she were feeling suicidal. She was living at school and traveling home periodically. This forced Julia to begin to address the family context. As I noted earlier, Julia was the third of four young adult children, all in their twenties. She came from an upper-middle-class Jewish family. Her parents had been married for 30 years. Her brother, Alan, 28, the oldest of the four children, had returned to school to study music. Her older sister, Suzanne, who had dropped out of high school, was working and living on her own. Her younger sister, Ruth, the "baby" of the family, was still living at home, had a long-term drug problem, and was presently in individual therapy. Julia described her parents as constantly fighting over their children. She stated that she was feeling increased apathy toward her family.

I wondered aloud if Julia's family knew how depressed she was. She thought not. I suggested that it might be helpful if we could all meet together, so that I could get a better sense of what was going on in her family and evaluate the connection of the family process to Julia's depression. She responded positively to my suggestion. Through my questioning, she began to recognize that perhaps her family and her position within it had some relevance to her depression. Since it appeared from her description of how things worked that dad had a key position in the family, the power to get everyone to come in for a family evaluation interview, and the tightest schedule, she and I agreed that she would talk to her father to organize a time and a place for the interview. Having the young adult make these arrangements represents the beginning of her empowerment.

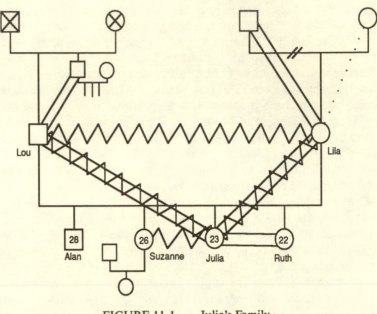

FIGURE 11.1   Julia's Family

The Family Interview

As predicted, Julia's father was able to gather the family for an evaluation interview, during which the family organization, themes, and stresses become more apparent. All the children agreed that there was a lack of clarity in the family relative to their parents' expectations of them and their moving on. Each gave a version of how this lack of clarity had affected his/her life. It seemed to the children that Julia's parents' laissez-faire attitude toward them had prevented them from defining a position and focus for their futures. Their concern about what would happen if they did move on rang clear: How could mom and dad survive? The feeling in the room was one of five children, rather than four, with dad acting the "distant" adult father and mom aligned with the children, especially Alan. Structurally, there appeared to be no boundary between the sibling system and part of the parental system. This boundary configuration, commonly seen in enmeshed families, makes it difficult for young adults to move on.

Exploring further, I discovered that dad worked very long hours and that mom had little to do other than look after the family. For years she had raised the children, calling dad in for emergency fix-ups when necessary. If the children were to move on, mom would be out of a job; furthermore, she would lose dad to the office, because there would no longer be any reason to call him in. Only in a crisis could she get dad involved with her.

This was the way the mother-father-children triangle seemed to work in this family. If the stakes seemed to keep getting higher, dad, much like Superman, would have to come in more frequently to save the day. Because of the nature of his work, he had access to experts. He would always get an expert for whatever ailed his family. The interaction in this interview confirmed my hypothesis. Father sat listening to his young adult children without responding. Mother was engaged in defending herself. In frustration, the son noted the difficulty that he experienced with his father's silence. He described how he had found that the only way to make his father react to him was to have a severe problem. This would then bring dad back home to take care of children and mother.

As the meeting ended, the central triangle was clear: These children were all stuck in a repetitive triangular pattern between themselves and their parents which served to keep dad involved with mom. The interview also revealed how conflicted the parental relationship was; the parents disagreed on how things should be with their children and vacillated between having no expectations and having many.

Education surfaced as an area that seemed to have a consistently high priority in the family, but the children had reacted to this in very different ways. Whereas Julia, like her brother, went to college, the other two girls were high school dropouts — a factor that contributed significantly to Julia's holding a different position in relation to her father from that of her sisters, setting up Lou's making her his confidante and her taking on for herself an "overresponsible" stance.

It is always a curiosity to me why one child presents and not the others. In this family, it looked as though each child was stuck — Alan, the eldest, was back in school and not quite sure what he would do upon graduation; Suzanne had never completed high school, to her father's distress, and was living with a young man and supporting herself by waitressing; and Ruth, the youngest, was fighting a drug problem. Julia appeared the most competent one of the clan, and therefore the overresponsible one. Feeling the pain for all of them, she had taken responsibility for getting help. She had called dad to tell him how badly she was feeling. Dad had called me, the expert, to fix things. With the family system apparently arrested at a crucial developmental point, Julia was voicing a cry for help for the entire family through her depression.

Julia had earlier turned to the cult as an answer to her depression, which stemmed from this central issue of separation, but paradoxically the cult turned out to be another family-like enmeshed system with no room for autonomy. The fact that Julia did not stay in a cult situation reflected her own strength and desire to move toward autonomy, as well as her recognition that that solution would not work. I saw this as another clue pointing to Julia's inner desire to separate and her potential capacity to work in a multigenerational model.

I decided to continue working with Julia alone and periodically with her family. Not only was she the one who presented, but it was also clear that she was the one motivated to work on resolving the problem. The first order of therapeutic business was clearly to help Julia with her depression. In order to do this I saw Julia alone on a regular basis and supplemented our one-to-one work with sessions attended by her parents, as necessary. Initially she needed to develop a keener understanding of herself in her present context at school and with the family. We would weave the family into that context by reflecting on the repeated patterns. I told her family that I wanted to leave the door open for potential future interviews.

FIRST PHASE OF TREATMENT

At the next individual session, it became clear that the family interview had had quite an impact upon Julia. She had never realized before that her siblings shared her thoughts and feelings, a realization that now provided her with some sense of relief. She was amazed at how quiet her father had been during the session and assured me that that was not his usual style. She was somewhat confused by his behavior. In addition, she was able to notice her own behavior as a listener/observer and "nonparticipant" in the family. This was the first theme that we would address in treatment. She was already beginning to see herself in the context of her family—the first step that needs to be taken in the therapeutic process.

During this first phase of treatment, I saw Julia 14 times over a period of six months. The goals of the therapy were to deal with the depression and isolation that she felt while at school, to deal with her depression in the context of her family, and to support her movement toward a clear goal— graduation. The family interview had not only helped to define her role in the family system but also shifted Julia's self-image. She realized that her depression was connected to issues within her family. She had been feeling responsible to her father to get her college degree, but did not know what to study. She was attending a school with little structure and few specific graduation requirements. She had asked for her dad's input, but had never been able to get it; she thus felt aimless and without a purpose for herself.

She was also aware that her relationship with her parents was quite disturbing to her. She loved them dearly, was financially and emotionally dependent upon them, but had no access to counsel, a need that was key at her stage of life. She also recognized that this was not just her problem but one that reverberated throughout the family. The only time one could get counsel or guidance in her family was in a crisis situation; otherwise the parents generally took a laissez-faire attitude. Both her involvement in a cult and now her depression had gotten her counsel in the form of referral to a professional.

This redefinition of the problem to include the family context was quite liberating for Julia. Although over the course of treatment she continued to go in and out of depression, her moods were less intense. We had begun to reverse the downward flow of her family emotional process and focus her goals in the here and now — to graduate and to come out of her isolation.

It did not take long for Julia to connect her spectator/nonparticipant behavior that had surfaced during the family interview to the isolation she had imposed on herself at school. Once we identified this repetitive pattern, Julia became quite motivated to reverse it. Relevance is the key to shifting from an individually oriented process to one that focuses on patterns and themes. She understood intellectually that placing herself in the "outside" position at school was very similar to what she had done in her family. We talked about the consequences of replicating that pattern at school, and gradually, with my coaching, she began to reach out to her peers and teachers in a productive way. This had a very positive emotional impact, since it gave her a sense of self-mastery and self-direction.

In using the multigenerational model, one of the major and clearest themes for the client-therapist relationship is developing the client's sense of taking responsibility for defining and changing his/her role in the interactional process. This is the beginning of the educational process that will enable the client to make changes within his/her family context. Initially the changes may be made in a work or social system, rather than in the family system. Such changes are often easier to accomplish because they carry less emotional baggage, and they often serve as "confidence builders" for the client.

Within the first two months, Julia's focus shifted from whether or not she would graduate to what she would do when she graduated. She became less and less depressed and more and more involved in her work. The moves she had made in school had had a positive effect. As Julia was getting better, there was another "uproar" in her family. This time the crisis was around her older sister, Suzanne. Julia's father called her to talk about the conflict around Suzanne's upcoming marriage. For the first time, Julia recognized how her father attempted to use her as his confidante in matters relating to her siblings. She realized that he was accustomed to calling her periodically to talk about their problems. This time she suggested that he discuss the problem with mom. She came into the next session feeling quite good, but also surprised at having, all by herself, recognized the triangling process and avoided taking part. This was her first detriangling move. It was then that Julia realized that she had not been just a spectator in her family; rather, she had also been serving as confidante to her father. Although she had stopped the process this time, she understood that it would happen again.

Taking a break soon after this incident, Julia stated that she needed to forego therapy in order to redirect her energies toward completing her work for graduation. I did not want therapy to interfere with one of my client's stated major goals. She realized that she still had to make changes relating to her family situation, but felt that she would be able to identify such changes herself. She also felt that she had learned enough to avoid any pitfalls that might obstruct her attempts at making such changes. As I thought that she had accomplished the initial goals of decreasing her depression, moving out of isolation, and recognizing how things worked for her in her family, we decided that she would take a break from treatment and return at a later date.

Some time later, I received a letter from Julia announcing her successful graduation and her future plans. She added:

> The reason I'm writing you is to say hello and thank you. I want you to know how much you've done for me. The work I did with you on my family . . . has enabled me to move beyond the barriers that held me back. . . . This has allowed me to relax, and enjoy who I am. . . . Now I believe in the value of counseling, especially your brand, and I advocate it highly. . . . I am getting along splendidly with mom and dad for the time being. . . . I hope to see you in the summer.

To me, this letter represented the end of the first phase of treatment for Julia. She had shifted enough in her perception of herself to move on with her own life. She had a beginning sense of her place within her family and a positive therapeutic experience, to which she knew she could return if she felt the need to continue. The seeds had been planted. Julia had completed her first phase of young adulthood, made a move in her family, and was moving toward differentiation. She obviously had used the time to integrate the changes she had made.

Working With the Parents

During the last two months of this first phase of Julia's treatment, we had discussed her feelings around my seeing her parents to help them focus on some of the difficulties that had surfaced in the family interview. This came about because Lila, Julia's mother, had called me to request an appointment for her and Lou. This seemed to come about after the crisis with Julia's sister, when Julia had told her father to talk to mom.

I felt it was time to see the parents. Julia had made progress in her thinking and view of herself in her family, but her progress clearly was not solidified. She was amenable to my suggestion that I could help her parents around their transition. It is quite appropriate for a systems clinician to see the family as a whole or to see individuals or dyads. Nevertheless, no matter whom one is seeing, holding onto a systemic perspective at all times is important.

After speaking with Julia, I called Lila back to set up an appointment for the couple. During the first session, they talked about the problems they were having in working out a satisfying relationship with their young adult children. After our family interview, they had recognized that they had not made their expectations clear to their children, and that somehow, as a couple, they had failed to help each other. They described their inability to resolve their terrible fights around child-related issues. I suggested that we work on some of those issues for three months and reevaluate how they were doing at that time.

One of my goals in working with Lila and Lou was to create a boundary between them and their children in order to diffuse the reactivity in the family system. I did this by helping them distinguish how and when to intervene with their children. During this time I encountered resistance whenever I attempted, as I often do, to connect their difficulties to their families of origin. In exploring their families of origin I had discovered that neither Lila nor Lou had made the young adult transition without complications. Lou's father had died when he was 20 years old; as a result, Lou had struggled during those years with issues of financial survival. Lila, on the other hand, had lived on a commune with her father, her mother having moved away when Lila was 12. Both Lila and Lou were reluctant to talk about these experiences, in spite of my repeated attempts to connect them to what their family was experiencing now. It became clear to me that, for the immediate future at least, therapy would need to be focused on their nuclear family.

We began by focusing on how things worked in their nuclear family and how and when escalations with the children occurred. I pointed out that, since mom was losing her "job" with the children, she needed to consider alternative interests other than trying to involve dad more and more. We also spoke about their beginning to agree on what they would or would not do for their children at this stage of life.

In the course of the three months, it became clear to me that both Lila and Lou would continue responding to the crises in their lives by looking for the latest expert outside of our therapeutic context or seeking a committed friend who would help them. The best I could hope for was to assist them in setting clearer boundaries between themselves and their children. That they did, in fact, begin to set such boundaries was reflected twice during the months that I saw them. First, when their youngest daughter escalated her drug problem, both parents worked hard at setting limits and disengaging themselves from their former "enabling position." Then, when their oldest child, their son, wanted to move back into their family home, Lila was able to say to Lou, "My children have reached an age where they should be independent and out of the house." Lila also realized that she needed to take care of herself. She became more involved in pursuing her avocation, writing. As part of the systemic move in this family, these two changes in the parental subsystem were quite important.

Middle Phase of Treatment

True to her letter, Julia returned to treatment in the late summer. Although she had been able to set up her own household, had gotten a job, and had become self-supporting, she had run into a problem when her sublet arrangement had ended. Having trouble finding a low-rent apartment in New York, she had found it necessary to move back into her parents' apartment. Her older sister, Suzanne, now married and pregnant, was also living there temporarily. Her younger sister, Ruth, was still battling her drug addiction.

Finding herself back in her central position in the family, Julia wanted to continue the work we had begun. The central triangle between her and her parents was still pulling at her, and the tension in her family was becoming unbearable. The other triangle between her parents, her siblings, and herself was becoming increasingly apparent and uncomfortable. She felt pulled into acting as she had before, as the one her father called upon to help with the other siblings, as the overresponsible one, the mediator.

These two triangles and Julia's role in them became the focus of our work during this phase of treatment. Julia was ready to shift her position. She had become more conscious of the pulls and tugs and was motivated to take responsibility for herself and shift her status and role in her family. She recognized that being between her parents and her sibs placed her on the "wrong" side of everyone. Her sibs resented her appearing superior and her parents perceived her as their "pet" and gave her little assistance.

Problems with both of her sisters, coupled with her own tendency toward accommodation and overresponsibility, forced Julia to work on her position relative to her siblings. My first intervention was to review with Julia the basic genogram information regarding the siblings in her family, in order to help her form better alliances with her siblings. Her position with her parents, the central triangle, tended to reinforce her conflicts with her siblings. It became clear that she and her brother, Alan, were considered the intelligent ones, while Suzanne and Ruth were considered the more attractive and social ones. This position had alienated Julia from her sisters and moved her to accommodate to Suzanne and to take care of Ruth in order to feel connected to them. She felt resentful toward Suzanne for bossing her around and making her feel less attractive. She felt motherly toward Ruth and rationalized her drug problem. Julia agreed that she was ready to change her behavior.

With Suzanne, Julia had difficulty saying "no." Suzanne was quite demanding and critical. She took a position of authority with Julia and others in the family. Julia felt that everyone in the family was afraid of Suzanne and no one ever denied her a request. In reviewing the varying roles that each member had assumed in the family, Julia recognized that Suzanne, being the oldest sister, had assumed an authoritarian position similar to the position her father would assume in his frustrated moments.

Julia and I talked at great length about how Suzanne's taking this authoritative stand worked, as well as the shadows the interaction carried for Julia. Julia noted that, the more intimidated she felt, the more commanding Suzanne became, to the point where Julia felt that she sacrificed her own needs to accommodate Suzanne's. Her biggest fear was that Suzanne would take advantage of her—she felt suffocated by this thought. This was reminiscent of the positions her parents took in their relationship.

We also clarified quite specifically how and when Suzanne approached Julia with requests. We reviewed Julia's reactions to Suzanne's demands and discussed what it would take to say "no" to Suzanne, as well as whether it would be possible for Julia to reverse the process and ask Suzanne to do something for her. This idea sounded quite enticing to Julia; she laughed as we discussed the prospect.

We planned Julia's request. She thought that she needed to approach the matter in two steps: first saying "no" to Suzanne's request that she go to the bank or the store for her at an inconvenient time; then at a later time making her own request, which was that Suzanne help her find an apartment. This had been an issue between them, because Suzanne was in a position to be quite helpful to Julia, but Julia had been reluctant to ask her for help. Our first task was to figure out how Julia would be able to say "no," creating a loss of authority for Suzanne, who would predictably try to maintain it. The next task was to help Julia define what she wanted Suzanne to do. As part of the process I got Julia to predict what Suzanne's reaction would be to both of these moves. We hypothesized many different reactions—each of them characterized by an attempt on Suzanne's part not to lose her "position of authority." These predictions were made to help Julia anticipate and maintain her new position.

Julia was shocked when she was able to say her first "no" and then make her first request. With the planning, preparing, and predicting done in the therapy sessions, she was able to shift her position in relation to Suzanne by experiencing herself differently in that relationship. She no longer felt com-pelled to do everything Suzanne asked. Nor did she feel intimidated by her. She also experienced Suzanne as listening to and responding to her request, rather than giving orders. Through this process, Julia began to feel less passive and more active for herself. She also experienced a more collabora-tive relationship with her sister, which she realized would help her resist her father's pursuit of her as a confidante around problems with her siblings.

The next focus was Julia's younger sister, Ruth, who had been fighting her drug addiction for many years and was presently in crisis. Julia had been Ruth's protector and caretaker. Here again Julia was maintaining her overre-sponsible position. As Ruth's problem escalated, Julia was able to shift from being jealous of all the attention that Ruth always got to recognizing how much trouble her sister was in. We were able to reframe Ruth's drug prob-lem, so that Julia could experience the full spectrum of emotions it evoked, ranging from sadness to frustration at her own sense of helplessness. When Ruth was hospitalized, for the first time Julia was able to tell her how sad she felt for her and how she had come to recognize that she could not rescue Ruth as she had tried so often to do in the past. Because of her work in therapy, Julia recognized the self-destructive quality of her and Ruth's past interaction: that her attempts to protect Ruth had only aided and promoted the drug problem.

With both her sisters, Julia was able to realign her position so that she no longer felt "locked in." With the use of the genogram, a reversal, and a redefinition, Julia was able to shift her relationship to her sisters so that she was able to say, "I don't have to go inside and stand like a shield because I'm afraid of their destruction. . . . I cannot invest myself in them anymore."

During the crisis with Ruth, Julia's father called her frequently to tell her how things were going and to discuss alternative plans. The triangle that had surfaced earlier in the beginning phase of treatment became more pro-nounced and clearer to Julia. Her father attempted to use her instead of his wife as his confidante and partner in parenting. As she recognized the pattern, Julia became aware of how uncomfortable she was in this position.

Again, we talked about her perception of her father and her relationship with him and with her mother. Julia realized that the pattern was not a new one; over the years, dad had called her and complain to her about her mother and her siblings. She also realized that she had few opportunities to talk to him about her own plans. Her anger and resentment surfaced as the triangle and its process became clearer.

We reviewed the process and talked about her emotional reactivity. Anger tends to surface when someone becomes more aware of the role he/she has played in the family system. It is important to address the anger and the underlying emotions, especially the feelings of being hurt and sad, before proceeding to the task of changing the client's position. In Julia's case, this was all part of the attempt to redefine her patterns with her parents. In our discussions, Julia realized that in the position of confidante to her father she felt obligated to be her mother's protector.

It was hard for Julia to imagine how things could work differently, and it took months for her to think about making another detriangling move. She talked about the betrayal she would feel toward her family, especially her father, if she did not respond to their/his needs. She felt an obligation inherent in her family membership to help in a crisis.

I talked a great deal with Julia about the benefits and costs, both to her and her family, of maintaining this position. As soon as she realized the consequences of her continuing in the same position, Julia felt comfortable in making her move. The next time her father called, she was able to tell him that she did not want to talk about her sister and to suggest that he talk to someone else — perhaps her mother or his brother — about the problem. This represented an important step and afterward she felt quite relieved. Later, while her mother was away in the country, she visited Ruth with her father. Afterward, she proudly announced how she had been empathic but had also set a boundary and would not let her father ask her advice or complain to her about her mother. He had respected her request. At the same time, she began to focus on how she would like things to be clearer between them. She was able to convey to him her empathy for the difficulty with Ruth, while at the same time stating that she did not feel that she could be helpful to them or to Ruth with this problem. This reflected her ability both to stay connected through empathy and to create a boundary for her autonomy. This was a major shift for Julia and, as was inevitable, resulted in a shift of the triangle. As an upshot of this, she decided it was time to reevaluate her relationship with her mother.

As noted above, Julia perceived herself as being her mother's protector, as well as her "fill-in." She alternately viewed her mother as emotionally needy and deprived or as "preachy" and negative. According to Julia, her "preachy" mother had a tendency to be critical and irrational. In this negative mode, she allowed no room for dialogue; as a result, when she talked, the other family members shut down and did not listen. Once Julia recognized her overly close position with her father and her distant and negative position with her mother, my goal was to help diffuse the negativity that Julia held toward her mom. I coached Julia to sit and observe her mother for a while as one might watch a play — without any personal response. This would give Julia some distance and ability to observe her own responses to her mother. I anticipated that mom would respond critically and negatively. I also wondered if Julia could thank her mom for the critique. I suggested as a potential second step the she talk to her mother about the things she was doing in her life. Julia thought that if mom did become critical, she might be able to listen without response.

Julia was able to make both steps and came into the next session declaring that her mother had "changed." Julia and I talked about her own responses, which were less reactive and more detached in terms of her perception of her mother. When her mom had responded with negativity, Julia had been able to listen without response. I was hopeful that in the future Julia would be able to respond with humor. We were not there yet. But because Julia had made just a slight move, she was able to have a different view of her mother.

It was not clear what additional work Julia was prepared to do with her mother, but as the therapy progressed she learned to identify the patterns in her family structure. She began to feel much more in charge of herself and to acknowledge that she had choices about what do and say to others in her family. It was not surprising, then, that in the late spring, after we had been talking about her mother, Julia told me that as part of her Mother's Day present she had invited her mother to lunch and an afternoon together. I asked to hear all of the details of Julia's plan for that day—the lunch, the time, place, and format—as part of our planning, preparing, and predicting process. As is often the case when the client experiences some success with his/her family work, he/she thinks he/she can "wing it." Julia was not exceptional; she had not prepared thoroughly for her day with her mother.

I led Julia back to the process of planning, preparing, and predicting what would or could happen. In coaching a client on family work, it is important to use this method to connect the emotional process to a given event. We reviewed carefully the structure and potential consequences of this date between Julia and her mother. We also discussed topics of conversation, what she wanted to talk about, and what she would and would not let happen. It was important to place Julia in a position where she was responsible for herself in relationship to her mother.

Julia came to her next appointment excited about how her date with her mother had turned out. We began to debrief around the event. She had shown her mother her work and her new apartment and had gotten some positive suggestions from her. This had all been part of our plan. Julia had not anticipated the suggestions, but her experience of the whole day had been so good that she realized that she was able to hear her mother's comments as suggestions rather than as criticisms. She was looking forward to doing it again. She recognized that the focus of her relationship with her mother shifted when they were alone together—without dad around—and Julia realized that she could look forward to an adult-adult relationship with her mother.

Results of Treatment

Clearly, the moves Julia had made represented the initial steps toward establishing a person-to-person, interdependent relationship with her parents. The central theme for Julia was around caretaking. As her therapist, I suggested that it would be interesting for her to shift her caretaking to herself rather than the family. Even though initially she considered such a move selfish, she nevertheless effected this shift with her two sisters and with both her parents; as a result, she felt better about her position in her family and about her ability to manage her life and her relationships with others. She had succeeded in disentangling herself from the central triangle, where the themes for her were caretaking and overresponsibility. She was now feeling free to concentrate her energies on the young adulthood tasks of becoming functionally independent through her world of work and relationships.

Presently, Julia is quite happy with her position in her family. She experiences herself as more actively involved in her own life. She has talked about how she felt pushed around in her family, experiencing herself as passive. She has taken a more appropriate, less overly responsible stance, and yet remains in contact with everyone. She is not overly involved in her family's day-to-day problems; instead, she channels her energies toward her own work and outside relationships. It took her a while to figure out what she needed to do to take care of herself. She has moved from early young adulthood to mid young adulthood, and is on the road to differentiation. In our last two sessions, she talked about a relationship with a man—her first potential long-term one. She proclaimed, "I am learning so much about myself in this relationship."

In working with a young adult, it is important to keep in mind the social and family contexts, as well as the normative issues of individual development. When I met Julia, she was a young 23-year-old, stuck in her development, feeling herself to be directionless, and enmeshed in a chaotic family. Our work together helped to change her position. It allowed her to take charge of her own life, while simultaneously maintaining contacts to her family.

Throughout the next few years, Julia will continue to redefine her relationships with her parents and her siblings. She has also committed herself to therapy. In keeping with her lack of self-focus and continued focus on others' needs, Julia had often declared that she thought therapy was self-indulgent; unless a crisis existed, she did not see why one should need therapy. But now, not only has she chosen to stay in treatment but she has also decided to pay for it herself—a major step toward her own functional and emotional independence.

CONCLUSION

The launching stage in the family life cycle is particularly complex because of its impact on at least two generations: the young adults who are — or, as sometimes happens, are not — being launched, and their middle-aged parents, who must adjust to this significant transition in family life. In encountering clients who are involved, either as parents or as children, in the launching stage of their family life cycle, the therapist needs to assess which member(s) of the family to see, when to see them, and how and when to deal with extended family issues. One sure rule, especially if the young adult is not yet completely out of the parental home, is to see everyone in the family in the initial phase of treatment to do a systemic evaluation.

The therapist who elects to coach a young adult must understand the young adult's need to distance him/herself from the therapist at times and must recognize the importance of creating a therapeutic experience to which the young adult will feel motivated to return when he/she is ready. The goal is to help the young adult "move out" into the world while maintaining his/her connectedness to the family as well as to the therapy.

Even though the therapist is working with the young adult, he/she should help the parents readjust their relationship to their children and to each other. Ultimately, every family member should benefit from the enriching experience that the launching stage of the family life cycle offers the family as it moves from adult-child to adult-adult relationships.

REFERENCES

Aylmer, R. (1989). The launching of the single young adult. In B. Carter & M. McGoldrick (Eds.), *The changing family life cycle; A framework for family therapy* (2nd ed.) (pp. 191–208). Boston: Allyn & Bacon.

Bowen, M. (1978). *Family therapy in clinical practice*. New York: Aronson.

Carter, B., & McGoldrick, M. (1989). *The changing family life cycle: A framework for family therapy* (2nd ed.). Boston: Allyn & Bacon.

Carter, E., & McGoldrick, M. (1980). *The family life cycle*. New York: Gardner.

Erikson, E. (1963). *Childhood and society* (2d ed.). New York: W. W. Norton.

Kerr, M., & Bowen, M. (1988). *Family evaluation*. New York: W. W. Norton.

McCullogh, P. (1980). Launching children and moving on. In E. A. Carter & M. McGoldrick (Eds.), *The family life cycle: A framework for family therapy*. New York: Gardner Press.

McGoldrick, M., & Gerson, R. (1985). *Genograms in family assessment*. New York: W. W. Norton.

Neugarten, B. (1968). *Middle age and aging*. Chicago: University of Chicago Press.

Simon, R. M. (1989). Family life cycle issues in the therapy system. In B. Carter & M. McGoldrick (Eds.), *The changing family life cycle: A framework for family therapy* (2nd ed.) (pp. 107–117). Boston: Allyn & Bacon.

12

Families in Later Life

DEMARIS A. JACOB

THERE DIDN'T USED TO BE a "later life." Average life expectancy was 18 in Ancient Greece, 33 in the year 1600, 42 in the Civil War era, and 47 in 1900. Now the average man will live 72 years, the average woman 78 (Silverstein & Hyman, 1982). This dramatic increase in our own, our children's, and our parents' life expectancies may be the most important single factor in changing the timing, the rhythm, and the context of family issues over the past 80 years. There was no "midlife crisis," no "sandwich generation," and no expectation on the part of young adults that they could count on two generations of self-sufficient, productive parents/grandparents above them for a long time to come.

Today each family has to break new territory in attempting to incorporate older generations into the family as a whole. There are few readily available, culturally mapped patterns and rituals that have been part of each family for generations to use as automatic guidelines. Only recently has the average family included active grandparents and great-grandparents.

The extended family of Francine, a 58-year-old woman whose therapy will be the focus of this chapter, is illustrative of the family context in which a typical person in later life is embedded (see Figure 12.1).

The first thing to notice is that there are four living generations: In addition to children and grandchildren, Francine has a 91-year-old father alive and living with her sister and brother-in-law. Secondly, her middle child, Susan, has recently divorced and, as do many single mothers, is having financial problems. Her youngest, John, is taking his time moving

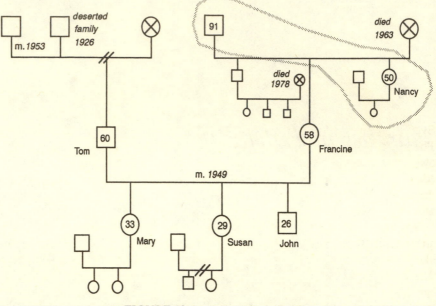

FIGURE 12.1   Francine's Family

out and Francine still takes care of him by cooking, doing his laundry, etc. Francine also works, as a secretary for a small company. She loves being a grandmother, and sees her grandchildren as often as she can.

Thus Francine, at this point in her life, is simultaneously a daughter with an elderly father, a mother with one child out and married, another out but temporarily more dependent on her for childcare and financial aid, and one still to launch. She is also a wife in a marriage now at the node of a life-cycle transition.

The family reorganizes to deal with later life issues, *when one spouse sets a definite date for permanent retirement and/or has an encounter with an illness serious enough to significantly alter general functioning or set up reverberations of foreseeable death.* The later life phase is thus ushered in by these observable, public notices of a shift toward the "end." Some people will continue to live a life of good health and active employment well into their seventies while others will, through fate or decision, enter the later life phase as early as their fifties. For instance, with Francine what defines her as in transition to the later phase is her husband, Tom. Tom has devoted his life to work; often working 14 hours a day, he built a successful retail business. Two years prior to Francine's coming for therapy, Tom suffered a serious stroke and underwent triple bypass surgery. He recovered well and returned to work, but this brush with death precipitated his setting a retirement date. At the time Francine began therapy, Tom was negotiating the sale of his business and looking forward to his dream — selling everything and spending his "last years" traveling with Francine.

MYTH AND STEREOTYPE: ISSUES FOR THE THERAPEUTIC ALLIANCE

Every therapy process is defined, and limited by, the vision of the therapist. Therapists working with individuals in this life phase must first explore their own inner blinders, particularly if they are somewhat removed from knowledge of how real people of this age live and think. That is, the younger the therapist or the more isolated he/she is from meaningful contact with the older generation, the more that therapist will be operating from stereotype.

Because older people continue to be very seriously underrepresented among those who receive mental health services, the average therapist is not likely to have the opportunity to expand knowledge of this age group through clinical practice. Surveys show (Roybal, 1988) that the older age group represents only 6 percent of people served by the community mental health centers and about 2 percent of those served by private therapists.

The media, therefore, provides most of our "information" about the place of older people in our culture. Walsh (1989) notes that the elderly in our society have often been "dismissed as old-fashioned, rigid, senile, boring, and burdensome." Media have presented mythological later life solutions, in which the older person "defies such negative cultural expectations" (e.g., *Harold and Maude* and *Harry and Tonto*). The problem is that nowhere "are options seen for healthy later life adjustment within the family and social context."

Recently there has been a shift toward more emphasis on successful aging in the media (Gatz & Pearson, 1988), spurred by the demographic revolution in our society. Those over 65 now make up 18 percent of the total population, and the group increasing proportionately the fastest is that of people aged 85 and older.

Contrary to myth, most older people *are* integrated into social and family networks with ongoing support and caregiving relationships. At any given time less than 8 percent of the older generation are in nursing homes (Silverstein & Hyman, 1982) and research (Halpern, 1988) indicates that families provide 80 to 90 percent of care for the older generation. While 70 percent of elderly women are widowed and live alone, most live less than 10 minutes away from one adult child and report contact with at least one child daily or every other day. The increase in longevity means that many of those entering the later life phase, like Francine, will be doing so with continued responsibility for the care of an elderly parent.

When older persons do come for therapy, they are often coming after a lifetime of coping; they are survivors of the usual life-cycle issues of work, marriage and childrearing. In addition, they may have lived through wars, illness, deaths, and economic depressions. These are strengths the therapist should remember when building the therapeutic alliance. Working with older persons multigenerationally is often extremely rewarding: besides a lifetime of coping, older persons generally come with high motivation to work in therapy. They are only too aware that they *don't* have all the time in the world to deal with individual and family issues and "put their house in order."

THE LATER LIFE PHASE: ISSUES AND TRANSITIONS

The therapist working with client(s) in later life needs to be aware of typical stressors and inquire about them in the assessment phase of the therapy. There are the *developmental stressors*, those changes that are part of the normative shift of the family at the node of a new life cycle phase, and *external stressors*, those changes that are part of aging itself.

Developmental Stressors

There are shifts in the family system as a whole, between generations, and within the marital and sibling subsystems.

IN FAMILY AS A WHOLE. With the public notice of permanent retirement and/ or serious illness that signals the mortality of the older generation and thus the beginning of the later life phase, the family feels pulled to start moving emotionally closer again. This shift toward greater intensity of family involvement is fueled by (1) practical considerations of decision-making and changes in caregiving patterns between the generations, (2) the emergence of unresolved emotional issues from the past with the awareness that time may be running out to resolve them, and (3) pressure on sibling and/or extended family subsystems to function jointly in new ways.

This centripetal shift (toward greater involvement) comes usually after years of family functioning in the centrifugal (toward less involvement) mode. Since the adolescent phase the family's thrust has been toward preparing everyone for separation and independent living. Parents and children all have had to move apart enough emotionally to allow for committed outside-the-family attachments and living arrangements. Now emotional intensity is rechanneled back towards the family of origin.

For Francine's family, it was Tom's specific retirement plan that heated up the emotional family temperature. Francine's anxiety about leaving her support systems (children and friends) and going off with Tom alone, together with the couple's inability to negotiate openly, led to Francine's increasing emotional pressure for herself *and* Tom to get closer to the children. Both daughters reacted to this by hostile distancing, thereby escalating the anxiety in the system.

Working on extended family relationships at this phase is usually viewed by older family members as highly relevant to how they see their problems. Thus, the therapist generally has to spend much less time at this life-cycle phase educating clients as to the import of multigenerational work. The hardest task for the therapist, in the usually heated emotional climate, is to be crystal clear about his/her own family-of-origin issues so as not to align with one subsystem against another.

BETWEEN THE GENERATIONS. Spurred by the shifts in caretaking patterns that are the sine qua non of this phase, the *emergence of unresolved dependency issues and of unresolved sibling competitions for parental favoritism* and the frequently accompanying rage, guilt, or fear provide the emotional ground for potential intergenerational battle. The arenas in which the family may fight about, rather than work through, these painful feelings are often time and/or money.

Intergenerational conflicts about the "right" use of time and money are exacerbated by the lack of any clear societal standard. Formerly clear-cut traditions, such as primogeniture, are being radically altered by the impact of feminism and other cultural changes, thus obliging each family to create its own "rules." On the one hand, the dream of the "golden years" is that the time after childrearing and retirement and before incapacity and death can be lived solely for one's own pleasure. On the other hand, as with Francine, there are usually children and/or siblings who may need and often expect the continued assistance of the older generation, and an elderly parent who needs assistance as well. If the members of the older generation enjoy good health after retirement, they have more available time. Should this time be used for self or for helping children? Should money be spent on self, saved for inheritance, or used to help children?

If the older generation is in poor health, however, it is the younger generation who have increased demands on their time and possibly money. Where should a child draw the line between self needs and parental needs? How much should you do to be a "good child"? How much should you expect from your siblings?

There are no clear answers to these questions, and this vacuum leaves the potential for bitter family conflict. In our society, as in many others, caretaker for the older generation usually means "daughter" (Brody, 1985). The daughter who has unresolved dependency issues toward her mother may become depressed at being expected to care for her. The son who has taken pride in self-sufficiency and "never asked anybody for anything" may erupt in rage to discover his sister has been given money because "she is more needy." The daughter who has diligently helped her parents while a distant beloved son got all the praise may launch an inheritance fight after her parents' death.

People are often unaware of the painful feelings that are at the bottom of these situations. It is much easier to fight battles over who should get/give the most money or time than to deal with unresolved emotional issues.

At the same time, there may be a shift in the balance of power between generations. This may be sudden, as in the event of incapacitating illness, or gradual, through the normative aging process. Either way, the next generation moves into a position of greater influence. The power derives from increased emotional reliance of the older generation on the younger. The reliance stems from waning capacity and energy and from the perceptions that continued contact with grandchildren depends on maintaining good relationships with one's own children and that good relationships with one's own children become increasingly necessary for the quality of the older generation's survival and well-being. While this shift in power may be handled with openness and mutual respect in some families, in others the shift is experienced as fearful and burdensome. The more the younger generation experiences the shift as a burden without a reward, the greater the possibility of abuse.

Unfortunately, tax laws and Medicare eligibility requirements act to accelerate this power shift. The more money the older generation has transferred into the names of their children or other relatives before their death, the better it is from a financial management point of view. This may stimulate powerful feelings of hurt, dependency, mistrust, or fear between the generations. If I give all my money now to my children, can I count on them to take care of me? Why are they hanging on to their money? Don't they trust me? Bitter fights over money and threats of will changes to "ensure" emotional family connectedness and the "power" to command respect and affection often erupt when basic issues of trust between the generations are in question.

Before planning a move the therapist working with a member of the older generation needs to assess *very carefully* the older client's current "power" in the family system, as well as the client's anxieties and the probable reactions of children. This may mean expecting smaller increments of change than in other phases of the life cycle, so as not to generate too much anxiety in the older client.

BETWEEN THE MARITAL DYAD. The post-retirement years may be viewed as a last chance to realize postponed dreams, particularly for those whose work has not been a source of satisfaction or for those, like Francine's husband Tom, who did not balance work with other meaningful attachments.

For those couples, like Francine and Tom, who have not had open communication and developed the means to resolve differences, the process of working out a joint definition of life meaning will be problematic. The differences between Francine's dream, i.e., more time for friendships, children and grandchildren, and Tom's, i.e., a marital world journey, are enormous. The negotiation of those differences will be one aspect of the work in therapy.

Along with redefining the meaning of the union, retirement also brings shifts in role definitions and the closeness-distance balance in relationships.

The retiree has more time available, and where and how this time is invested can either enrich or dislocate and threaten the emotional life of the spouse. The therapist working with a family with a retiree needs to track this change very closely, as it may have reverberations down to the next generation, who may be the ones presenting the problem.

Mostly, the shift is for husband and wife to move closer to one another, and this works smoothly when the marriage is basically sound. Realignments that may lead to symptomatology are those where there is movement of the retiree into the territory of the spouse, without that spouse seeing some emotional gain. With Francine, Tom's illness and retirement plan confronted her with the prospect of increased emotional contact with and reliance on her husband, with whom she had had a highly conflicted and distant relationship for years.

Early phases of therapy usually involve educating clients about the relevance to their emotional pain of shifts in closeness and distance among family members at retirement time.

BETWEEN SIBLINGS. In the typical family, sibling positions are usually frozen in time at the point they were when each child left home. Rarely do siblings actively work on shifting their interrelationships once they reach adulthood. The "responsible one" continues being responsible in relation to a "carefree" younger sibling. Daughters may continue being more in touch with the emotional life of the family than sons. The shift in caregiving patterns that is a part of the normative process in the older generation generally puts strain on underdeveloped and outmoded sibling bonds and positions. Francine and her sister Nancy maintained fixed emotional positions in relation to their father: Nancy was "tougher" and could handle him, Francine was too "sensitive"; therefore, Nancy got the job.

The "responsible one" may not want to shoulder most of the care for the parent while the "carefree one" breezes in for a visit once in a while. The "carefree" sibling may not want to directly challenge the "responsible" one, but instead expresses concern as well-meant advice to the responsible sibling on how to do it better.

Many siblings with conflictual relationships continue to look to the parental generation to "right the wrongs" between them. One common way siblings may detour their issues through a parent is to seek a favored position in a will or to initiate legal action to contest a will. Detouring such sibling conflicts and rivalries through parents or courts rigidifies emotional positions and generally leads to cutoff. The therapist, therefore, needs to be alert to whether children are assuming responsibility for their own issues or are counting on third "powers," which may often include the therapist, to form an alliance with them against another sibling.

In families where there is a large estate and sibling relationships have been competitive and triangled through parents in the past, the forces toward cutoff are strong. In families where children have formed an earlier alliance, the forces toward closeness are strong. Our culture provides almost no ritual to facilitate maintenance of sibling bonds (e.g., there is no Sisters or Brothers Day). This is left to the commitment and energy of each individual.

Specifically, the maintenance of sibling bonds requires not only a reworking of old emotional positions, but also an assumption of roles previously held by a parent. For example, the main way children hear about each other is often through the mother-grapevine. When mother dies, will it be automatic that children start calling each other directly? Maybe, and maybe not. Children may often make great efforts to visit parents at important holidays. Will they make the same effort to visit a brother or a sister? Maybe.

External Stressors

The external stressors of later life usually involve loss. When doing an evaluation/assessment the therapist should not only note the loss itself, but also track the meaning of the loss to the individual and the family.

There are a variety of losses that can occur, including the death of a spouse, physical and mental incapacity, death or incapacity of long-time friends, loss of a driver's license, and loss of one's home. The complexities of individual and family reactions to death and chronic illness are worthy of their own chapters (see Herz Brown, 1989).

For Francine and Tom, the meaning of Tom's heart surgery for the couple expressed itself as follows: Francine viewed it as an opportunity to nurture her husband (e.g., by cooking proper meals, going with him to doctors). Tom, a lifelong model of self-sufficiency and counterdependency, refused any help. Francine interpreted this refusal as further evidence that he didn't value and love her, thereby adding to the hostile distancing already prevalent.

THE THERAPY OF AN OLDER ADULT: FRANCINE

Initial Phase: Defining the Foreground

When Francine, a 58-year-old woman of Italian background, came for therapy for the first time, she reported that she was crying "at the drop of a hat" every day now and had been depressed a "long time before that." She couldn't figure out why. Her troubles were "nothing big" and she thought she might be going crazy.

She said what she wanted from therapy was to "Grow up! I've always been very sensitive, a people-pleaser. I need to get strong." While Francine cried throughout the first session, she also had a vitality and sense of humor that were clear strengths. Her depression had not affected her care for her appearance—she was stylishly dressed and made-up neatly. She had told her husband she was coming for therapy, but was emphatic in telling me she was too angry to include him and wanted this time for herself. We agreed that, after her anger was down, he would become a participant in the therapy.

Multigenerational therapy begins when the therapist decides this will be the model of treatment. It is not a technique that can be immediately applied, but a decision that influences the way assessment is done and shapes the work on the presenting problem. Francine's statement of her therapy goal boded well for this type of work; it implied that she realized *she* would have to make some changes. Even though depressed, she didn't view patienthood as passive. Francine had also lived for 58 years—successfully raising three children and working competently at a job she enjoyed. She brought considerable coping experience, which suggested basic ego strengths.

"You can't do coaching until the client's head is above water!" (E. Carter, personal comment). This means first alleviating the presenting problem—with Francine, her depression. I decided against a referral for medication because her energy level was fine; she was functioning at work and maintaining her home, her friendships, and herself. However, it is also important to note that, in working with those in later life, the therapist needs to be alert to the possible contribution of physical, hormonal, or endocrinological imbalance to the presenting problem. Many older patients take a variety of medications, sometimes not in the prescribed dosages, which may have negative interactions. The hormonal changes associated with menopause may be another contributory factor. Some, especially those living alone, may not be eating adequately and so have anemia or dietary insufficiency. If there is any question about physiological status, an adjunctive referral to a physician should be a part of responding to the presenting problem. Francine felt that postmenopausal changes were not a problem to her. She had regular checkups with a good physician and was in good health.

Next the therapist inquired about the people important in the client's life, and what changes had occurred within the past few years. "The biggest change is that my husband Tom and I are getting along; we're talking to each other now," stated Francine. "This is a first in our 37 years of marriage." When asked what they were talking about, it turned out the sole subject was their daughter, Mary. Here Francine began to cry steadily. About eight months ago, Mary quit her job at Tom's business and told them both her therapist said she should distance from her mother; since then they had not spoken.

Tom and Francine were engaged in a mutual exploration of how Francine had gone wrong as a mother. Both of them believed that the emotional life of the family was the responsibility of a mother, and Francine was mired in guilt, self-blame, and self-pity: "I know I dumped too many of my problems with Tom on Mary. She's angry at me for that, and there's nothing I can do. I can't erase the past, and she can't forgive me for it." The cutoff with Mary also blocked Francine's access to those grandchildren. Contact had been daily phone calls and drop-in visits several times a week; now it was reduced to a strained weekly phone call to the grandchildren. Mary and Francine lived within two blocks of each other.

Francine's relationships with her other two children seemed basically fine: "We can say what's on our mind to each other and no hard feelings. But I'm upset at Susan, because she refused to help me with Mary. I'm mad at John now too because his girlfriend practically lives with us. I do laundry and cooking for both." Francine had not spoken directly to John about her displeasure: "I shouldn't have to. John should know I don't like it."

As for Tom: "I've been angry with him from the day we married! He never consulted me on anything. We moved into his mother's one-bedroom apartment, and he took her side in everything. She was a difficult woman. She was crippled from polio, but she could get around. She just didn't want to. She'd lie in bed giving me orders, get depressed, and then Tom would tell me I wasn't being good enough to her. I left him, but my mother made me go back."

The pattern in the marriage has been one of distance punctuated by intense quarrels and long silences. "But I like it when we're not talking to each other. Only then do I have the courage to do what *I* want. If we're talking, I just crumple and do what *he* says."

We may now map the triangles in Francine's nuclear family (see Figure 12.2). The emotional patterns of closeness and distance had been fairly rigid through the years:

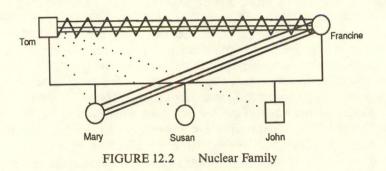

FIGURE 12.2   Nuclear Family

The marital dyad, as depicted by Francine's extreme reactivity to Tom, seems fused and conflictual. By her own statement, she used cutoffs (not speaking) as a means of dealing with the fusion and to gain a pseudo-independence. It seems that the main couple in the family had been Francine and Mary, both allied by their belief in Tom's insensitivity. Tom, relying on Francine to provide his link with his children, had distant and underdeveloped relationships with them. While Tom and Francine were now talking, the major triangle had not changed: Francine was still intensively child-focused and joined with Tom only to discuss Mary.

The pattern of women being more closely connected to children and extended family, and men being more involved in work and out-of-home activities (with the marital dyad remaining somewhat distant) is not uncommon, especially in Italian families (McGoldrick, Pearce, & Giordano, 1982). What made Francine's situation dysfunctional was the rigidity of the triangles over time, the intensity of the fusion, and the almost exclusive use of cutoffs to handle conflict and gain "autonomy."

Into this system came the change that moved Francine and Tom into the further stresses involved in the later life phase transition. Recovering from heart surgery years prior, Tom was moving to execute his retirement dream — to be alone with Francine at last. He was selling his business, wanted to sell the house, move away and have fun together. To Francine, however, this meant only loss. She feared being alone with him and did not want to deprive herself of her most important emotional ties (children and friends). However, Francine had never directly spoken to Tom about any of this.

In exploring Francine's extended family, it was no surprise to find more cutoffs; she had not spoken to her sister Nancy or her sister-in-law Judy for five years. "After all I've done for them. They couldn't stand each other and I always worked it out. Now they're as thick as thieves and don't invite me. I am very hurt." This cutoff includes Nancy's nuclear family and Francine's father, who lives with Nancy, as well. Regarding her father, Francine said,

"That's no loss. He's a mean bastard and I've always been afraid of him. I always stay out of his way." Francine's only connection to her extended family had been her cousin, who died two years previously. With such distance and negative reactivity toward her father, one might foresee that Francine had been extremely close to her mother: For the first 13 years of her marriage (until her mother's death) she had gone daily to her mother's house, where they cooked and ate dinner together. Her mother "didn't like" to be alone with her father. Francine then took a plate home for Tom to eat later. The main emotional couple in the family at that time was her mother and herself. One can speculate that after her mother's death Francine shifted to Mary as her "partner," thus repeating the main triangle in the next generation (see Figure 12.3).

During the assessment phase, the therapist not only collected information but fed it back to the client to promote an awareness of patterns in her family, for example, "looks like Mary handled her difficulties with you the same way you did with Nancy and Tom." Stimulating a kind of "family system detective" stance on the client's part is important, and using the genogram can be a powerful tool in achieving this. Francine's emotional pull would probably have been to enlist me as a nurturing person allied with her against her "difficult" husband (i.e., to fill the vacuum left by Mary). The genogram helps both therapist and client remember that the task of therapy

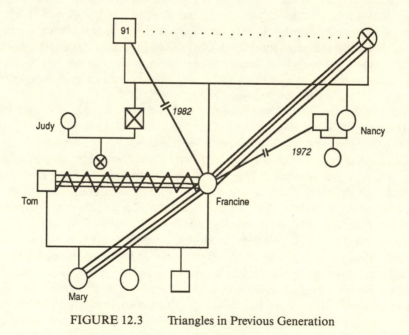

FIGURE 12.3   Triangles in Previous Generation

is to rework relationships "out there," not to make up for them in the therapy itself.

For Francine, seeing where she stood in her family was an eye-opener: for the first time it became clear to her why she was so depressed and that the problem was more complicated than how to get back with Mary again. We both confirmed Francine's original diagnosis: She did need to grow up! It wasn't working for her to be the "good little girl" (who works hard and does her chores), expecting to be financially cared for by a husband who would love her from a distance and leave her alone to enjoy her most important relationship (she and her daughter). Viewing Francine's depression as a result of her own and her family's inability to maintain successful, connected relationships meant that we defined the work of therapy from the start as nuclear and family-of-origin relationship-reworking. Only after these building blocks were in place could she contemplate retirement with her husband as anything other than exile to a penal colony.

The therapy continued with education of Francine about her family's process, the triangles, and her part in them, as we prepared for the coaching to come. In teaching the way the triangles worked, it also became apparent that Francine's family had a "rule" that, when there was upset in a relationship or a request to be made, no one did it directly. Communications were passed through a third person. This was the basis for Francine's anger at Susan for refusing to discuss Mary with her. By detriangling herself from the Francine-Mary upset, Susan had violated a basic family operational principle. The emotional underpinning of this rule for this enmeshed system was the belief that a request was a test of love; to say "no" meant emotional abandonment. With this foundation, the therapist made two predictions: (1) When Mary and Francine did reestablish contact, the marital dyad would return to angry outbursts/long silences, and (2) unless Francine quit pushing Susan to mediate her upset with Mary, Susan would probably distance from Francine too.

In an intense, enmeshed system such as Francine's, it is usually better to begin with the relationships that are relatively calm rather than go straight for the most toxic ones. That way the client can make doable changes without anxiety building too high. Since any move creates anxiety, and thus resistance, it is frequently better to keep two or three potential moves in mind, to be able to shift if resistance is too strong.

The first move the therapist tried with Francine was to have her tell Susan a little of what we'd talked about (the family triangles) and say that, while it would be hard for Francine, she thought Susan was right not to talk about Mary. Francine was going to keep her upset just between her and Mary.

In making the suggestion, the therapist has to remember that it is more like planting a seed that will bear fruit later than lighting a firecracker. The client will usually resist at first, so then you back off for a while and look at something else. This is what happened with Francine: It led to her refocusing on Mary, and a tirade about Susan not being a good daughter.

The other move was to invite Tom to come in for joint sessions. The purpose was to take advantage of their probably brief rapproachement and use Francine's stated goal of wanting all the family to be closer to introduce Tom to the therapy and see if some structural shifts could be made. I didn't have much hope for any shift to be made easily, but at least my including Tom might undercut Francine's tendency to ally with women against men.

Tom was rather as Francine described—brusk, opinionated, clearly used to being in charge, but also intelligent and well-meaning. We had two joint sessions, going over the patterns of their family life with emphasis on the very separate territories and distance between them the two had evolved and on the fact that Tom's relationships with his children were uniformly mediated through Francine—so much so that he rarely spoke to them directly and only saw them when Francine was present. Tom agreed that this was so, and we spoke of how difficult it must be for him to know what a father does, his own having left when he was eight years old. As Tom's own goal was to move closer to Francine and get the children more distanced, he didn't totally buy the idea that establishing his own relationship with his children would help the marriage, but said he'd do it. The homework was that he would initiate separate contact with Susan and John each week, however brief it might be. Francine's part was to put Tom on the phone when Susan called (after she'd finished her talk). The result was that Tom was saying "a few sentences" to Susan, but began a lot more contact with John.

Meanwhile, as Francine continued to pressure Susan about Mary, Susan told her mother she wouldn't talk to her anymore at all. It's always nice to have a prediction come true because it makes it hard for the client to continue resisting. So we dusted off the old suggestions (that Francine tell Susan she was right to not talk about Mary) and tried to predict what Susan's reaction to it might be. It is always difficult to be accurate in these predictions, especially on the first move, when you're not that clear how the system works. Francine thought Susan would just be shocked: "I never told her she was right before!" My guess was that Susan might unleash a flood of information about Mary, Susan being a bona fide family member too. So we planned that if that happened, Francine would interrupt her, thank her for wanting to help, but tell her she was right not to talk about it.

It turned out we were both wrong. Susan just replied, "Oh good," and changed the subject. But the grapevine worked because a few days later Mary called Francine. She was brief, explaining that she was depressed, that on the advice of her therapist she was spending more time with her husband and kids, and that she didn't want to talk about what happened because it would only start a fight. Francine handled it well on the phone, but boomeranged back emotionally to an intense refocus on Mary. With the reconnection, Tom and Francine's relationship deteriorated; they had a fight where Francine bitterly blamed him for Mary's depression and were now back to reactive silence.

As neither Tom nor Francine wanted to be in the same room with the other, we agreed that marital sessions would resume only after Francine was more "grown up" — defined as being able to tolerate upset in a relationship without becoming an angry, sulking child. We would shift to work on other relationships less toxic than the marital.

Middle Phase: Reweaving the Tapestry

It was important that Francine not start to "pile in" on Mary, and she was able to accept grudgingly that the best tack for now was to continue amiable, superficial conversations with her. The next sessions were spent coming to grips with a central family theme: Daughters are supposed to maintain their primary attachment to mothers, *not* husbands. Mary broke this tradition of who the "real" emotional couple should be by choosing her husband *instead* of her mother, thereby unbalancing the system. One therapy task was for Francine to figure out a way for mothers and daughters to be committed to husbands *and* families of origin *and* children — not to have to choose between them.

Meanwhile, Francine's irritation at John was increasing, and that provided the opportunity for us to work on her setting some limits with him. She didn't want John's girlfriend staying overnight anymore. Francine had no experience with taking an I-position. She had usually retreated into hurt, angry silence, in the belief that if John loved her he would know she didn't want it and would not do it. If angry withdrawal failed, she would launch a scathing attack or get Tom to be her mouthpiece, which served to cement his distant "bad guy" position with the children. The therapist needs to go slowly in preparing someone like Francine for a new position.

First she needed to be very clear about why the old way wouldn't work *for her*. Second, both therapist and client needed to understand what is feared by changing. Francine had two fears: that John's feelings would be hurt and he'd never speak to her again, and/or that he would refuse to obey, thereby "proving" that he didn't love her. Once the fears behind the anger are acknowledged, the client may see the extent to which responsibility for self is avoided by anger at the other.

Francine's homework was first to ask Tom for his backing and agreement with her that John should tell his girlfriend she could no longer stay overnight. The chances that he would not go along were very slim, as Tom wanted Francine to do less for the children. It also set the stage for a functional parental alliance for perhaps the first time in the marriage. The second part was for Francine herself to speak to John. We planned this very carefully: writing a script together about what she would say, predicting John's possible responses, and preparing what she would say in return. Francine's anxiety was high but she did it and it went smoothly. John agreed to her request, Tom even complimented her, and Francine got a taste of a new way to do things.

Along about this time fate lent a therapeutic hand in the form of a frantic phone call to Francine from her sister Nancy. Things had exploded over there: Either Francine had to take their father to live with her or Nancy was going to have him committed. This ended the five-year cutoff, and Francine's stockpile of hurt and anger at Nancy reemerged in the therapy. One source was the family money: Nancy's house was bought with, renovated with, and continued to be partially financed with Dad's money. This meant there would be no inheritance for Francine. Francine said in the therapy that it was Nancy's lying about it and pretending the house was earned through her own hard work that was the hurt. Of course, neither sister had ever talked directly to the other about either their mutual knowledge or their feelings about it. Another element of hurt in the sisterhood was an old rivalry as to which one had it toughest in life and, therefore, which one now deserved the most sympathy and attention. They had also been, before the cutoff, united in a rigid coalition against Tom.

The therapist's goal was for Francine to reconnect with Nancy without triangulation and without dumping her anger on her. Since Francine certainly didn't want her father living with her, and it was dishonor in this family to put him in a home, she was motivated. Now she had to finally face the "tyrant father" from whom she had been running.

The second phase of treatment had begun; therapy now moved to her family of origin, where it stayed for about nine months, with sessions usually every two or three weeks. In this system, Francine had always been on the outside of the dad-Nancy relationship, preferring to remain in her alliance with her mother. With dad she had been reactively distanced throughout her life, and much of the emotional glue in her relationship with Nancy had been through joining her against Tom.

The first goal was to have Francine move toward Nancy in a supportive rather than hostile and competitive way. To this end Francine was not to approach Nancy as an "older sister" (telling her what she was doing wrong with dad and giving advice on how to do it better), but to ask what kind of help she needed and attempt to give it. This was hard for Francine because, to her way of thinking, Nancy had it easier and should be helping her.

Francine was not to mention her anger or the cutoff to Nancy at all for now. The leverage for this intervention was provided by Francine's fear that she would have to take her father if Nancy wouldn't.

Francine did admirably. What Nancy wanted was for Francine to let her father "blow off steam" to her, so that Nancy didn't have to absorb it all. Francine spent many hours with her "dreaded" father and discovered that he was not as powerful as she'd feared.

Through being in the household Francine also got a better understanding of the price Nancy was paying for her father's financial help. This understanding made it possible to open up the toxic money issue in a healing way. Francine told Nancy that she had always known about the money and thought Nancy had earned every penny of it! The hardest part of opening it up for Francine was asking Nancy why she had been afraid to tell her. Nancy said she'd always been afraid because then Francine would get hurt and never speak to her again. This information was enormously important for Francine to hear. She had no inkling how powerful and intimidating her withdrawal into hurt cutoff was.

While she and Nancy were building bridges, Francine was getting bored with, rather than terrified by, her father's tirades against Nancy, herself, fate, etc. She was encouraged to be more active in shaping the conversation, rather than passively listening to it. Slowly she was able to interrupt him, asking him about his childhood and earlier years, and eventually letting him know how scared she'd been of him all her life. Their relationship couldn't be considered warm, since there had basically been no close prior ground to reestablish. But closeness was not the goal; the goal was for Francine to spend time with her dad without shrinking into a scared, hurt child. She finally even grew indifferent to wanting him to admit what a terrible father he had been to her and gained some understanding of what childhood and life forces had shaped her father into the person he was.

All shifts in families, even positive ones, create additional issues. The reconciliation with Nancy and her father, which included her sister-in-law as well, brought expectations on their part of once again getting together a couple of times a week. Francine, discovering that she didn't want that much time together anymore, had to face the very difficult issue in her enmeshed family of how to say "no," stay connected, and not precipitate a cutoff again. At this time in her therapy she chose her age-old solution of blaming it on Tom — she would love to but Tom "wouldn't let her."

Needless to say, Tom and Francine's extended family had had a 30-year history of mutual rancor. At the least, this time Francine understood the process: her own fear, and the problems of enmeshed systems. We were able to use Francine's trouble with negotiating Nancy's wanting to be "too" close as a parallel for Mary. Francine wanted to be "too" close to Mary, and Mary couldn't negotiate it any better than Francine could. So the women blamed it on the men instead.

It is hard to convey the flavor of multigenerational work. Reading this it may seem that things flow in a straight line, and we proceed with one issue at a time. That is rarely the case. The client will go back and forth between wanting to work on one issue rather than another and resisting work. In Francine's case this meant often sliding into using the therapy as a place to talk safely about her stockpile of hurts. Also, when the client does move in one direction, there are shifts occurring in the rest of the system. So the work, while reflecting core issues, fluctuates back and forth between one family member and another.

Thus, while Francine was able to keep focused on work with her sister/ father, she was much less reactive to Mary and Tom. Mary had, in the meantime, reestablished regular phone calls, and Francine was better able to tolerate the greater emotional distance between them. She was seeing her grandchildren again, and her own children had reestablished contact with their grandfather. Her son John had rented his own apartment nearby. Tom had a much closer relationship with him, and was also talking more to Susan. Francine's depression had lifted some months previously. The marital relationship was still very problematic, but not as intensely filled with bitter fights and silent wars. They had lived separate lives for 38 years of marriage: hadn't slept together for 15 years, didn't eat together, and had a pattern where Tom didn't even inform Francine when he was going out of town or to the hospital. Francine was speaking about wanting to work on more closeness in the marriage — soon, but not yet. We agreed on a three-month vacation from therapy before resuming work on her tightest relationships: with Mary and with Tom.

Final Phase: Three Months Later

The coaching on her relationship with Mary meant that Francine needed to take a serious look at the intensity of the bond between mothers and daughters in her family, where the primary commitment lay. Only after this was shifted would there be room in Francine's life for Tom. In reexamining her relationship with her own mother, Francine discovered a deep well of sadness that they had never been emotionally close, just overconnected. They had spend a lot of time together, but mostly working side by side. Francine felt they had never really known each other. She carried enormous resentment that her mother had so briskly sent her back to her husband when she left him early in their marriage. Francine was given the task of writing a letter to her mother — getting in touch first with her anger, and later with her sadness at missed opportunities in the relationship. The expression of anger at her mother was very difficult for Francine, and it took some weeks for her to make a start at it. Eventually, Francine wrote a final version of her letter, where her feelings were more at peace. The culmination of her coaching work here was for her to go alone to the cemetery and read her letter to her mother. In this way she began finally to mourn her mother's death.

Now that Francine no longer sought an unrealistic mother-daughter relationship, it seemed a good time to approach Mary. Francine gave thought to what she expected from her daughter, and much to her surprise it turned out to be not that much. Basically she wanted them to exchange family news, feel comfortable dropping in every week or so, spend some time at holidays together, and principally learn how to say "no" to each other directly. Francine sent this off in a letter, and Mary responded by a drop-in visit three weeks later. While they both agreed it was better not to talk about the past yet, they began to make plans for a family Thanksgiving. They were still walking on eggs with each other, but a new process had begun.

We took another break from the therapy here. It was clear to Francine that, even though she felt more comfortable in the marriage, there were still problems that needed addressing.

A year and a half elapsed before I heard from Francine again. The children had taken the position that, while they would be happy to see each parent separately, they were not willing to endure the cold wars and running power struggles when both parents were together. This meant no gatherings as a family, putting great pressure on Tom and Francine to do something different. As of this writing, they have been in couples therapy for two months, with the work going slowly but well.

CONCLUSION

The hope in writing this chapter is to convey a sense that, far from being invisible and hopeless relics, people in the later life stage continue to be engaged in the same processes and shifts as everyone else: how to derive meaning from life and relationships, how to be connected to others and independent, and how to rework generational ties and boundaries as the family moves through time. They bring a lifetime of experience to the therapy, and a perspective not yet evolved in younger generations on what's important and what's not. Perhaps on some level we agreed with Leonard Sagan (1988), who postulates that the increase in human longevity is due not to medical advances, but to a decrease in daily life stress and an increase in the nurturance and support provided by family relationships. Good health, he states, "is as much a social and psychological achievement as a physical one, and the preservation of the family is not (only) a moral issue but a medical one."

REFERENCES

Brody, E. (1985). Parent care as a normative family stress. *The Gerontologist, 25(1)*, 19–29.

Gatz, M. & Pearson, C. (1988). Ageism revised and the provision of psychological services. *American Psychologist, 43(3)*, 184–188.

Halpern, J. (1988). The reluctant caretaker. In R. Simon (Ed.), *Family Therapy Networker, 12(4)*, 43–46.

Herz Brown, F. (1989). The impact of death and serious illness on the family life cycle. In E. Carter & M. McGoldrick (Eds.), *The changing family life cycle* (2nd ed.) (pp. 457–482). Boston: Allyn & Bacon.

McGoldrick, M., Pearce, J. K. & Giordano, J. (Eds.). (1982). *Ethnicity and family therapy*. New York: Guilford.

Roybal, J. (1988). Mental health and aging. *American Psychologist, 43(3)*, 189–194.

Sagan, L. (1988). Family ties. *The Sciences, Mar/Apr*, 20–29, New York Academy of Sciences.

Silverstein, B., & Hyman, H. (1982). *You and your aging parent*. New York: Pantheon Books.

Walsh, F. (1989). The family in later life. In B. Carter & M. McGoldrick (Eds.), *The changing family life cycle* (2nd ed.) (pp. 311–332). Boston: Allyn & Bacon.

❧ III ❧

WORKING WITH FAMILIES
WITH DISRUPTIONS IN
THE LIFE CYCLE

Families in the Divorce and Post-divorce Process

JUDITH STERN PECK

FREDDA HERZ BROWN

DIVORCE INTERFERES WITH the flow of family through its life cycle (Carter & McGoldrick, 1980, 1989a, b; Herz Brown, 1989; Peck, 1988/89). We believe that the process begins when one of the spouses starts to think about the possibility of divorce and continues through five or six more stages, until it ends, usually three to five years later, when the family has reorganized into whatever form works for it (Ahrons, 1980; Herz Brown, 1989; Hetherington, Cox, & Cox, 1977).

Divorce creates a crisis in the family life cycle—a state of disequilibrium experienced by all members throughout the nuclear and extended family system (Peck, 1988/89; Peck & Manocherian, 1989). The process continues through a series of stages that require varying tasks by the family. As a result, marriage, divorce, a single-parent household, and/or remarriage are simply points on a continuum for most families.

The divorce process intersects with the family's life cycle, and each ensuing life cycle phase is affected by this, thus creating a multitude of complex and far-reaching issues. Therefore, subsequent symptoms in all family members must be viewed within the dual context of the stage itself and the residual effects of the divorce experience (Carter & McGoldrick, 1980; Wal-

The authors shared equally in the writing of this chapter. The order of authorship was decided by a flip of the coin.

lerstein & Kelly, 1980), in addition to the impact of future shifts in the family system.

The first three stages of the divorce process encompass (1) the decision-making process, (2) the ability to begin to articulate the reasons for the dissolution of the marriage, and (3) the planning for the actual separation (Ahrons & Rodgers, 1987; Carter & McGoldrick, 1989b). The stages that follow require redefinition and reorganization for the family, including shifts in boundaries, roles, and membership of the entire system; it is usually during these stages that families confront difficulties in stabilizing and re-aligning.

For the family experiencing divorce, there are tasks to be mastered in addition to the usual tasks involved in growing up in a family (Carter & McGoldrick, 1989b). The accomplishment of these additional tasks takes time, and frequently families experience their normal life as a state of suspended animation in terms of progress through the life cycle. From the authors' clinical experience, there appears to be little that the family or the clinician can do to speed up the process, which seems to move at its own rate. However, there are numerous things that the family can do to handle the process and make the reorganization work more smoothly.

In addition to understanding family emotional process in general, clients seeking help in a divorce situation must also begin to understand the emotional process of divorce and how to negotiate it so that they can get back on track with the least amount of upset in their lives. In our clinical experience, we have found that understanding the interplay of the divorce process with the family's emotional process allows for a more comprehensive clinical assessment to determine an appropriate treatment plan. Most families present themselves post-divorce and we view this as part of the last stages of the divorce process.

INTRODUCTION TO FAMILY

Josie appeared for treatment complaining that her son and daughter were acting up, not obeying curfews, and generally getting into trouble with their friends. Although the trouble was not serious, it was enough that, with her impending remarriage, Josie was feeling overwhelmed (see Figure 13.1). Kevin, 11 years of age, and Jane, 13, both felt that their mother had not been spending enough time with them since her relationship with Peter had become serious and Peter had begun living with the family, a year and a half earlier. Since that time, both Kevin and Jane thought that Peter had started to take over in disciplining them, telling them what to do or not do. They felt that their mother said little to Peter about what she thought should happen with the kids. They both felt resentful of Peter's interference in their lives.

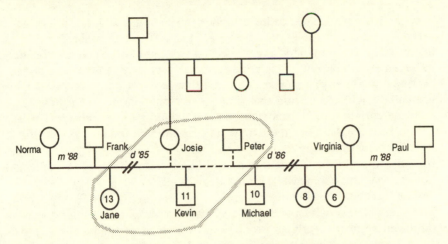

FIGURE 13.1   The Taylor Family

Even though they liked him a lot, they felt that he was not respectful of the fact that they had been a family before he came into their lives.

Jane had gotten to the point that she was threatening to live with her father, even though that meant moving away from her long-term friends. Kevin did not want to move, but was continually in a battle with Peter; he seemed very much connected to his mother and yet caught in his allegiance to his older, parental sibling, who was pushing him to come with her to their father's. Amidst the children's rapid talk, Josie just looked perplexed about what to do and what to say. She frequently looked at the therapist as if to say, "Help!"

Divorce is common in families with young children, and dealing with it during this life-cycle phase is different from dealing with divorce when the couple is in early marriage or after the children have been launched — the other two most frequent times for divorce (Glick, 1984). One needs to go back to the time of the actual separation to understand how relationships shifted. At the same time, one cannot jump into assisting the adults in achieving an emotional divorce, the process that identifies the emotions connected to the breakup of the old marriage, without first paying attention to the current state of the children in relation to both their parents (Goldsmith, 1982).

In this instance, it is clear that the children are viewed as the presenting problem, and their relationship to the rest of the system is important to explore with the family. We begin with issues of membership roles and boundaries.

In the initial phone call, Josie had talked only of the problems she was having with her children and never mentioned the relationship with Peter.

Had the therapist known of his presence in the household, she might have asked him to be at the initial interview. It is difficult to make the clinical decision about whom to include in the first session with a remarried (or soon to be remarried) family. To include Peter would have helped the therapist see firsthand the family's struggles. On the other hand, it would probably have prevented the children from speaking up so frankly about their difficulties with the current family constellation and dynamics. In his absence, it was possible for the therapist to see how the single-parent household functioned without "a man," taking into consideration that this family had transitioned from divorce to a single-parent household and was on its way to a remarried one and was stuck somewhere in that transition.

The therapist was able to explore the functioning of the family for the four years following the parental divorce and to see what triangles may have stabilized during the early disaster phases of divorce, the phase referred to as "the aftermath." The relationship of the children to their father and the mother's relationship with her ex-husband were also explored. The openness of the system was further examined by exploring the family's relationship with both extended families. The therapist noted which triangles had rigidified and began to formulate a hypothesis for future work with this family.

Josie stated that she frequently spoke with her ex-husband regarding the children's welfare. He was living one town away from their household, with his new wife, Norma. The children maintained weekly visitation with their father. Throughout the separation and divorce, Josie had called Frank to help with the children when they became too much for her. When asked how frequently that would happen, she said that at least once a week one of the kids would not listen to her and she would then call Frank, who would either discuss the difficulty with the child on the phone or, if it could not be settled in that way, come over to the house. When asked if this was still occurring, Josie said that it had begun to stop when Frank's wife began to complain of his frequent visits. This had happened about one year ago. Josie felt upset by this, but also felt that it had given Peter a chance to become a member of the household; she then increasingly involved Peter in the disciplining of the children. The therapist noted the timing of entry into and exiting from the process on the part of the two men.

Josie had maintained contact with her ex-husband's extended family, making sure that the children visited their paternal grandparents regularly. The grandparents also felt comfortable calling the children at Josie's home, as well as their father's home. Josie had infrequent contact with her own family; she stated that she found them generally unhelpful in her separation and divorce. She was unable to ask them for much help with family matters, since they—especially her mother—used such requests as opportunities to criticize her way of handling her life and her children. While she wished that she could be closer to them, she was unwilling to open herself up to their criticism; initiating a phone call to her mother inevitably made her feel worse rather than better.

In evaluating a family coming to treatment in some stage of the divorce process, it is important to examine how family members have moved through that process up to the present time and how they have negotiated the specific tasks of each stage. Current difficulties are frequently related to the family's failure to negotiate an earlier task of the process (Carter & McGoldrick, 1980, 1989a, b). In this case, it was becoming clear to the interviewer that the Taylor family had never truly reorganized as a single-parent household able to function on its own (Herz Brown, 1989). This is one of the critical tasks of a single-parent household—to manage as one.

Earlier, in order to cope with the immense pressures of raising two children alone and going to work for the first time, Josie understandably relied on, first, her ex-husband, and then, her soon-to-be new husband, to deal with the children. Her daughter, Jane, functioned as a parental child who helped raise her sibling brother while her mother went to work. Certainly, one could expect that Jane would help her mother; after all, older children do help with younger ones. However, when the child acts to take a burden off the mother (or father), without the parent's ongoing direction or charge, we see the beginnings of difficulties for the family. When this happens, the child begins to serve a quasi-parenting function for the parent, as well as for the other child or children. Older children thus burdened frequently do not experience or ask for any caretaking themselves, and their contact with the parent centers around the reporting of caretaking responsibilities.

Meanwhile, the other child or children may have little direct access to the parent, and the parent who initially and realistically felt overwhelmed with the divorce now has fewer and fewer functions to carry out with the children; this only serves to increase the parent's ongoing sense of not being able to manage on his/her own. What starts out to be helpful during one phase becomes part of the problem during another phase.

Until now, we have not seen Jane's functioning as the parental child in any manifestation other than her pull on her brother to come with her to their father's, rather than stay with their mother. She seems to be in somewhat of a competitive relationship with her mother, if not with Peter. To get a clearer sense of how things worked at home, the therapist asked how the family conducts a typical day. It was Jane rather than Josie who answered.

Jane described how she awakens not only her brother but her mother, who often oversleeps. "Mother usually rushes out the door to get to work on time, and I make breakfast for Kevin and me," Jane said. Kevin chimed in that he hates what his sister makes and that she frequently hollers at him for his tardiness. After school, both children are involved in extracurricular activities and arrive home about an hour before their mother does. Josie makes dinner, with the children assisting in setting the table and making the salad.

Josie reported that she spent a good deal of her time getting the children to stop annoying each other. When asked to describe how this went, Josie said that Jane was always trying to be helpful by telling Kevin what to do; Kevin objected, and a fight broke out between them, with Kevin teasing Jane and Jane yelling back or poking him.

Josie said that she wished that they would stop and that she had tried sending them both to their rooms, but that Kevin was usually so wound up by that time that he continued to harass Jane from his room, across the hall from hers. Before Peter's presence in the house, Josie would eventually get angry enough to punish both kids.

Now it seemed that Peter would arrive home just as Josie sent the children to their rooms, and he would get annoyed as the noise continued. When asked what she would do now, Josie stated that she would tell Peter to go up and change for dinner, but he would find that hard to do without stopping along the way to discipline the children further. Josie added that, when Peter's kids would arrive, every Wednesday and every other weekend, matters got even worse, with all five children involved in the dinnertime shenanigans.

When this happened, Jane would refuse to respond to their mother's request that she make the rest of the children stop their antics. Peter's children were six, eight, and ten years of age. The scene appeared to be quite chaotic.

It was clear that Josie had relied on Jane a great deal over the course of the separation and divorce for the normal functioning of the household. Jane had been more than willing to help her mother out — first, because she sensed that her mother needed assistance, and second, because she was struggling herself to develop an appropriate role with her mother, since she had always been "daddy's girl."

While the role of parental child has some power, it certainly lacks authority. Thus, it is not unexpected that Jane either struggles with getting the kids to listen or refuses to help mother with them. While her power is in her direct access to her mother, her relationship with the other children is hampered; she becomes a child who is not a child, nor is she a parent. She has no place on either side of the generational boundary and may in fact begin to struggle with Peter for his position.

In this instance, Jane is at least able to maintain her position as the oldest child when Peter's children arrive. Just imagine the struggle that might ensue for Jane if Peter's oldest child were older than she. If that were the case, the only potential solution would be for Jane to become "buddies" with the child and less interested in being involved with the other children's lives.

Jane needs the opportunity to be a child in the current family structure, or she will continue to threaten to leave or actually leave. Such a move would only solidify the family difficulties, as much more effort would have to go into resolving the mother-daughter issues. Josie, meanwhile, needs the opportunity to view herself as capable of functioning with or without the assistance of a man.

The therapist checked on how the family was doing in other areas of life—school, work, friends, and of course, extended family. She began by asking Josie about her children's school lives.

THERAPIST: Josie, how are the children doing in school?

JOSIE: I think they are doing okay. Jane is a very good student, but she is the class busybody. Kevin has more difficulties in school than this sister. He doesn't like to do his homework and often fools around in class. He is a real smart kid, though . . .

JANE: You don't make sure that he does his homework. He gets away with murder with you. He doesn't do his homework, and you don't do anything to him. You'd "kill" me if I did what he does. (It certainly is clear who knows what is going on!)

KEVIN: That's not true. Mom, tell her to be quiet. I do my work.

THERAPIST: How do you usually deal with them at home when they begin to banter back and forth like they are now?

JOSIE: I send them to their rooms.

THERAPIST: Both of them? (Mom shakes her head yes.) That's great. Do they go? (Again yes from Mom.) And how long do they have to stay there?

JOSIE: I usually have them stay there for half an hour. That seems long enough for them to calm down. I just wish that Jane would stop interfering with Kevin. Then I wouldn't have to send either of them to their rooms and I could deal with Kevin's lack of schoolwork. As it is, by the time they come out of their rooms and we eat dinner, I have totally forgotten the reason for their being sent there in the first place.

THERAPIST: Kids certainly have a way of doing that kind of thing to us busy parents. How were you as a kid, Josie?

JOSIE: I was a good kid. I was the oldest of four children; I had a younger sister and two younger brothers. I took care of them all. Mom worked with dad in the store and I took care of my siblings for as long as I can remember. I made sure that they did their homework and their housework. Of course, they didn't always want to listen to me, so we would fight and I would always get held responsible for anything that wasn't done. My brothers hated school and refused to do their homework. I was always struggling with them, and mom was always telling me that I had to get them to do better. I swore that I wasn't going to do that with my children, and I don't want to, but somehow it is happening without my understanding how. When I was a kid, my mother would get so angry at me and I would feel terrible for not being better able to help her. Dad would always be on my side. He would always tell mom to go easy on me — that it wasn't my fault that the boys wouldn't listen. But neither of them would ever tell the kids to get into shape.

As is true in many instances, the things that we try the hardest not to repeat become part of our ongoing life. According to Bowenian theory, patterns and themes are often repeated in families. Here, Josie reveals that she once basically functioned in a role similar to her daughter's; it is clear that she will understand the dilemmas posed for her daughter when the therapist guides her to do so. She tries not to do what her parents did in terms of their expectations of her caretaking; she claims, at least, that she wants Jane to stop interfering with Kevin so that she will be able to deal with him. Although one might argue that she is ambivalent about this desire, it is certainly a strength which the therapist should encourage.

It is also clear that this single-parent household has not accomplished the tasks necessary to move on to the phase of remarriage (Ahrons & Rodgers, 1987; McGoldrick & Carter, 1989b). In order to do so, the family must be able to function as a household unto itself without the ongoing experience of a power gap in its functioning. Otherwise Peter is likely to fall into the trap of trying to close the gap in the family functioning. Since he is a newcomer to the system, it will be an impossible task. He will run headlong into Jane's (or Kevin's) resistance to the idea. It is really up to Josie to deal with the issues related to her children until Peter has earned the right to deal with them.

We often tell stepparents that initially they will do better if they perceive themselves as an aunt or uncle, and that they will have earned the right to deal with child-related issues when the children have reached double the age they are when the stepparent enters the scene. It may be an exaggeration, but it serves to make the point that kids do not readily accept another adult trying to act like their parent. They are more likely to accept that adult initially functioning as their friend and gradually earning the right to discipline them (McGoldrick & Carter, 1989b).

In this family, Jane has stabilized the family's functioning by her position as the parental child; she has become part of a triangle consisting of herself, her mother, and her brother, which serves to keep her brother behaving the way he does. It also keeps Jane necessary in the family's functioning and mom feeling overwhelmed by the family dynamics. This is basically a single-parent household in the stage of realignment, struggling to move on toward stabilization, the next phase. The stabilization cannot come from the remarriage, however, or matters will be made more difficult for everyone.

THERAPIST: So you didn't find your role/job in your childhood family to be something that you could do. Do you know how your daughter got a similar role in this family?

JOSIE: Now that you mention it, she does have a very similar role. I guess she got it because after the divorce I was totally overwhelmed by the idea of raising the kids alone and having to find a job to support us. I had not worked since the children were born and had had no intention of beginning until Kevin got out of junior high school. I was shocked when their father told me that he was in love with someone else and that he was moving out of the house. It took me months of work and upset to settle into the idea that I would be doing this alone. During this time, Jane was very helpful. Even though she was only nine years old, she was more than willing to help out. In fact, she did so without my asking her. It was such a relief in the beginning, I didn't stop to ask how come she seemed able to do so — what was going on with her . . .

During the first phase after separation, "the aftermath," family members struggle with the immense disruption that they feel to their ongoing life (Herz Brown, 1989). Often, as in this family, some relationships are established whose major focus is organizing the system. Problems begin when these relationships become permanently realigned in a triangle during the second phase, called "realignment" (Herz Brown, 1989).

In order for therapy to assist Josie and her children, the family must be able to move forward without its functioning being impeded by triangles. With the current structure, adding a new person only adds another potential triangle to the system. If the current structure is changed so that the mother can be the head of her household and the children free to be children, then the addition of a new person adds to the complexity and the richness of the system but not to the dysfunction.

Just as becoming a new household occurs in stages, so does therapy; let's follow the therapeutic process from stage 1 to stage 3.

TREATMENT

Stage 1: Defining and Working on the Foreground

During the first stage of treatment, the therapeutic goals are to stay relevant to the presenting problem and, at the same time, to place it in a context that is broad and systemic enough to enable the family to work on multigenerational issues. In this case, it is important to see the problem with Jane and Kevin as related both to their life-cycle phase and also to the additional stressors of divorce and remarriage on their lives. One has to embed the presenting problem not only in the context of the developmental process, but also in the context of the divorce process. This includes a redefinition that involves nuclear family process and extended family process; in addition, these systems have been expanded to include several households — the children's father's home and Peter's children's home.

It is important to start where family members are, in terms of their definition of the problem. In this instance, the mother has defined the problem to include her children's fighting, which results (in our redefinition) from her daughter's trying to intervene between her mother and her brother. This triangle is the one that is keeping the behavioral symptoms active in the family (see Figure 13.2).

There are several other interlocking triangles that serve to keep this one active. The first involves mother, father, and daughter, whereby the father's ongoing involvement in the mother's household helps to keep the children behaving as they do (see Figure 13.2). As long as they behave as they do, and as long as the mother or the daughter informs him of the goings-on, he will stay involved as if it were still a two-parent household. This is a fairly common triangle in single-parent post-divorce situations; usually it is the father's girlfriend or new wife who begins to put a stop to it, much as Norma did in this case.

In this case, being willing to take his daughter from the mother's household is one way the father, Frank, shows his involvement with the children. It is also a way of inadvertently undermining the mother's sense of power with the children. Every time Josie tries to get things straightened out, Jane runs to call her dad to complain. When asked if she has talked to Frank about this difficulty, Josie says that she hasn't.

The ability of Frank and Josie to co-parent after their divorce is essential if the children are to feel that both parents care about them (Goldsmith, 1980). When the balance is such that dad is called constantly, we see the undermining of mom's competence. It is clear to the therapist that having a

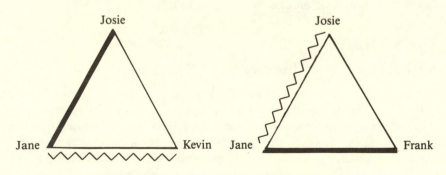

FIGURE 13.2   The Nuclear Family Triangles

session with Frank and Josie might be very useful later on, but the timing would be everything, because moving too quickly might make the mother feel less rather than more powerful with the situation. Therefore, it was decided that initially the work with Josie would include her taking control of the situation with Frank. There was evidence that she would be able to do this, based on some of her comments regarding his support of her with the children.

Other triangles that interlock with the two that have been described involve Peter. The first has to do with Peter's relationship to the children vis-à-vis his and their relationship to Josie (see Figure 13.3). Peter feels that he must help Josie control the children; the kids resent this. This situation places Peter in a bad position and eventually leads to fights between him and Josie. It is clear that Peter's involvement in the therapy process will be important.

A second triangle involving Peter has to do with Josie's children feeling caught between letting him into their lives and retaining their loyalty to their father (see Figure 13.3). They clearly like Peter but hesitate to accept him as a member of their household. Loyalty is always a factor in the relationships that children have toward the new adults in their parents' lives.

Peter's relationship with his own children must also be suffering from the same kinds of loyalty questions, with his kids questioning how loyal he is to them when he lives with these two other children. We have seen children test their parents' "loyalty" by continually setting up situations — ongoing loyalty battles — in which their parents are asked to choose between their own children and their stepchildren.

Added to these already important triangles are the extended family triangles, which serve to further rigidify this situation. Josie's relationship to her parents is based on her continued sense of incompetence vis-à-vis her children. It continues to allow them to interact with her in a familiar way. Josie is expected to care for them and not be in need of any caretaking herself.

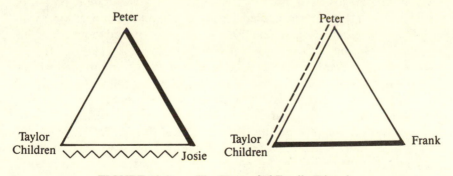

FIGURE 13.3   The Remarried Family Triangle

Asking for their help only confirms her parents' view that she can't manage her children and that she as a woman should have been able to keep the marriage together.

It is fairly common in our experience that women encounter this kind of gender-based reaction from their mothers, who have struggled for years to keep their own marriages together. A divorce in their children's marriage brings into question all the issues, costs, and rewards of staying in their own marriages. In addition, divorce raises the question of a different relationship with one's grandchildren and one's son- or daughter-in-law. It is also difficult for the older generation to deal with the increasing financial costs, as it is not unusual for the adult children and their children to go to live with the grandparents for some period of time or to rely on them financially.

What, then, is one to do with this complex, very interconnected situation, in which the presenting problem is embedded in many interlocking triangles, all of which crisscross through the emotional divorce and extended family process? In our experience it is better for the therapist to move simply in ways that will increase the mother's sense of power over her situation. Unless she is empowered the therapist will fall into the trap of acting like another caretaker telling her what to do or doing it for her.

In this situation, Josie was applauded for her sensitivity to the children's needs, especially her daughter's need to be a teenager rather than a parentified child. It was suggested that the way she was keeping Jane from dealing with Kevin was excellent and that, in fact, what she needed was her ex-husband's support in the process. We asked if she could call Frank and enlist his assistance in helping Jane to act like a teenager.

We checked out these needs with Jane, who assured the therapist and her mother that she did not want to deal with her brother, that she wanted to be free to go out with her friends. Asked if she thought it would be helpful to have her father's support in this, she agreed. Josie was to call Frank and ask him to direct Jane back to her when she called him with complaints about Kevin and Josie. Josie was also to suggest that Frank spend more time with Jane, since as a teenager she needed her father's input in her decisions; with all his having to help Josie, he hadn't had the opportunity to give Jane his individual attention.

Josie thought Frank would love the idea, and she was more than willing to call him. She also made it clear to her daughter that she understood how hard the process of divorce had been on her and assured her that she was ready to be even more of a parent than she had been up to this point. Jane expressed her doubt that her mother would be able to do so. With the therapist's encouragement, Josie assured Jane that she was certainly going to try, and that she needed for Jane to give her a chance. Josie also expressed her desire to spend more time with Jane in ways that were not oriented around things to do about the house. Jane and she agreed on some time together that was to be their special time outside of the house. Josie suggested that Kevin could use some time with his father, and Kevin readily agreed.

While the therapeutic aim was mainly to deal with the nuclear family triangle among mother, daughter, and son, it was clear that in order to do that it was important to understand the other triangles that interlocked with this one. The intervention would serve to help the therapist assess the ability of this family to shift in response to the shifting life-cycle and membership issues.

Josie came into the therapist's office with Kevin and Jane, announcing that the last two weeks had been the calmest weeks she had enjoyed with her children since her separation from Frank. She had spoken to Frank about not responding to Jane's complaints about Kevin. Frank had complied, and indeed, on two occasions when Jane had called her father because Kevin was not attending to his homework or he had created some other mischief in the house, Frank had told his daughter that she needed to speak to her mother about these things because, after all, she was living in her mother's household and her mother was quite capable of handling the problem.

Josie went on to tell the therapist that her conversation with Frank had been enlightening to her. Frank had always thought that Josie wanted his support from the outside. As he understood it, he was being helpful to her in managing the children. He also told Josie that he always felt she was much more capable than he in managing the children. After all, she had had so much experience with her own family, and he had counted on her for so much, based on that history.

Needless to say, Josie was quite taken aback by Frank's commentary. She had never realized how much he respected her parenting skills. Josie reported that initially she had needed Frank's support, but at some point she had begun to experience his "help" as more of an undermining of her handling of the children. She had never recognized it as such until the last time she and the children had been in the therapist's office and the therapist had commented on Josie's sensitivity to her children's needs and her capacity to be responsive to them. It had been at that moment and in reflection later that Josie had realized that, once the initial crisis of the divorce had ended for her, she had never disengaged from the initial pattern that had been set up with Frank and her and the children. She realized that she was quite capable of disciplining the children; after all, when she was married, she had been the one in charge most of the time.

Josie went on to tell the therapist how helpful it had been to think about the divorce in stages and how her response to that approach had been very positive. She had always felt guilty for her feelings after the separation and her need to call upon her daughter and her ex-husband to help her out during that time of crisis. Once she had gotten through that difficult period, she never knew how to get back on track with her children, how to get Jane to take a step backwards and be a child again. She realized how caught she had gotten in these patterns with all the people in her life. Her greatest concern now was how to maintain the newer pattern she was beginning to establish with Frank and Jane, as well as how to deal with Peter.

Josie was concerned that, if she asked Peter to stay out of her struggles with her children, he would not feel a part of their household. Before moving on to the issues around the potential remarried family, the therapist questioned Josie about her children's views. Jane started to respond, but Josie interrupted her and answered the therapist's question. She then signaled to Jane that it was her turn to speak. This was a decidedly different interaction from that of the previous visit, when Jane independently responded to the therapist's queries. Josie was clearly feeling much more in charge of her family. The therapist continued to check on daily routines to reconfirm her sense that Josie indeed was experiencing herself as competent and capable of handling her household without always calling upon an outsider to help her.

In the Taylor family, it did not take a major intervention to begin the process of stabilizing the current family organization. This does not occur so smoothly in most families we have seen. At some level, the mother had been disturbed by what had been happening to her. She had not been able to articulate or define it for herself. She was now quite confirmed in her belief that she could handle her children and her job. Her major focus became her new relationship and the integration of Peter into their family life. She understood that she and her children were a unit with boundaries that she had allowed to be too permeable. She didn't want that to happen again, and she was grateful that she had been able to come to therapy.

The problem had been redefined from the children's behavior to her handling of the various transitions in the divorce, single-parent, and remarriage process. The intersection of the shifting family life cycle from young children to adolescents and the unfinished divorcing process had revealed the potential collision course for the Taylor family. The first two triangles had been addressed successfully. Mother had moved back into her parenting role, using friends, Peter, and ex-husband Frank when needed for counsel. Frank had agreed to spend time alone with Jane so that she did not need to go to him with Kevin's problems to get his attention. Frank and Josie had realigned as co-parents.

The other issue that needed more time was Josie's ability to maintain her new position. The feelings of incompetence that she brought with her from her own childhood experience with her siblings could potentially interfere with the process. While the first intervention had redefined the presenting problem and calmed down the family system, the central theme for Josie remained her challenge to maintain her level of competence in her single-parent household and her ability to create a context in which her children would continue on their developmental track. The next task for the therapist was to address the triangle operating with Peter, Josie, and the children. The therapist also thought that a phone call to Frank or an invitation for him to call her was in order.

THERAPIST: Josie, you seem to be quite comfortable with your ability to handle the children's day-to-day problems and your knowing when to call on Frank for help.

JOSIE: I feel quite good about that. The fighting has really stopped, for the most part, except when Peter is around. I haven't quite figured out what that is all about. Jane doesn't call her father anymore to complain about Kevin, and she and I are spending more time together doing fun activities.

JANE: Except when Peter is around. Somehow, when he enters the scene, things get all messed up again. Maybe he just shouldn't be around.

KEVIN: Jane, don't say that! You know how upset mom gets when you suggest that. He's not a bad guy. I kind of like having him around. He's the only one who knows anything about sports that I can talk to!

JANE: I don't care about you and your sports. I don't like his being there, and furthermore, I can't stand it when his kids come to visit. They invade our house.

JOSIE: Kevin, Jane, stop fighting!

THERAPIST: I guess they haven't given up fighting altogether. There are still some things that we all need to talk about. It seems like it might be good if you agree for me to meet Peter. Perhaps the three of us could meet next time.

JOSIE: I think that is a good idea. He was wondering when he would get to meet you. Oh, as you suggested, I also told Frank that the children and I had come to see you, and he said that he would be available if and when you felt he could be helpful.

THERAPIST: For the time being, judging from the kids' fight, I believe it might be better to talk with everyone who currently lives in your home first. I do think I'll call Frank and set an appointment with him in about two weeks. Meanwhile, let's set up a tentative date that you can check with Peter, and Jane and Kevin can meet again with mom after that.

The boundaries have been redefined in this intervention. The presenting problem surfaced in the mother's household, and it is important to stay with

that subsystem initially. The initial intervention served to create the necessary boundary by redefining Frank's role. His willingness to come in and
hers to have him are reflective of his involvement vis-à-vis the children. Since
the central issue is to help Josie with her household, the clinical choice at
this time seems to be to address the third triangle noted in the evaluation
session—Peter, Josie, and the children.

Although the therapist attempted to define Peter's role in the first interview, it will now be important for him to become involved. Peter's perceptions of what occurs in the household will be very useful. The issues of
membership, roles, and boundaries are all so ambiguous in a post-divorce
family that considerable confusion can be created for the therapist. The
therapist needs to investigate the issues around Peter's divorce and his extended family. Josie appears to have recaptured her strength for parenting
without the constant assistance of Frank, and it appears that Peter may be
drawn into the same position as Frank's.

Peter tells the therapist how pleased he is to have the opportunity to shed
light on what he sees happening in the Taylor household. He starts out by
agreeing with the children's view, saying that Josie appears to be much more
in charge of things until he walks through the door. He doesn't know what it
is all about, and he certainly hopes that the therapist will be able to help.

He describes a sense of being drawn like a magnet into getting involved
between Josie and her children. Although he has become involved with the
children, he experiences himself as always disciplining them. The only time
he experiences himself as relating is when he and Kevin talk about sports or
watch a game together. He goes on to describe the havoc that occurs when
his children enter the scene. He has begun to dread those weekends with all
five of the children together. He had thought that they would be like the
Brady Bunch—if only it were so!

Peter goes on to say that he has never been to a therapist before and never
believed that he would be looking for advice. He had always lived his life
without seeking help from others. His parents had imbued in him a sense of
confidence that he could make decisions and act on them. He had learned
early in his life that you make mistakes, you fall down, and then you get up.

When he discovered that he had made a mistake in his first marriage, he
decided unilaterally to get out. He did not need to seek anyone's advice. His
children seemed to be doing fine until he moved into Josie's home. It was
right after that that they started acting up with him. He had even said to
Josie a while back that he was contemplating moving out, but then he
thought about that and felt as if his children were ruling his life. It all felt
very muddled to him. When Josie had told him how helpful the initial
session with the therapist had been, he had decided to join her. He figured

that maybe one session would help him deal with his and Josie's children better.

It is clear that Peter never thought he would be in therapy, and that he is a man used to solving his own problems. The therapist would be trapped if she attempted to tell Peter what to do. She anticipates that Peter would be quite defiant, given the hint of how he has always made his own decisions. Instead of tackling him head on, she decides to offer Peter some reading materials she has in her office and to encourage him to return to discuss the materials.

The challenge for the therapist is to get Peter out from between Josie and her children, so that Josie can continue to manage her children. Additional tasks are to address the loyalty conflicts that surface with Peter, his children, and Josie's children, as well as the conflicts that Jane and Kevin feel as Peter becomes more involved in their lives.

THERAPIST: It sounds as though you, like others in your position, are really feeling muddled about this, Peter. Tell me some more about how you decided to get divorced and how that has been for you and your family.

PETER: Three years ago, I decided to leave my wife. My youngest child was three years old, and I figured that Virginia could handle things without me. Our marriage had deteriorated right after our oldest son was born. Virginia kept wanting me to go to a marriage counselor, but I refused. I've always been one to fix my own problems. I wasn't having an affair or anything like that, I was just terribly unhappy in this marriage. She just didn't seem to love me anymore, once the kids started coming. She always asked me to help with the kids, with disciplining them, taking them to the playground, picking them up from friends. I began to feel like a babysitter.

THERAPIST: Does it ever feel like that when you discipline Kevin and Jane?

PETER: Not really. You see, the difference is that Josie doesn't try to tell me what to do. Virginia always told me what to do with the kids and what to say to them. With Josie's children, I just do what I think will help Josie. She seems to need my support, whereas Virginia made me feel like a babysitter. Virginia even tries to tell me what do when the children come to our house. My own kids say to me, "Mommy said that you should. . . . " It drives me crazy. It feels like more of why I got out of the marriage.

THERAPIST: So if Josie were to tell you what she wanted you to do vis-à-vis her kids, it might seem like the old days with Virginia?

PETER: I'm not sure what you mean by that.

JOSIE: I think she's trying to point out to me that it would be hard for me to tell you what you should or should not do with Kevin and Jane. If I did, it might bring back the old feelings you had with Virginia, and you might be out the door without ever talking to me about it. (To therapist:) I guess you are right. I never realized that before. Peter has always made that point so clear every time he talks about Virginia that I go overboard the other way in never saying anything to him about what he says or does with the children. I love Peter so much, I don't want to lose him, and yet I cannot stand what happens with Kevin and Jane when he walks through the door. I know he means well, but he tries to act like their father, and that just doesn't work for them or for me.

PETER: I am totally confused. Josie, you've told me often how helpful it is to you to have me around the children.

JOSIE: Peter, that's true, but I'm beginning to realize that it's good to have you there as another adult to talk with, not one who takes so much of the responsibility.

THERAPIST: Perhaps, Peter, it would be helpful if I repeated some of the things I said to Josie about the role a stepparent can play initially . . .

As so often happens in remarried families, the roles are unclear and become even more ambiguous when overshadowed by issues from other experiences, either in a previous marriage or in an extended family (McGoldrick & Carter, 1989). Peter was trying to do things differently with Josie and her children, and Josie had not interfered. She did not realize the effect that this had on her relationship with her children. Josie was reliving the position she had had with her own siblings, and so she and Peter had complemented each other in this pattern, each playing out a position similar to or reactive to past experiences. The interweaving of all these factors had created a complicated process.

For the moment the therapist decided to focus again on the present household. She reviewed with Peter the notion that, in the children's view, it would take quite a while for him to earn the right to discipline them. She also noted that he had taken on quite a responsibility. She suggested that he read the materials she was giving him and that they meet again to talk about his response. She noted that, because of the structural issues of remarried situations, most people become as confused as he appeared to be, and she reassured him that once he had a perspective on this process, he would be back on his own course of decision-making.

Peter was grateful for the reading material and pulled out his date book to set up another appointment. He also asked if the therapist thought it would be advisable if he backed off somewhat from Kevin and Jane. He really did not like intervening in their fights. He asked Josie if she would object to his doing that. They all concluded that it would be a good thing to try and see how things would work. Josie stated that it would be helpful to her if he just watched.

Peter came to the next session three weeks later, with a list of questions about the reading he had done; he carefully reviewed each one with the therapist. Then he stated what a relief it was for him not to come home anymore feeling as though he were entering a battleground where he had to be the referee. If he heard the children fighting, he called Josie to have her handle it.

Initially, Kevin and Jane had been shocked, but they were now getting used to Peter and Josie's handling things in this new way. Josie said that it had been hard for her, too, but she had discovered that she could talk to Peter about what she should or should not do either before or after the event. She said that as long as she had his support in that way, she was quite content to do the disciplining of Kevin and Jane. Things had calmed down in their household, and both Josie and Peter agreed that the therapist had helped them in making their present home much less chaotic. Jane was no longer talking about going to live at Frank's home, and Kevin was starting to take responsibility in completing his schoolwork.

The difficulty that they all still experienced was with the entry and exit of Peter's children. When they came for visits, not only was there fighting among the children but there was also more tension between Peter and his own children. They still brought orders from Virginia for him, and Peter was furious about that and often yelled at his oldest son, who was the message bearer. Peter turned to the therapist and asked if that had anything to do with him and Virginia. He had read something about an emotional divorce, and that triggered so much anger for him. He felt so furious at Virginia and didn't know why. After all, he said, he had been the one who had decided to leave. He had been the one who had refused to go for therapy. Why should he be so angry with her?

Stage 2: Reweaving the Family Tapestry

During the second phase of treatment, the therapeutic goals are to assist the family in weaving the presenting problems into the extended family patterns, triangles, and themes. In families where a major disruption, such as divorce or death, has occurred, it is frequently necessary and important to attend first to the processes around that disruption. In this case, the therapist has the opportunity to do some work around the divorce process and the future remarriage in an attempt to prevent the couple from reliving old patterns and themes that had gotten them into trouble in their previous marriages.

Once the boundary has been set around Josie, Peter, Jane, and Kevin, and the initial presenting problem of the children's fighting has subsided, it is appropriate for the therapy to move to this stage, in which the complexities of the context are assessed and both Peter and Josie become more aware of their role in the family's emotional process. Weaving back and forth will be required as the therapist connects for Josie and Peter the issues that relate to their own personal family experiences. At times of high stress, the initial problem(s) may reappear; the therapist will then need to attend to the initial problem to determine whether the problem is still there or the client is using it as resistance to further change.

It is important for the therapist to confirm for her/himself that the initial two triangles have been attended to. These were identified earlier as:

1. Mother, father, and daughter—in which the father's ongoing involvement in the mother's household helped to maintain the children's fighting. It appears from all signs that mom has now taken control of the situation with her children and Frank.
2. Mother, children and Peter. Basically, Josie has been able to maintain her position with Peter in their household. The open issue for Josie is how long that will last before she attempts to pull Peter into the triangle. To do so would allow Josie to attend to Peter's desire to be more in charge in this household than he had been in his first marriage, as well as to deal with her own sense of needing an authority to tell her that she is or isn't a competent, effective parent. Each of these factors relates to Josie's desire to be "nice" and gain approval: a typical woman's issue made more complicated by the extended family and divorce process.

During the course of therapy, the issue of loyalty for both Josie's children and Peter's children is likely to surface repeatedly. Clearly, from what has been stated, both sets of children feel the tugs and pulls between their natural parents and their parents' present and potential spouses. Kevin and Jane do not know how to relate to Peter while remaining loyal to their father, Frank. When Peter's children enter the household, they react to their father's relationship to Kevin and Jane. After all, Peter is living day-to-day with them. Peter's children, meanwhile, are living with another man, Virginia's husband, day to day.

All these relationships contain the potential for loyalty conflicts. Although the therapist has not met Peter's children, it is reported that they bring with them their mother's messages. The therapist needs to evaluate the extent to which that triangle interferes in the Taylor family household. This can be part of the process of engaging Peter in the task of reworking the divorce script. It would be helpful to investigate further into Peter's extended family drama to obtain some clues as well.

Throughout this stage of treatment, it is helpful for the therapist to maintain her/his focus on who the original clients are; this will help to organize the clinical thinking and lend clarity to the interventions. In this case, one could define the Taylor household as the client. The others in the larger, extended family system need to be considered in that context — in relation to their impact on the primary household.

During this session, Peter questioned the therapist on many of the issues discussed in the literature she had given him. The focus for most of the questions was around his children, as well as Josie's. He challenged the therapist on the notion that he should relate to Kevin and Jane as if he were a "good uncle." After all, he was living with these children, and he needed to be able to say something to them beyond just talking about the weather.

The therapist talked to Peter about his own children and wondered what it had been like for Peter when he had left his family home and was not living with them daily. Peter claimed that that was an irrelevant issue. The therapist backed off and asked Peter what his reaction had been when his ex-wife Virginia had remarried and there was another man in "his" old household. Peter looked at Josie, and she at him. Josie responded for Peter that it had been a very difficult time for him. They had met just around the time that Virginia had remarried, and Peter was always complaining about her to Josie. He was calling his children quite frequently during that time, and they always wondered what he wanted. It was during those first few months of Peter and Josie's courtship that Josie had become aware of how much Peter missed being a father on a daily basis. He had even told her how displaced he felt when he and Virginia had separated. No matter what he did to fill up his time, he always felt this loss in his life.

When he met Josie and she was so willing to take him into her household, he felt needed again as the man of the house. They had never thought what all this would mean for the children. Josie thought it would be good for everybody — a help to her, a man in the house for her children, and a fulfillment for Peter.

At this moment, Peter turned to Josie and asked her if she had ever thought about whether she might have brought him into her family because she felt that she could not handle things alone. Josie responded that she had not been aware of how much that issue had affected her thinking. Certainly, she thought she was taking care of everyone else, as usual, without attending to herself.

Josie and Peter then started to talk about events with both sets of children.

In addressing the issue of loyalty conflicts with parents and their spouses, it is important to get a handle on what messages are being communicated to the children about the former spouse/natural parent or the new spouse/future stepparent. All too often, there are roles and relationships that the children are asked to play out that are in direct conflict with their natural instincts, e.g., calling the stepfather or stepmother "dad" or "mom." No matter what the relationship might be with the natural parent, the children feel a strong commitment and loyalty to that parent over and above the new stepparent, no matter how well they get along with the latter and no matter how much more they may have in common with the stepparent.

All too often, stepparents are drawn in by children's positive responses, combining with their own personal need and desire to have the children fill their own void. An effective way to deal with loyalty issues is to work with the adults in the family, educating them about the effects of loyalty issues and helping them become more aware of personal issues that might be clouding their judgment. This does not mean that close relationships cannot or should not be formed with stepparents — only that these relationships need to be considered within the context of the loyalty children feel toward their natural parents.

THERAPIST: Peter, let's talk about what it is like for you when your children come to your present household. You have described chaos and conflict, with all of the children fighting. I am wondering about you. How do you respond to Kevin's wanting to watch the game with you while your son wants you to play soccer with him?

PETER: Funny you should ask that specific question. That is precisely what happened this past weekend. I had promised Kevin that we would watch this important football game on Sunday, and my son, Michael, came in demanding that I play soccer with him. I couldn't understand what was happening, and I got very angry with Michael for his tone. I even threatened never to play soccer with him again. I felt terrible afterwards, but I felt caught between a rock and a hard place. I don't like to go against my word, and I had made a promise to Kevin.

THERAPIST: I guess that was one of those terrible moments when you felt you had to choose between your own child and Josie's. It's interesting that you found a reason to get angry at Michael to solve your problem. Don't get me wrong, I am not defending Michael's attitude. I am attempting to retrace with you how it all happened and what your piece of the action was.

Throughout this session, the therapist tracked the loyalty issue as it affected Peter in the triangle with his children and Josie's children, as well as the triangle consisting of him, Josie's children, and Frank. As the therapist posed the questions and moved from his children back to Josie's, it became apparent to both Peter and Josie how the loyalty issue interfered in so much of what went on in their household. Josie began to comment about her relationship with Peter's children and how difficult a time she had with them. Not only did her issue of competence get played out with her own children, but she felt doubly incompetent when Peter's children walked through the door. They were always saying to her that their mother did things differently—for example, that their bedtime was later when they were home. Josie wanted so badly to be the "good mom" when they were there, but instead, she experienced herself as the shrew, and lately she found herself hoping that they wouldn't come at all. She liked them, but she had such a hard time when they were there.

The therapist commiserated with her and reiterated how hard Josie worked at trying to take care of everyone. This is not unusual among women, who frequently view caretaking in general as their primary calling. The session ended with the therapist's trying to help Josie and Peter create yet another boundary for themselves. She advised them that for the next month they should be in charge of their own children, much as Josie had done earlier with Kevin and Jane. Peter should take care of his children and their activities on the weekends that they spent visiting the Taylor household. He should not make any specific plans with Kevin and Jane. He and Josie should talk ahead of time about mealtimes, bedtime, and other activities. If Peter's children questioned Josie about what she was doing, she should refer them to Peter.

This exaggerated task was intended to begin to make Peter and Josie more aware of the roles they played respectively in escalating the loyalty conflict triangles. They looked at the therapist and at each other and stated that they would certainly try it out for a couple of weeks to see how they would manage.

The therapist also asked if Peter would call Virginia before the children came, to find out if there were any specific things he needed to know, thereby avoiding having his son function as the message bearer. Peter had never done that before. As a matter of fact, he said that he spoke quite infrequently to Virginia. He felt that they had little to say to each other. He always felt so angry at her.

The therapist queried whether he would be able to make this phone call without getting annoyed with Virginia. Peter said he would try. He was beginning to understand that part of the difficulty he had with his children related to his residue of anger toward Virginia. He looked at the therapist and said, "This is the 'emotional divorce piece' that they referred to in that article you had me read." The therapist just looked and nodded. Peter walked out of the office, then walked back in and made another appointment, saying, "I really appreciate this."

When the couple arrived three weeks later for the next session, both seemed somewhat weary. When asked about their appearance, Josie began in the following manner:

JOSIE: Well, what you had us do was really difficult; we had the opportunity to try it for the two weekends that both sets of kids were at the house. Of course, we had the weekend in between alone as sort of a recoup time and, boy, did we ever need it! The kids tested us in every way—they fought with each other, asking each of us to take sides with our own kids—I guess that was the worst!

THERAPIST: It sounds like they were their most clever selves! How did the two of you do with all of the hurdles that they posed?

PETER: After all is said and done, I think we did pretty well. I'm not sure I would have said that then if you had asked me, but after Josie and I talked I began to realize that, although I felt upset, it had not really gone that badly. No one got hurt, physically or emotionally—at least I don't think so. Wouldn't you agree, Josie?

JOSIE: Yes, I think Peter's right. Things were really hectic, and we both felt under siege at times, but in the end I think we felt the worst. The kids all seemed okay about the weekends.

THERAPIST: What did you two do to deal with the kids? For instance, in the situation that Josie presented as the worst one?

PETER: We refused to take sides along biological lines—that sounds so funny to say! Instead we both gathered information on what had happened from our own and each other's kids, and then, together in consultation with the children, decided what to do. In fact, we decided that all the kids were involved in the brawl equally, and that all should suffer the consequences equally—we had several chores that really needed their participation so we gave them those to do. In order to complete the tasks, like cleaning the basement and yard, they had to cooperate. It was very interesting to watch how they handled it when they knew that they needed each other and that neither of us was going to get involved in their tasks or in any arguments that started.

JOSIE: Pretty soon they were laughing and joking around with each other, and several times we even heard them jointly making fun of Peter and me. Even when one of our children rose to our defense, the other kids would just joke and jibe with them. It was great to hear—I actually felt like we might be able to become a family—not like each of us had originally thought we would, but a family in a different way.

THERAPIST: Is there anything that still stands in the way of your becoming a family that can function in such a complex way?

JOSIE: Yes—two things. Peter seems unfinished about his divorce and I think I still need to feel competent with my family. The kids are beginning to see me in that way, but my parents and my siblings still view me as a helpless little girl who needs to get married to get help in managing my household. I don't think they even recognize that I hold a very important and demanding job that I am able to handle well.

THERAPIST: Sounds like you're pretty clear about the work that is necessary, Josie. Do you agree, Peter?

PETER: Yes, I did speak to Virginia as you had suggested. She was more than shocked that I called ahead of time to discuss the children's weekend and any issues that she might need for me to know about. It was a really tense but useful conversation. I was really nervous calling her and suddenly had a sense that this was what I had avoided by telling the kids instead of her. I feel angry and guilty and sad all at once. When I realize that she even has my family believing I'm a bastard I get even more upset. I always feel so trapped when I speak with her.

THERAPIST: Wow! Sounds like the two of you have gotten a start on a lot of work in a short time and even identified the work still to be done. You've already gone through the flames, so this work you've each mapped out for yourselves will seem like a piece of cake.

It was clear that this couple was ready to begin the reweaving of the family tapestry. Each was at a different phase in the process—Josie was ready to begin work on her family-of-origin issues, while Peter had to deal first with the issues of his first marriage. As one can see from what Peter says, the work on his marriage/divorce would necessarily lead to his working on his own family issues—e.g., why would his family be so likely to side with Virginia regarding culpability in the divorce?

Josie, typical of the way most women are socialized, was ready to accept most of the responsibility for the failure of her marriage; she was willing to start examining and changing one of the most central issues of her personal life—the way in which she presented herself to others.

The therapist decided to spend some time asking Peter more about his relationship with Virginia and what the marriage and divorce were like. It was clear that Peter still felt very angry about the divorce and the problems in the marriage, and it was obvious that he would be unable to accomplish an emotional divorce until he was able to get over the anger and hurt.

THERAPIST: Peter, I want you to write a letter to Virginia which is not to be mailed under any circumstances; this is just for you to do. I want you to let Virginia know in this letter the reasons you remain so angry with her — and make sure that you let her know all of them. Now, you probably will think the letter is finished after the first time that you write it, but I want you to sit down the next day or two days later and reread the letter and make sure it describes all of the reasons that you remain angry at Virginia. There is no way that you will be able to be finished with Virginia and your marriage unless you first get clear on why you are so angry. Will you do this?

PETER: Yeah, I'll do it. I'm not going to like it, but I'll do it. I try to forget what happened in that marriage. I just want to go on and have a better life with Josie.

THERAPIST: That's pretty hard to do when you have so much unfinished business from your first marriage. Without you being aware of the issues that are left over from that one, it will be hard for you to keep them out of the way in your new relationship.

PETER: I get it. It's just not something I'm going to enjoy doing.

Josie sat expectantly and listened to the exchange between the therapist and Peter. She was not at all clear what was in store for her when the therapist asked her about her relationships with her siblings. Often siblings are forgotten members of the family with whom our relationships remain frozen in time from when we left home. For Josie, it was no different. She was fairly distant from her siblings, and when she did interact with them, it was to help them with some problem that they were experiencing. She never asked them for assistance with her difficulties in life, nor did she discuss her divorce or impending remarriage with any of them.

Part of the reason for this distance was that Josie had been a parental child in her family and thus had never functioned as one of the siblings. In addition, such a position created a tendency on the part of her parents not only to rely on her for some caretaking of themselves and the children but also to have very high expectations of Josie's ability to handle all kinds of difficulties in her own life. Thus, with her divorce, Josie's parents had experienced her for the first time as being helpless. Not only did they not know what to do to help her, but they got angry with her for not doing what she had always done before — that is, hold things together.

The therapist thought that talking to her siblings would help to place Josie on the appropriate level, sibling to sibling, and at the same time provide her with some emotional support. This would aid her in the next family moves, which would entail dealing with her parental triangle. When the therapist asked Josie which of her siblings she wanted to start talking with, Josie had no difficulty in suggesting her youngest sibling, the one to whom she felt closest.

The next several therapy sessions were scheduled a month apart so that both Peter and Josie could accomplish their tasks. It is not unusual for this to be the case during this stage of therapy, when so much of the work demands thinking, planning, and carrying out tasks with extended family members who do not live close to the nuclear family.

Peter wrote his letter to Virginia, and in the process became much clearer about what his expectations had been for the marriage and what his disappointments were. He also became clearer about which of his expectations had been unrealistic and which were realistic. He decided that he needed to do some work on those expectations that he still held that were unrealistic. He also decided that he needed to have a conversation with Virginia regarding his upcoming marriage to Josie and some acknowledgment of what had gone wrong in their marriage. He was not planning on confronting her about her behavior, but instead wanted to focus on what he had done wrong in the marriage — his contribution to its demise.

The therapist thought he had a good idea, but that he needed some practice in focusing on his part in the marriage. She therefore suggested that he now write a preparatory letter to Virginia, again not to be mailed, which would focus on what he thought was his contribution to the failure of the marriage. He would also focus on what he had wished for the two of them. He agreed to do so, adding that he would also focus on what he had learned from the breakup of the marriage.

Josie, meanwhile, had spoken to each of her siblings and had experienced how difficult it was for her to talk about her own difficulties and for her siblings to hear her discuss such matters with them. In varying degrees, each of the siblings had expressed shock that she, of all of them, was having a difficult time. Josie said that it was easy for her to feel as if she shouldn't go on, but she forced herself to do so.

The therapist applauded her work, along with Peter's, and asked her to describe how she got herself to continue talking with her siblings. In the process of describing what had transpired, she mentioned that her parents had expressed their surprise that she had been speaking with her siblings. They even began to ask Josie what was going on with her and if she needed their assistance. Josie was so shocked by their offer that she didn't know how to respond. She discussed possible responses with the therapist and decided that she might begin by telling her mother about her concerns around getting married again.

Conclusion

It is obvious that this couple is well on their way to reworking their family themes and dances. After both sets of current tasks are accomplished, they may, as frequently happens, drop out of treatment for a while.

Having achieved more than symptom relief, Josie and Peter have done more than most couples do: They have begun to change lifelong patterns that affect the manner in which they relate to each other and others with whom they are or will be intimate. They will probably continue their work later, after the marriage takes place and there is some time and energy (and need) to devote to their ongoing work.

They will then enter stage 3 of therapy—reweaving their own tapestries. From the current level of their work, it is clear that divorce adds several steps to the process of coaching, but in addition may assist people in focusing on their life patterns and triangles that need work.

From life's tragedies and failures often come some important and far-reaching learning. Such was the case with both Peter and Josie and their respective families. They are probably going to need some further assistance in dealing with remarried family issues; it is a complex situation that will need their attention for a while. This will also spur them on in the ongoing family-of-origin portion of their work.

REFERENCES

Ahrons, C. R. (1980). Divorce: A crisis of family transition and change. *Family Relations, 29.*

Ahrons, C. R., & Rodgers, R. H. (1987). *Divorced families: A multidisciplinary developmental view.* New York: W. W. Norton.

Carter, B., & McGoldrick, M. (1980). *The family life cycle.* New York: Gardner.

Carter, B., & McGoldrick, M. (1989a). *The changing family life cycle: A framework for family therapy* (2nd ed.). Boston: Allyn & Bacon.

Carter, B., & McGoldrick, M. (1989b). Overview: The changing family life cycle—A framework for family therapy. In B. Carter & M. McGoldrick (Eds.), *The changing family life cycle: A framework for family therapy* (2nd ed.) (pp. 3–28). Boston: Allyn & Bacon.

Glick, P. (1984). Marriage, divorce, and living arrangements. *Journal of Family Issues,* 5(1): 7–26.

Goldsmith, J. (1982). The postdivorce family system. In F. Walsh (Ed.), *Normal family process.* New York: Guilford.

Goldsmith, J. (1980). Relationships between former spouses: Descriptive findings. *Journal of Divorce, 4.*

Herz Brown, F. (1989). The postdivorce family. In B. Carter & M. McGoldrick (Eds.), *The changing family life cycle* (2nd ed.) (pp. 371–398). Boston: Allyn & Bacon.

Hetherington, E. M., Cox, M., & Cox, R. (1977). The aftermath of divorce. In J. H. Stevens, Jr., & M. Mathews (Eds.), *Mother-child, father-child relations.* Washington, DC: National Association for the Education of Young Children.

McGoldrick, M. & Carter, B. (1989). Forming a remarried family. In B. Carter & M. McGoldrick (Eds.), *The changing family life cycle* (2nd ed.) (pp. 399–429). Boston: Allyn & Bacon.

Peck, J. S. (1988/89). The impact of divorce on children at various stages of the family life cycle. *Journal of Divorce,* 12(2/3), 81–106.

Peck, J. S. & Manocherian, J. (1989). Divorce in the changing family life cycle. In B. Carter & M. McGoldrick (Eds.), *The changing family life cycle* (2nd ed.) (pp. 335–370). Boston: Allyn & Bacon.

Wallerstein, J. & Kelly, J. B. (1980). *Surviving the breakup: How children and parents cope with divorce.* New York: Basic Books.

Alcohol in the Family System

GAIL S. LEDERER

ISSUES RELATED TO ALCOHOL take precedence and color all behavior within a family system. Consequently, attempting to deal with the family relationships without acknowledging the impact of alcohol on them only leads to continuance of dysfunctional patterns (Berenson, 1976; Jesse, 1989; Stanton, Todd et al., 1982; Treadway, 1989). Working on any issue without actively attending to the issue of alcohol creates anxiety for the family and, as soon as a family's anxiety goes up a notch, the drinker will drink. Whatever issue caused the anxiety to go up is then forgotten, as the family refocuses on the drinking behavior.

ALCOHOL-RELATED ISSUES

Whenever a family with an alcoholic member enters treatment, even if the active alcoholic is one or two generations in the past, the therapist should automatically think of the difficulties that distinguish alcoholic families from other families (Elkin, 1984; Treadway, 1989). The most common problems are: reciprocal extremes of behavior, lack of a model of normalcy, power imbalances in family organization, a strong sense of pride and shame (Fossum & Mason, 1986), and thus a constant risk of family members' becoming alcoholic. As the reader will note, these issues tend to be interrelated.

Reciprocal Extremes of Behavior

Relationally, alcoholic systems tend to be closed systems with rigid family rules. Members relate in a polarized fashion, swinging back and forth be-

tween complementary extremes of behavior, such as over- and underresponsibility, fusion and cutoffs, intensely alive and emotionally deadened feelings (Bepko & Krestan, 1985). The operating style of any one individual is
formed in the family of origin. These positions can flip as issues change. In
a given family, which issues will become toxic and which reciprocal positions
family members will take are determined by a number of factors. Some of
these factors are: the life cycle of the family at the time of onset of drinking
(Kestan & Bepko, 1989), gender and ethnic considerations (Bepko, 1989),
sibling position (Jesse, 1988), generational themes, and family messages
(Fossum & Mason, 1986). The following scenario illustrates how some of
these factors might be at work.

In a family with three daughters, the father begins drinking alcoholically
the year his 18-year-old goes away to college. As dad's drinking increases,
the mother begins to use her 15-year-old as a confidante and co-parent,
depending on her to help with the care of the 12-year-old. In this example,
one could hypothesize that the oldest daughter, being already out of the
house, will be the least affected by dad's drinking. The 15-year-old will be
the most triangled in and will most likely take on an overresponsible operating style around issues of caretaking. Her 12-year-old sister might become
daddy's little girl to balance the family and take on characteristics of irresponsibility, eventually drinking alcoholically as a way of continuing her
alliance with dad.

The alcoholic did not come into this world already an active alcoholic.
While current thinking points to the possibility that the addiction, alcoholism, may be genetically predetermined (Altman, 1988; Goodwin, 1976; Vaillant, 1983), it does not speak to the function of alcohol and how it gets
incorporated into the coping styles of a given family. It may be that alcoholism is transmitted to the next generation by the high degree of reactivity
family members have to the toxic issues related to alcohol. Alcoholic drinking, as well as the family's response to the drinking, seems to serve two
functional roles in the family's system. First, it appears to facilitate *expression of feelings*, whether good or bad, that are unacceptable due to family
messages and cultural injunctions. Second, it appears to *relieve anxiety* that
is created when an individual tries to meet unrealistic expectations, both
functionally in the task arena and emotionally in the relationship arena
(Bepko & Krestan, 1985).

Having unrealistic expectations leads to under- or overresponsible behavior. When an individual tries to attain an unrealistic, unspoken goal, he/she
is trying to do the impossible. It is impossible partly because it is conditional
on other people's responding in accordance with the individual's unspoken
wishes. This sets up conditions for failure, since people rarely do what is not
voiced directly. Then, when failure inevitably occurs, the individual blames

him/herself, deciding that he/she did not do it perfectly enough; rather than saying, "I'm trying to do the impossible." he/she says, "I guess I should try harder." He/she then takes on more responsibility in an attempt to achieve the impossible. This leads to more failure. The harder he/she tries, the greater the sense of failure. The greater the sense of failure, the harder he/she tries. It is a symmetrical escalation, with each person doing more of the same (Bepko & Krestan, 1985).

When two people are in an over- and underresponsible pattern of reciprocity, it creates a climate in which alcoholism can occur (Bepko & Krestan, 1985; Elkin, 1984; Steinglass et al., 1987). The less responsible an individual is, the more responsible the other person becomes, in an effort to take up the slack. Being over- or underresponsible is not a personality defect. It is a response to a given situation. An individual can be totally overresponsible in one area and underresponsible in another. However, once these responses become fixed in the system, they may become individual problems as well as a function of the system. Not all over- and underresponsible relationships produce alcoholism. It may be that the extreme degree of polarity, combined with a genetic and emotional predisposition and/or patterning, produces alcoholism. When alcoholism does occur, we frequently see one of two patterns. Either the underresponsible individual becomes alcoholic to maintain his/her irresponsible position, or the overresponsible individual, to relieve the ever-increasing anxiety that comes from trying to meet unrealistic expectations, swings to the other extreme and seeks relief through drinking (Bepko & Krestan, 1985). The following is a brief illustration of the second variety of problem.

Kelly, 38, the only daughter of alcoholic parents, was upset over a family feud between her brothers and her parents. In the past, her role had always been to smooth things out in the family. Lately, she had been trying not to be so overresponsible for everyone. This was causing her considerable anxiety. The pull to homeostasis in the family system for Kelly to remain overresponsible was so strong that for the first time in her life she actually thought about getting drunk. Kelly said, "I feel wiped out . . . emotionally. I mean, thank God I went to the movies Friday night. Because otherwise, I swear, for the first time I can remember, I would have gone home and gotten drunk, ripping, on purpose. I mean, I've had too much to drink in my life, but not intentionally, premeditated."

For Kelly, "the responsible person," not attempting to solve the family feud felt like a dereliction of family duty and created a great deal of anxiety for her. In her family, when the anxiety from being in an overresponsible position became too high, the solution was to seek relief through drinking. Thus, Kelly, as her own anxiety increased, found herself thinking about getting drunk. In an alcoholic system, all family members are at risk of becoming alcoholic in response to either extreme position of over- or under-responsibility (Bepko & Krestan, 1985). Consequently, the alcoholic system tends to produce children who either become alcoholic or marry someone who will become alcoholic — as a way to maintain the system's continuity of reciprocal behaviors over time. The process itself may become reinforcing, with the alcohol reinforcing the extremes of behavior.

No Model of Normalcy

Another major difficulty that is related to the behavioral extremes of the alcoholic system is that the individual tends to have a distorted view of "normal." Normal family patterns and rituals are disrupted as the family attempts to adapt to the alcoholic's drinking. As these normal family processes break down, the boundary lines between the family as a whole and the larger social context become more rigidly drawn. This creates a sense of isolation for the family and hinders socialization. The family tries to protect itself by keeping the family secret — that there is an alcoholic in their midst — from their friends, school or work. This pull to close ranks does not allow the individual family members to interact enough with others (Fossum & Mason, 1986; Steinglass et al., 1987). As a result, they are unable to measure themselves against other families and do not gain a firm sense of what normal is. Not knowing what "normal" is, the individual then makes it up, basically creating his/her own version of what he/she thinks normal might be.

For instance, Ginny, a 49-year-old housewife, had grown up with an alcoholic father who was always "rip-roaring drunk." She was explaining how she didn't think she was normal, but she tries to appear normal: "My method of dealing with it is to pretend to be normal. I study what is all right and then I try to make myself into that. I have this sort of vague notion about being normal and I know I want to be that, but if you asked me to define it, I don't think I could."

In trying to appear normal, the individual may develop an outer façade for the world that masks his/her internal self. This creates a fear of being unmasked, with the "real" person being revealed as inadequate. The longer the individual is successful at maintaining this façade, the greater the fear of exposure. This sets in motion another symmetrical escalation in which the individual overfunctions more and more, as he/she tries to manage the ever-increasing anxiety of eventual exposure (Bepko & Krestan, 1985).

Pride and Shame

Years of projecting a strong exterior to the family and the world at large, while at the same time being ashamed of and making sure that no one sees "the real me," sap the individual of emotional energy. At the same time as the individual fears exposure, he/she also takes great pride in having been able to maintain a façade of normalcy (Bepko & Krestan, 1985). After all, this façade has protected him/her for many years from being vulnerable or hurt. It has been a method of survival in an unpredictable environment. The clinician must be aware of this self-protective behavior and not push the client to be more self-revealing than the client is ready to handle. Any suggestion that the client drop this façade creates intense anxiety and needs to be carefully planned, so that the client won't react by shifting to the underresponsible position and drink or leave therapy in order to maintain the façade.

Imbalances of Power and Hierarchy

In contrast to the rigid boundaries between the family and the larger social context, the boundary lines between the generational subsystems tend to be diffuse (Fossum & Mason, 1986). Hierarchy is skewed, with cross-generational alliances between parent and child. Children often take on rigid roles in an attempt to take care of each other and their parents. Either way, children miss out on a part of childhood because they have to assume adult behavior and adult duties at a time when they should be accomplishing their own age-appropriate developmental tasks. When normal individual developmental tasks become derailed, all other subsequent developmental stages are affected, creating a gap in emotional and functional skills (Jesse, 1989).

One young woman, Polly, age 17, should have been dating boys and transferring most of her allegiance to peers, as she moved along the separation-individuation continuum of adolescence. Instead, many evenings she would have to accompany her father on business functions such as cocktail parties, because her mother would be too drunk to go. As a result, by age 21, when she moved away, Polly had skipped over an important developmental stage in which she should have been practicing social and relational skills with her peers. It was not surprising that she would present at age 43, with a series of failures in the social and relational area, as well as concerns about her own drinking.

WHY USE THIS METHOD?

Multigenerational therapy may be useful in bringing about change in an alcoholic system. Often, in alcoholic families, the therapist is not lucky enough to get the whole family to come in for treatment. Unlike methods of family therapy that need the whole family present, multigenerational therapy enables the therapist to work with either a couple or an individual in a family systems context. In addition, it permits the therapist to move from a nonalcoholic symptom in the family to a redefinition of the family difficulties as alcohol-related.

Nevertheless, multigenerational therapy, like all other types of therapy, does not get people to stop drinking. AA is still the most successful method in this regard. However, in my opinion, AA may enable the drinker to stop drinking but have little effect on entrenched family patterns. Furthermore, AA meetings can become triangled into the family system as a replacement for the bottle. While it does attempt to deal with enabling and codependent behavior, in general AA does not address the generational transmission process that continues alcoholism into the next generation. Multigenerational therapy complements AA's work in stopping drinking and also creates the climate for changing the alcoholic patterns that have been incorporated into the family system's coping style.

AA and Alanon give the messages: You are powerless against alcohol and you are responsible for change. Multigenerational theory gives a similar message as the AA programs: You are powerless against alcohol and the only person you can change is yourself. With its emphasis on only changing one's own behavior, and not on changing the other person, it is a rich methodology for restructuring hierarchy, repairing developmental gaps, blocking enabling behavior, and addressing denial.

A major part of multigenerational work is carrying out tasks designed to help shift the process in family relationships. The individual defines his/her role in the family system and then strategizes on how to change that role. Tasks can only be done successfully when the individual has lowered his/her level of emotional reactivity. Alcoholic systems tend to be highly reactive (Elkin, 1984; Treadway, 1989); the careful planning and predicting that characterize tasks help to lower the system's reactivity. The emphasis on thinking, rather than being emotionally reactive, maximizes the possibility for change. As we will see in the case that follows, helping a client figure out how his/her family system works broadens perspective. This larger perspective decreases personalization and blaming, and therefore lowers the individual's reactivity to the other person's behavior. Once reactivity is lowered, it is possible to create new patterns of behavior that allow for the expression of previously taboo subjects.

In the case that follows, it is clear that the tasks require the client to take responsibility for her own ideas, beliefs, and values. When there is an active alcoholic in the family, teaching the nondrinker to be more responsible for self and less responsible for the alcoholic's drinking blocks enabling behavior. It also prevents the use of denial by removing the protection that comes from being more responsible for another person than that person is for him/ herself. When this protection is removed, the *possibility* of the alcoholic's taking more responsibility for his/her own drinking increases. Taking responsibility for oneself and not for the other person does not mean not caring about the other person. Many clients, especially women, worry that expressing or meeting one's own needs is selfish. On the contrary, stating your own needs clearly relieves the other person of having to guess what will make you happy. It also gives others the opportunity of knowing that their actions are going to match your needs and be pleasing.

THE CASE OF THE PERFECT DAUGHTER

Stage 1. The Presenting Problem

Carol, age 26, first came to see me at the time of separation and impending divorce from her husband Hank, age 28. Carol and Hank had only been married for three years when they decided to separate. They had no children. If they had, the issues of dealing with divorce and parenthood might have taken precedence over the issues of couplehood that Carol presented alone. The problems confronting Carol and Hank were money, career, sex, and drinking. On an individual level, Carol expressed feelings of failure. She felt she had failed in her marriage; also, despite being a superachiever at work, tackling all tasks and working late hours, she felt she had failed with her career. These failures compounded her sense of having disappointed her parents in her career choice and her ultimate failure at not being able to help mom cure dad's drinking problem.

As is often the case, divorce is a prime time for therapy because the person experiencing divorce is in crisis and motivated to feel better. In order to resolve the divorce, it is necessary to figure out what went wrong in the marriage. One step in accomplishing this involves examining the patterns in one's parents' marriage and in one's own marriage, to understand how these patterns have been replicated. The initial contract was to help Carol understand her feelings of failure regarding her marriage and career. Within the context of her extended family, she would explore how her family had affected her current behavior and how it had influenced her expectations and disappointments of Hank and marriage, so that future relationships would be free of the same mistakes. If Hank had been present, the issue of alcohol might have been in the forefront of the therapeutic contract, as it was a major issue affecting them as a couple.

Part of stage 1 is to redefine the presenting problem, which is usually done in the very first session. Carol had come in saying, in essence, "I am a failure because I couldn't make my marriage work, and I am not a good enough daughter because I have disappointed my parents with my career choice and not saved my father from drinking." The way this is presented, it is not a problem that can be easily changed. Also, by the time a client asks for help, he/she has already tried to solve the problem and failed. The client feels hopeless that a solution is possible, since he/she has already exhausted everything that he/she can think of. The therapist must reframe the problem into one that offers new possibilities for a solution, thus providing the client with a renewed sense of hope. By putting Carol's sense of failure within the larger context of the extended family, we reframed the problem from one of individual inability to succeed to one that relates to family patterns of behavior. Family patterns can be reshaped more easily than individual failure can be changed.

Despite the emphasis in multigenerational therapy on family-of-origin work, it is important that the clinician stay focused on a client's presenting problem. Family-of-origin questions should be asked only in relation to helping the therapist and client better understand the presenting problem. If questions are not relevant, you are likely to hear, "What does my father have to do with my divorce?" Since Carol had presented the problem of her marriage ending, I began with gathering information on the history of the marriage. Carol had met Hank in her junior year of college and had married him as soon as she graduated. She had never lived on her own away from her family. She had skipped over the life-cycle phase in which the young adult practices being an individual who is separate from but still connected to the family (Carter & McGoldrick, 1989; Meyer, 1980). Therefore, it is not surprising that she was unable to negotiate well the next life-cycle phase, which involves forming a new couple (McGoldrick, 1989). Carol and Hank had not built any kind of couple foundation in the three years they had been married.

In the courtship period, Carol had seen Hank as someone to lean on, to be a success and go far. He was to be "the perfect man," who came from "the perfect family," one in which family life was always placid and nice and his father was a "real daddy." This pull of Carol's to seek the perfect family evolves out of the alcoholic family's isolation and lack of knowing what is normal. The idea of normalcy goes astray and becomes idealized as perfection. By marrying Hank, Carol expected to have "the perfect marriage." However, she was soon disappointed. Hank was unable to communicate feelings, coming from a polite WASP family. So far, he was not earning much money and seemed on his way to being a personal failure like her own father. What's more, Hank had all the earmarks of a drinking problem. While Carol spent most of her waking hours climbing the corporate ladder, Hank spent much of his time with the boys, drinking and partying, and the rest of his time eking out a living. Since Carol had grown up with an alcoholic father, the last thing she wanted was to find that she was married to an alcoholic-in-training.

However, when engaged to Hank, Carol was positively sure Hank was the perfect man for her. She does remember that the honeymoon wasn't good and that at the end of six months she found herself saying "Oh my God, did I marry the wrong man?" Before marriage, Carol felt sex had been satisfactory, but after marriage she found herself repulsed by Hank; she said that she would physically curl up inside when he touched her. Approximately one in four times that they would have sex, she would throw up immediately afterwards. Carol was a beautiful girl, with a beautiful figure, and dressed in very tailored, conservative suits. At first, I assumed this was due to her working in a corporate environment and trying to look like one of the guys. However, it turned out that she had been dressing down her female appearance since puberty at age 12, in order to try and look unattractive sexually, so her dad wouldn't look at her "that way." She had no actual memory of him having abused her sexually, but she did not rule it out as a possibility.

An important aspect of stage 1 is to educate the client about how emotional systems work. So, in trying to resolve Carol's presenting problem, the therapist would need to teach her about alcoholic systems and how her experience as a child related to her quest for the perfect marriage. Carol would need to work on the nuclear level to understand how she had looked to Hank to provide what had been missing in her own family. She would also need to understand her own part in the relationship that kept the myth of perfection going and perpetuated the difficulties between them. Otherwise, Carol would run into the same difficulties in the next relationship. She agreed, admitting that she was already having some problems in a new relationship with a man she was dating at work.

ABOUT THE FAMILY (SEE FIGURE 14.1). Carol was one of five children. She had an older brother Howard, Jr., 29, who was married with two children. He had moved far away from the family home and refused to talk about his father with any member of the family. When he did speak with family members, it was only to communicate on an impersonal level. Effectively, he had cut himself off from the problem. Of all the children, he was the most allied with his mother. Carol labeled him, "the obedient son"; in her opinion, he was at risk of becoming alcoholic. He was a compulsive worker and suffered from ulcers. Carol, 26, was next. Her label was "the perfect daughter (see Table 14.1 for family roles). Carol only drank occasionally. Next came a brother, John, 25, married with one child. He, like Howard, had moved far away. John was a teetotaler and his label was "the spokesman," since he always took a strong stand on issues, as if he were on a soap box. Then came Lisa, 24, married with no children. She was also a teetotaler, grew up as "daddy's little girl," and was the most connected of the sibs to dad. The last one was Jennie, age 21, still living at home. She was labeled

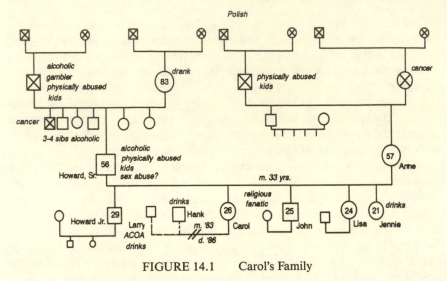

FIGURE 14.1   Carol's Family

"the unwanted child." Jennie was the most like dad and drank, often excessively, but denied it was a problem. No one challenged her.

Carol's mother, Anne, 57, was devoutly Catholic and labeled "the buffer." Her credo in life was "stand by your man." Mom worked as a nurse. She had only one sibling, an older brother. She had been physically abused by her father as a child, and her mother had not stepped in to protect her. However, she came from a Polish-American family and Polish-Americans, culturally, often believe in physically punishing kids, sometimes harshly, if they have broken rules of behavior (Mondykowski, 1982).

Carol's father, Howard, Sr., 56, had been alcoholic all of Carol's life. His family label was "the central character." He was one of 10 kids and the

TABLE 14.1
The Family Roles

Howard, Sr. — the Central Character
Anne — the Buffer
Howard, Jr. — the Obedient Son
Carol — the Perfect Daughter
John — the Spokesman
Lisa — Daddy's Little Girl
Jennie — the Unwanted Child
Hank — the Perfect Man

---

youngest boy. Several of his siblings were alcoholic. He, too, came from a Polish-American family and had been physically abused by his father. He was also physically abusive with his own kids, especially the three oldest. Howard, Sr.'s parents were both alcoholic. He described his mother as incredibly mean. His dad had been a professional gambler and never worked a day in his life. As a result, Howard, Sr. had worked from age 13 on to help support his family. Of all his sibs, Howard, Sr. felt as if he had given the most to his family and yet was the least appreciated. Therefore, he had completely cut off from his family of origin.

Carol described being afraid of her dad as a young child, never knowing when he would be physically abusive; later, as an adolescent, she dreaded his coming home because his sexual looks always made her feel so uncomfortable. She also recalled trying always to keep "the family secret" that dad was an alcoholic. Though this is quite common in alcoholic families, it was also culturally sanctioned, since in Polish-American families, "family loyalty and mistrust of outsiders is strong" (Mondykowski, 1982). Carol never had friends over because, as she said, she never knew which dad she'd find at home—the drunk one or the sober one. Trying to contain the "secret" within boundaries of the immediate family and portray the family myth that everyone was fine created an enormous sense of isolation and differentness in Carol. Even within the family, dad's drinking was not discussed, so Carol (and probably other family members) often felt as if she were the only one struggling with these problems.

AA GROUPS. Until recently, adult children of alcoholics did not usually present alcohol as the problem, nor did they see the problems they presented as related in any way to alcohol. Now, with all the recent popular literature (e.g., Woititz, 1983), alcoholism in the family and codependence are much more "acceptable" ways to enter therapy. Still, many ACOAs are quite surprised to hear the extent to which their current problems are connected to alcoholic issues. They often think that because they are now adult and on their own, the effects of living with an alcoholic are behind them. Therefore, it was suggested to Carol that she go to an Adult Children of Alcoholics group.

Initially, I encourage ACOAs to go to ACOA meetings because group meetings tend to normalize behavior. By providing an opportunity to be with people who are dealing with similar alcoholic issues, it also decreases the sense of isolation. Attending meetings also decreases the use of denial, as it indicates acceptance of the ongoing effects of growing up in an alcoholic system. Joining a group helps expand a client's view of the problem. Instead of seeing problems as one's own individual failure, the client comes to see that all people growing up in an alcoholic system struggle with the same issues. While alcohol was still active in Carol's family, it was not a part of her ongoing daily life. If it were, she would have benefited more from the work of an Alanon group, which focuses on living with an active alcoholic.

Much of the first eight months was spent teaching Carol about characteristics of alcoholic systems and how they related to her own family's emotional system. I usually recommend to clients that they read about alcoholism and its effects on the family. There are several good books for this purpose (see, e.g., Woititz, 1983, and Beattie, 1987). Reading is one way to help clients realize that many of the problems they are dealing with are shared by other people in alcoholic systems. Also, when a client first begins to attend AA, Alanon or ACOA meetings, I ask what the client's reactions were to the topic that was discussed and, whenever possible, connect the topic to the client's emotional system. In these ways, Carol learned about the difficulties children of alcoholics encounter in their adult life. She also began to learn which types of behavior resulted in enabling the alcoholic and which types represented taking a stand.

Then there were family systems concepts to be taught, such as how triangles work, how patterns are transmitted down through the generations, and how to shift her role within the family system (Bowen, 1978). The way to teach a client these concepts is twofold. One way is by the comments you make when the client talks about an incident. As an example, Carol talked about how her mother called her all the time and complained that her father was drinking more heavily. She said that that made her worry about dad's health and at the same time she felt sorry for her mother. The therapist might respond by saying, "So you get stuck in a triangle between your mom and your dad. You feel like your mom needs you as her ally and wants you to take her side against dad, but part of you wants to be on dad's side since you worry about his health." This introduces the concept of triangles. It also begins to describe the process of interaction within the triangle. The other way to teach is by the question you ask the client. Using the same example, the therapist might ask, "Do you think your mom felt she needed to be your grandmother's ally against your grandfather when he would be abusive?" This introduces the concept of three-generational patterns and how they repeat over time.

THE PRIMARY TRIANGLE. Carol remembered that, growing up, she would try to help mom with dad when he was drunk. Carol thought that mom was a saint to put up with dad and his drinking. This unbalanced view of her parents, one as "saint" and the other as "sinner," illustrates the degree to which mom overfunctioned for dad, who underfunctioned. It also signifies a triangle. Carol is allied with her mom for putting up with dad, the alcoholic. She is distant and conflictual with her dad for causing her mom grief with his drinking. A triangle exists in that the view of one parent is dependent upon the view of the other. If dad were to stop drinking, mom would lose her saint status since dad would no longer be the sinner. The fact that this triangle is organized around the issue of drinking defines it as an alcoholic system (Steinglass, 1976).

LIKE MOTHER, LIKE DAUGHTER. An important goal in the first stage is connecting the present problem to a three-generational theme. For Carol, this meant tracking the issues of a failed marriage, career choice, and alcoholic patterns back a couple of generations to see what the patterns and myths were in her extended family.

In describing what her expectations of Hank and marriage had been, two themes emerged. One was the theme of "perfection vs. settling," and the other was "stand by your man no matter what." Developing themes provides both therapist and client with a focus for treatment and a way to track three-generational patterns and issues in the family system.

Carol began tracking these themes by asking her mother questions about her growing-up years. She learned how her grandmother had been unable to stand up to her grandfather's harsh physical abuse of the children. She began to see her mother not merely as a parental figure but as a woman who was the product of her own family system. This added a human quality to her mother. Her mother's inability to stand up to Carol's father, with regard to his drinking and abuse of Carol, was understandable in light of her mother's growing-up experiences. Carol began to see how her own marriage to Hank had replicated her parents' marriage. She, like her mother, had been unable to take a stand with Hank about his drinking and partying with the boys. Carol was also able to see that she was on her way to repeating the same pattern once again by now dating a fellow worker who drank a lot and came from an alcoholic system in which both parents drank. Carol realized that her alliance with mom against dad and his drinking was training her to "stand by your man no matter what." Overfunctioning emotionally for her dad was teaching her to overfunction for men in general. She understood that, unless she changed her role of mom's ally against dad, she would continue to pick alcoholic men who needed a woman to stand by them. Overfunctioning for others would also put her at risk of becoming alcoholic, as a way to stop overfunctioning.

GETTING THE CLIENT INTERESTED IN MULTIGENERATIONAL ISSUES. Stage 1 ends once the client connects current behavior with extended family process, is able to define her part differently, and begins to be clear about what role she plays in the extended family. Carol expressed a desire to work on herself in her family, in order to break the cycle of women marrying alcoholics and prevent the transmission process to the next generation. She no longer viewed "the problem" as linear: "I marry the wrong kind of man." Her perspective had changed to a systemic view of: "Women in our family pick a man they can stand by, no matter what." They marry an alcoholic who behaves irresponsibly, which provides the climate in which the woman can overfunction and seem strong, thus filling the bill of standing by her man no matter what. These themes of "stand by your man," and "perfection vs. settling" not only are connected, but are gender issues as well. The reality for women is that the alternative to standing by your man is to leave and be on your own. This is not an attractive alternative to women who have children to care for and lack sufficient job skills to make them financially independent. Thus, many women choose to "settle" and to "stand by their man."

As Carol developed a systemic view of her family, she began to shift her focus. Instead of wondering how Hank could have behaved differently in the marriage, she began to wonder how she herself could have done things differently, and what she could change about herself so that future relationships would have a positive outcome. This represents a shift away from other and towards self. Carol was no longer holding Hank responsible for the failure of the marriage. She was holding herself responsible for following the family pattern of women who married men they could "stand by no matter what." This new self-focus became possible when Carol was able to connect that her role as mom's ally had trained her to "stand by her man" in her marriage with Hank. She was now ready to begin the work of detriangling from the parental triangle.

Stage 2: Studying the Patterns

In therapy, tasks are designed to promote change by reversing the movement in a given triangle, so that the client can begin to have more personal relationships with family members, on a one-to-one basis. The therapist suggests a task to the client that will help her understand the family process so she can plan new responses to old, conflictual issues. However, before the client can figure out a new response, she has to figure out the old responses.

At Thanksgiving time, I asked Carol to observe how her family acted before and after dad drank. The purpose of this task was to begin to teach Carol about the family relational patterns and about the function of alcohol in allowing expression of emotions that otherwise would be considered unacceptable. I warned her to be sure to only observe, not to do anything differently. Because alcoholic systems are fused and rigid, exhibiting a high degree of reactivity, the therapist must be careful to go very slowly. It is important that early tasks given to clients be successful. These successes encourage clients to try more active tasks later on. If a task is too difficult, that is, too anxiety-provoking, the client will either not do the task or will do the task and fail.

Carol's observations of how her family behaved and her part in the process began on her visit home for Thanksgiving. However, she was not able to observe pre- and post-drinking behavior as her dad was in one of his nondrinking periods. Instead, she decided to pay close attention to her dad's behavior and was surprised to see how he had to get into all conversations and be part of everything. She also said that her mom sat so close to her dad at the dinner table, "She was practically on top of him." Watching her parents, Carol imagined hearing each of them comment on her separation from Hank. In her imagination, she heard her mother say to her, "You should have been satisfied with what you had." And she imagined she could hear her dad saying, "If you'd been satisfied with Hank, he would have been a success." Here we begin to see a picture of Carol's emotional system and how the primary relationships work. It was clear that mom's message was; "You should settle," and that dad placed responsibility for self onto others, since he held Carol, not Hank, responsible for Hank's lack of business success.

Carol complained that all she ever got from her dad was criticism. Since childhood, Carol had tried to gain dad's approval and failed. In college, Carol tried to get top grades, but somehow even A's didn't seem to please dad because she was not in the right field of study. He wanted her to become a doctor; when she did not go into pre-med, he made it clear that he was disappointed in her. In her marriage, Carol shifted from dad to her husband, Hank, in her search for approval; as with her dad, she met only criticism. This would usually cause her to try even harder and do more for Hank, anticipating his responses ahead of time, so she could please even more. Of course, this did not work because she never could anticipate him quite right, not being a mind reader.

Carol had distanced herself emotionally from her dad in reaction to his disapproval of her. Carol's closeness with her mom was reactive to the approval she felt as mom's ally. The amount of distance between Carol and her dad was directly related to the amount of closeness between Carol and her mom. Conversely, Carol's closeness with her mom was conditional on Carol's being distant from dad. As long as Carol maintained this view of dad as the bad husband and critical father who should get his act together and mom as the saintly wife and good mother for putting up with dad's drinking, she would remain a little girl instead of an adult in charge of getting her own needs met.

SHIFTING THE TRIANGLE. Carol's big shift came on her visit home at Christmas. Between Thanksgiving and Christmas, she had prepared strategies for shifting her position in the primary triangle so that she would not be so tight with mom at dad's expense. When her mother tried to pull her in tight by expressing some worry about dad's drinking or his health, Carol was to shake her head and sympathize, but only by commenting on how tough that must be for her mom and not by volunteering her own worries or trying to "help" with suggestions. Afterwards, Carol reported feeling indifferent and cutoff emotionally from her mom. Initially, the lack of differentiation in any relationship that an individual is trying to change makes it difficult to detach without experiencing some degree of cutoff. Carol perceived herself as having cutoff when, in fact, she had actually taken the first steps in the detriangling process, first moves towards redefining herself. By sympathizing with mom but not offering "help," she was playing a different role, one in which she could be on her mother's side without having to be against her father. In first attempts to detach, the client needs a lot of reassurance that he/she can still stay connected despite detaching emotionally.

On Carol's next visit home, dad was drinking again, which gave Carol an opportunity to practice taking a stand about what *her* limits would be to *his* drinking. She decided she would talk with him only if he wasn't drinking for the day yet. The tough part for Carol would be how to stay connected to her dad and still take a position in regard to his drinking episodes. When she spoke with him and it was obvious he'd been drinking, she was to say, "I can't talk to you, dad, when you've been drinking, so I'll speak to you another time when you're sober." This would be very different from her responses in the past, when she would respond to his drinking cycle by cutting off the entire relationship, whether he was drunk or sober. Carol was able to take this new position with her dad. When they did talk, she told him that he had done a good job supporting the family and working so hard. He admitted that taking care of the family financially weighed heavily on him. He told her about having taken care of one family or another since he was a child.

Carol's view shifted and she reported looking at her dad on this visit and seeing a sad sack instead of a sinner. She also found herself angry, for the first time, with her mother for not appreciating how hard her dad had worked. Now it was Carol's mom who was the sinner. This kind of flip-flop from one end of the spectrum to the other is typical of alcoholic systems. It is necessary to help a client shift a position without flip-flopping. If Carol is to develop a balanced view of marriage, she will need to continue to see dad as more human — and see mom that way too.

Carol's next task was to sympathize with mom about dad without giving advice *or* distancing emotionally. This time she was to try and stay emotionally connected. To help Carol stay connected, the therapist suggested Carol tell her mom about how she now viewed dad as a sad sack. If Carol talked about her own feelings, in response to mom's worry, she would not be able to cut off emotionally. Because Carol's dad was drinking again, she didn't have long to wait before her mom called. Carol did the task and reported that this time she was able to stay emotionally connected even though she wasn't offering any advice or help. And to her surprise, instead of agreeing with her that dad was a sad sack, her mom ended up praising him for how much he had done for the family, putting five kids through college.

Seeing her dad in a more understanding light meant Carol was less distant with him. No longer acting as confidante for her mom meant she was less allied with her. The primary triangle between mother, father, and daughter had shifted to a more balanced position.

THE CAT IS OUT OF THE BAG. Approximately one year after we had begun working, a nodal event occurred that caused the system to shift further. Carol's dad was out west visiting John, his teetotaling son. He had decided to stop drinking for 24 hours and as a result had a seizure. John, who had previously distanced himself from the family, was forced to discuss dad's drinking. The family secret — dad is an alcoholic and we are not "fine" — was now out in the open and all family members were finally talking to each other about dad's drinking, instead of denying it as a problem. The myth of "the perfect family" had been debunked.

Next, Carol wanted to work on changing her role as "the perfect executive," who could do everything right. She had just taken a new job within the corporation. I suggested she talk to her mother, who, after years of keeping the family secret, must surely be an expert on trying to be perfect. So Carol asked her mom's advice on how she could stop worrying about making mistakes or knowing all the right answers. Her mother told her she shouldn't be afraid to make mistakes. She said Carol was too hard on herself, expecting to know all there was to know the first month of a new job. Her mother also told her she was confident that Carol would do a great job because she was so capable. This was the first time Carol had ever had a direct vote of confidence from her mom. She said that as a result she felt closer to her mom, in a person-to-person way, totally separate from what was going on in her relationship with dad.

WORKING BOTH SIDES OF THE TRIANGLE. The next task was to balance the movement that Carol had made with her mom by making a reciprocal move with her dad. Carol's relationship with dad had been primarily distant and critical. They had never just spent time together, father to daughter, having fun. To begin to reverse this, Carol was asked what she could do to allow her dad to father her positively. She said her dad loved to cook and she could ask him for one of his recipes. Since her dad was still drinking, Carol would need to be sure he was sober when she spoke with him. Carol did the task and reported that her dad had been very receptive. Not only had he given her the recipe, telling her several times to be sure to follow all the steps, but he also asked her to call and tell him how it had turned out. Carol called to thank her dad and tell him what a success his recipe was. Her dad said how glad he was she had done such a good job and to call him anytime she wanted another recipe. Carol said she felt as if her dad had acted like the kind of father other people had and expressed hope that, even though he was drinking, maybe she could still have a relationship with him during his sober times.

However, Carol's concept of being parented was based on old childhood feelings. The kind of parenting she had missed as a child was no longer possible to have, since she was no longer a child. Besides, as an adult she had different needs. Carol had to take responsibility for letting her parents know what she needed as an adult daughter. She began with her dad. Carol had yet to take the risk of finding out whether her dad would accept her as an adult daughter who wasn't "perfect." Did he still want her to be "the perfect daughter," that is, to be who she wasn't and never could be, or would he be able to accept her for who she was? I suggested she write a letter to her dad about her personal feelings regarding her relationship with him.

Next, Carol planned how she would handle his response. She decided that the worst thing he might say to her would be that he was disappointed in her for not being satisfied with Hank. If he said this, she planned to say, "I'm sorry you're disappointed, but I did what I had to do for me." This response shows a good degree of differentiation because she's now able to let her dad have his reaction, while she feels entitled to have her own reaction, and it is OK for them to differ.

Carol sent the letter to her dad and received a phone call a week later. Her dad thanked her for the letter and said that as far as he was concerned, she was just the daughter he wanted and she shouldn't think he was disappointed in her. Carol was thrilled because this was the first noncritical, out and out supportive statement she could remember hearing from him. It was the first time she felt he approved of her for herself and not just for what she did.

Carol continued to work on her relationship with her mom and her sibs. However, in this model of therapy, the client works not only on the family-of-origin issues but also on the nuclear relationships. Carol continued to weave back and forth between extended family and current relationships, with the goal always of defining herself within each relationship. Therefore, Carol worked on not being perfect not only with her parents but also in her relationships at work and with her boyfriend, Larry. Carol had been upset over her relationship with her boyfriend and feeling more and more as if he was "Mr. Wrong" instead of "Mr. Right," especially since it was becoming increasingly clear that not only did he drink too much, but he also never took responsibility for his drinking, denying that it was a problem. Carol decided she would take a stand with Larry and tell him that on nights when he drank too much, she would not stay at his apartment but would go back to her own place. She also called her sister Jennie, who also had a boyfriend who had a drinking problem that was denied, as was Jennie's own drinking. Carol asked Jennie how she might figure out whether Larry really had a drinking problem or she was just overreacting. Jennie not only said it sounded like a problem but for the first time admitted that she worried that she, too, had a drinking problem.

THE TIDE HAS TURNED. Halfway through the treatment, Carol's paternal grandmother died. Her dad went home for the funeral. This was dad's first contact with his family in over 10 years. Despite having been dry for the past four months, he began drinking again soon after he came home from the funeral. When Carol heard her dad was drinking again, she responded in a nonreactive, appropriate fashion. She did not rush in to commiserate with her mom. Though she felt sad and concerned that her dad was ill, she had gained enough perspective to see her dad as a person in his own context. She realized that her dad's inability to express feelings of loss and sadness for his mother's death had led to a resumption of his drinking, and she was able to take the news of dad's drinking in stride without feeling less for it. In fact, she now was able to trust the process of therapy and felt sure she would be able to achieve any changes she still wanted to make. Carol felt confident and in charge of herself. Despite dad's drinking, she was able to remain responsible for herself and leave the responsibility for her dad's drinking where it belonged — with him. She had a much clearer sense of herself.

Stage 3: Confronting the Alcohol

In stage 3, the client is able to come up with many of her own tasks. She now has a clear idea of how the family system works and a clear idea of what she is trying to accomplish with each family member. So, even though Carol was able to accept that her dad was drinking again, she still wanted to tell him how sad it made her. Carol planned another weekend home, with the goal of talking to her dad during a sober time. Her plan was to tell him how much she had enjoyed having a father during his dry spell. She wanted him to know how sad it made her to see him drinking again, because she still needed a father. Carol also planned to tell her mom that she felt sad about dad's drinking again and how nice it had been having a father for a while. Because Carol now saw her mother as a person, she found herself curious to know if her mother felt sad as she did and missed her husband. These two moves were very different for Carol. This would be the first time she talked to her dad directly about his drinking and the first time she spoke to her mom about dad's drinking only on behalf of her own feelings and not in response to her mother's worries.

THE SYSTEM SHIFTS. Exactly four weeks after Carol's visit home, her mom went to Alanon for the first time. And two weeks after that, dad called AA and asked for help, admitting himself to a detox hospital. At the same time, her sister Jennie stopped drinking and, though she did not go to AA, she began joining her mother at Alanon meetings. Because Carol's primary triangle was no longer operative, the system shifted; mom was now free to decide for herself to go to Alanon thus removing the last bit of protection from Carol's dad. This allowed him to hit bottom and call an AA contact for help in getting into a detox unit. As a result, Jennie no longer needed to ally with dad through drinking and was able to take responsibility for her own drinking problem.

CALLING A SPADE A "BOTTLE" (TALKING ABOUT THE FORBIDDEN SUBJECT). The last two tasks that Carol did before leaving therapy were major ones. Though Carol had dealt with her father and his alcoholism in the present, she had yet to resolve incidents that had occurred in the past. Tasks up to this point had been designed around the here and now relationships, even though they were based on generational themes. Certainly, all the work on the here and now had affected Carol's perceptions of her parents and sibs, but that is not the same as, nor should it get confused with, actually talking with a parent about unresolved issues that took place in the past, in an attempt to resolve them once and for all.

Carol was to write another letter to her dad. This letter was to enable Carol to return to "the scene of the crime" and resolve the outcome of an old issue in a new way. However, she would discuss this issue not as the 12-year-old she was when it happened but as the 26-year-old she was now. Carol had never told anyone in her family how upset she used to get as a child when her dad, drunk, would scream and curse at her and say abusive and hurtful things. I suggested she write an "I used to think . . . " letter* to father. This is a method that enables a person to talk about an incident that occurred in the past without accusations and blame. The client writes a letter pretending the hurt and angry feelings are in the past and uses this vehicle as a way to talk about the issue. By writing all about the angry and hurt feelings but

---

*This is a technique I learned from Betty Carter, who in turn learned it from Philip Guerin.

stating that those feelings are in the past, the client relieves the recipient of the letter from having to defend or explain his/her past behavior.

Therefore, Carol was asked to write a letter saying how as a child she used to think her dad didn't love her when he would drink, yell, curse, and call her abusive names. Then she was to add that now, as an adult, she realizes he really did love her and didn't mean any of those things. In this way, a person can bring up a highly toxic issue with a family member and express his/her true feelings without confronting or accusing the other person. This is not to be confused with blaming the alcohol for the poor behavior. The alcohol might be the reason a person gives for behaving inappropriately, but alcohol doesn't "make" a person "do" anything. Drunk or not, it is still the person and not the alcohol who is talking. Externalizing behavior to the bottle is an underresponsible-for-self position.

Because the topic of her dad's past verbal abuse was so highly charged, writing the letter turned out to be an extremely difficult task for Carol. In fact, Carol had to write several drafts, over a four-month period, before she was able to come up with a letter that stated her feelings clearly, put them truly in the past, and was devoid of anything confrontational. Before she mailed the letter, we discussed the possible responses she might get from her father and how she would handle them. Carol received a letter from her dad three weeks later, in which he apologized for all the verbal abuse and said he had always loved her. In processing the results of this task, Carol said that, though she would never forget the abusive incidents, she no longer felt that they were so important. They really were in the past now.

By summer, Carol's father began drinking again but this time, after only four weeks off the wagon, he readmitted himself to a 30-day detox program. Carol said she was finally coming to grips with being the child of an alcoholic. She even began questioning the possibility of their having been some sexual abuse as a child, even though she couldn't remember anything specific. By September, she finally took that last step with her boyfriend Larry and broke up with him. She then accepted a promotion at work which necessitated moving to the West Coast. Carol began the process of ending therapy.

Summary

Carol felt confident that she would be able to tackle a new job, in a balanced way this time, without falling back into her old pattern of trying to do the job perfectly. She also felt that she would be able to form new relationships without being overresponsible for the relationship's success. Carol planned to hook up with Alanon and find another ACOA group when she moved. She said she liked the supportive environment a group provided for checking out personal issues. Carol said she planned to continue working on family issues, as she felt she had one last important issue to settle. The issue was the sexual overtones of her relationship with her dad and the possibility of sexual abuse. She thought it was likely that the sexual problems she had when she was married to Hank were related to these unresolved feelings and worried that if she remarried these problems would recur. However, she felt she would take a break from therapy for a while.

In the three years Carol was in therapy, she learned how to have a personal relationship with her dad during his sober periods and to connect with other family members around personal issues instead of around dad's drinking. Her original role in the family of the perfect daughter had kept her allied with mom and distant from dad. This primary triangle of Carol, mother and father was organized around a rigidly fixed perspective. Dad was the sinner, who should have just shaped up and gotten his act together. Mom was the saint, who "stood by her man." Carol was the perfect daughter, who never quite got it right. As Carol shifted her position in this triangle, she came to see her mom as a person with her own difficulties and strengths and her dad as a sick man who felt overburdened with the care of his family. This new perspective allowed her to become an adult daughter to both her parents and to form peer relationships with her siblings that were developmentally and structurally appropriate. In the process, she learned to take responsibility for herself and her own needs, instead of being too responsible for others and not responsible enough for herself.

By redefining herself within the family system, Carol was able to gain true personal power, rather than pseudo power, over the shape of her life. In my opinion, to be in charge of the direction of your life is a gift well worth the hard work that multigenerational therapy requires.

REFERENCES

Altman, L. (1988, December 22). Test may show genetic tie to alcoholism. *The New York Times.*

Beattie, M. (1987). *Codependent no more.* New York: Harper & Row.

Bepko, C., & Krestan, J. A. (1985). *The responsibility trap.* New York: Free Press.

Berenson, D. (1976). Alcohol and the family system. In P. Guerin (Ed.), *Family therapy: Theory and practice.* New York: Gardner.

Bowen, M. (1978). *Family therapy in clinical practice.* New York: Aronson.

Carter, B., & McGoldrick, M. (1989). Overview: The changing family life cycle — A framework for family therapy. In B. Carter & M. McGoldrick (Eds.), *The changing family life cycle: A framework for family therapy* (2nd ed.) (pp. 3-28). Boston: Allyn & Bacon.

Elkin, M. (1984). *Families under the influence.* New York: Norton.

Fossum, M., & Mason, M. (1986). *Facing shame: Families in recovery.* New York: Norton.

Goodwin, D. (1976). *Is alcoholism hereditary?* New York: Oxford University Press.

Jesse, R. C. (1988). Children of alcoholics: Their sibling world. In. M. Kahn & K. G. Lewis (Eds.), *Siblings in therapy.* (pp. 228-252). New York: Norton.

Jesse, R. C. (1989). *Children in recovery*. New York: Norton.

Krestan, J., & Bepko, C. (1989). Alcohol problems and the family life cycle. In B. Carter & M. McGoldrick (Eds.), *The changing family life cycle: A framework for family therapy* (2nd ed.) (pp. 483–511). Boston: Allyn & Bacon.

McGoldrick, M. (1989). The joining of families through marriage: The new couple. In B. Carter & M. McGoldrick (Eds.), *The changing family life cycle: A framework for family therapy* (2nd ed.) (pp. 209–232). Boston: Allyn & Bacon.

Meyer, P. (1980). Between families: The unattached young adult. In B. Carter & M. McGoldrick (Eds.), *The family life cycle*. New York: Gardner.

Mondykowski, S. (1982). Polish families. In M. McGoldrick, J. K. Pearce, & J. Giordano (Eds.), *Ethnicity and family therapy*. New York: Guilford.

Stanton, M. D., Todd, T. C., & Associates (1982). *The family therapy of drug abuse and addiction*. New York: Guilford.

Steinglass, P. (1976). Experimenting with family treatment approaches to alcoholism, 1950–1975: A review. *Family Process, 16*, 97–123.

Steinglass (1979). Family therapy with alcoholics: A review. In E. Kaufman & P. N. Kaufman (Eds.), *Family therapy of drug and alcohol abuse* (pp. 147–186). New York: Gardner.

Steinglass, P. et al. (1987). *The alcoholic family*. New York: Basic Books.

Treadway, D. (1989). *Before it's too late: Working with substance abuse in the family*. New York: W. W. Norton.

Vaillant, G. (1983). *The natural history of alcoholism*. Cambridge, MA: Harvard University Press.

Woititz, J. (1983). *Adult children of alcoholics*. Deerfield Beach, FL: Health Communications.

❦15

Families With a Medically Ill Member

JANE S. JACOBS

CHRONIC MEDICAL ILLNESS is a special life circumstance that seriously affects a family's everyday practices and long-term priorities. Anxiety about the ill member's well-being, the burden of constant caretaking, and the loss of family income are common illness-related experiences straining family coping abilities. A triangle can emerge around the management of the illness if care responsibilities are assumed more and more exclusively by one family member and relinquished by others. Preoccupation with illness needs can shape or delay critical life-cycle tasks; decisions about whom to marry, when to leave home, and whether to have children can be powerfully influenced by the presence of a medical illness (Carter & McGoldrick 1989; Rolland, 1989). In this chapter we will consider the special challenges posed to families by chronic illness and describe the steps involved in treating families who are facing these dilemmas.

The particular effect of medical illness on a family depends on several interrelated factors (Rolland, 1984, 1987a, b, 1989) (see Table 15.1):

1. the phase and characteristics of the illness;
2. the contribution of important extrafamilial systems such as the medical caregiving system and the financial reimbursement system; and
3. the horizontal and vertical stressors within the family (Carter & McGoldrick, 1989).

TABLE 15.1
Key Factors in the Impact of Chronic Illness on the Family

I. *Illness Factors*
    A. Illness phase: Family tasks during acute and chronic phases
    B. Illness characteristics: Degree of predictability, monitoring, disability, stigma, nature
       of prognosis
II. *Extrafamilial Systems*
    A. Medical system
    B. Financial reimbursement system
III. *Intrafamilial System*
    A. Horizontal stressors: Triangles and life cycle issues
    B. Vertical stressors: Under/overfunctioning, conflict, separation

---

ILLNESS PHASE AND CHARACTERISTICS

Illness Phase

The tasks faced by family members in the acute phase of chronic medical illness are very different from those to be negotiated in the chronic phase (Jacobs, in press). The acute phase includes the initial period of diagnosis and medical interventions aimed at controlling symptomatology and preventing the further progression of the disease. The major tasks for a family during this time are to incorporate accurate information about the disorder as quickly as possible and to mobilize itself to deal with the immediate crisis. The illness becomes the main priority of family business; household tasks, work obligations, and social commitments are typically put on the back burner. While this high level of mobilization is not "normal," it is adaptive for families temporarily to narrow their focus of activity to cope with the illness crisis.

The chronic phase begins after the initial treatments have controlled the disease process to the extent possible. Depending on the illness, the chronic phase may involve, on the one hand, minimizing exacerbations through medications, diet, monitoring of patient activity or episodic hospitalizations, or, on the other, providing social supports for a stable or deteriorating level of disability. The caretaking tasks during the chronic phase may be great or minimal, but by a certain point they are known. It is important during the chronic phase of the illness that family members find a balance between illness demands and other family priorities.

Illness Characteristics

There is a growing literature on the impact of specific medical disorders on families (Hobbs & Perrin, 1985). Rolland (1984, 1987a, b) has also classified illnesses by similarities in onset, course, and prognosis. It is useful to think of the specific characteristics among medical illnesses that are likely to pose particular challenges to family life. Five examples of such characteristics are:

1. *Unpredictability*. Illnesses with unpredictable episodes, such as asthma, Crohn's disease, and sickle cell anemia, constantly disrupt a family's short- and long-term plans, including mealtimes, vacations, and special family events. These family members are no longer able to count on the rituals and traditions that so often give families a sense of stability and coherence.

2. *Intensive monitoring*. Serious conditions requiring close daily supervision, such as diabetes and renal disease, create dilemmas about the degree of involvement family members should have in the care of the patient. When the patient is an adolescent or when family members believe that the patient is not exercising adequate self-care, conflicts about the patient's level of autonomy arise.

3. *Uncertain prognosis*. End-stage renal disease, cancer, and congenital heart problems leave family members uncertain about the future. Family members may have difficulty realistically discussing plans for a time in which the patient will be deceased or in a nursing home. In addition, family activities may be extensively curtailed by fears of exacerbating the condition.

4. *Extensive disability*. Illnesses such as spina bifida and cystic fibrosis require an extraordinary degree of daily caretaking from family members. Often there is no ideal way of allocating care responsibilities. If one person assumes the lion's share, she has an impossible burden; if the responsibilities are shared, all family members' activities are regularly curtailed. Children and siblings of the disabled family member often feel guilty about leaving the family to pursue work or education in another location.

5. *Stigmatizing conditions*. Disfiguring conditions, such as pediatric craniofacial abnormalities, can interfere with the attachment process between the child and the rest of the family and with the patient's getting proper care. Stigmatizing illnesses, such as AIDS, affect family boundaries; family members are less likely to discuss their problems or ask for help from coworkers, friends and neighbors.

EXTRAFAMILIAL SYSTEMS

The unique requirements of a chronic medical illness bring the family into intimate and enduring relationships with other caregiving systems. The pattern of the family's response to the illness often shifts in reaction to changes in these separate but interlocking systems.

Medical System

Because of the expert role of medical professionals in diagnosing and treating the disorder, and because of the long-term relationships that develop between medical and family caregivers, family members often become highly attuned to issues and triangles within the medical system. Unacknowledged disagreements among the medical team may surface in the form of increased anxiety in family members, and difficulties encountered by the medical team in accepting their powerlessness over the illness may be reflected in similar feelings within the family. The exclusive focus of the medical team on the care of the patient may induce family members to further reorganize their priorities around illness requirements.

Financial Reimbursement System

The pattern of reimbursement by third-party payers to families with a chronically ill member will affect the nature of family organization around the illness. Public and private reimbursement systems typically pay for hospitalization and outpatient medical visits but rarely for such maintenance functions as transportation to specialty care facilities, special equipment needed at home, child care, social services and respite care (Hobbs, Perrin, & Ireys, 1985).

Such payment priorities force families to make difficult financial and moral decisions about how to allocate limited family resources. For example, should one spouse cut back on his full-time job, forfeiting some of the family income, so he can drive his daughter on a daily basis to an excellent long-term rehabilitation center? The lack of coverage for maintenance services tend to encourage heroic caretaking efforts on the part of family members.

HORIZONTAL AND VERTICAL STRESSORS WITHIN FAMILIES

Horizontal Stressor: Triangles in the Context of Chronic Medical Illness

Triangles that develop in families with a medical illness most frequently develop around (1) access to information, (2) responsibility for care, and (3) power to make decisions about the ill family member. The insider(s) in the triangle are privy to "special" information from the medical team or are thought to possess special expertise in the care of the illness. They are empowered to determine how the illness is progressing, how much the patient can do, and what can be discussed. They also often feel tremendously burdened by the responsibilities they have assumed. The outsider(s) in the triangle are not given, and do not seek, extensive information about the ill member. Neither do they seek additional caretaking responsibilities or decision-making authority. They are likely to feel isolated but may also feel relieved and somewhat guilty about their disengagement from the illness issues.

Horizontal Stressor: Chronic Illness and the Family Life Cycle

The appearance of a serious chronic illness can delay or distort ordinary life-cycle processes (Carter & McGoldrick, 1989; Rolland, 1989). Following are some of the most common examples of the ways in which this can happen.

Young adulthood. Young adulthood in most cultures involves a process of identification of values and goals that are similar to, or distinct from, those of one's origin family. Young adults typically make these distinctions through a choice of vocation, a decision to pursue advanced training in a particular field, and/or a serious commitment to an intimate relationship. Often the young adult goes through a series of such commitments before arriving at the "right" one.

The presence of a chronic illness during this period of development can constrain this process. The young adult may perceive, accurately or inaccurately, that fewer options are open and that a decision about work and an intimate commitment must be made quickly. Parental anxiety about the young person's well-being may add to this perception. As a result, the young adult may permit herself only a truncated period of exploration, a decision that may result in subsequent dissatisfaction with one's choices.

Committed couple relationship. Intimate relationships formed during this period may be organized around the illness and may set troublesome precedents, particularly in the area of underfunctioning/overfunctioning. Because anxiety about the illness may intensify the typical anxiety about one's ability to care for oneself at this stage, the young adult may select a partner who is prepared to be a permanent caretaker.

For instance, Sharon was diagnosed with Crohn's disease at age 19. Despite the episodic nature of the illness she and her parents came to view her as an invalid. At 24 she married Phil, a man who had been the caretaker of his asthmatic mother through much of his childhood. He was attracted by Sharon's consistent receptivity to his offers to support her financially and protect her from stress.

One of the tasks of the committed couple stage is the decision about whether and when to have children. The appearance of an illness with a strong genetic component, such as sickle cell anemia or Parkinson's disease, or with pervasive caretaking requirements, such as lupus or multiple sclerosis, may result in the couple's deciding not to have children.

Among homosexual partnerships, the stigma associated with the relationship can further isolate and burden the couple. The partner of the ill person often does not feel free to confide in any but the closest of friends about the illness circumstances. If the ill person is not insured, the partner usually cannot include the patient on his or her insurance policy and must shoulder major illness costs.

The family with young children. A family with young children is negotiating one of the most stressful periods of the life cycle. The time and energy it takes to care for young children must compete with a period in which the parents are usually striving to establish themselves in the workplace. If the partners are young, they usually do not have enough discretionary income to provide a great deal of childcare. It is a period when the partners are focused inward towards the rearing of the children.

The appearance of a serious illness during this phase can create an overwhelming pile-up of responsibilities. If one of the parents becomes significantly disabled, the family may lose its ability to provide adequate income or adequate childcare to its members. An ill child or parent diverts energy from the nurturing of the couple's relationship, a relationship that is at risk under any circumstances during this child-centered phase. If a disabling illness occurs to a single parent or to the custodial parent in a divorced family, some structural rearrangement will be necessary to provide both adequate income and child care.

Although Nick and Rita had been divorced for two years, much anger remained. When Rita was diagnosed with Hodgkin's disease, Nick immediately tried to gain custody of their daughter despite Rita's optimistic prognosis. After their daughter developed school problems, Nick and Rita were referred to a therapist who helped them see how the illness was triggering old unresolved conflicts that interfered with their co-parenting abilities. After many difficult months, they reached an agreement in which Rita remained the custodial parent and some of the child support money was earmarked for assistance for Rita during treatment periods or possible relapses.

The family with adolescents. During this phase the family is negotiating a more autonomous arrangement between parents and children. A serious illness in a child or parent can potentially interfere with this process. When the adolescent has a serious illness, especially one that requires extensive monitoring, there is a disruption of the mutual disengagement process. Under normal circumstances the adolescent sends out inconsistent signals as to how involved the parents should be in decision-making; similarly, parents are trying, through trial and error, to find the "right" degree of supervision. The presence of a serious or life-threatening illness raises the stakes of these negotiations to an exasperating level. When one of the parents has a serious illness, the ease with which the adolescent can separate is affected. The adolescent, who is ambivalent under any circumstance, may fear that neglecting his parent or getting into any kind of trouble may exacerbate the illness. The normal process of experimentation, conflict, and separation becomes disrupted for both generations.

The family with children leaving home. During this phase, the process of independence between the parents and children accelerates; the young adult children increasingly feel free to leave their origin family to pursue education, work, or an intimate relationship, and the parent(s) feel free to reaffirm the importance of their intimate relationships, their friendships, and their individual work and recreational interests.

If the young adult child has a chronic illness, the parents may be too anxious to support their offspring in his or her quest for independence; by conveying their fears or by providing excessive assistance, they may make it difficult for the child to separate. Reciprocally, the young adult may subtly communicate an inability to care for himself or herself, raising the parental level of anxiety. If a parent is the one with the medical illness, the child may feel guilty about leaving home; particularly if one spouse feels overwhelmed by the responsibility or the ill spouse conveys disappointment with her partner's competence, the child may be triangled in.

The parents' relationship may have been weakened by preoccupation with the illness. If much time was devoted to caring for a disabled child, the parents will feel anxious about being left alone. If the non-ill children are all in the process of leaving, and only the child with the illness will remain, there is a danger that the parents will become even more solicitous of the remaining child.

The couple in later life. The task of this phase is to deal with the process of retirement, aging, and death as successfully as possible. Medical illness in one partner can disrupt long-held plans for retirement. If much enjoyment was postponed to the retirement phase, then this change of plans can engender bitterness. In the post retirement period, the couple usually has to adjust to heightened contact; the presence of a serious illness greatly intensifies such an adjustment. If anxiety about illness management increases, the couple's children may be pulled in to diffuse the tension. The adult children are usually involved at this stage in the stressful task of raising young or adolescent children. The pressure of being inducted into the parents' conflicts may cause intolerable stress, which may surface in the adult children's marriage or in the next generation.

Vertical Stressors: Intergenerational Issues

Underfunctioning/overfunctioning relationships. When normal complementarity in a relationship becomes distorted, a situation may result in which one partner assumes much more than her share of the ongoing responsibilities in the relationship and the other partner assumes much less (Rolland, 1984). This may take the form of one partner's assuming the major financial responsibility, performing most of the household tasks, and worrying more about "how things in the relationship are going." These patterns are often repeated in the next generation in the following way: a parent who is overresponsible may raise a child who rarely has to worry about taking care of his own needs; this child is likely to select an overresponsible mate who will take over the role previously played by the parent.

When a serious medical illness is involved, this process can escalate rapidly. The legitimate needs of the illness make it easier for the non-ill partner to take over, and for the ill partner to relinquish, more and more responsibilities. The presence of the illness makes it more difficult for either partner to confront the imbalance in the relationship.

Level of conflict. Permission to disagree, and periodically to fight, is one of the most important contracts between individuals in an intimate relationship (Bowen, 1978). Disagreements are inevitable if both partners are able to take an "I" position. When a couple never fights, one partner is usually "giving up self" in order to accommodate to the other. Rules about acceptable levels of disagreement and the circumstances under which disagreements can take place are often transmitted to the next generation.

A chronic illness is likely to increase the constraints a family already feels about expressing conflict. When there is a serious illness, family members are often afraid to disagree or fight with the patient, for fear of triggering a relapse, or to fight with other family members, for fear of upsetting the patient. Family members begin to accommodate to the patient, creating a situation over time in which the patient becomes a tyrant and the family members willing victims. One of the children may become the focus for criticism or concern, in order to distract attention from unexpressed conflicts between the patient and other family members. Excessive concern for the patient can also be a cover for anger. The illness itself can become the third point on the triangle, diffusing tension between the ill person and another family member.

Separation issues. Unresolved issues in previous generations with regard to separation, loss, and death can be played out through illness management problems in the current generation. Unfinished business around a death in a previous generation may inhibit family members from addressing critical issues with a dying relative in the current generation. When separations historically are considered abandonments, children, spouses, or siblings of a chronically ill family member may feel that they cannot leave home to get married, to get divorced, or to go away to school because such an act would be morally unacceptable.

CASE ILLUSTRATION

The following will describe in some detail the therapy of a family with a 15-year-old diabetic boy over a period of about two years. Psychotherapy initially addressed the immediate conflicts in the nuclear family and then moved to a coaching model primarily with the boy's mother and, to a limited extent, with his father. The case illustrates the ways in which the specific nature of the illness, the quality of medical care, and horizontal and vertical stressors in the family all play a role in a family's response to a chronic medical illness.

Presenting Problem

Vicky O'Connell called me on the advice of her son's guidance counselor. Dennis, aged 15, was missing school and his grades were dropping sharply. All the members of the O'Connell household came to the first meeting. They included Vicky, 35, George, 36, Glen, 18, Dennis, Sally, 13, and Donna, 11 (see Figure 15.1).

While George remained quiet, Vicky described the fights that often erupted between Dennis and herself. The fights were usually about Dennis' compliance (or lack of it) with his daily diabetes regimen, which included urine and blood sugar tests and injections. According to Vicky, Dennis frequently ate high-sugar foods and then neglected to test his blood sugar. With the exception of one episode of ketoacidosis, his symptoms usually included lightheadedness, irritability, and dehydration.

Questioning revealed that George, Glen, and Donna were mostly unaware of Dennis' dietary practices and usually heard details about the fights from Vicky or from Sally, who sometimes jumped in to try to calm things down. Dennis said that he occasionally "strayed from the straight and narrow" of his diet but that he was not putting himself in serious danger and that his mother was "constantly following me around."

I inquired about Dennis' medical care arrangements and learned that he had regular appointments with the family pediatrician, who was responsible for monitoring his diabetes. All family members had confidence in the pediatrician.

Because the presenting problem involved management of Dennis' diabetes, I asked a series of questions in the initial session about the presence of

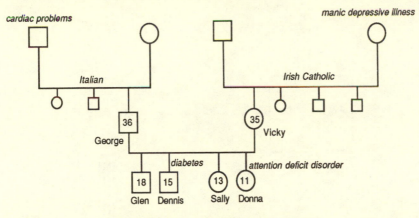

FIGURE 15.1   The O'Connell Family

medical illness in both parents' origin families (a problem-centered geno-gram). George's father had a chronic cardiac condition, and Vicky's mother had manic-depressive illness. Each spouse described his/her parent's illness as serious but currently under control.

The Foreground: Working With the Nuclear Family Triangle

I hypothesized that the primary triangle in the nuclear family consisted of an overly close conflictual relationship between Dennis and Vicky with George on the outside. After acknowledging the special stresses inherent in dealing with a chronic illness, I began to question each family member about the three positions in the primary triangle. George said that at one time he had been more actively involved with parenting the children, but that "I don't know as much about diabetes as my wife." Vicky said that George had become disengaged from all the children and that she felt com-pelled to "make up for his disinterest" with Dennis because of the risks connected with the illness.

I then asked all family members what they understood about Vicky's "insider" and George's "outsider" position in relation to the children. After a moment's silence, Glen volunteered that he thought his father had gotten less involved because of his drinking, and hastened to say, " . . . but he hasn't had a drink in years."

In tracing the alcohol history in the family, I observed an important link between the alcoholism and the management of the illness (see Figure 15.2). According to family members, Dennis' diabetes had been diagnosed five years ago, when George was still actively drinking. Taking primary responsi-bility for Dennis' care was only one of many parenting tasks Vicky had taken

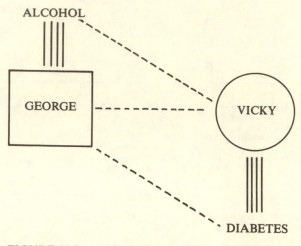

FIGURE 15.2   Alcoholism and Illness Management

over. Four years ago, George had made a decision to stop drinking and, with the help of regular AA meetings, he had remained sober ever since. However, the family never addressed the systemic effects of the alcoholism on the family, namely that George had become progressively more disengaged from the management of family business, while Vicky had taken on more and more household and parenting responsibilities. Glen had immersed himself in basketball and school activities to protect himself from being pulled in to fill the void, while Sally had taken on the role of "mother's helper" in parenting the remaining children. Although Glen and Sally both thought that their mother was monitoring Dennis too closely, they were afraid to say anything for fear of causing a serious medical crisis.

Reframing the Presenting Problem in Systems Terms

I began by emphasizing the family's strengths—the four years of sobriety and the concern of family members for each other and especially for Dennis. Then I described some characteristics of the O'Connell family that were common in families with adolescents and typical of families with a chronically ill member. I started with this information as a way of normalizing the family's dilemmas in the context of a serious illness and of the developmental tasks facing the family.

I emphasized that all parents face a dilemma in deciding how much independence to encourage in their adolescents, especially when teenagers give their parents mixed messages. When the adolescent has a serious illness, the stakes become much higher. In addition, other family members are more reluctant to talk about the illness management problems out of fear of triggering a dangerous medical episode. Finally, I mentioned, the period of alcoholism in the family had left the family with an inside and outside parent; they were not currently well positioned to address these difficult dilemmas as a team.

First Steps: The Parental Unit and the Diabetic Adolescent

Deciding to begin family-centered work with the primary triangle, I set up a series of meetings with the parents as a couple, with Dennis alone, and with the three family members together.

The purpose of the couple sessions was to provide a private setting for George and Vicky to discuss ways they might function more effectively as parents. Although I guessed that there were probably significant marital problems, my contract with the family at this stage was around illness management and I chose to focus discussions of their relationship around the illness issue.

As the parents began to talk, two interlocking triangles emerged: (1) Vicky, George, and the alcoholism, and (2) Vicky, George, and the illness. In the context of the alcoholism, George had fallen through on many commitments and Vicky had developed a view of George as incompetent; when the diabetes was diagnosed, she believed that only she could be trusted to handle such an important issue. After he became sober, George felt guilty and useless to his family. He made timid attempts to "get back in" to the center of family life, but he was intimidated by the seriousness of the diabetes. He too became convinced that only Vicky could be trusted, and he remained disengaged.

Both parents expressed interest in trying to change the current arrangement. They began tentatively to work on the process of sharing family responsibilities, including the illness, more equally.

The purpose of meeting separately with Dennis was to give him some space to articulate his own feelings about the illness as well as other important issues. He felt that the constant fights about the diabetes management had given the illness too great a role in his life. He couldn't tell how worried he really was about himself because his mother always worried for him. He admitted to provoking his mother at times by being secretive about his self-care practices. He also wanted to talk to his parents about colleges, but didn't know how to make contact with his father and wanted greater distance from his mother.

In the joint sessions, I helped the three family members to construct a different pattern of dealing with each other around the illness. I encouraged Dennis to use his physician as a primary resource to clarify the details of illness management and recommended that George, Vicky, and Dennis come to an agreement about which aspects of the illness were Dennis' responsibility and which were the parents'. It was decided that almost all care practices were Dennis' responsibility, with the consultation of his physician. Dennis, however, would take responsibility for giving his parents brief reports on his regular checkups. It was agreed that his parents needed to be involved with a few details; for example, the medical insurance system was very complicated, and Dennis needed his parents' help in making sure that he received maximum reimbursements. I suggested that Dennis get help from George in taking care of the insurance forms.

Any time a therapist recommends an important change in a family system, he or she must anticipate the consequences of change in the rest of the system. In this case I asked each family member in the triangle to anticipate what might happen as a result of these changes. All three expressed fears: Vicky that Dennis' diabetes would go out of control, George that he would make mistakes in his new role, and Dennis that he might forget to take urine or blood tests. I helped them to plan the way they would deal with these anxieties, encouraging the parents to talk to each other about their fears and Dennis to talk to his physician or to a friend of his who also had diabetes.

Over a period of two months, things began to change between Vicky, George, and Dennis. There were fewer fights between Vicky and Dennis, and more contact between Vicky and George and between Dennis and George. These changes were directly connected to my original formulation of the primary nuclear triangle.

The Background: Working With Multigenerational Processes

Although much of the family work was focused on Dennis, George, and Vicky, I had meetings of the entire family periodically to assess further consequences of change in the primary triangle. Just when it appeared that family members had grown comfortable with the new patterns, I began to notice a troublesome sign: Vicky began to talk more and more about Donna's attention deficit disorder. George, now more involved, was able to point out that the condition was being successfully handled through special services at Donna's school.

In discussing this further, Vicky reported that she had been feeling intense anxiety as she had been backing off from Dennis' care and had only felt relief when she immersed herself in Donna's learning problems. She confessed that, although she was successful in staying out of Dennis' day-to-day care, she had found furtive ways to watch him closely.

The initial problem-centered genogram had revealed that both spouses had parents with serious illnesses. I now decided to pursue this information further to determine whether intergenerational processes were interfering with Vicky's ability to relax her vigilance over her children's chronic conditions. Further questioning revealed that, although Vicky's mother was currently on medication, she had had terrifying manic episodes when her children were young, shouting obscenities at them and often beating them. Her father had sometimes intervened but had often seemed frightened of her mother as well.

Currently, when her symptoms were not in good control, Vicky's mother would call her occasionally on the telephone and hurl sharp criticisms at her. These episodes would bring back the terror of the early days. As Vicky described these events, her eyes opened wide with fear and she began to tremble slightly.

George explained that he had long known about Vicky's intense fear, but he had never felt permission to bring it up because the belief between them for so many years had been that he was "the one with the problem." He complained that his efforts to become closer to Vicky in recent months had sometimes been thwarted by her preoccupation with her mother. Vicky began to cry with relief, saying that the role of "the healthy one" had become an unbearable burden to her. She suddenly recognized that her vigilance with Dennis, and now with Donna, were efforts not to allow them to lose control, because loss of control with her mother had inevitably turned into a nightmare.

I asked if Vicky would be interested in doing some work on her own family of origin. She expressed trepidation but said she had to do it or she knew that she would never be able to let her children handle their disorders on their own.

The Background: Working With Vicky

The next phase of therapy involved meetings with Vicky every two to three weeks, interspersed with family meetings about every six weeks. Vicky first produced a detailed family genogram (see Figure 15.3). She came from a middle-class Irish Catholic family; she was the oldest of four children, with a sister two years younger and two brothers, four and five years younger. Both of her parents were still alive.

Because her father did not intervene decisively with her mother's illness, Vicky felt responsible for protecting herself and her siblings from her mother's rages. She spent much of her energy trying to keep peace by keeping everything running smoothly in the house. She called her sister's and brothers' teachers when they were sick and kept problems with the other children from both of her parents.

Vicky identified her major problem as one of trying to keep everything

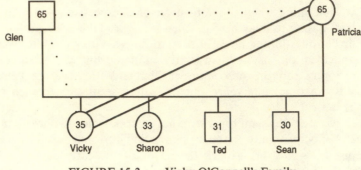

FIGURE 15.3   Vicky O'Connell's Family

stable by controlling any potential threats in her environment. She saw
herself as the only source of solutions. She wanted to handle the family-of-
origin work in the same intensely assertive way. I encouraged her to slow
down and to try to get help from other people along the way.

As a first goal, Vicky planned a trip to her parents' home simply to
experience how it felt to be in their presence as an adult. This step was
difficult because Vicky rarely visited them and then only with George and
her children as protection. She did go, however, and experienced intense
anxiety and the constant desire to control her circumstances, e.g., to invite
other people over or to check whether her mother had taken her medication.

We talked for several sessions about Vicky's need to be strong and to rely
only on herself. Vicky insisted that she could never rely on anyone in her
family. I encouraged her to look through her genogram to see if she could
"discover" a family member to talk with. Reluctantly, Vicky said that her
sister was someone who might understand. They were in frequent communication, with Vicky in the "helper" position, but they never discussed their
growing up years. It was many weeks before Vicky could bring herself to
contact her sister in a different context. She finally decided to write to her
and briefly to share some of the difficulties she was having in her own
family. Admitting that she didn't always "have it together" was one of the
hardest things she had ever done.

Her sister responded warmly, calling her immediately and offering support. Vicky was surprised to find that she felt very panicky; she realized
that, when the tables were turned, she herself felt out of control. She began
to learn that not every way of losing control was bad. She began to call her
sister regularly. After several months, she and her sister began to talk about
the frightening circumstances of their childhoods. It was helpful to have her
experiences validated.

Meanwhile, back in the family sessions, Vicky's new experiences with allowing herself to depend on other people were generating changes between herself and George. She was able to notice and accept more of his strengths and to share more of her feelings with him. This was what George had been asking for over the past few months, but when she allowed more closeness he was not sure what to do with it. I had in part anticipated this turn of events and, in noticing the changes in Vicky, begun to tease George with the question, "What if you should get what you want?" It was hard for George to stay in close, but he was able to talk about it in the periodic couple sessions.

In the next stage of coaching, Vicky began to talk about approaching her parents with some of the issues she had been working on. She decided to approach her father, as he was by far the less scary parent. She set a clear goal: to be able to share with him some of the issues she was working on currently without trying to protect him from any feelings he might have in hearing this information. In the beginning she wanted to blame him for her problems and hoped that he would apologize to her. It took her four sessions to give up on trying to orchestrate a certain outcome. I emphasized that she could only control her own experience in the encounter. Vicky eventually set as a goal that she would only talk about her own struggles and would concentrate on noticing her own feelings in the conversation. I helped her to anticipate her father's most likely reactions and to plan how she could deal with them.

When she visited her parents and told her father about some of the things she was struggling with, he became defensive. Even though she did not blame him, he was visibly shaken and angry. Although the preparation for the encounter had helped to some degree, Vicky still felt responsible afterwards for upsetting him and went through two weeks of depression. Finally, she began to realize that she could only be responsible for her own feelings; she could not control his or anyone else's. Gradually, her depression lifted. This was a turning point in her work.

Soon after this phase of the work a medical crisis erupted with Dennis, which tested Vicky's progress. The pediatrician with whom Dennis had worked so successfully moved to another city and Dennis began to see another physician who believed in much tighter control of the diabetes. Dennis rebelled against this strict regimen, taking his insulin sporadically, and developed ketoacidosis. Vicky was surprised by her ability to stay calm and to advise Dennis that this was an issue that he needed to address with his new doctor. Laughter erupted in the family session when it became apparent that George knew more details about Dennis' condition than Vicky.

Vicky is currently involved in the most difficult phase of her work — changing her relationship with her mother. Her goals are to feel in control of her own well-being when she is in contact with her mother. She has made several changes. In an effort to move away from a reactive position, she now calls her mother as often as her mother calls her. Some of the conversations are relatively satisfying, and Vicky is learning simply to experience the possibilities of their relationship. When her mother becomes intensely critical, Vicky tells her firmly that she does not want to talk to her under these circumstances, tells her that she would welcome a call when her mother is calmer, and then terminates the conversation. Vicky believes that this is a long-term undertaking, and anticipates continuing therapy sessions every three to four months for the next few years.

The Background: Working With George

For the most part, George followed Vicky's efforts with considerable interest but without as great a desire to work with his own family. During one phase of Vicky's journey, however, George had some dramatic insights which he did follow up with some family-of-origin work of his own. When Vicky began to see George's strengths and to seek his support and guidance, George was surprised to find that he was filled with sadness. He met with the therapist several times and began to explore his own position in his family (see Figure 15.4). George was the youngest of three children with an older sister and brother in a blue-collar Italian family. He recalled that during his father's illnesses and other family crises, both his parents tended to look to his sister for emotional and practical support. The boys were seen as unreliable. He did not think that his parents ever told him about his father's symptoms or prognosis, nor did he ask, even when he was a young

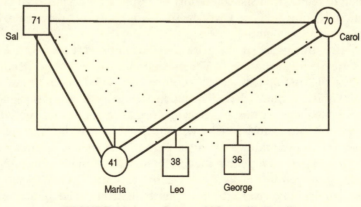

FIGURE 15.4   George O'Connell's Family

adult. When Vicky looked to him for help, it was the first time that anyone close to him thought he might be capable of it.

Having observed Vicky's work with her family, George decided to try to take a more responsible position with respect to members of his family of origin. He chose not to talk extensively with his family about this, but rather to try to change his behavior. He remembered that his parents had complained recently that their heating system was breaking down. He went to a local bookstore and sent them a consumer book on repairing and replacing heating systems. Next time they spoke to him they thanked him, but nothing more was said. Two months later, some weeks after his father's brother had died, he called his father to see how he was doing. Again, his father seemed appreciative but no further comments were made.

Several weeks later, his mother called him to ask if he knew anything about retirement communities. They were talking about selling their house and were trying to get some information on different options. George called someone at work whose parents had moved into a retirement community and got their telephone number for his parents. After these three events, George's parents began to ask him for advice periodically. He felt enormously gratified by these calls, and his success with his parents seemed to reinforce his ability in his own family to provide information and guidance.

Case Summary

In this case I began by identifying the primary triangle in the nuclear family around the presenting problem, that of the management of an adolescent's diabetes. In this triangle the adolescent and his mother had an overly close, conflictual relationship, while the father remained on the periphery. The level of conflict was exacerbated by the specific nature of diabetes, which requires close monitoring, and by the life-cycle phase of the family, in which the development of autonomy was a central task. Initial moves included placing the family's problems in a larger developmental context and helping each family member in the primary triangle to understand his or her role in the problem.

Although the level of anxiety in the original triangle was reduced, hints of a new triangle with another child suggested that toxic intergenerational processes might be at work. A multigenerational interlocking triangle emerged on the mother's side of the family; the violent pattern resulting from her mother's uncontrolled illness, her father's passivity, and her own overresponsible position was now replicated as she assumed the same overresponsible position with her rebellious diabetic son and her withdrawn husband.

Through extensive multigenerational work the mother eventually learned the consequences of her overresponsible position and began to relate to her family of origin in new ways. These changes in turn had consequences for the work in the mother's own family.

Although in less extensive ways than the mother, the father followed up on changes emerging in the family work by exploring some of the roots of his underresponsible behavior. He was able to change his role in his family of origin to some extent by assuming greater responsibilities with his aging parents. These changes in turn reinforced the parents' more equal relationship with regard to their son's illness. The father was able to become more appropriately involved, while the mother was able to allow her son to deal more independently with problems around management of the diabetes.

CONCLUSION

This chapter has presented the ways in which a particular life stressor, chronic medical illness, affects critical organizational processes within families. In this circumstance, a biological "given" – the illness – emerges in the context of a particular set of triangles, life-cycle issues, and intergenerational themes. These factors influence the beliefs the family develops about the illness and the methods through which family members allocate care responsibilities. While all chronic illnesses force families to make decisions about balancing illness demands and other family priorities, specific illnesses pose particular dilemmas about planning activities, monitoring the patient, including outsiders, and setting limits on illness responsibilities.

The family therapist who works with a family facing this circumstance must identify the specific requirements of the illness, the current family life-cycle tasks, the primary triangles operating in the management of the illness, toxic intergenerational issues influencing illness beliefs, and the impact of the medical caregiving and financial reimbursement systems. The therapist's initial goal will be to help the family members in the primary triangle to shift their positions with regard to illness management and to deal with the consequences of these changes in the family system. Subsequently, one or more family members may elect to explore the implications of such changes within their origin families; this objective will involve long-term coaching with the family therapist, with the client taking on more and more responsibility for treatment goals and strategies.

REFERENCES

Bowen, M. (1978). *Family therapy in clinical practice*. New York: Aronson.
Carter, B., & McGoldrick, M. (1989). *The changing family life cycle: A framework for family therapy* (2nd ed.). Boston: Allyn & Bacon.

Hobbs, N., & Perrin, J. (Eds.). (1985). *Issues in the care of children with chronic illness: A sourcebook on problems, services and policies.* San Francisco: Jossey-Bass.

Hobbs, N., Perrin, J. & Ireys, H. (Eds.). (1985). *Chronically ill children and their families: Problems, prospects, and proposals from the Vanderbilt study.* New York: Jossey-Bass.

Jacobs, J. (in press). Family therapy in the context of child medical illness. In A. Stoudemire & B. Fogel (Eds.), *Medical psychiatric practice.* Washington, DC: American Psychiatric Press.

Rolland, J. (1984). Toward a psychosocial typology of chronic illness. *Family Systems Medicine, 2,* 245–262.

Rolland, J. (1987a). Chronic illness and the life cycle: A conceptual framework. *Family Process, 26:* 203–221.

Rolland, J. (1987b). Family illness paradigms: Evolution and significance. *Family Systems Medicine, 5:* 467–486.

Rolland, J. (1989). Chronic illness and the family life cycle. In B. Carter and M. McGoldrick (Eds.), *The changing family life cycle: A framework for family therapy* (2nd ed.) (pp. 433–456). Boston: Allyn & Bacon.

16

Families Facing Terminal Illness

ELLIOTT J. ROSEN

THERE IS PROBABLY NO more dramatic point in the life cycle when individuals need to attend to the resolution of unfinished family business than when a family member is suffering from life-threatening illness. There is, of course, an irony inherent in this period, since an enormous amount of emotional and physical energy is likely to be expended in family caretaking functions, leaving little for the difficult tasks required with nuclear and extended family members. However, it is important for the clinician to see this time as both a necessary and opportune moment for coaching. The climate in the family changes dramatically in the face of serious illness and imminent death; this creates special opportunities for individuals to make realignments in family relationships (Bowen, 1976). It is also important to note that there is no more urgent time for changes to take place in family relationships than when a family member is about to die. The prevailing feeling of "last chance" that accompanies terminal illness often creates an atmosphere in which individuals feel free to make moves they might otherwise resist (Paul, 1967; Rosen, 1990).

It is also helpful to keep in mind that coaching in most circumstances promotes an "imposed process" of grieving. Since the primary goal of coaching is to potentiate the individuation necessary for growth and development, the method, when used properly, serves to create a natural process of mourning. Coaching involves the giving up of old relationship patterns and the reconstruction of the emotional process in the family system. Given this reality, there is a loss which the individual suffers when making these necessary moves. It has been suggested that genuine change can take place only when individuals become profoundly aware of their aloneness (Fogarty, 1976). This is, indeed, akin to the experience of one who is grieving the actual loss of a loved one. Changing relationship patterns can often feel like a kind of death has occurred; thus, coaching is a method particularly well suited to cases where a family faces imminent loss.

This chapter will consider three basic issues in coaching individual family members in times of terminal illness:

1. the impact of imminent death on the family system at various stages of the life cycle;
2. coaching as a tool for facilitating anticipatory grief and for reallocation of family roles at different life-cycle stages; and
3. the impact of previous family losses and the implications for coaching.

In addition, we will examine a specific treatment case as a model for understanding the role of coaching in families dealing with life-threatening illness.

IMMINENT DEATH AND THE FAMILY SYSTEM

When a family is dealing with the terminal illness of one of its members, it is also facing an imminent reorganization of the entire system (Cohen, Dizenhuz, & Winget, 1977). The family's universe is about to suffer a dramatic blow and individual members have begun to brace themselves for the moment when the family will cease to be what it has always been. Needless to say, the function of the patient in the family's emotional life will have a bearing upon how family members anticipate the future (Hare-Mustin, 1979; Herz Brown, 1989), but regardless of who is about to die the family will never be the same. Families facing terminal illness are likely dealing with a multitude of systems issues, many of them far too complex for discussion here. However, it is helpful to point out four general areas of family reactivity to terminal illness:

1. a high level of disorganization, likely related to shock and denial, which are particularly prominent in early stages of diagnosis;
2. fear and anxiety, particularly related to the uncertainty that serious illness creates in terms of caretaking roles, as well as concern for the future of the family;
3. varying intensity of emotional lability in family members; and

4. a "closing-up" or turning inward of the nuclear family, which may include cutoffs both within the family and with extended family members.

Although these issues are common to some degree in most cases of impending death, there are fundamental differences in the ways in which families will experience loss at various stages of the family life cycle. There are stages of the life cycle during which the primary tasks have to do with disengagement and leaving; other stages have as their focus the need for consolidation and drawing inward (Hoffman, 1989; Rolland, 1989). It must be noted that the family's ability to accommodate to the potential loss of significant members is highly correlated with its developmental stage.

At "centrifugal" stages of the family life cycle, such as adolescence and young adulthood, when the necessary emotional tasks are to help family members to disengage themselves from the system, terminal illness and imminent death may have the effect of creating an impediment to the natural leave-taking expected at this time in the family developmental process.

For the Ahearns, an Irish-Catholic family, the eldest daughter Bridget experienced enormous conflict with her fiancé, which began shortly after her mother's diagnosis of cancer. Within months of the diagnosis her engagement had been broken, Elizabeth, her younger sister, decided to transfer to a local college and move back home, and James, the youngest of the children, began making plans to join his father in the latter's construction business rather than go off to college. None of the three Ahearn children made a connection between what was happening in their lives and their mother's illness.

Coaching work with this family took into account ethnic background and the implicit cultural expectation that the eldest female child, in particular, would become the caretaker for her mother. A primary clinical intervention involved coaching mother to "release" her children from a caretaking role by having her connect with members of her family of origin—primarily her older, widowed sister and a favorite aunt—and invite them to help nurse her during her illness. Also, the family was helped to accept the services of the local community hospice program so that the children could more critically examine some of the decisions they had made about their own lives.

In families who are in "centripetal" periods of the life cycle, such as newly married couples, families with young children, or families who have launched their children, the impact of terminal illness may be to create a developmental arrest in the family process. In the case of young families, members may be unable to carry out tasks appropriate to the necessary individuation from their family of origin. Or, in the case of families where children have been launched, the couple may find themselves unable to establish a strong, new bond as a marital dyad. Fatal illnesses at early stages of the life cycle may contribute to a sense of despair about the future, as well as confusion as to where to turn for support. On the other hand, losses at the launching phase of the life cycle—a centrifugal stage—may create a despair about the past and a refusal to continue with life's tasks.

The following case illustrates the issues facing a young couple in the first stages of forming a new family. It is important to note that even in a new marriage, where the emotional process is clearly centripetal, each new spouse has only recently been part of a family where the tasks of the launching stage may have been set in motion but are not yet fully accomplished.

The Hartmans, a newly married couple in their twenties, were referred for marital therapy soon after the wife, Margo, was diagnosed with a life-threatening cancer a few months after the marriage. It was clear that both her and her husband Tom's anxiety around the illness made visits to the doctor and planning for treatment quite difficult for both of them. In addition, Margo's mother and her father (a physician) had become very involved with their daughter's illness, and a great deal of conflict, both overt and covert, had begun to develop in the family.

A primary treatment goal was to encourage Margo to continue the process of differentiation from her parents which she had begun when she moved from her home a year or so before her marriage to Tom. By carefully coaching her to include her parents in discussions about the illness, to use her father's contacts in the medical community when appropriate, and to specifically invite her mother to be with her when she needed support and Tom was unavailable, I helped Margo and Tom to reconstruct the boundaries they had begun to develop when they married. The ease with which Margo could ignore Tom and turn to her parents for help at this transitional stage of the life cycle had to be countered by enabling the two young people to establish strong boundaries and define themselves as a couple.

The Ahearn and Hartman cases both suggest that, regardless of the stage of the life cycle a family is in when it faces terminal illness, a likely complication will be family members' difficulty in mastering the process of individuation. In the case of the Ahearns, mother's illness threatened all three children's separation (i.e., the primary task of the centrifugal stage of launching) and a state of developmental arrest had come about. Margo Hartman had been able to begin the process of individuation by marrying and leaving home. But since healthy separation is not a singular event, magically achieved when one marries, but rather a complicated and often long-term process, her illness threatened to bring that process to a halt. While the clinical intervention with each family might seem quite different, in both cases the essential aim was to help the family to establish appropriate boundaries, a vital dimension of the coaching process. With the Ahearns, the mother was strongly encouraged to look beyond her nuclear family for support, thus allowing her children to feel safe in continuing their still embryonic moves toward differentiation. By coaching the Hartmans to include Margo's parents in her medical treatment, I empowered the young couple to set the boundaries for themselves, rather than feeling overwhelmed by the intrusion of the maternal in-laws.

COACHING AND ANTICIPATORY GRIEF

The onset of grief reactions during the period preceding a likely death has been well documented in the literature (Fulton & Gottesman, 1980; Glick, Weiss, & Parkes, 1974; Rando, 1986; Schoenberg et al. 1974). Anticipatory grief is a complex phenomenon that has seldom been explored from the vantage point of the family systems clinician. While highly valued and much examined as a valuable emotional preparation for loss in both patients and their loved ones from an individual perspective, anticipatory grief may also be viewed from a systems perspective (Lebow, 1976; Rosen, 1990). What this means, of course, is that process of grieving in anticipation of a loss is one that involves not only the individual and his/her intrapsychic process but also the nuclear family and its ability to perform certain important tasks. In addition, viewed from a systems perspective, the process works bidirectionally, including both the impact of the loss upon extended family and the ways in which family-of-origin issues influence the family in the present. Bowen (1976) has called this process an "emotional shock wave."

Following the death of significant persons, the family is faced with the demand for fundamental reorganization, functionally as well as emotionally (Herz Brown, 1989). Depending upon the place of the deceased in the system, as well as the family's phase in the life cycle, this reorganization may be relatively uncomplicated or highly disruptive and dysfunctional. If the family is in a centripetal phase of the life cycle (such as the family with young children), many functional tasks will need to be performed. In more centrifugal phases (such as the family in later points in the life cycle), while there will surely be some demand for performance of functional tasks, greater stress will be placed on the emotional equilibrium of the family (Rolland, 1989).

Anticipation of the need for reorganization, functional or emotional, as well as the recognition of what may be expected of family members when their loved one has died, may begin at the point of diagnosis of life-threatening illness. However, it is important to note that anticipatory grief, as a recognizable entity, does not automatically ensue at the time of diagnosis (Rando, 1986). The processes of denial may impede the family's ability to begin the actual tasks of anticipatory grief; thus, the clinician cannot assume that families immediately begin thinking about the need for reorganization. Depending upon the openness of the family, these feelings may be acknowledged by family members or kept secret.

From clinical observation it would appear as though there exists a natural tendency on the part of the system to "close up" in the face of fatal illness and death, and this has been documented in the literature (Bowen, 1976; Evans, 1976). This is not a unique phenomenon; in fact, family systems theory suggests that at extremely stressful points in the life cycle most systems will turn inward (Guerin, Fay, Burden, & Kautto, 1987; Hoffman, 1989). Family members may withdraw and feel awkward and uncomfortable in discussing the situation they face. An implicit agreement to protect "vulnerable" family members, such as children, the elderly, or those perceived as emotionally unstable, is often forged and has the net effect of closing the system, thus protecting no one (Gerber et al., 1975; McGoldrick & Walsh, 1983). Coaching a family at the earliest stages of fatal illness can be extremely valuable, particularly in terms of opening lines of communication and encouraging family members to confront their apprehension about what the future might bring.

Although choosing to use coaching as a method of treatment may be indicated in a variety of situations, with tasks as varied as individuating from an enmeshed system to reconnecting with a disengaged one, for a family facing the imminent death of a significant member the process is likely to focus upon the opening up of the nuclear and extended family systems (Rosen, 1987). We shall examine here an example of work with a nuclear family, where it was important to give members a way in which to communicate openly among themselves their concerns and fears about the future of the family and their place in what is surely to be a reorganized family structure.

The Kamens, an upper-middle-class Jewish family, were first seen on a hospice-related home visit during the final few months of Laurie Kamen's life. Having suffered for two years from amyotrophic lateral sclerosis, Laurie, 47, had virtually no muscle control, although she remained lucid and capable of communicating via complicated electronic means. Her husband, Jules, had participated actively in her physical care and their four children (Scott, 20, Michael, 18, Lisa, 13, and Rebecca, 7) were also involved in caring for their mother. While the Kamens appeared to be a warm and open family, closer examination revealed that they were more verbal than communicative. The two younger children seemed somewhat confused by their mother's illness and Rebecca seemed quite naive about the fact that her mother had little more than a few months to live. Lisa spent much time in helping around the house (the Kamens had a full-time live-in housekeeper who had been with them since Rebecca's birth) but not a great deal of time with her mother. Michael seemed depressed, and I only met Scott once during his vacation from college.

Coaching with the Kamens was short-term (approximately eight meetings) and was based on the premise that a shift to a more open family function was vital to their future survival. The work had three specific goals: (1) helping to open up the system, allowing for increased communication about the nature of mother's illness and the imminence of her death; (2) discussing the implications for the future of the family without mother's presence — the beginning of the reallocation of roles; and (3) planning together with the entire family the funeral and subsequent mourning period.

It should be noted here that this case demonstrates work within the nuclear family. In contrast, coaching a family toward work with extended family members involves a different approach, focusing not so much on the internal functioning of the nuclear family as upon cutoffs in the families of origin. This approach will be explored more closely when we examine a specific case in greater depth. While the nature of relations with extended family members shifts in response to life-threatening illness, it is in the nuclear family system where there is the keenest awareness that, among other things, there is likely to be an important shift in members' roles in the family.

It has been pointed out that " . . . to prepare for or anticipate the death of a loved one brings forth deliberation about role functioning after death" (Gerber, 1974, p. 27). How such deliberations are processed within the family system — among family members — is an important concern of the family therapist and a significant component of the process of coaching. Clinical observation would suggest that families in which there is greater openness, including a less rigid, non-gender-related allocation of roles, will find it easier to contemplate future structural changes in the family. In families where there is less flexibility in the allocation of roles, where family hierarchy is rigidly stratified, and where communication is not open, one is likely to find fewer, and less successful, attempts at role reallocation, particularly following the death of a mother (Kuhn, 1981; McGoldrick & Walsh, 1988).

In conjunction with this, Vess, Moreland, and Schwebel (1985–86), in a study of role reallocation following a death, found that the family's life-cycle stage was a highly significant variable in performing the tasks necessary to shift family roles. For example, the death of a young spouse before the birth of children is likely to leave the surviving spouse fairly well equipped to deal with the changes that must come about in his/her status as a young widow; however, in a family where a young mother has died, leaving the care of children to a surviving father, the complicated demands of child-rearing, housekeeping, and the maintenance of a professional life might prove overwhelming. In our culture men have not been expected to learn the skills of maintaining open relationships, communicating feelings, or nurturing children—all important tasks following a significant family loss—particularly that of the mother. Thus, the life cycle stage of the family and the gender of the surviving spouse, as well as the openness of the system, are primary components of future functioning for the family facing life-threatening illness, particularly when the patient has served a central role, functionally or emotionally, in the family (Herz Brown, 1989; Kuhn, 1981; Rosen, 1990; Sanders, 1979).

PREVIOUS LOSSES IN THE FAMILY

In a previous clinical study (Rosen, 1988–89), I described a strong relationship between the development of pathological grief reactions and the presence of unresolved losses in the family system. It was Paul and Grosser (1965) who first suggested a family systems orientation—"operational mourning"—for working with families in which dysfunction might be connected to a previous loss in the family. Many observers, representing a wide variety of therapeutic orientations, have addressed this connection (Paul & Paul, 1982; Reilly, 1978; Sanders, 1979; Walsh, 1978). Unresolved grief in the family's past is likely to have most impact at major transitional points in the life cycle, when issues of loss are prominent (Herz Brown, 1989; McGoldrick & Walsh, 1988). It follows, then, that whenever a family is dealing with terminal illness it becomes vital for the clinician to take a careful history and construct a good three-generational genogram to assess the presence of past losses and the ways in which these losses were dealt with.

The presence of previous, unresolved losses in the family also has powerful implications for our consideration of coaching family members facing the imminent death of a loved one. Contrary to popular belief, time, by itself, does not heal. When requisite grief work is done and the meaning of any loss, past or present, is understood and integrated, one can be said to have achieved resolution. It is not unusual for losses at early stages of development to remain unresolved, well into adulthood.

It is helpful to very briefly examine two important factors that may account for the irresolution of early stage loss in the family life cycle: the nature of child-rearing and ethnicity. For children, in particular, the grieving process is often complicated, and indirect symptoms of a child's grief are likely to be identified as a presenting problem to the family therapist. It remains common practice in many families for children to be protected from the rawer aspects of the grieving process (Grollman, 1967; Raphael, 1983), such as attendance at funerals, presence in the grieving household, viewing of the deceased, or permission to discuss the loss or openly express volatile emotions.

Such protection may be related to the family's ethnic background, which is a vitally important factor to consider, both when investigating family members' experience with previous losses (Herz Brown, 1989; McGoldrick & Walsh, 1988) and when helping them to prepare themselves for the process of grieving and reallocating family roles (Rosen, 1988, 1990). Some ethnic groups remain more in touch with the implications of the emotional flow of life and death than others. Thus, family members are more likely to be heir to appropriate rituals and ceremonies for coping with loss, and better able to adjust than in families where children are typically kept from wakes, funerals, and the expression of grief. This is not to suggest, however, that one's participation in a funeral ritual is, in itself, sufficient for a mourning process to be set in motion or for a functional grief process to take place. One study (Doka, 1984–85) suggests that prior expectation of a death is a more important factor in subsequent adjustment than participation in a funeral or other rites, and such prior information would be more characteristic of an open system. Of course, personalizing and utilizing rituals are important facets of successful mourning. However, the clinician should be aware that a child's participation in these rituals may not in itself be sufficient to assure good adjustment.

When, through examination of a family's history, it becomes evident that there are losses in previous generations that may interfere with the family's ability to adjust to the death now imminent, it is important to view this as an important indicator for coaching. A basic systems orientation demands that we not perceive any death in a vacuum but as part of an evolutionary, circular component of the family's history across at least three generations (Herz Brown, 1989). It should be pointed out that "loss" in the family can be defined in a variety of ways. A death in the present or an earlier generation is an obvious example of loss; however, the clinician should be aware of the presence of other kinds of losses, such as divorce or emotional cutoffs from family members, which may also have a potentially devastating impact on the family, as in the following case.

Albert Graham, 41, had become the primary caretaker for his mother, Alice, in the wake of her terminal cancer. The Grahams were referred for a consultation by a hospice social worker, who had been struggling with what she identified as their resistance and denial of the seriousness of Mrs. Graham's illness. Another son, Martin, 50, was an infrequent visitor due, it was explained, to his severe emphysema and his uncooperative wife.

In an initial interview there was clearly a refusal to accept the prognosis of Mrs. Graham's imminent death; also, the patient stated that she was afraid of what would happen to Albert afterwards. Whenever she alluded to her death, Albert became visibly upset and, in fact, needed periodically to leave the room. The social worker had indicated that the three Grahams comprised the entire family; the father had died some 25 years before, shortly after the Grahams' divorce. However, when a careful history was taken, it was discovered that there was an eldest, third son, Eugene, who had been cut off from the family since early adulthood. Having left home after a bitter dispute with his mother (whom he apparently blamed for "throwing his father out"), Eugene had no contact with any family member and was, of course, unaware of his mother's illness. Careful questioning of Mrs. Graham revealed that she had never ceased "mourning" this loss.

Albert's role in this family drama had been to never leave home, providing mother with a solid caretaker on whom she could depend. As is often the case, there were extended family members who knew of Eugene's whereabouts (he was married with three grown children and a number of grandchildren) and, in fact, he had attempted to make contact with his mother on a few occasions some years before.

The unresolved cutoff with Eugene was a clear indicator for coaching with the Grahams. Mrs. Graham was prescient in her concern for Albert, since his undisputed role as her only caretaker and the patterns of cutoffs in the family were likely to leave him with a grief that would not be easily resolved. Any "frontal assault" on the family's reconnecting with Eugene would have been met with complete resistance; however, bringing Albert and Martin together for a series of meetings initially designed to strengthen their sibling alliance allowed Albert some respite from his constant care of mother. It also resulted in discussion between the brothers and with mother regarding their elder brother and whether he should be informed of his mother's illness.

Suggesting some contact with Eugene involved delicate negotiations and initially involved merely finding out where he was and who in the extended family actually had contact with him. There then followed an exchange of letters between the brothers and, while Eugene did not get to see his mother before she died, they did speak on the telephone. Opening the family system in this way was intended to provide Albert with a larger framework within which to cope with his loss, particularly since Eugene's cutoff from the family represented one significant aspect of the family's reaction to father's death a quarter century earlier. Some months later Albert reported that he had been invited to California to visit with his brother and that he was seriously considering making the trip.

This case was an example of how coaching of family members in anticipation of a death can be an important factor in preparing them to grieve without symptomatic complications, particularly in cases where previous losses may have resulted in closing down the system or creating cutoffs. In cases where there are previously unresolved losses, as with the Grahams, the coaching must first address those losses and enable family members to make some changes in the system.

We will now examine the coaching process with one adult sibling in a family where a number of important systemic factors converge to intensify the experience, among them a repetitive, destructive response to previous loss, cutoffs among siblings, power struggles, geographic distance, ethnic complications, and issues of gender and birth order.

CASE EXAMPLE: THE MCCULLUM/GORMAN FAMILY

Ellen Gorman McCullum and her husband John had come for treatment around some marital issues that had been troubling them both for about four years. Issues of power, particularly around the handling of money in the family, Ellen's depression and nagging of John, and John's remoteness and lack of involvement with their children were the presenting problems. John was the eldest of two sons from a Boston Irish family and Ellen was the eldest daughter and second of six children in a Catholic family from Texas (see Figure 16.1).

Four years before the beginning of treatment Ellen's father had died after a two-year bout with cancer and her mother had been diagnosed with Alzheimer's disease. At the time of her father's death only two of the six Gorman children—the unmarried ones—were still living in the Houston area: Jack, the eldest son, 47, and Sally, 37, the youngest daughter. Jack lived with his mother in the original family home and had become her primary caretaker when she first began to develop symptoms of Alzhei-

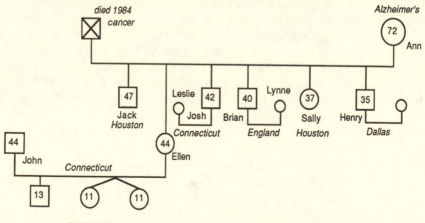

FIGURE 16.1   The McCullum and Gorman Families

mer's. Sally was actively on the scene and, having been the child closest to her father, completely took over her mother's finances after his death. This included a role as executor of the estate, control over monies which would ultimately be divided among the children, and specifically, a quasi-parental role with her underfunctioning brother Jack, in which she supervised a month allowance which he had received for many years.

Josh, 42, with whom Ellen had the most conflictual relationship, lived with his wife and children just a few miles from the McCullums; Brian, 40, Ellen's closest sibling, had recently moved with his family to England, and Henry, the youngest, was married and lived in Dallas. Before her illness, mother had served as the center of the family and had regularly corresponded with all her children and kept them apprised as to their siblings' lives. The family had been almost always successful in getting together for Christmas and the Fourth of July each year, but after father's death and mother's diagnosis this custom was no longer maintained. No one seemed clear as to why those holiday celebrations no longer took place, but it would appear that the mother's illness had left the family bereft of an emotional center. Some siblings had not seen each other for more than a year and there seemed little prospect of getting the family back together.

It emerged shortly into marital treatment that Ellen was quite sad about not having been in Texas at the time of her father's death and was very disturbed that she had barely visited her mother in the past four years. She had seen little of her father during his illness, partly because of distance and the responsibility of her own young children but also because "it was too painful to see daddy dying that way." Mother's illness was very difficult for Ellen to discuss and, in fact, John did much of the updating of her rapidly deteriorating condition with his sister-in-law, Sally, parsing out the information sparingly so as not to "depress Ellen even more." Although I determined at this early point in treatment that the loss of Ellen's father was probably a significant factor in the marital dysfunction, we needed to lay some groundwork before such a connection could be directly suggested.

Needless to say, Ellen herself made little connection between the sadness about her parents and her estrangement from most of her siblings and the issues she was struggling with in her marriage. Effective marital therapy involves more than merely addressing immediate issues in the marital dyad; it demands in-depth examination of the individuals themselves. Only when spouses come to understand the ways in which they duplicate patterns of behavior learned in their families of origin can they effectively bring about real change in the present generation. Ellen, for example, operated in her marriage in accordance with old patterns of dealing with conflict learned in her family: in particular, a tendency toward not expressing her feelings and withdrawing emotionally in the presence of conflict. This created a workable complementarity in which John, who was raised in a similarly non-expressive family, was able to play the role of "martyred husband" to Ellen's depression and withdrawal. Interestingly, in a session in which I helped Ellen to express her sad—and unresolved—feelings about the loss of her father, John indicated some surprise about his wife's feelings, commenting that he had assumed that she "was over that a long time ago." Ellen was not particularly disturbed by her husband's not knowing how she felt. What she did express, however, was a firm belief that no matter how angry and frustrated John might get about her behavior he would never leave. John concurred, indicating that, like his father, he prided himself on his loyalty, so she had nothing to fear. Thus, the repetition of old scripts, including unexpressed anger, irresolution of conflict, and emotional cutoffs indicated that neither of these individuals had ever fully individuated from their families of origin.

After a number of weeks spent calming down the open conflict in the marriage and fostering a solid therapeutic alliance, I suggested to Ellen that there were particular issues in her family which seemed to be unresolved. Rather than immediately address her father's death, however, it was suggested instead that the cutoffs from a number of her siblings must be a disturbing factor for her. She agreed that she was not happy with this state of affairs and allowed that her situation with some of her brothers and sisters could be connected to how she was handling her own children. In addition, John was able to point out that he worried that she would disengage from him in the same way she had disengaged from her brother Josh. I suggested that there might even be some value in working on these family-of-origin issues in order to better cope with her marriage and children. She was not convinced (few clients initially are!) but agreed that it was not entirely impossible that such a connection might exist. She doubted her ability to address either generation effectively and, in talking about her parents and siblings, commented: "I was in psychotherapy for years and never was able to figure out what they're all about and why they make me so crazy." However, she indicated that she was willing to try.

The decision to encourage Ellen's working on her family of origin is central to Bowenian family systems thinking as well as a central concept in the process of coaching (Bowen, 1976). Ellen's depression seemed very much related to unresolved issues in her family, and triangles that included her husband and various siblings were undoubtedly at the root of some of the marital difficulties. Despite the fact that working on family-of-origin issues is an important dimension of marital treatment, it is not always easy to accomplish. In my experience it is not that clients are specifically resistant to the idea that what happened in their families years before is of much importance in the present; rather, what they resist is the notion that there is anything they can do in the present that would change things. This is most frequently expressed in terms of the popular (and sound) psychological notion that you can't change anyone else. The corollary notion that one can, however, change oneself in that family system and have that make a difference is not an easy concept to convey. Thus, one frequently needs to proceed patiently with a couple, secure in the knowledge that a propitious opportunity will present itself and make it possible to address the three-generational issues in a way that can be meaningful. In this case that occasion was Ellen's mother's Alzheimer's disease, an illness which was quite rapidly diminishing her mental capacities, and a number of accompanying physical illnesses, which made a long survival unlikely.

An excerpt from an early session discussing her role in the family and what might need to be done is an example of how the therapist might set the stage for beginning the process of coaching. People often have fantasies about making things "perfect" or recreating some idealized picture of the "good old days"; in this case, disenchanting them of this notion may be seen as a beginning point in coaching.

ELLEN: Well, I agree with you, first of all, about Jack and I do worry about what is going to happen; but I don't know what to do about it. I don't know whether it makes any difference. And I guess you're saying that now is our time to do it — to re-group and support each other.

The therapist had questioned whether the siblings had discussed what Jack's situation would be after mother's death; Ellen begins to discuss the communication patterns in the family, providing what will be a propitious opening for coaching.

ELLEN: We just didn't communicate. Can you believe that? We lived together and we interacted — we didn't talk about feelings or emotions or whatever. So I don't know. It's funny . . . you talk about being close with people and then all of a sudden you wonder whether you're close to people or what's there anyway.
THERAPIST: Well, there's loving people and there's being close to people and they're not always the same thing.
ELLEN: Sometimes there are barriers that you feel and you can't . . . you can't get beyond, or you can't identify, but they're there.
THERAPIST: And sometimes we can never remove those barriers, although there still may be ways to love people and even communicate despite the barriers.

(The therapist lays the groundwork for coaching not in terms of creating the idealized, close family, but rather in terms of communicating and getting a job done. Essentially, coaching involves helping people to be themselves in their families, not making the family "better.")

The family's (and the therapist's) ethnic background is an important indicator of how the process of coaching should proceed (Rosen, 1988, 1990; McGoldrick, 1982). In Ellen's family of origin, sibling position (Toman, 1976), ethnicity (McGoldrick, 1982), and particularly the position of the daughters, reflected an important aspect of their functioning. One interesting aspect of Ellen's family was the fact that none of the siblings seemed to be operating in predictable ways, given their relative positions and traditional Irish Catholic background. Jack, the eldest son, functioned at a minimal level and presently lived in his mother's apartment alone. Josh, the next eldest son, was essentially cut off from his siblings and played almost no active role in family life. It was Sally, the next to youngest of the six children (and youngest daughter), who assumed an important leadership function in the family, despite the fact that she had three older brothers. Ellen, who was the eldest daughter, had not assumed a very important role as an emotional caretaker (although she had operated more in that role when she was younger), and there was an emotional void in the family since mother's illness. One aspect of the coaching process will be to encourage Ellen to assume a more appropriate sibling position.

THERAPIST: . . . If Sally was the sibling who kind of took charge, and took things in hand . . . and indeed everyone agreed — except perhaps for Jack — that there was a need for somebody to do that . . . Sally took that.

ELLEN: At one point, at dad's death, Josh attempted to take some kind of role as head of the household but he couldn't pull it off. And you know Henry and Brian are not going to take charge of anything.

THERAPIST: If I'm counting right that leaves one other person we haven't mentioned.

ELLEN: (Laughing) John?

THERAPIST: No, besides John.

ELLEN: The oldest daughter.

THERAPIST: Yep, the oldest daughter. What's your family's ethnic background?

ELLEN: WASC!

THERAPIST: WASC! White Anglo-Saxon Catholic, huh?

JOHN: I never heard that expression.

ELLEN: English-Irish Catholic.

THERAPIST: And in Texas, too.

ELLEN: But dad was, well, his roots were Texas and my mom's family, some from Pennsylvania, and of course from the old country.

THERAPIST: She was Irish too, huh?

JOHN: Born on St. Patrick's Day.

ELLEN: Well, her mother never left Ireland.

THERAPIST: Mmm.

ELLEN: Old, old.

THERAPIST: Well in such families, you know, the oldest daughter often-times does take on a responsibility of kind of riding herd on the emotional life of the family. Sometimes she does it as a nun. You didn't make that decision. But it doesn't . . .

ELLEN: (Smiling at John) Close?

THERAPIST: I won't touch that one! But really, as I went through the family in my mind as we're talking, it does seem as though it leaves you with a certain responsibility. Who really does take charge when taking charge is necessary?

ELLEN: One of the two daughters.

It is indeed fascinating that no one in this family seems to have ever looked to a man (father or brother) to perform any particularly significant emotional tasks. In terms of their marriage, Ellen's dissatisfaction with John often centers around his lack of emotional support; yet she seldom chooses to share with him what she is thinking or feeling. Ellen feels very uncared for but seems at a loss as to how to get what she wants.

THERAPIST: Yep. And it seems to me that this daughter needs to take charge of the "other piece"—if we call Sally's the "business piece" (and of course it's more than just business—it involves a lot of other stuff) . . . but if we call it, for argument's sake, the "business piece," maybe the other piece is the . . .

ELLEN: The "peacemaker" piece?

THERAPIST: Yeah. The "peace piece." In some way there's going to be a need for one of the other siblings to help to reorganize the family without mom at the center. And I'm wondering if you feel up to that task.

I explored the ethnic background of the family and Ellen's sibling position. Interestingly, Ellen hadn't a clue as to why she had not been her father's favorite. I suggested that when she had the opportunity she should discuss this with Sally, who might have a better sense of how she had come to assume the role commonly assigned to the eldest. Once again there is an opportunity to make the process of coaching congruent with the client's background and experience. Here we can see that Ellen may be willing to take on the task of working on her family because it so clearly fits her notion of her role in the system. This is not to say that Ellen is completely comfortable with the task; it is necessary to validate the actual value of doing work with her family.

ELLEN: I don't know if I am up to it . . . right now I'm having a hard enough time coping with my own family.

THERAPIST: Would it sound absolutely insane if I said to you that sometimes when people find it hard coping with their own families working on their families of origin makes it easier? 'Cause sometimes when they straighten that stuff out, the stuff in their own families straightens out even better.

It is seldom an easy task to have clients make the connection between their present family's function and what they bring from their families of origin. To convince individuals of this — and then to have them do something about it — may be an arduous task and it is a psychoeducational aspect of the therapy. In fact, it may be said that, in a certain sense, the process of coaching is in many ways a course of re-education.

ELLEN: Yeah, you told me that. Well, I think I can do it. Maybe some of the things that John and I are fighting about are connected with all that stuff. I feel very strongly that everyone should have his or her say-so . . . that everyone should be on an equal level. It would be nice if we could all get along, anyway. I don't know if I could get anybody to do more than that.

THERAPIST: Maybe that's one of the things you need to examine: that the goal may not be a close, communicative, loving, idyllic family.

ELLEN: Right.

Here Ellen makes an even stronger connection between her marriage and the need to get things straightened out with her siblings. The therapist reiterates for her that her goals for working on her family need to be relatively modest and realistic. This theme will be repeated again when specific tasks are developed.

There is, of course, a particular urgency in facilitating Ellen's work with her family. Ellen's mother is dying of a variety of medical problems and her Alzheimer's has rendered her virtually noncommunicative. Without mother at the center, little semblance of the Gorman family is likely to survive unless her children develop some basis upon which to keep the system intact. In fact, since her illness and her husband's death the regular family get-togethers have ceased. Ellen is distressed by this and there is every reason to believe that her siblings are pained by the dissolution of the family as well. The essential goal in families where there is an imminent death is to examine carefully the likely emotional reverberations and attempt to develop possibilities for adjustment and role reallocation. In addition, in this family there is a pattern of reacting to loss with emotional or geographic cutoffs. Ellen's mother, born in Ireland, left the old country at the time of her mother's death and never saw two of her siblings again. At a young age her father was orphaned and separated from his sisters, only one of whom he ever saw again, many years later. The present situation has the potential of perpetuating that pattern.

Thus, for the Gormans there appear to be four important tasks to be accomplished: (1) a reallocation of family roles, which would address the desire of all six siblings to keep the family intact, including the development of a formal mechanism to provide for communication among them; (2) consensus on how to deal with Jack, including a consideration of what to do with the ancestral home; (3) a clarification of Sally's fiduciary role, particularly in terms of how a very complicated will is to be interpreted and a great deal of money distributed; (4) some consideration of funeral arrangements with an eye toward how the family might incorporate a period of grieving for mother which would be helpful to all of them in "moving on."

Obviously Ellen herself could not be expected to take responsibility for all of these tasks. All she could really do was make some change for herself and hope that there might be some resonance in the system that would allow for a healthier adjustment after mother died. It would be a mistake to burden Ellen with the basic responsibility for changing the family. Coaching helps an individual to assume a different, and hopefully, more appropriate and empowered role in his/her family system. Since systems theory assumes that the move of any one person in a system will have resonance in the larger system, it is reasonable to assume that the moves encouraged in the process of coaching will have a wide impact. Often it is not even necessary to share this concept with the client.

Since there was an indeterminate, but short, amount of time left before mother's death, and given Ellen's role in her family of origin, it was mutually decided that a specific coaching task would be to have Ellen assume some role as the connecting link among her siblings (mother's traditional position, unfilled in four years). It was posited that this role, if assumed effectively, would accomplish a number of purposes: (1) It would help Ellen to address some of the unresolved issues attendant to her father's death, since it appeared that, not having visited him when he was dying, she remained conflicted about her relationship with him and had not as yet addressed her grief; (2) it would impose upon her the necessity of seeing her mother — something which she was clearly avoiding and which could ultimately result in conflict over this parent's death as well; (3) it would reconnect her with her siblings and help to ameliorate some of the alienation she was feeling from her family; and (4) it would mobilize her to take some action in her family of origin rather than standing by as a distant, passive observer. This last point, of course, is one essential belief of the systems therapist: Change in the family of origin creates change in the family of procreation.

It was further suggested that Ellen stay in particularly close contact with her sister to avoid the latter's feeling "upstaged" by Ellen's sudden involvement. One important aspect of coaching is to help the individual prepare for the impact that his/her moves might have on others — how they might react and how the person can respond. To facilitate the individual's success it is often helpful to encourage him/her to predict potential responses to the moves that are going to be made. Often the individual is unable to do this; this, in itself, can be a powerful diagnostic indicator that the coaching task(s) are likely to be successful. If one is unable to foresee the impact of one's action on intimate others, it is reasonable to assume that there is an emotional connection with those others which has not been made, and the coaching task will facilitate a new connection. Of course, the ultimate goal of coaching with Ellen would be to alleviate some of her depression, since there did seem to be some relationship between her affective state and issues in her family of origin, specifically her unresolved grief for her father, the impending loss of her mother, the cutoffs from her siblings, and her sense of powerlessness and alienation from her family.

After a number of sessions of preparation, which involved extensive discussions of family history, Ellen concluded that an appropriate task would be to write a letter to her brothers and sister, catching them up on all the news she knew, and then inviting them to get together in Texas on July 4th weekend. Excerpts from the session in which this strategy was developed follow.

ELLEN: I'm just afraid that if we all get together it could be a gigantic flop. I'd look ridiculous getting everybody together and then having some awful argument break out or Sally refusing to talk to Brian or something.

THERAPIST: Well, maybe it has to do with what your goal is. Maybe it should just be that no one gets cut adrift from the family.

ELLEN: Everybody can give or take whatever . . . we can never be intimate friends, like with Josh and Leslie [her brother and sister-in-law] . . . But if we can be civil to one another . . .

Once again, it becomes necessary to keep expectations low and reassure Ellen that if she does so there is little danger of anything too terrible happening. The conversation later turns to how mother's illness has been like a death; Ellen wonders whether in getting together as a family they will find it even more difficult to deal with the horror of mother's condition.

ELLEN: But are we going to have to go through the grief all over again?
THERAPIST: Well, in one way the answer is yes, of course you will, because illness, no matter how grave, is still not death. But it's my firm belief . . . that the pain of grief is heightened if we're cut off from the family. The less cut off, the easier the grief. If there's a way for the six of you to stay in close enough contact, then I think you'll be able to bear the pain of mother's death. And it will be shorter in duration because part of connecting with all these people will be some part of the grief process. Now the question is: How do you do that?

A rationale for bringing the family together is presented to Ellen but the actual method is left to be developed together with her. When she talks about her relationship with her brother Brian, who is in England, she begins to clarify what she needs to do.

ELLEN: . . . I feel as though (Brian and Lynne) have been ocean-hopping for years. So they're a little bit removed. However, I don't think we'll ever cut off contact because . . . our families are very close and I think we all work hard to show that. . . . I feel there's a family there and I try to keep that part of the family working well.
THERAPIST: So it's interesting that your feeling is that the piece of the family that's the furthest away is the piece of the family in least danger of being cut off.
ELLEN: As far as I can see.
THERAPIST: Yeah, so I'm saying that distance doesn't mean a thing. Physical distance is not the issue.
ELLEN: On the contrary, the proximity of my other brother . . .
THERAPIST: Right, you and Josh . . . are at the greatest distance and you're ten minutes from each other.

Ellen continues to discuss possibilities for changing what is presently happening in the family and toward the end of the session it is suggested that she personally contact Sally (up until now it was her husband, John, who had been making most of the contact) and discuss mother's condition. Ellen was urged to keep the conversation "light" and simply catch up with her sister on what was happening in Texas. A next meeting was scheduled for two weeks hence. She reported that her mother continued to deteriorate and that Sally had been pleasant and expressed her uncertainty about how to handle the problem of Jack now that mother had been put in a nursing home.

ELLEN: Yeah, so now I wonder whether or not I should go to Texas. Josh told Sally that he was planning to come down the end of the month or the beginning of July. He wanted to know whether anyone else was planning to come down. Sally said he asked whether I was going. . . . In my mind I'm not sure I want to go.

THERAPIST: You mean you're not sure you want to see mother in that condition?

ELLEN: Because since she's in the nursing home she's gone down drastically. And Brian saw her last Thanksgiving. . . . Maybe he's planning to come back this summer and we could . . . I'm not sure that I need to go. I'm not sure I want to go or I can . . .

Ellen is obviously ambivalent about whether she wishes to see her mother again in her present condition. She discusses her father and the difficulty she had with handling his illness and death and questions whether she can bear to see her mother.

THERAPIST: I'm not sure there's an answer to that. I think the answer lies in the question, will it be all right for you if mother dies without your having seen her again? And that only you can answer. There are no books . . .

ELLEN: Will it be all right for her?

THERAPIST: Will it be all right for *you*? At this point she may not even recognize you and it's impossible to know what your presence will mean. Is it all right for you if mother dies without your having seen her again? The answer is a very personal one.

ELLEN: Well, I think if I feel the need I will.

Ellen is also not sure about whether she wants to be there if Josh is there. She begins to devise a plan that might include all the siblings and this develops into what will become a major reunion of the family and, ultimately, the last time she will see her mother.

JOHN: Well, maybe you should call Josh and ask him whether he'd like to go and maybe whether you should contact Brian so he could make plans for them . . .

ELLEN: Yeah . . . but we'd have to make sure everyone . . . well, I'm a little afraid that stuff might get all stirred up if Josh . . .

THERAPIST: You want to write another letter?

JOHN: Right. You could let them all know that this was clearly not for business.

ELLEN: If we made it July 4th weekend, then . . .

THERAPIST: Kind of like the way it used to . . .

ELLEN: Yes, if we all got together and they perceived that it . . . well . . . not necessarily for some huge reconciliation, but . . .

THERAPIST: You're coming together not to discuss business, but . . .

ELLEN: We're gonna come down and PLAY!

THERAPIST: And anyway, the business is mostly taken care of and you can leave it to Sally. She's pretty competent. All the rest of you would also be saying to Sally and Jack in Houston — you guys aren't in this alone. We're here too.

ELLEN: So Josh would come, Brian could come . . .

THERAPIST: And why not spouses and kids and . . .

ELLEN: Yeah! We'll have a party.

JOHN: You know the Irish. They always have good parties.

THERAPIST: It's not so outrageous. You might want to even have a party with mother. Even if she didn't know what the party was about she'd probably enjoy a party and a piece of cake. . . . Also, I think that siblings who are in place geographically where a parent is sick or dying . . . no matter how loving, no matter how open, or understanding or whatever . . . they can't help but feel some degree of resentment for those siblings who aren't around. They can't help but feel, well, you know, where are you? How come you're not here more?

ELLEN: Yeah, why not? I'm going to definitely do it. We can call Brian and I'll invite everyone . . .

Ellen did, in fact, arrange for the big party and on July 4th weekend every sibling and his/her family showed up in Houston. Mother joined the festivities and, while she was unable to communicate very well, she apparently did understand that she was with her family and that they were having a party. Two months later she died.

Ellen continued to stay connected with all her siblings and quite naturally adopted the role of writing a family letter every few months to keep everyone informed. She also began meeting with her siblings and their families more frequently, planning a number of trips and visits. The financial and estate difficulties that had concerned Ellen and her siblings were addressed more easily than expected in the warmer atmosphere which had been created as mother was dying.

Ellen's depression, which had been a significant symptom for four years, did seem to be connected to the unresolved issues that had been set in motion at her father's death. She was now better able to cope with the loss of both her parents; John and she were now prepared to address some of their marital issues. As Ellen worked on the relationships with her siblings she began to experience a greater sense of potency in other spheres of her life as well—particularly her marriage. Her marital relationship was further enhanced by her ability to recognize the patterns in her family of origin which she was reenacting in her marriage. Armed with this knowledge and a sense of achievement in changing her role with her siblings, Ellen was now able to approach John in a new role that she herself described as "grownup." John, having been an active part of the coaching process, was able to tolerate the changes his wife was making and become an active partner in changing the patterns in their marriage.

REFERENCES

Bowen, M. (1976). Family reaction to death. In P. Guerin (Ed.), *Family therapy, theory and practice* (pp. 335–348). New York: Gardner.

Carter, B., & McGoldrick, M. (Eds.). (1989). *The changing family life cycle: A framework for family therapy* (2nd ed.). Boston: Allyn & Bacon.

Cohen P., Dizenhuz, I. M., & Winget, C. (1977). Family adaptation to terminal illness and death of a parent. *Social Casework, 58*(4), 223–228.

Doka, K. J. (1984–85). Expectation of death, participation in funeral arrangements, and grief adjustment. *Omega: Journal of Death and Dying, 15*(2), 119–129.

Evans, N. S. (1976). Mourning as a family secret. *Journal of the American Academy of Child Psychiatry, 15*, 502–509.

Fogarty, T. (1976). On emptiness and closeness: Part I. *The Family, 3*(1), 3–12.

Fulton, R. & Gottesman, D. J. (1980). Anticipatory grief: A psychosocial concept reconsidered. *British Journal of Psychiatry, 137*, 45–54.

Gerber, I. (1974). Anticipatory bereavement. In B. Schoenberg, A. C. Carr, A. H. Kutscher, D. Peretz, & I. K. Goldberg (Eds.), *Anticipatory grief* (pp. 26–30). New York: Columbia University Press.

Gerber, I., Rusalem, R., Hannon, N., Battin, D., & Arkin, A. (1975). Anticipatory grief and aged widows and widowers. *Journal of Gerontology, 30*(2), 225–229.

Glick, I., Weiss, R., & Parkes, M. (1974). *The first year of bereavement*. New York: Wiley.

Grollman, E. (1967). *Explaining death to children*. Boston: Beacon.

Guerin, P. J., Fay, L. F., Burden, S. L., & Kautto, J. G. (1987). *The evaluation and treatment of marital conflict*. New York: Basic Books.

Hare-Mustin, R. (1979). Family therapy following the death of a child. *Journal of Marital and Family Therapy, 5*(2), 51–59.

Herz Brown, F. (1989). The impact of death and serious illness on the family life cycle. In B. Carter & M. McGoldrick (Eds.), *The changing family life cycle: A framework for family therapy* (2nd ed.) (pp. 457–482). Boston: Allyn & Bacon.

Hoffman, L. (1989). The family life cycle and discontinuous change. In B. Carter & M. McGoldrick (Eds.), *The changing family life cycle: A framework for family therapy* (2nd ed.) (pp. 91–105). Boston: Allyn & Bacon.

Kuhn, J. (1981). Realignment of family emotional forces following loss. *The Family, 5*, 19–24.

Lebow, G. H. (1976). Facilitating adaptation in anticipatory mourning. *Social Casework*, (July), 458–465.

McGoldrick, M. (1982). Ethnicity and family therapy: An overview. In M. McGoldrick, J. K. Pearce, & J. Giordano (Eds), *Ethnicity and family therapy* (pp. 3–30). New York: Guilford.

McGoldrick, M., & Walsh, F. (1983). A systemic view of family history and loss. In M. Aronson (Ed.), *Group and family therapy*. New York: Brunner/Mazel.

McGoldrick, M., & Walsh, F. (1988). Loss and the family life cycle. In C. J. Falicov (Ed.), *Family transitions: Continuity and change over the life cycle*. New York: Guilford.

Paul, N. (1967). The role of mourning and empathy in conjoint family therapy. In G. Zuk & I. Boszormenyi-Nagy (Eds.), *Family therapy and disturbed families*. Palo Alto, CA: Science and Behavior Books.

Paul, N. L. & Paul, B. B. (1982). Death and changes in sexual behavior. In F. Walsh (Ed.), *Normal family process*. New York: Guilford.

Paul, N. L. & Grosser, G. H. (1965). Operational mourning and its role in conjoint family therapy. *Community Mental Health Journal, 1*, 339–345.

Rando, T. A. (1986). *Loss and anticipatory grief*. Lexington, MA: Lexington Books.

Raphael, B. (1983). *The anatomy of bereavement*. New York: Basic Books.

Reilly, D. M. (1978). Death propensity, dying and bereavement: A family systems perspective. *Family Therapy, 5*(1), 35–55.

Rolland, J. (1989). Chronic illness and the family life cycle. In B. Carter & M. McGoldrick (Eds.), *The changing family life cycle: A framework for family therapy* (pp. 433–456). Boston: Allyn & Bacon.

Rosen, E. J. (1987). Teaching family therapy concepts to the hospice team. *American Journal of Hospice Care, 4*(4), 39–44.

Rosen, E. J. (1988–89). Family therapy in cases of interminable grief for the loss of a child. *Omega: Journal of Death and Dying, 19*(3), 187–202.

Rosen, E. J. (1988). The ethnic and cultural dimensions of work with hospice families. *American Journal of Hospice Care, 5*(4), 16–21.

Rosen, E. J. (1990). *Families facing death: Family dynamics of terminal illness*. Lexington, MA: Lexington Books.

Sanders, C. M. (1979). A comparison of adult bereavement in the death of a spouse, child and parent. *Omega: Journal of Death and Dying, 10*(4), 303–322.

Schoenberg, B., Carr, A. C., Kutscher, A. H., Peretz, D., & Goldberg, I. K. (1974). *Anticipatory grief*. New York: Columbia University Press.

Toman, W. (1976). *Family constellation* (3rd ed.). New York: Springer.

Vess, J., Moreland, J., & Schwebel, A. I. (1985–86). Understanding family role allocation following a death: A theoretical framework. *Omega: Journal of Death and Dying, 16*(2), 115–128.

Walsh, F. (1978). Concurrent grandparent death and birth of schizophrenic offspring: An intriguing finding. *Family Process, 17*, 457–463.

17

Families With Affective Disorders

DAVID A. MOLTZ

> The curious and unbiased clinician is always perplexed by
> the depressive patient, sensing the biology behind the dy-
> namics, and the dynamics behind the biology.
> (Lansky, 1988, p. 220)

COACHING—IN FACT, ANY family-oriented treatment of an affective disorder—
requires exceptional flexibility and conceptual dexterity on the part of the
therapist. He or she must work simultaneously from two different perspectives, the biologic/medical and the family/systemic. With a kind of binocular
vision, the two perspectives must be kept separate, and at the same time
overlaid and merged, in order to give depth and subtlety to the view.

On the one hand, in the presence of mania or severe depression, it is
essential for the therapist to acknowledge the reality of the illness.* The
individual and the family know that something is wrong, that what they are
dealing with is outside the usual realm of their experience, and it is important to validate this reality and to help them deal with it.

I would like to thank Ronald Taffel, Ph.D., for his critical review of an earlier draft of this
chapter.

*Throughout this discussion, I use the term "affective disorder" to refer to episodes of mania
and/or severe depression, which are assumed to be at least in part biologically-based and which
are experienced by the individual and the family as extreme deviations from their usual ways of
being. I do not refer to the more ordinary elations and depressions of everyday life. I use the
term "illness" to emphasize the intensity and differentness of these experiences.

On the other hand, it is important that the therapist not be hypnotized by the illness, as the family and the individual often are. The individual is more than his illness, and the family has issues and problems which, while perhaps magnified through the lens of the illness, exist separately from it. The affective episode creates a crisis which can allow access to the heart of the family, and if the therapist thinks only of treating an illness and alleviating symptoms, he will miss an opportunity to be of real help to the individual and to the family in their ongoing process of development.

An episode of mania or of depression can be a devastating experience for a family. The person who is affected changes dramatically, essentially taking on a new personality. The family's usual ways of dealing interpersonally no longer hold. Roles and functions shift for everyone. Suicide, violence, or personally destructive behavior may be present. Poor judgment may lead to social or financial disasters. While recovery from the episode may be complete, the threat of recurrence will hang over the family, especially after several episodes have occurred (Moltz, 1986).

The episode is a crisis for the family, and like all crises it can lead to increased rigidity in the system or it can help open the way to change and development. As the episode unfolds, preexisting issues in the family are highlighted and intensified. Stresses are increased, and triangles that may have been latent become activated. The family experiences a degree of urgency and distress, which may be converted into readiness for change.

The dynamics of the illness and the dynamics of the family are inextricably intertwined. The shape of the family is determined by the illness as much as the shape of the illness is determined by the family; the treatment must reflect and respect this reciprocal interaction and interdependence. Medical treatment and family treatment are not contradictory; rather, they can complement and enhance each other (Clarkin, Haas, & Glick, 1988; Mayo, O'Connell & O'Brien, 1979). Questions of diagnosis and prognosis, of medication, and of hospitalization can be approached in ways that empower the individual and the family, eliciting strengths and resources. In the course of dealing with these "medical" questions, family patterns, conflicts and triangles emerge and can be explored, and so the treatment of the family becomes inextricably intertwined with the treatment of the illness.

MULTIGENERATIONAL THERAPY

How is multigenerational work relevant to this process? During the acute episode, coaching in the formal sense is not possible. Mania and severe depression, almost by definition (American Psychiatric Association, 1987), involve distortion of judgment and paralysis of will, and the individual in the midst of an affective episode is not able to engage in the difficult and demanding process of consciously changing his or her position in the family. In addition, the entire family is in crisis during the episode, and coaching is not possible when anxiety in a system is very high. Thus, formal coaching must wait until the episode is resolving.

However, the theory and concepts underlying multigenerational work can be extremely useful from the very beginning of treatment, both in understanding important aspects of family interaction in affective disorders and in guiding interventions to modify these interactions. While these interventions are initially directed toward relieving the manifestations and effects of the illness, they also decrease anxiety, address underlying family issues, and help engage the family in treatment. In doing so they constitute the first phase of coaching.

Individuals and families who are struggling with an affective illness present certain characteristic issues and dilemmas, which arise from the nature of the illness. For example, during an affective episode, emotional reactivity in the system is intense. The individual has no distance from his emotional state; whether it is despair or elation, it is the whole and only truth, and it determines his or her reactions to all events. Family members react strongly as well. They may be frightened and confused by a dramatic change in the individual's personality and functioning. They may be humiliated and angry, or helpless and perplexed. When suicide, assault, or other potentially disastrous behaviors are threatened, emotional reactivity can be overwhelming. In addition, the mood changes in affective disorder are "contagious"; it is a painful, upsetting experience to interact with someone who is manic or depressed (Coyne, 1984; Janowsky, Leff, & Epstein, 1970), and family members have to struggle with their own intense reactions as well as with the individual's. The multigenerational model emphasizes the importance of decreasing the emotional reactivity of the system, and its principles and techniques are very helpful in dealing with the extreme reactivity of acute affective episodes.

Over time, another difficulty commonly develops for individuals and families with affective disorders: because of the painful consequences of the affective episodes, the intense fear of relapse, and the similarity between affective symptoms and normal emotional states, they may become frightened of any intense emotional expression (Davenport, Adland, Gold, & Goodwin, 1979; Moltz, 1986). Anger, sadness — any unusual or intense emotion — can be seen as a premonition of coming disaster, and the system may not be able to tolerate its expression. However, such emotions may also be an integral part of the process of the individual's, or the family's, moving through a developmental stage in the life cycle (Carter & McGoldrick, 1989); if their expression is not allowed, this development may be impeded, with serious consequences for all (Davenport et al., 1979). Multigenerational work, with its focus on facilitating development and differentiation in the family system, can be very helpful in addressing this problem.

In the multigenerational model, a major aspect of differentiating is developing the ability to be responsible for oneself in a relationship system: The individual is helped to define his or her own thoughts, perceptions, feelings, and needs, and to take a position in a given relationship or system that is congruent with these definitions (Bowen, 1972; Carter & McGoldrick Orfanidis, 1976). In a family during an affective episode, this is extremely difficult to do. People who are manic or depressed tend to act in ways which make others feel (often correctly) that they cannot be responsible for themselves. Poor judgment and grandiosity in mania, for example, or paralysis of will or suicidal threats in depression make family members feel that they have to be responsible for the individual in ways in which he or she is not. This may lead to interactions that are resented by the individual and experienced as intrusive; however, he or she may not be able or willing to act in ways that would reassure the family that this is not necessary.

At the same time, family members may have trouble taking positions for themselves; they may be afraid that doing or saying the wrong thing will make the illness worse, that even ordinary demands, expectations, or rules of behavior will precipitate further collapse in depression or escalation of arguing and agitation in mania. They may be afraid to take any action without the individual's consent and agreement, at the same time that they feel that he or she is unable to act responsibly.

These problems can create escalating tensions and turmoil, which will exacerbate and prolong the affective episode (Hooley, Orley, & Teasdale, 1986; Miklowitz, Goldstein, Nuechterlein, Snyder, & Mintz, 1988). Multigenerational therapy can provide a guide and a framework for addressing and resolving these dilemmas, even in the early phases of the work.

In this chapter a case study will be used to illustrate the interplay of individual illness and family dynamics in affective disorder and to demonstrate how a multigenerational model can be used to facilitate change and growth in the individual and the family. The effects of an affective episode in the context of the family will depend on characteristics of the episode, such as its type, duration and intensity, the degree of disruptiveness and danger, and the previous course of the illness, *and* on characteristics of the system, such as the stage in the family life cycle, the roles and functions of the affected person in the family and the triangles (Bowen, 1966, 1972) that are activated in the immediate and extended family.

Using one case necessarily emphasizes one set of circumstances and of choices and not others. For example, the treatment of a married couple in which one member has a recurrent affective disorder will raise different issues than will this case, in which a young person leaving home has her first major affective episode. Nevertheless, the two cases will also have many themes in common, and it is hoped that the advantages of following one case from start to finish and exploring the changing shape of the treatment over time will outweigh the disadvantages of this approach.

THE CASE

Kathy Snyder was a 19-year-old woman who had become depressed during her first year at college. While she was home in New York for winter vacation, her mother's psychiatrist had prescribed an antidepressant for her, and in the month after her return to school in Pennsylvania she had become manic. She slept only a few hours a night and felt no need for more sleep. Her mood was elated. Her mind was racing with thoughts and ideas; while she had previously had a great deal of trouble keeping up with her studies, she now felt that she was learning *too* easily. She spent more money than she had, paying with credit cards and with checks that later bounced. She was excited and grandiose. She talked incessantly to friends, and when they expressed concern about her condition she became irritable and contemptuous. Though she stopped taking the antidepressants, her excitement continued. She felt tremendous physical energy and restlessness, and in a week she walked an estimated 400 miles on country roads around her school. She wore out her hiking boots, and the nails in the heels cut into her feet, but she kept on walking, and her feet became bleeding and swollen. Her parents, called by the school, came to take her home. Though Kathy told them that she didn't want to go home, she didn't resist, and they drove the six hours back to New York together, arguing all the way. Mrs. Snyder had been given my name before they went to get Kathy, and she called to arrange an evaluation as soon as they returned. I met with Kathy and her family early the next morning.

Although the initial focus of treatment may of necessity be on the illness and its medical treatment, it is essential to include the family in the process from the very beginning. Frequently, the individual in an affective episode, whether manic or depressed, is difficult to engage, and involvement of the family can be crucial in providing the traction that is required for beginning treatment. In addition, family members are deeply affected by the episode, and their perceptions and concerns need to be acknowledged and addressed from the outset.

The family's presence is also an important counterweight to the pull of the individual's symptoms and problems; it helps the therapist to maintain a contextual focus while dealing with the illness. The interactions of the individual and family members as they discuss the illness will suggest hypotheses about the interplay of illness and context in the particular case. Patterns of behavior that are maintaining and exacerbating the situation will become apparent and can be modified. In addition, the presence of the family allows an assessment of the system's strengths and resources, as well as its potential weaknesses and difficulties, which is essential in developing a plan for treatment. In this case, organizing and mobilizing the family were essential first steps in the treatment.

Defining and Working on the Foreground: Using the Crisis to Lay the Foundation for Multigenerational Work

My first meeting with the Snyders included Kathy and both her parents, Joan and Richard. At this time, because of the pressure of the crisis, I obtained only the bare outlines of the family's history. Joan and Richard had separated three years before and divorced one year later. Joan and Kathy moved to New York City, while Richard remained in a small town not far away, where the family had lived before the separation and where he practiced as a dentist. Since the separation, Richard and Joan had been very angry with each other and at this point they had practically no direct contact, though both remained actively involved with Kathy.

The first session was very intense. Kathy was grandiose and excited. She wanted to organize and shape the session, and she put herself in the center of every interaction. She tried to calm her father when he got upset, and she tried to calm me when she thought I was getting too excited. She encouraged her parents to discuss their disagreements, saying that it would be therapeutic for them if they could "get into it" with each other. She dismissed any concern about herself or her condition and acted as if she were there to help everyone else.

Kathy's parents contributed their own intensity to the session. Richard could barely speak to Joan, he was so furious at her. He insisted that Joan was a big part of Kathy's problems, that she fed her neediness and insecurity, and that her interactions were toxic and destructive to Kathy. Joan said that Richard denied and minimized Kathy's problems and that he was unreasonable in his expectations of his daughter. In response to his attacks, Joan acted hurt and misunderstood, and conveyed by her behavior that he was irrational, overbearing, and impossible to deal with.

At this point, a crucial triangle in the family, exaggerated and amplified by the intensity of the crisis, was apparent: Joan and Richard were in an intensely conflicted relationship, and the conflict was routed through Kathy, who was involved with both of them but in an alliance with Joan (Figure 17.1). As Kathy put it, with manic clarity: "My parents both use me, and by putting their conflicts on me they make me stronger than either of them, and it drives me crazy."

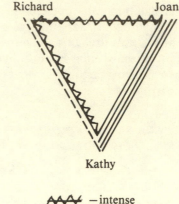

Key:
hostility/conflict
distance
intense closeness

AAAA — intense
AAAA — less intense
- - - -
=====

FIGURE 17.1   Changes in One Relationship in the Triangle Leading to Changes in Another Relationship in the Triangle.

My goal at this point was specific and immediate: to arrange a secure and containing environment for Kathy, so that she could be stabilized on medication without having to be hospitalized. For this to be possible, Joan and Richard would have to set aside their anger and mutual distrust; instead of playing out their conflicts through Kathy, they would have to cooperate and join forces to control and contain her.

Thus, the earliest stages of treating Kathy and her illness required addressing, and altering, the family's usual patterns of interaction. I told Joan and Richard that Kathy could not be responsible for herself right now. Medication would probably help her a great deal but would take up to a week to start working, and she needed close supervision and care until then. I said that neither of them would be able to provide that care without the other's support and assistance, and that if they were not able to work together on this, the only alternative would be hospitalization. I made it clear that I was not asking them to resolve their conflicts, but only to set them aside temporarily in order to work together to help Kathy.

As we discussed this, Kathy interrupted to announce that there was nothing wrong with her and that she was returning to school the next day; if she stayed in New York "my parents would weaken me, rip me apart." Joan and Richard responded with upset and alarm and began to argue, with Kathy and between themselves. They were diverted from their discussion, and were in danger of losing the thread completely. I did not respond directly to Kathy's statement, instead helping her parents to return to the questions we were discussing about handling and containing her over the next few days. As they continued their discussion, Kathy calmed down and did not press the point, and they were able to complete their arrangements. By the end of the session, Kathy had agreed to start taking lithium* and to stay at Joan's house at least for the next few days, and Richard and Joan had had an experience of collaborating on her care.

In this session, right at the beginning of treatment, the process of multi-generational work began. Richard and Joan were each caught in reactivity; they helplessly and reflexively responded to each other in highly patterned ways. The crisis created by Kathy's behavior, as well as their mutual concern for her, required them each to take a different position and to change their usual reactions. They didn't change their feelings about each other, but they were able to set them aside and act differently in spite of them; they did this consciously and toward a specific goal, which was to protect and care for Kathy. They were able to move away from reactivity toward a more self-responsible, conscious position, which is the beginning of differentiating.

An acute affective episode, especially a manic one, is an emergency for a family. Events move fast and unpredictably. Hour by hour there are crises to handle, limits to set, decisions to be made. The manic person constantly pushes against limits and boundaries (Janowsky et al., 1970), and because of impaired judgment and its consequences, the family must remain alert and involved. Hospitalization may be necessary to relieve this intensity, and making this decision can sometimes be empowering for the family; however, it is often experienced as a failure and defeat, adding to the family's sense of helplessness and incompetence. In addition, because the crisis is defused, an opportunity for change and growth may be lost. However, if the therapist and the family decide to work together to avoid hospitalization, it will require an extraordinary amount of commitment and energy from all concerned.

Over the next week and a half, I met with the Snyders every other day, with many phone calls between sessions. With great difficulty, and only under the pressure of the emergency with which they were confronted, Richard and Joan did work to control their anger and to reach agreements about the immediate handling of Kathy, such as where she would stay and how they could contain her behavior and ensure her safety. I was actively involved in these negotiations and continued to develop the themes that had been set in the first meeting.

---

*Kathy, for all her grandiosity, and in spite of her insistence that the problems were in others, did not object to taking medication. She felt that she was over-energized and out of control of herself, and she recognized the need to calm herself down.

Kathy was "commuting" between the two households every few days, which meant that Richard and Joan alternated being the primary person in charge. This arrangement gave them each a break from the intensity of dealing with Kathy, but it also required more consultation and coordination between them, as they each in turn took over and then relinquished control.

In the process of encouraging and supporting this process, I began to develop a theme which ran through my work with the Snyders and which is a fundamental concept in multigenerational therapy: that each person in the system must be responsible for his or her own position in the relationship. When Joan complained that Richard wanted her to be more restrictive with Kathy than she herself felt was appropriate, I helped her to negotiate with Kathy to set up rules and limits which made sense to her, Joan, for when Kathy was staying with her, and then to communicate the new understandings to Richard. This was different from either helplessly accepting Richard's wishes or changing them behind his back, which were her usual ways of dealing with conflict with him. When Joan turned to Richard for advice about handling Kathy and he said to do whatever she wanted, I pushed him to take a position and to tell her what he thought. When Kathy complained about her parents' not trusting her, I told her that it was up to her to act in such a way that they would start to trust her again.

It is a tenet of the multigenerational model that as one relationship in a triangle changes, the system will exert a pull to return to the previous configuration (Bowen, 1972; Carter & McGoldrick Orfanidis, 1976). As Richard and Joan began in fact to work together, Kathy escalated her challenges to their new arrangement. While staying with Richard she fingered knife blades threateningly, stole small objects from him, and even hit him. At Joan's, she threatened to jump out of the window if Joan tried to tell her what to do. Joan and Richard did stay in touch with each other, and with a great deal of difficulty (and encouragement from me), they were able to collaborate and to support each other. Hospitalization was left open as a possibility, and I checked with Richard and Joan frequently as to whether they felt that they could not handle Kathy; in spite of her challenges, they agreed that for the moment they were able to continue.

If the change in the relationship persists in spite of the pull to return to the status quo, changes will begin to occur in other legs of the triangle; the system accommodates to the change, and a new, more stable configuration emerges (Bowen, 1972; Carter & McGoldrick Orfanidis, 1976). A week after the beginning of therapy, there was a meeting in which such a shift began to occur.

The session began with Kathy's saying that she couldn't possibly stay any longer with her mother, who was driving her crazy. Richard would not back Joan, even though he had agreed to the arrangement; he said that he refused to be "set up" by Joan to be the "mad bull" while she remained helpless and placating, as usual. When I insisted that he and Joan had to decide together where Kathy would stay, he tried to give the choice to Kathy. I again pushed the parents to work it out together, saying that they had to decide which of them she would stay with or decide to hospitalize her. Under this pressure, they decided that Kathy would in fact stay at Joan's. Kathy refused, but her parents stuck to their decision.

At this point Kathy began to scream at her parents. She screamed that she was capable of killing someone, that she could "permanently change both your faces!" Then she screamed that maybe she *should* be in a hospital. In spite of this fearsome escalation, Richard and Joan remained firm in their decision. We discussed how they could assure Kathy's safety for that evening, until we met again on the following day. As in our first meeting, they were able with my help to maintain their focus and their agenda, without being deflected and defeated by Kathy's challenges. By setting aside their conflicts and mistrust and working together, they were changing their part in the triangle that bound them all. In response to that change, Kathy escalated her challenge, attempting to return the triangle to its usual conformation, in which she and Joan, and not Joan and Richard, were joined. When her parents maintained their position in spite of Kathy's strongest efforts to dislodge them, it was clear that a real change was taking place. Then, in response to this change, and confirming it, there was a shift in another leg of the triangle: Joan, not Richard, got angry at Kathy; she told her that she was irresponsible, that she was acting badly, and that she had to stop (Figure 17.2). This session was a turning point; it marked the height of the crisis, as well as the beginning of real changes in the family.

Depression and Differentiation: Working With the Individual

Within a week of that session, the serum lithium was at therapeutic levels, the mania had ended, and Kathy was depressed. At this point, treatment entered a new phase. The family was still in crisis, but the shape of the crisis had changed. Although Joan and Richard were still directly involved in the treatment, it was more focused on Kathy herself, and most of the work was with her alone. The work on changing the major triangles continued, but it shifted from a direct attack on the usual patterns to the more subtle and long-term process of coaching Kathy in changing her relationship with each of her parents, that is, in differentiating.

In this phase of treatment the depression was a central focus. It was seen both as an illness to be treated and as an expression of conflicts and struggles in her life, which should be respected. The depression was keeping Kathy locked into old patterns of dependence, but it was also part of her

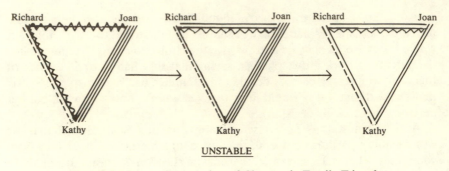

UNSTABLE

FIGURE 17.2   Progression of Changes in Family Triangle

attempt to separate from these patterns and to define herself. It was an impediment to her development and at the same time an expression of her attempts to change and differentiate.

During this period, which lasted approximately four months, I saw Kathy twice weekly, usually alone, but also at intervals with one or both of her parents. This decision was determined primarily by life-cycle considerations (McCullough & Rutenberg, 1989). The family's developmental task was to "launch" Kathy; Kathy's task was to define herself in the world, separate from her family. Working with Kathy individually would help focus on these issues. In addition, because of her depression she was extremely vulnerable to her parent's input and could think more clearly and less reactively in their absence. At the same time, seeing her at times with her parents allowed me to monitor their interactions and to continue to develop the themes we had started in the earlier sessions.

As the acute situation calmed down, I was able to learn more about the family's history. Richard had grown up during the Depression, the oldest son in an Orthodox Jewish family. His father had been psychiatrically impaired, probably manic-depressive, and had been hospitalized several times.

Richard himself had mood swings, though he had never been hospitalized. He had periods of depression, which responded to antidepressants, and though he had never had any clearly manic periods, he had what Kathy described as a "high idling speed." He was a forceful, aggressive person, who talked fast, had a bad temper, and was very demanding of those around him (during the early part of the therapy, when we were meeting every other day and talking on the phone on the other days, Richard angrily accused me of not being available enough when I wouldn't meet with the family on a Sunday!).

Joan was the youngest of two daughters. Her mother was described as "a dominating personality" and her father as "obedient." Joan's personality was complementary to Richard's; she was meek and ingratiating, made few overt demands, and tended to feel victimized by life.

After their marriage, Richard and Joan settled in a small town near Joan's parents. Richard, a dentist, was starting his practice, and Joan worked as a magazine editor. When Kathy was born she gave up this work and stayed home to care for her; she did not resume outside work as Kathy grew older.

As Kathy saw it, the organizing factor in her family's life had been Richard's temper. Although he was not physically violent, he had explosive temper outbursts, mostly directed at Joan. Kathy had generally been able to avoid being the target of his anger and even felt herself to be favored by him. However, as she got older she came to feel more and more bound to Joan, in an alliance against Richard. Joan talked to her about her unhappiness and helplessness in her marriage, and Kathy advised her on how to handle Richard. Kathy saw herself as Joan's peer, her confidante and protector. In return, Joan protected her; she let her stay home from school when she wanted, helped her with her papers and homework, and generally tried to shield her from life's stresses.

When Kathy was 16, Joan left Richard, taking Kathy with her. Kathy felt that both her parents leaned on her during the separation. As she became more overtly allied with Joan, it seemed to her that Richard was disappointed and felt let down by her. At this time she became depressed for several months. Her depression lifted when she went to boarding school the following fall, and she did fairly well for the next two years, until she went to college.

Her boarding school had been very supportive and comfortable, and Kathy was unprepared for the rigorous demands of college. As she fell behind in her work, she became more and more depressed and turned to Joan for support and help. Joan responded with sympathy and concern and helped her write her papers, but this only made Kathy feel more helpless and inadequate; while Richard's pushing and "encouragement" made her feel even worse. It was at this point, while Kathy was home on a visit, that Joan's psychiatrist prescribed the antidepressants which led to the manic episode.* Now, with the mania resolved by lithium, Kathy was depressed. She slept too much, she cried frequently, and she felt helpless and vulnerable. She also became increasingly preoccupied with thoughts of suicide.

Kathy's depression could be understood simply as a physiological event: She had a genetic predisposition to bipolar affective disorder; the antide-

---

*Although there is some debate over the question, it is quite likely that antidepressants can precipitate mania or "rapid-cycling" illness in susceptible individuals. See Wehr and Goodwin (1987) for a review and discussion of this issue.

pressant medication had triggered a manic episode, which the lithium resolved; and she was now in another depressive phase of the illness. But from another perspective, her depression was rooted in her struggles to develop a sense of self. She felt that her previous life, and self, had been invalidated: She had failed at college, had been irresponsible financially, and, in the grandiosity and arrogance she had displayed to her friends, had acted in ways that were foreign to her and which she could not own. And now she was living at home, dependent on her parents, with no idea of how to reconstruct her sense of self in a more stable way. She felt unable to return to her former self but did not know any alternatives: "I don't want to be who I was, but I don't know who else to be."

It was important here, as throughout the treatment, to maintain a binocular view and to respect both of these perspectives. Kathy was in a deep depression, and we continued to use the language of illness to discuss her state. At the same time she was struggling with individual and family issues, which we also addressed.

An important aspect of Kathy's depression was her intense experience of helplessness in relation to her parents. Joan predictably responded to Kathy's depression with worry and concern and with attempts to comfort her and cheer her up. While Kathy elicited these responses by talking to Joan about her misery and helplessness and her wish to die, she then resented her mother for being intrusive and over-accommodating. Richard, equally predictably, responded to her distress by pushing and challenging her, insisting that she get out of bed and help him in his office; Kathy resented this as well. She felt weakened and burdened by Joan's concern but unable to separate from her emotionally; she felt that Richard wanted too much closeness and intimacy, but she didn't know how to keep him away without totally cutting off from him. She was unable to modulate her relationships, to establish a comfortable proximity with either of her parents. Although this problem was highlighted by her depression, it was an exaggeration of her ongoing problems with differentiating in her family.

A related issue was Kathy's inability during this period to make any decisions concerning herself. This is a classic symptom of depression (American Psychiatric Association, 1987), but it was also an expression of her difficulty in her family: She was unable to take any position for herself. Making a choice was experienced as a capitulation, as giving in to Joan and her concern or to Richard and his pushing. To both of them she was only able to say no; this was the closest she could come to defining herself. But while her negation and refusal were attempts to protect and insulate herself, they in fact drew her parents closer to her, eliciting exactly the responses she was trying to avoid. Joan became more concerned and more protective, and Richard became more insistent and demanding.

These patterns were played out most forcefully around the issue of suicide. Even during the mania Kathy had made suicidal threats, but in her depression this became more and more of a preoccupation with her. The idea of suicide was an expression of her hopelessness and her inability to move forward in her life; at the same time it was a way to declare her autonomy—it was a position she *could* take, an assertion of self-determination. And finally, it was an expression of her overwhelming wish to be *left alone*. No one could get to her, or expect anything from her, if she were dead.

Unfortunately, since she talked to her parents about these thoughts, she only pulled them in more and made it harder for herself to define any areas of autonomy separate from them. The threat or possibility of suicide is absolutely compelling to family members and makes it far more difficult for them to be less reactive or to maintain more distance from the individual. Kathy would talk to Richard and Joan about her impulses toward suicide and then complain that they weren't letting her be free, that they were forcing her to stay in New York and in therapy. She and her parents were caught in binds that got tighter the more they struggled with them.

As I worked with Kathy and each of her parents to help them loosen these binds, the therapy moved more toward active coaching. I encouraged Joan to see Kathy's depression as hers, Kathy's, which she would have to deal with herself; however, Joan had difficulty doing this and continued to try to rescue Kathy by coddling or cheerful encouragement. Joan also found it very difficult to take positions that Kathy might not agree with or that might anger her; though she attributed this reluctance to worries about Kathy's condition, it was clearly a long-standing pattern.

Richard, for his part, found it difficult to develop a personal relationship with Kathy separate from his relationship with Joan. Since he blamed Joan for Kathy's distress, the more depressed Kathy became the angrier he got at Joan. He heard things Kathy said to him as if they were coming from Joan, not from her; and he felt that Joan's insistence on being "nice" pushed him into the role of "heavy" in relation to Kathy. Perhaps because he was more distant from Kathy than Joan was, he was better able to look at these patterns, and as we discussed them he worked to modify his behavior.

But most of the work was with Kathy, who was struggling with her own questions about autonomy and identity. Over and over in this period we discussed how she could actively change her relationships with her parents by changing her behavior, rather than helplessly waiting for her parents to change. Because of her sense of helplessness, which came both from her depression and from her position in her family, this was slow going; however, her focus gradually shifted from what they were doing to her to what she could do to change it. She was able to see how her expressions of distress brought Joan closer, and she experimented with keeping her despair to herself; by not telling Joan when she felt hopeless or suicidal, she took a first step toward creating a boundary between them. She also became aware of how her silence and withdrawal activated Richard, and she made small steps toward dealing more directly with him; for example, she negotiated with him the conditions under which she would stay at his house, rather than either passively and resentfully accepting his terms or rebelling against them, as she had done before. As we continued this work, her depression gradually began to resolve, and the focus of the therapy changed again.

"Coming Out": Active Engagement in the Work

As Kathy's depression lifted, the focus of treatment continued to move away from managing an illness and toward questions of differentiation and self-definition, of coming out or emerging from her family and consolidating an identity separate from her parents. She continued to work on changing her relationships with her parents, and at the same time she began to define herself in the world.

As she started to feel better, she found pleasure in some of her old activities, such as bicycling, walking, and playing music. She began to consider the possibility that some of her old life could be salvaged, that she did not have to recreate herself from scratch. At the same time, she consolidated a new aspect of herself and her identity: She "came out" as a lesbian. While she had previously had a few sexual experiences with women and had been strongly attracted to a woman friend when she was manic, this was the first time she had identified herself as a lesbian. She experienced this as a major step toward defining herself in the world in a way that was congruent with who she felt herself to be. However, it also presented her with a problem: She did not want to hide this information from her parents and pretend to be someone she was not; she was very concerned that her parents, especially Joan, would use it to intrude more in her life. As we talked about this dilemma, Kathy worked out how and when she would talk to each of her parents about her sexual orientation. In fact, she waited four months to tell Joan, until she felt more confident of her own ability to handle herself in their relationship, and she waited even longer before telling Richard. This decision was an important step not only in defining herself but also in taking responsibility for her relationships.

One result of this "coming out" was that she quickly developed a network of friends and acquaintances who were separate both from her family and from her previous life. She felt for the first time in her life that her friends were more important than her mother. She also became involved in a series of relationships with women in which she found herself confronting questions of merging and separateness, of competence and overresponsibility, at the same time that she was dealing with these issues in relation to Joan.

Although Kathy's mood was more stable at this time, the preceding mania and depression continued to cast a shadow over her. As she became more actively involved with people and with activities, her moods naturally tended to vary. However, because of her recent painful experiences with both highs and lows, she was wary about these changes; when she felt very good, or when she felt very bad, she was afraid that she might be becoming manic or depressed again.

Such uncertainty or ambiguity is a common problem in affective disorders, both for the individual and for the family (Moltz, 1986). Because affective symptoms, especially at the start of an episode, may so closely resemble normal mood changes, it is often difficult to decide whether a given experience is simply a normal variation in mood or a warning sign of an impending manic or depressive episode. This problem complicates the process of differentiation and self-definition; it is difficult to take a position based on your own thoughts, feelings, and perceptions when you don't know for sure if they are expressions of your "real" self or manifestations of pathology, and it is equally difficult for family members to know which they are responding to.

As Kathy talked about her uncertainty, I was sometimes not certain myself whether her moods marked the beginning of another episode or not. We talked about how she was feeling and the relation of her feelings to events; we watched for physiological signs, such as changes in sleep, appetite, or activity level; and we waited to see what would develop. In this process, Kathy learned how to monitor her moods herself. She discovered that she could be high or low without losing herself and falling into mania or depression, that she could own and control her moods, and this was important to her emerging sense of competence.

As she began to develop and define a life of her own outside of her family, Kathy continued to work on changing her relationships with her parents. Now that the depression had lifted, she was able to be engaged in this process as a more active agent, and the coaching became more active as well.

Changing proved to be most difficult in relation to Joan. Overly close relationships are generally more difficult to change than are overly distant ones, and this generalization was especially relevant for Kathy because at this point she was living full-time with her mother. She was still responding in old ways to Joan, and she still felt bound to her, by loyalty as much as by need. She felt that Joan was lonely, that she hadn't developed her own life after leaving Richard, and that she needed Kathy to somehow complete her life for her. Kathy was also still feeling the pull of her alliance with Joan against Richard, and as she began to change her relationship with Richard she felt guilty, as if she were betraying Joan. In fact, she felt this sense of betrayal about moving forward in her life in any way: managing money, making decisions, having her own friends — all meant to her that she was abandoning Joan.

Kathy responded to this guilt with anger. She blamed Joan for her own difficulty separating from her, and she continued to react angrily to what she saw as her intrusiveness. But her blaming and anger made it more difficult to change her own part in the relationship. In our sessions we worked to shift her focus away from Joan's actions and onto her own responses, so that she could see that she had some choice in how she responded. Joan's actions were Joan's, and Kathy's responses were Kathy's, and one did not have to follow from the other. This theme was a constant thread in the therapy, starting with the earliest sessions with the family. As we developed it in relation to her and her mother, Kathy began to get some measure of distance from her reactions, and she also became less angry at Joan. She began to see the possibility of responding differently herself, even if Joan didn't change.

While Kathy's work with Joan focused on getting more distance in the relationship, her problem with Richard continued to be how to get closer to him without feeling overwhelmed. She felt that he was demanding and overly critical, that he wanted too much from her emotionally, and that she had to "watch him" to maintain safe boundaries. As with Joan, she felt that she had no control over her relationship with Richard and no choice in her responses to him; as with Joan, the first step in changing the relationship was to develop her sense of the possibility of choice, of options in her responses. However, because this relationship was more distant and less enveloped in guilt, the process of change was not as difficult.

Kathy's struggles with Richard centered on money. As part of his divorce settlement with Joan, he was supporting Kathy financially. The settlement had provided very little for Joan directly and she had been working in advertising since the divorce. Kathy thought of her money as "alimony" that she was getting from Richard in Joan's place — a strong statement of her alliance with her mother. Although Kathy was now working as a salesperson in a clothing store, she needed her father's financial support since she was unable to support herself on her salary. She experienced the money as a way that Richard controlled her, and she felt bound and obligated by it. In addition, she thought of the money as really being Joan's, and she felt strongly that she would be betraying her mother if she didn't take it. She was unable to refuse the money, but she was equally unable to accept it comfortably, and she could not discuss the issue with her father at all. Whenever she had to ask him for money, or whenever he offered her something extra, such as to pay for a trip or to lend her his car, she would become angry and resentful and attack him personally.

As a start toward introducing new possibilities into the relationship, I suggested that Kathy practice saying no to Richard in a way that would not offend or alienate him. We talked many times about how to decline his offers without attacking him; yet Kathy still felt too vulnerable to him to be able to do this. She was too afraid of Richard's taking her over and controlling her and could only protect herself by angry, resentful attacks on him. Finally, in frustration at her repeated attacks, Richard decided that he needed to temporarily break off contact with Kathy. However, rather than do this explosively, as he would have before, he called me to discuss it first and to say that he was not doing it punitively but to provide some space and time for them both.

This was a real change for Richard; he was taking a position in a less reactive way. If he had angrily and accusingly broken off contact, it would have caused an escalation in their battle; instead, because it was not an attack, it allowed Kathy to see that Richard had a need of his own for distance, and it gave her the space to start moving toward him on her own.

It took her some time to test this new situation and to see that Richard was really going to leave her alone. Eventually, however, Kathy was ready to take a step herself. I helped her to construct a letter to Richard in which, without defending herself or attacking him, she discussed her financial needs and asked him to help her in defined and specific ways. This letter broke new ground: It was personal, about her and him and not about Joan; and it was a request, not an attack or a demand. Richard responded positively, agreeing to help her, but he also maintained his distance, limiting his response to the specifics of her request. This helped to reassure Kathy that she could take a step forward in their relationship without being overwhelmed in response.

Kathy felt somewhat more in charge of herself in relation to Richard as a result of this interchange, but it was only a first step. She continued to fear that he would use the money to intrude on her and control her, and she wanted assurances from him that there would be no obligations attached to what he gave her. She still saw the money as a trap and wanted him to take care of her fears about it.

As the next step in opening their relationship, I suggested to Kathy that she ask Richard for something without demanding guarantees that he wouldn't use it against her. I told her that as long as she needed such guarantees (which he couldn't give her anyway), she was making him responsible for their relationship and she would continue to feel helpless herself. After much discussion, she was able to ask Richard for the use of his car for a weekend trip, without attaching any conditions to the request. Since the request did not contain an attack hidden in it, Richard responded positively, and Kathy used the car for the weekend, without incident. The success of this interchange led over time to others like it, and Kathy gradually began to believe that she could have a more open relationship with Richard without being overwhelmed by him.

Leaving Home (Again)

At this point, a year and a half after starting treatment, Kathy decided that she wanted to stop taking lithium. She was experiencing bothersome side effects, and she wanted to be more in charge of herself and her physiology. She wanted to see how she functioned on her own, without medicine to back her up. She also wanted to be free to stop therapy when she felt ready, and thought that she should test herself off medication before making that decision. Since I thought that she was making this decision in a reasonable, thoughtful way, I agreed to try it.

At around the same time, Kathy began to talk seriously about returning to school. This was a big change for her, because she had experienced college not only as the scene of her failure and humiliation but also as a capitulation to her parents and their demands. Rather than returning to the same school, she wanted to choose one for herself, where she thought she would be comfortable. In the process of doing this, her relationship with Richard continued to improve. He paid for a trip to California so she could look at schools there. As she made concrete plans and worked on applications, she found that she could use his advice and could talk to him about her doubts and fears without his taking her over. At moments of doubt or depression she even found herself "using his voice" to help her through.

Her relationship with Joan was changing more slowly. She still felt responsible for her mother, and as she made plans to move away to school she again felt that she was betraying and abandoning her.

As she struggled with this conflict and prepared to leave, Kathy again became intensely depressed, with strong suicidal impulses and fantasies. However, she dealt with this very differently from her earlier depressions. Where before she had been sullen, angry, and withdrawn, this time she was actively involved in handling her depression. She collaborated with me in planning her treatment: We decided together whether hospitalization or medication was required (neither was); we developed a plan for structuring her days; and she did things which she knew from experience helped her feel better, such as exercising and modifying her diet.

This episode also served to test the changes in her relationships with her parents. She kept herself from pulling Joan in; for example, she didn't talk to her about her suicidal preoccupations. On the other hand, she found that she was able to talk to Richard more easily about how she was feeling; she felt that he could listen without pushing or prying. She was even able to use his "pep talks" to help herself get going, rather than responding by digging in her heels.

Although this depression was similar to previous episodes, she handled it differently and as a result she emerged from it with a stronger sense of herself as a competent and effective person. Although she felt she still had much to do in relation to Joan, she said that her relationship with Richard had changed so much that she found it hard to believe.

In the few months before she left for school, Kathy focused on changing her relationship with her mother. She was able to do this in part because of the work she had done with Richard. In any triangle, changes in one relationship facilitate changes in others; as she developed a more personal relationship with Richard, the intensity of her alliance with Joan was lessened, and she could work on their relationship more directly and personally. This process was a continuation of the work she had already begun; as she became more responsible for her relationship with Joan, she could also be responsible for changing it.

As she felt stronger and prepared to leave, Kathy became increasingly concerned about Joan's ability to care for herself without her. She felt that Joan was becoming more frail; she had been mugged in the subway, she seemed easily confused, and she was having memory trouble. Kathy worried about Joan's ability to take care of herself both financially and practically. Because of her intense guilt and ambivalence about giving up her caretaking relationship with Joan, she was unable to talk with her about these concerns. She was afraid that if she did talk to Joan, she would not be able to leave.

I suggested that, if she could open up this topic with Joan, it would be "detoxified" and she might be able to see it differently. We talked about how she could bring up her concerns in a way that was safe for her. After much discussion and rehearsal, Kathy was able to tell her mother, in the course of a "casual" conversation, that she would feel better about leaving if she knew that Joan would be able to take care of herself. Joan responded that she *was* taking care of herself, and in the discussion that followed Kathy realized that this was true, that while Kathy worried about her, Joan was in fact managing on her own. In addition to reassuring Kathy about leaving, the experience showed her that she could actively work on changing her relationship with Joan.

Talking to her mother about her worries about her was an important step in opening their relationship without being engulfed by it. However, to be truly personal and to reverse the process of "mothering her mother," Kathy would have to be able to talk about herself as well. She had been having her own anxieties about leaving and about starting school again, apart from her worries about Joan. She was afraid that, if she talked to Joan about these worries, they would get blown up out of proportion and she would "fall into" worrying and weakness with her mother. In reaction to this fear, she had been keeping her anxieties completely closed to Joan, communicating only a cheerful, confident optimism.

We discussed the possibility of telling Joan about her anxieties and acknowledging her difficulties leaving, without asking for help or pulling Joan in. Although this was a new idea for Kathy, because of her recent success in opening up a difficult topic with Joan, she was less reluctant to try. After more planning and discussion, she talked to Joan, again in a casual way, about some of her own anxieties. She was able to do this without asking for help or rescue, and Joan listened without getting alarmed or trying too hard to reassure her. And then, as often happens in coaching when the person is actively engaged in the work, Kathy took the task a crucial step further: She thanked her mother for sheltering her and caring for her and told her that the two years she had been home had been useful to her. That she was able to say this without feeling that she would lose herself as a result marked a real change for Kathy. It showed a new level of freedom and of differentiation in her relationship with her mother, and it helped her to leave home in a better way.

Follow-up

Soon after, Kathy left for school in California and the therapy ended. She was off lithium and her mood was stable, but she was somewhat apprehensive about how she would manage the stresses of college. I had no further contact with Kathy or with her parents. Four and one-half years later, on follow-up by telephone, Kathy said she was doing well. She had completed college without taking more time off, earning an undergraduate degree in biology. In her second year she had become depressed and had gotten through it with the help of individual therapy, without medication. Now she was living in California, working in her field, and living in a stable relationship with a female lover.

She said that her relationship with Richard continued to go well. He had remarried and seemed to be doing well. He was supportive of Kathy and was a source of "parental help" and good advice. He didn't try to change her, and she didn't try to change him: For example, if he lost his temper in public, she didn't feel she had to stop him. She felt her relationship with him was more open, with less reserve than before, and she felt good about it.

Kathy felt that she had maintained her gains with Joan, but that their relationship had not developed much further. Joan was living alone in New

York City and not doing well financially or socially, and Kathy saw her as lonely, needy, and not doing well in her life. Kathy continued to struggle with guilt, a sense of obligation, and a fear of enmeshment: "It takes some degree of assertion to have my own life." Nevertheless, she felt that she was doing this; in spite of her worries about Joan, she was living her own life and functioning well in it.

CONCLUSION

This case has been presented in some detail, in order to demonstrate the use of multigenerational therapy in the treatment of affective disorders. Over time, the shape and emphasis of the therapy changed in many ways: from treating a medical illness to facilitating personal growth and development; from intensive family crisis intervention to long-term work with the individual on family issues; from interventions guided in a general way by principles of multigenerational work to more direct applications of coaching techniques. However, all of these movements occurred within a broad framework which remained constant: the recognition of the multiple realities of biology, the individual, and the family, and of their reciprocal interaction. Each level influenced the others in important ways. The acute episode of the (biological) affective disorder was precipitated by individual and family life-cycle stresses (the parents' divorce and Kathy's leaving home) and by pre-existing family issues (the tight protectiveness between Joan and Kathy and their triangle with Richard). At the same time, the family and individual issues were intensified and brought to crisis by the affective episode.

Treatment also reflected this reciprocal interaction. In order to treat the affective disorder it was essential to intervene with the family, and major shifts in the usual patterns of family interaction were required. At the same time, treatment of the family was possible only because the affective episode had amplified and exacerbated preexisting family patterns to the point where they had to be addressed. In addition the changes necessary to improve family functioning were the same as those required to manage the affective episode and to prevent or minimize future episodes. Thus, just as biological, individual, and interpersonal events interacted to create the crisis of the affective episode, interventions at all three levels interacted to resolve it.

REFERENCES

American Psychiatric Association (1987). *Diagnostic and statistical manual of mental disorders* (3rd ed., rev.). Washington, DC: Author.

Bowen, M. (1966). The use of family theory in clinical practice. *Comprehensive Psychiatry, 7,* 345–374.

Bowen, M. (Anonymous) (1972). On the differentiation of self. In J. Framo (Ed.), *Family interaction: A dialogue between family researchers and family therapists*. New York: Springer.

Carter, B., & McGoldrick, M. (1989). Overview: The changing family life cycle—a framework for family therapy. In B. Carter & M. McGoldrick (Eds.), *The changing family life cycle* (2nd ed.) (pp. 3–28). Boston: Allyn & Bacon.

Carter, E. A., & McGoldrick Orfanidis, M. (1976). Family therapy with one person and the family therapist's own family. In P. Guerin, Jr. (Ed.), *Family therapy: Theory and practice* (pp. 193–219). New York: Gardner.

Clarkin, J. F., Haas, G. L., & Glick, I. D. (Eds.) (1988). *Affective disorders and the family: Assessment and treatment*. New York: Guilford.

Coyne, J. C. (1984). Strategic therapy with depressed married persons: Initial agenda, themes and interventions. *Journal of Marital and Family Therapy, 10*, 53–62.

Davenport, Y. B., Adland, M. L., Gold, P. W., & Goodwin, F. K. (1979). Manic-depressive illness: Psychodynamic features of multigenerational families. *American Journal of Orthopsychiatry, 49*, 24–35.

Hooley, J. M., Orley, J., & Teasdale, J. D. (1986). Levels of expressed emotion and relapse in depressed patients. *British Journal of Psychiatry, 148*, 642–647.

Janowsky, D. S., Leff, M., & Epstein, R. S. (1970). Playing the manic game: Interpersonal maneuvers of the acutely manic patient. *Archives of General Psychiatry, 22*, 252–261.

Lansky, M. R. (1988). Common clinical predicaments. In J. F. Clarkin, G. L. Haas, & I. D. Glick (Eds.), *Affective disorders and the family: Assessment and treatment* (pp. 213–238). New York: Guilford.

Mayo, J. A., O'Connell, R. A., & O'Brien, J. D. (1979). Families of manic-depressive patients: Effect of treatment. *American Journal of Psychiatry, 136*, 1535–1539.

McCullough, P. G., & Rutenberg, S. K. (1989). Launching children and moving on. In B. Carter & M. McGoldrick (Eds.), *The changing family life cycle: A framework for family therapy* (2nd ed.) (pp. 285–309). Boston: Allyn & Bacon.

Miklowitz, D. J., Goldstein, M. J., Nuechterlein, K. H., Snyder, K. S., & Mintz, J. (1988). Family factors and the course of bipolar affective disorder. *Archives of General Psychiatry, 45*, 225–231.

Moltz, D. A. (1986, June). *Bipolar illness and family functioning*. Paper presented at the Interest Group on Cognitive, Behavioral and Psychoeducational Approaches, American Family Therapy Association Annual Meeting, Washington, D.C.

Wehr, T. A., & Goodwin, F. K. (1987). Can antidepressants cause mania and worsen the course of affective illness? *American Journal of Psychiatry, 144*, 1403–1411.

Index

AA, 224, 229–300, 238, 252
Ackerman, N. J., 133, 135
ACOA, 229–30
acute illness, as a phase of chronic medical
    illness, 243
Adland, M. L., 288
adolescents:
    families with, 11, 131–48
    and medical illness, 247–48, 252–53
adulthood, stereotypes about, 80
adults, single, 77–93
affective disorders, 286–308
Ahrons, C. R., 191, 192, 198
AIDS, family impact of, 244
Alanon, 224, 230, 238
Alcoholics Anonymous, see AA
alcoholic system, 219–41
    and management of a medical problem,
    251
Altman, L., 220
Alzheimer's disease, 272, 275
American Psychiatric Association, 287, 298
Anderson, C. M., 3, 114, 116, 117
anxiety:
    alcohol's role in, 220
    decreasing, 49–50
    about the emotional separation of the adult
        child, 80–81
    in families with affective disorders, 288
    of families with dependent young adults,
        79–80
    reducing in therapy, 27
Arkin, A., 267
assessment, 43–49
    of adolescents, 135–38
    of families with young children, 118–22
    feedback during, 180–81
assignments:
    homework, 183–84
    see also tasks

authoritarian position of an oldest sibling, 163
authority, and power, 196
autonomy, 244
    and attachment for young adults, 151
    and connectedness, 165
    and suicide threats, 299
    of young adults, 79
Aylmer, R., 78, 79, 80, 95, 150

baggage, see emotional systems, baggage in
Battin, D., 267
Beattie, M., 230
Bepko, C., 98, 219, 220, 221, 222, 223
Berenson, D., 219
Bernard, J., 95
bipolar affective disorder, genetic predisposi-
    tion to, 297–98
Boscolo, L., 51, 62
boundaries:
    issues for couples, 117, 265–66
    negotiating parent-child, 132, 161–62
Bowen, M., 5, 6, 7, 8, 13, 14, 15, 17, 18, 22,
    24, 38, 46, 50, 54, 64, 65, 67, 69, 78, 84,
    95, 117, 137, 139, 152, 153, 154, 249,
    262, 266, 267, 274, 289, 294
Bradt, J., 114, 115
Braverman, L., 116
Brody, E., 174
Brown, F. H., 103
Burden, S. L., 3, 56, 267

caretaking:
    across generations, 167, 246–47
    and disability, 244
    as woman's role, 213
Carl, D., 98
Carr, A. C., 266
Carter, B., 3, 5, 6, 9, 10, 11, 13, 15, 17, 39,
    69, 70, 78, 81, 94, 117, 134, 150, 191,
    192, 195, 198, 208, 226, 242, 246, 288

Carter, E. A., 16, 17, 18, 22, 30, 61, 63, 65,
     87, 89, 139, 146, 177, 289, 294
case examples:
     adolescence, 139–48
     affective disorders, 290–307
     an alcoholic family, 225–39
     facing terminal illness, 272–84
     medical illness, 250–59
     older adults, 177–87
     single young adults, 82–93
     transition to couplehood, 99
     young adults, 154–68
     young children, 118–29
Cecchin, G., 51, 62
centrifugal/centripetal periods, 12
     death's impact on, 264
change:
     evolutionary nature of, 39–40
     expectations of, 57
     in the family system, 16–19
     opportunities for, 57–58
          in managing a terminal illness, 262
          in medical illness, 259–60
     planning preparing, predicting and process-
          ing, 58–60, 166
     resistance to, 29–30
     transition as an opportunity for, 69–70
change agent:
     the client as, 22, 70–72
     in the multigenerational model, 26
     in the structural model, 26
     the therapist as, 16
child–centered family, 86, 87–88
children:
     families with young, 114–30
     and grieving, 269–70
     and medical illness in the family, 247
circular questions, 25, 34, 46
Clarkin, J. F., 287
class, 3
     and couplehood, 98–99
     and the family life cycle, 12
     see also ethnicity
client:
     as a change agent, 22, 70–72
     characteristics of, 26–30
     as a detective, 71
     responsibility for change, 4
     teaching to understand extended family,
          54–57
     as weaver, 67–73
closeness/distance:
     and relatedness, 8, 12–13
     redefining in retirement, 175
     and valence, 16
closing up on facing terminal illness, 267–
     68

coach, the therapist as, 22, 24
coaching, 3–4, 159, 165–66, 177
     an anticipatory grief, 262, 266–69
     with families in later life, 186–87
     with families facing terminal illness, 262–
          63
     with families with medical illness, 257
     planning in, 166
     preparation for, 181
     to prepare for feedback from change, 280
     setting the stage for, 275–76
     for young adults, 152
Cohen, P., 263
Colon, F., 70
Combrinck, Graham, L., 12
coming out, 300–301
community groups /workshops:
     role in therapy, 50–51
     utilizing in therapy, 229–30
conflict:
     in an intimate relationship, 249
     patterns learned in the family, 273–74
confrontation, 17
     over alcoholism, 237–39
connectedness:
     and autonomy, 165
     and the life cycle, 12–14
     and self, 152
connecting:
     with the family, 35, 45
     the problem and the three–generational
          process, 46–49
consultant:
     the therapist as, 20, 22, 25–26
contexts, creating, 64–66
co–parents, alignment in divorce, 204
couplehood, 94–113
     case study, an alcoholic family, 225
     in families with young children, 115–17
     medical illness's impact on, 246
Cox, M., 39, 191
Cox, R., 39, 191
Coyne, J. C., 288
crisis:
     developmental, 81
     and life–cycle tasks, 11
Crohn's disease, 246
cutoffs, 55, 84, 125, 179–80, 184–85
     and deaths in the family, 270–71, 279

Dance of Anger, The (Lerner), 24
Dance of Intimacy, The (Lerner), 24
Davenport, Y. B., 288
death:
     and the family system, 11, 263–66
     reorganization around, 170
     see also terminal illness

decision making, and genetically related ill-
    ness, 247
denial:
    of imminent death, 270–71
    in terminal illness, 266–67
dependency:
    overreaction to, 79
    between parents and young adults, 151–52,
        167
depression, 286
    and differentiation, 295–300
    in later life, 177–87
    responsibility for, 304–5
    and unresolved family issues, 274–75
    and unresolved issues over death, 283
    in young adults, 153, 154–68
detective:
    the client as, 71, 180
    the therapist as, 25
detriangling, 61–62, 160, see also triangulation
developmental stressors, 172–76
diabetes, 250–59
differences, types of, in marriage, 96–97
differentiation:
    and depression, 295–300
    and separation of young adults, 78, 153–54
director, the therapist as, 26
disability, and caretaking, 244
distance:
    and triangles, 13, 16
    see also closeness/distance; relatedness
distancer–pursuer combination, 3
divorce, 11, 39, 191–218
Dizenhuz, I. M., 263
Doering, D. P., 116
Doka, K. J., 270
drug problem, 164
dyads, instability of, 13

Elkin, M., 219, 221, 224
emotional shock wave, 266
emotional systems:
    baggage in, 6–7, 17, 119–20, 126
    basic relationship of, 6
    in divorce, 192
    individual contributions to, 37
    maturity and triangles, 8–9
    teaching about, 50–51
enmeshed systems, 156–57
    in later life, 181–82, 185–86
Entwistle, S. G., 116
Epstein, R. S., 288, 293
equality, myth of, 105–6
Erikson, E., 151
ethnicity, 3
    and the family life cycle, 12
    and grieving, 269–70

Irish family, 255, 264, 272, 276–78
Italian family, 179, 258–59
Jewish family, 84, 120–21, 123–24, 228, 267
Polish–American family, 228–29
therapist's, 276
WASC, 276–78
and young adulthood, 82
evaluation:
    format for, 44–45
    during therapy, 41–42
Evans, N. S., 267
expectations and behavior, 220–21
expression of feelings, 220
extended family:
    identifying issues in, 40–41
    tracking from the nuclear family, 3
    see also genogram; nuclear family; trian-
        gles
external stressors, 172
    of later life, 176–77
extremes, in an alcoholic system, 234

families with young children, 114–30
family:
    the language of the, 34–35
    principles of operation, 5–14
Family Business (film), 7, 8
family democracy, myth of, 141–42
family of origin:
    changing self in the, 20
    and couplehood issues, 108–11
    as the primary influence on individual de-
        velopment, 5–6
    problems in families with young children,
        117–18
family secret, alcoholism as, 229
family tapestry:
    introducing, 34–36
    see also tapestry
Fay, L. F., 3, 56, 267
Ferran, E., 12
flexibility:
    and distance, 14
    and history, 9
focus
    early in therapy, 51–52
    second and third stages of therapy, 67–68
Fogarty, T., 3, 8, 13, 17, 57, 61, 263
following through, 28
foreground:
    couplehood case study, 99–107
    families in divorce, 199–209
    families with affective disorders, 291–95
    families with young children, 118–22
    the nuclear family triangle, 251–52
    working with adolescents, 135–38
    young adult case study, 154–55

Fossum, M., 219, 220, 222, 223
Friedenberg, E. Z., 137
Friedman, E., 65, 67, 69, 70
Fulmer, R., 12, 98
Fulton, R., 266

Gatz, M., 171
gender, 3
    and caretaking, 173–74, 264
    and family functioning, 276–78
    and family functioning, terminal illness,
        269
    and family themes, 232
    issues in marriage, 95–96
    and relatedness in therapy, 35
    and relationship time, 56–57
    and responsibility for self, 13, 225
    specific roles in marriage, 115
    taking sides in the family, 182
    tracking roles multigenerationally, 8–9
    and young adulthood, 82
genetic predisposition to bipolar affective dis-
        order, 297–98
genogram, 34, 45, 52, 97, 99, 101, 118, 120,
        142, 144, 153, 156, 162, 170, 179, 180,
        193, 228, 251, 254–56, 258, 272
    for connecting to family–of–origin issues,
        48
    and family history, 55–56
    mapping triangles on, 85
Gerber, I., 267, 268
Gerson, R., 45, 153
Gilligan, C., 82
Giordano, J., 3, 12, 179
Glick, I. D., 266, 287
Glick, P., 193
goals:
    in the assessment process, 43–44
    authentic self–to–self relationships, 18
    in collecting information, 56
    focus on therapeutic, 41–42, 49, 152
    of the model, 4
Gold, P. W., 288
Goldberg, I. K., 266
Goldner, V., 9
Goldsmith, J., 193, 200
Goldstein, M. J., 289
Goodwin, D., 220
Goodwin, F. K., 288, 297n
Gottesman, D. J., 266
grief, 39
    anticipatory, and coaching, 262, 266–69,
        271–72
    operational mourning, 128, 269
    pathological, and unresolved losses in the
        family, 269
Grollman, E., 269

Grosser, G. H., 65, 269
Guerin, K., 136
Guerin, P., 3, 8, 13, 17, 53, 56, 136, 267

Haas, G. L., 287
Haley, J., 11, 15
Halpern, J., 171
Hannon, N., 267
Hare–Mustin, R., 263
health, components of, 187–88
Herz Brown, F., 70, 118, 176, 191, 195, 199,
        263, 266, 269, 270
Hetherington, E. M., 39, 191
Hidalgo, H., 98
hierarchy in alcoholic families, 223
Hines, P., 98
Hobbs, N., 243, 245
Hodgkin's disease, 247
Hoffman, G., 51, 62
Hoffman, L., 264, 267
Holder, D., 116
homosexuality, 300–301
    and medical illness, 247
    and tasks of the transition to a couple,
        98
Hooley, J. M., 289
horizontal stressors, in the context of chronic
        medical illness, 245–48
Howard, K. L., 138
Hyman, H., 169, 171

Imber–Black, E., 65–66, 69, 70
Inclan, J., 12
individual work:
    with adolescents, 137, 143
    with affective disorders, 295–300
    with young adults, 158
intergenerational issues and medical illness,
        249–50
interventions:
    direct, 51
    strategic, 51
intimacy issues, case example, 82–93
"I" position, 183
    adolescents' difficulty with, 137
    and conflict, 249
    evolving in therapy, 68–69
    of family members, 50
    prior to family–of–origin work, 146–47
    therapist's, 24, 35
Ireys, H., 243, 245
issues, process–oriented, 39

Jacobs, J., 243
Janowsky. D. S., 288, 293
Jesse, R. C., 219, 220, 223
judgment in affective disorders, 293

Kautto, J. G., 3, 56, 267
Kelly, J. B., 191–92
Kerr, M. E., 5, 6, 7, 8–9, 13, 15, 16, 17, 46, 49, 78, 84, 154
Krestan, J. A., 98, 219, 220, 221, 222, 223
Kuhn, J., 268, 269
Kutscher, A. H., 266

language, therapeutic, 34
Lansky, M. R., 286
later life:
    families in, 169–88
    responses in medical illness, 248
launching phase, 304–6
    death at the times of, 265
    depression in, 296
    families of young adults, 149–68
    of the family life cycle, 150
learner, the client as, 22
Lebow, G. H., 266
Leff, M., 288, 293
lens:
    of affective disorders, 287
    finding a new strategic, 62–63
    therapeutic, 115
    for viewing families, 6
Lerner, H. G., 24
letter writing, 64–65
    case examples
        an alcoholic family, 236, 238
        couplehood, 107
        facing terminal illness, 280
        families in later life, 186–87
        family with young children, 126
        families with affective disorders, 303
Levinson, D., 79
life cycle:
    corollaries of negotiating, 10–12
    launching phase of, 150
    and opportunity for change, 58, 69–70
    phases, and roles after a death, 268–69
    timing and the ability to accommodate change, 121–22
    transition in, 136
life-cycle issues, 3
light bulb therapy, 25
limit setting for adolescents, 139
lithium (medication), 293
living together, and family issues, 98
loyalty:
    and differentiation, 302
    in divorce and remarriage, 201, 207, 210–13
lupus, 247

McCullough, P. G., 150, 296
McGoldrick, M. (McGoldrick Orfanidis, M.), 3, 6, 12, 16, 17, 18, 39, 45, 81, 82, 94–95, 114–115, 117, 118, 134, 139, 146, 153, 179, 198, 208, 267, 268, 269, 270, 276, 289, 294
mania, 286
Manocherian, J., 191
marital difficulties during a child's adolescence, 133–34
Mason, M., 219, 220, 222, 223
Masters, R., 34, 39
Mayo, J. A., 287
medical illness, 242–61
    reorganization around, 11, 170
medical system, 245
meta position for planning change, 18
meta statement, one-liners, 24
Meyer, P., 226
Miklowitz, D. J., 289
Mintz, J., 289
Minuchin, S., 136
model, the therapist as, 24
models:
    of multigenerational therapy, 3–21
    of normalcy in alcoholic families, 222
Moltz, D. A., 287, 288, 301
Mondykowski, S., 228, 229
monitoring medical illness, 244
Moreland, J., 268
multigenerational therapy, 3–21
    change agent in, 26
    principles that guide the practice of, 33–42
multiple sclerosis, 247
myths:
    of equality, 105–6
    of gender roles, 8
    of later life, 171–72
    of family democracy, 141–42

negation as protection, 298
negotiation in marriage, 97
Neugarten, B., 151
Nicholson, S., 136
nodal events:
    connecting to family-of-origin issues, 48
    identifying, 153
normalization of a family's patterns, 45, 46–47, 252–53
nuclear family process, connecting with the extended family, 4, 40
Nuechterlein, K. H., 289

objectivity about the family, 87
O'Brien, J. D., 287
O'Connell, R. A., 287

Offer, D., 138
one–liners, meta statements, 24
openness and functioning in a family facing
     terminal illness, 269
Orley, J., 289
Ostrove, E., 138

Papp, P., 3, 9, 13, 51, 117
paradox:
    and adolescent independence, 132
    emancipation and connectedness, 152
    in the multigenerational model, 35
    therapeutic, 51
parental child, 195–98, 216
parents:
    symptoms in, 134–35
    working with, 138–39
    working with young adults', 160–62
Parkes, M., 266
Parkinson's disease, 247
patterns in alcoholic families, 232–37
Paul, B. B., 269
Paul, N. L., 65, 262, 269
Pearce, J., 3, 12, 179
Pearson, C., 171
Peck, J. S., 191
Penn, P., 51, 62
Peretz, A. H., 266
performer, the client as, 22
Perrin, J., 243, 245
Peterson, T. L., 98
physiological status, 177–78
planning, 58–60
    for change, 18
    in therapy, 37–38
power:
    in alcoholic families, 219, 223
    and authority, 196
    balance between generations, 174
    within couples, 102
prediction, role in planning, 59
preparation for change, 59–60
presenting problem:
    defining, 45–46
    focus on, 19–20
    mapping of, 52
Preto, N. G., 135, 136
pride, in alcoholic families, 222–23
problems, tracking within the family system,
     84–88
process:
    of normalization, 36–37, 45
    of repetition of the past, 7–9
    of therapy, 19–20
processing change, 60
process–oriented issues, 39

quality time, 56
questions, therapeutic use of, 41

race, 3
    and the family life cycle, 12
Rando, T. A., 266
Raphael, B., 269
reactivity:
    of acute affective episodes, 288
    in alcoholic families, 224
    and focus, 50
    to terminal illness, 263–64
reality, accurate reporting of, 27
reciprocal extremes of behavior, alcoholic
     families, 219–22
reciprocity, 37, 139
redefining self in the family system, 164, 240
reframing, 62
    case example, couplehood, 111
    in medical illness, 252–53
    to offer possibilities of solution, 226
Reilly, D. M., 269
relabeling, 62–63
relatedness, the closeness/distance dimension,
     8, 12–13
relationships:
    establishing person–to–person, 54–55
    intimate versus fused, 95
    among siblings with later–life parents, 175–
     76
    see also closeness/distance; emotional sys-
     tems; enmeshed systems
relationship time, 56
relevancy, maintaining in therapy, 33–36, 129
repetition, multigenerational, 198
resistance, 29–30
resources, allocating in the presence of medi-
     cal illness, 245
responsibility:
    client's, 159
    for self, 13, 17–18, 224–25
        and medical illness, 253–54
    and socialization by gender, 215
    for a spouse in marriage, 98
    in therapy, 22–23, 37–39, 71–72
retirement, reorganization around, 170
reversal, 63–64, 164
rituals, 65–66
    surrounding death, 270
    in the third stage of therapy, 70
Roberts, J., 65–66, 69, 70
Rodgers, R. H., 192, 198
Rolland, J., 242, 243, 246, 249, 264, 266
Rosen, E. J., 65, 70, 118, 262, 266, 267, 269,
     270, 276
Roth, S., 98

Roybal, J., 171
Rusalem, R., 267
Rutenberg, S. K., 296

Sagan, L., 187
Sanders, C. M., 269
Schoenberg, B., 266
Schwebel, A. I., 268
self:
    completion through a spouse, 95
    developing a sense of, 49–50
    focus on, 27–28
    redefining in the family system, 240
    responsibility for, 13, 17–18, 224–25, 253–
        54
    sense of, and depression, 298
    in terms of other family members, 9
self–direction, 8
self–esteem and parenthood, 116
separation:
    "the aftermath" for the family, 199
    and the life cycle, 12–14
    and medical illness, 249–50
    see also divorce; death
shame in alcoholic families, 222–23
siblings
    relationships among, 175–76
    symptoms in, 134
sickle cell anemia, 247
Silverstein, B., 169, 171
Silverstein, O., 3, 9, 13, 117
Simon, R. M., 153
single young adults, 77–93
situational issues, and separation of young
    adults, 81–82
Snyder, K. S., 289
social context of the family, 115, 150–52, 167,
    171–72
socioeconomic status and young adulthood,
    82
Stanton, M. D., 219
Stein, P., 80
Steinglass, P., 221, 222, 231
stepparents, 198
    in families with adolescents, 134
stereotypes:
    of adulthood, 80
    of later life, 171–72
stigmatizing conditions, 244
strategy for detriangling, 61–62
strengths, focus on family's, 36–37
stress:
    level and separation of young adults, 78
    and transitions to adulthood, 79
structural issues of remarried situations, 208–
    9

structural model of therapy, 26
suicide, 299
symptoms:
    in adolescents, 135
    formation of, 14–19
    in parents of adolescents, 134–35
    in siblings of adolescents, 134
    as unsuccessful solutions to tasks, 11
systems:
    alignment of marriage in, 94
    relationships outside the family, 47–48
    rigidity of, 19
    shifts in an alcoholic family, 238–39
    see also emotional systems; enmeshed sys-
        tems

Taffel, R., 34, 39, 286
tapestry:
    of the family of origin, 52
    reweaving
        adolescent example, 146–47
        in divorce and remarriage, 209–17
        couplehood example, 107–12
        in later life, 183–86
        as a phase of treatment, 53–66
        young adult example, 88–93
    weaving a theme into, 36–37
tasks:
    assigned, following through on, 28
    assignment of, 51
    creating for clients, 60–64
    imposed by divorce, 192
    life–cycle, 10
    symptoms as unsuccessful solutions to, 15
    see also assignments; letter writing
teacher, the therapist as, 23–24, 139
Teasdale, J. D., 289
tension, 68
terminal illness, 262–85
termination of therapy, 306–7
    at the reweaving stage, 93
themes:
    developing multigenerational, 231
    in multigenerational patterns of relating, 8
    weaving for relatedness, 35–36
therapeutic process, phases of, 4–5
therapeutic relationship, 22–32
    changing nature of, 72
therapist:
    as an agent of change, 16
    distancing from the, 168
    own–family issues, 31, 173
    own life–cycle stage, 153
    as a person, 30–32
    roles of, 19–20, 22–32, 129, 139
    vision of the, 171

therapy:
  contraindications, 28–29
  session as a play, 38
  see also assessment; background; foreground; treatment
time:
  moving horizontally and vertically in, 9–12
  past-in-the-present, 52
repeating the past, 6–9, 10–11
timing:
  life cycle, and accommodating change, 121–22
Todd, T. C., 219
Toman, W., 9, 98, 276
transitions:
  in adolescence, 148
  to couplehood, 94–113
Treadway, D., 219, 224
treatment:
  dealing with previous, 82, 83–84
  early stages of, 49–52
  families in divorce, 199–218
  families with adolescents, 132–33
  families with young children, 122–29
  initial moves, 104–7
  plan for, 48–49, 103–4
  results of, 167
  second phase of, 53–66, 88–93, 209–17
  and symptom definition, 15
  third stage of, 67–73
  young adult case study, 158–67
  see also assessment; background; client; foreground; therapist; therapy
triangles, 6, 178–79
  AA in, 224
  in alcoholic systems, 230–31, 253
  in the context of chronic medical illness, 245–48, 253
  in a divorced family, 200–201
  in the extended family, 54
  identifying, 45–46

in-law, 117
mapping, 47
and repetition of the past, 7–8
and symptoms, 11
therapeutic use of, 23
triangulation:
  in families of adolescents, 136
  symptoms resulting from, 15
  of the therapist, 31–32
  see also detriangling
trust between the generations, 174

uncertainty:
  and medical illness, 244
  about mood shifts and affective disorders, 301

Vaillant, G., 220
valence, and closeness/distance, 16
vertical stressors, and medical illness, 249–50
Vess, J., 268
visits as opportunities, 65

Wallerstein, J., 191–92
Walsh, F., 3, 114, 117, 171, 267, 268, 269, 270
Walters, M., 3, 9, 13, 117
Wehr, T. A., 297n
Weiss, R., 266
Whiting, R., 65–66, 69, 70
Winget, C., 263
Woititz, J., 229, 230
Woodman, N. J., 98

young adulthood, medical illness's impact on, 246
young adults:
  families launching, 149–68
  responses in medical illness, 248

zero expectations, 57